Occasional Paper 94

Excavations at Barnfield Pit, Swanscombe, 1968-72

Edited by Bernard Conway,
John McNabb and Nick Ashton

Illustrations by Phil Dean

Department of Prehistoric and Romano-British Antiquities
1996

BRITISH MUSEUM OCCASIONAL PAPERS

Publishers: The British Museum
                       Great Russell Street
                       London WC1B 3DG

Production Editor: Josephine Turquet

Distributors: British Museum Press
                       46 Bloomsbury Street
                       London WC1B 3QQ

Front cover: Schematic section through the Lower Loam showing the knapping floor with hypothetical human activities (see Figure 16.10). Drawn by Phil Dean.

Occasional Paper No. 94, 1996
Excavations at Barnfield Pit, Swanscombe, 1968-72

Edited by Bernard Conway, John McNabb and Nick Ashton

ISBN 0 86159 094 5
ISSN 0142 4815

Orders should be sent to British Museum Press.
Cheques and postal orders should be made payable to
British Museum Company Ltd and sent to
46 Bloomsbury Street, London, WC1B 3QQ.
Access, American Express, Barclaycard and Visa cards are accepted.

Printed and bound by The Chameleon Press Limited, 5–25 Burr Road, London SW18 4SG

The late John d'Arcy Waechter, 1915-1977

CONTENTS

CONTRIBUTORS

Nick Ashton   Department Prehistoric and Romano-British Antiquities, British Museum, 38 Orsman Road, London N1 5QJ

Bernard Conway   58 Broadway Gardens, Mitcham, Surrey CR4 4EE

Andrew Currant   Department of Palaeontology, Natural History Museum, Cromwell Road, London SW7 5BD

Peter Davis   Polvean, Freshwater Lane, St Mawes, Cornwall TR2 5AR

Richard Hubbard   Palaeobiology Research Unit, University of East London, Romford Road, London E15 4LZ

Brian Irving   19 Hebden Avenue, Keld Park, Carlisle, Cumbria CA2 6TW

John McNabb   Department of Prehistory, Institute of Archaeology, 31-34 Gordon Square, London WC1H OPY

Steven Parry   Department of Zoology, University College London, Gower Street, London WC1E 6BT

Eric Robinson   Department of Geology, University College London, Gower Street, London WC1E 6BT

Danielle Schreve   Department of Zoology, University College London, Gower Street, London WC1E 6BT

Alan Walker   Department of Cell Biology and Anatomy, The John Hopkins University, School of Medicine, 725 North Wolfe Street, Baltimore, MD 21205, USA

ACKNOWLEDGMENTS

The editors would like to express their thanks to Dr Ian Longworth, Dr Tim Potter and to the staff of the Quaternary Section of the Department of Prehistoric and Romano-British Antiquities for their support of the publication of the project. We also thank the funders of the original fieldwork: the Royal Anthropological Institute; the Institute of Archaeology; the British Museum; the Natural History Museum; and the British Academy. In a project of this scale and of this duration a great many people from differing institutions will have contributed. Unfortunately in the quarter of a century that has passed since excavations were initiated, it is now difficult to trace all those who helped, but we thank them all.

Bernard Conway thanks Kenneth Hutcheson and Simon Conway for the least squares and temperature computation in Chapter 8, and Steven Parry thanks Dr Colin Harrison, Dr Adrian Lister, Cyril Walker, Andrew Currant, Danielle Schreve for advice and assistance, and Sandra Chapman, Dr R Prys Jones, J Bailey and M Walters for assistance at Tring. Dr John McNabb would also like to thank Angus and Jane McNabb for considerable support during the early stages of the Swanscombe analysis.

1. INTRODUCTION

Bernard Conway, John McNabb and Nick Ashton

Barnfield pit, Swanscombe, Kent has been a site of archaeological and geological research since the turn of the century. The former chalk pit with its overburden of sand and gravel lies on the southern flank of the Lower Thames basin, 5 km to the east of Dartford (TQ 598743) (see Figure 1.1). The Pleistocene deposits at the site consist of a series of gravels, sands and loams (see Chapters 3, 6-8), mapped as Boyn Hill terrace by the Geological Survey, which rest on an eroded surface of Thanet Sand and Chalk.

It was during the extraction of the sands and gravels in the latter part of the 19th century that flint artefacts and bones were first discovered. However, it was not until the seminal work of Smith and Dewey (1913) that the importance of Swanscombe was recognised and it took its place at the centre of British Lower Palaeolithic research (see Chapters 3 and 4); not only could the site be placed into a regional geological sequence, but there were a series of stratified flint industries that paralleled the evolutionary models being developed on the Continent, and in particular in the Somme Valley in France. From this time on, the pit was the subject of extensive collecting and some geological recording and excavation. Most of the endeavours were aimed at the biface-bearing deposits of the Middle Gravels and the deposits above, and this research was taken up with renewed vigour when the first skull fragment was found in the Upper Middle Gravel by Marston in 1935. Meanwhile, the Lower Gravel, containing a core and flake industry, and the Lower Loam which was thought to be sterile, received scant attention.

It was with the intention of examining the Lower Gravel and Lower Loam, that the late John Waechter initiated his excavations in 1968. These excavations ran seasonally until 1972 (see Chapter 5) and interim reports were published each year in the *Journal of the Royal Anthropological Institute* (Waechter 1968; Waechter and Conway 1969; Waechter *et al.* 1970; Waechter *et al.* 1971). Due to Waechter's untimely death in 1977 the full excavation report remained unpublished.

The present volume, initiated in 1992, has taken reports previously written, principally on the geology and pollen, and added to these new reports on the archaeology, fauna and footprint surfaces. In addition, previously unpublished details on the history of the site have been added to provide a context and background for the excavation. Some of these chapters have been written by those involved in the original excavations (Chapters 2, 3, 6-8, 12-15), while the remainder have been written by specialists fresh to the site.

The volume can be broadly divided into four sections: the history of the site concluding with the description of the Waechter excavations (Chapters 2-5); the geological descriptions, context and interpretation of the site (Chapters 6-8); the environmental studies including fauna, footprints and pollen (Chapters 9-15); and the archaeology of the site (Chapter 16). There are also two appendices, the first of which is an explanation of the methodology used for the flint analysis, and the second is a previously unpublished paper by Marston, written in 1937 and critical to his understanding of the geology of the site.

In over twenty years some information has certainly been lost. Hence Chapter 5 on the description of the excavation is a reconstruction of events based on field notebooks, other archive material, interim reports and in some instances memory. The same is true for Chapter 14 on the footprint surfaces. Equally, the flint report (Chapter 16) is based on those collections that have survived the years; there are undoubtedly some pieces missing, and where findsbook numbers and artefact markings do not always tally, a degree of guesswork has been necessary. These inconsistencies are clearly noted in the text.

The result is a near-complete excavation report that hopefully provides a coherent source of information and guide to the site. Over the last ten years, other sites and other excavations have taken much of the limelight away from Swanscombe. Through this volume, however, it is demonstrated that Swanscombe remains one of the most important Lower Palaeolithic sites in Britain and it will make a significant addition to the growing number of multidisciplinary reports for the period.

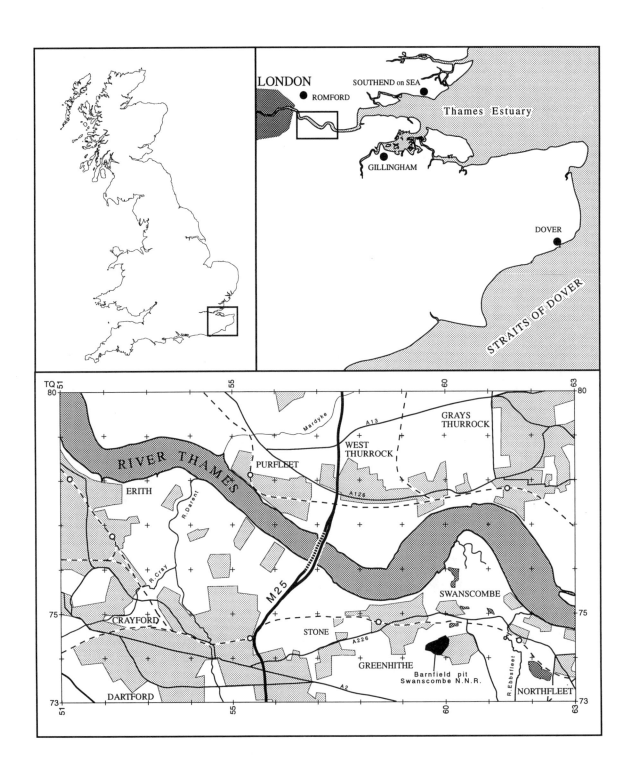

Fig. 1.1. Location of Barnfield Pit, Swanscombe

2. A HISTORY OF QUARRYING IN THE SWANSCOMBE AREA

Bernard Conway

The many archaeological finds and geological discoveries made in the Swanscombe area in the past century have been as a direct result of the development of the cement industry. Chalk has been quarried in the Dartford/Northfleet area using picks, shovels and crow-bars, for many hundreds of years; one of the earliest lime kilns, dating to the mid 17th century, was sited near to the West Hill Hospital, Dartford. This shallow surface working satisfied demand whilst it was restricted to supplying purely local needs.

The population of England and Wales, after being relatively stable at between three and five million people from the 16th century, began to rise sharply from the mid 18th century (Wrigley and Schofield 1981). London attracted more than its fair share of this increase, including migration from a wide provincial catchment area, and grew at a phenomenal pace. From being a major European city of nearly a million people in 1800, it became the biggest city in the world by 1900 with over four million inhabitants (Weightman and Humphries 1983). Such a population increase generated the requirement for massive building programmes which were largely unplanned and mostly speculative.

Large building and construction enterprises required basic raw materials in ever-increasing quantities at cost effective prices. Cement, sand and gravel were raw materials much in demand, but sources were required in as close proximity to London as possible in order to keep transport costs low and prices competitive. The Dartford/Northfleet area proved to be ideal for this purpose with the presence of almost unlimited supplies of the constituents of cement (chalk and clay), the facility for obtaining fuel by sea (coal from the Durham coalfield) and the distribution and export of the manufactured cement by river and sea (Bamber 1908). Of secondary, but by no means minor importance was the sand and gravel generated as a by-product of removing the overburden from chalk workings.

Figure 2.1 shows the geology of the Swanscombe area as it would have appeared *ca.* 1800, based on parts of the Geological Survey 6-inch to one mile maps Kent 9 NE, SE and 10 NW, SW with some boundaries reconstructed over the quarried areas. At that time 'the Thames below Dartford must have presented an attractive piece of country overlooking a busy river. The chalk coming close to the river's edge was still largely open downland falling steeply to a narrow apron of green marshes', (Millward and Robinson 1971).

James Frost of Finchley established a cement works at Swanscombe in 1825 and was the first commercial manufacturer in the London area. Frost took out patents for 'British Cement' in 1822 and 1823 and managed the works at Swanscombe until 1833 when it was taken over by J.B. White and Son (Guy 1975). Shortly after 1840 I.C. Johnson, White's manager, developed and refined Frost's process making a product which he called 'Portland cement'.

In 1824 Joseph Aspdin, a Yorkshire brick-maker and builder, took out a patent for 'Portland cement' produced by firing a carefully proportioned mixture of limestone and clay which he claimed to have been making since 1811. The name was given because he thought that the set cement resembled Portland stone! Aspdin's patent saw a variety of applications for his cement - particularly for the mid-Victorian fashion of stuccoing the exterior surfaces of buildings, but also engineering projects, water works, bridges, harbours etc.. Aspdin opened a works at Wakefield in West Yorkshire and commenced production on a modest scale.

There was a great deal of competition between rival cement manufacturers, concrete and mortar based on cement being essential to the rapidly expanding building industry. Portland cement eventually came to be recognised as the best of the 'hydraulic' cements, so-called because of their ability to set and develop strength under water. Portland cement came to the public notice in the late 1840s as rivalry built up between Frost and Aspdin. There had been repeated failures of both 'British'

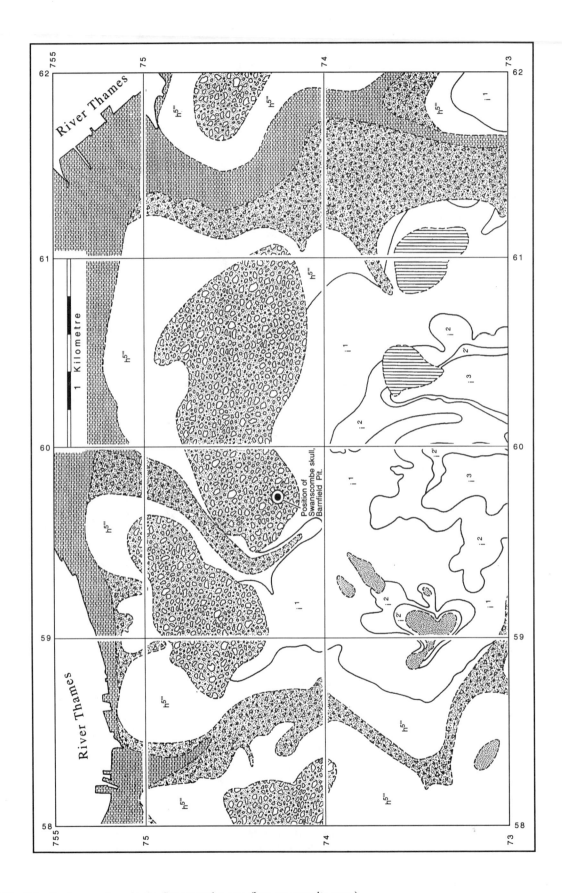

Fig. 2.1. Surface geology in the Swanscombe area (key on opposite page)

Key

	Thickness	Stratigraphic Unit	General Lithology
	5 - 15 m.	Alluvium	Silty clays with variable thicknesses of peat
	5 - 14 m.	Boyn Hill Gravel	Sandy gravels, sands and loams
	1 - 3 m.	Head	Stiff sandy clay with angular chalk and flint clasts
	2 - 6 m.	Plateau Gravel	Gravel in a sand or clayey sand matrix

	Thickness	Stratigraphic Unit	General Lithology
i³	to 90 m.	London Clays	Stiff dark clays with some silt and horizons of septarian noduls
i²'	0 - 24 m.	Blackheath Beds	Sands and pebbles
i²	2 -18 m.	Woolwich Beds	Clays, sands, loams and pebbles
i¹	18 -24 m.	Thanet Sand	Fine silty sand with basal layer of flint cobbles
h⁵'''	97 m.	Upper Chalk	Soft white earthy limestone with nodular and tabular flint in lower half

Landslip

⊙   Find position of Swanscombe skull, Barnfield Pit

Plate 2.1. Barnfield pit, Swanscombe 1937, looking north. Note the railway, handscreening frames and the steam navvy (Photo M.A.Cotton)

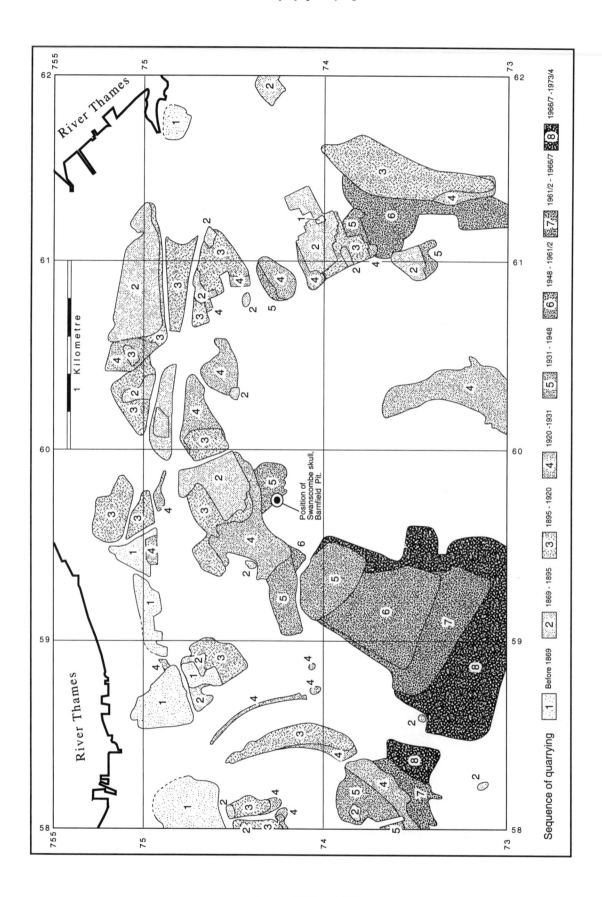

Fig. 2.2. Progress of quarrying in the Swanscombe area 1869 to 1975

and 'Roman' cements and eventually Portland cement came to be seen as superior.

William Aspdin, younger son of Joseph, saw great commercial possibilities in his father's cement and left Yorkshire to set up a cement works at Rotherhithe around 1846 and later another at Northfleet Creek where he traded as Robins, Maude and Aspdin. In the battle to market his cement young Aspdin had the good fortune to meet Isombard Kingdom Brunel as the latter was completing his ill-fated Thames tunnel. At one point when the roof of the tunnel collapsed because it was made using inferior cement Brunel dumped many tons of Aspdin's Portland cement in the river above the damage. This sealed the break in the tunnel roof and Brunel was able to pump the tunnel dry, he then rebuilt it using Portland cement for the lining (Pugh 1988).

Even with this very public display of the superiority of Aspdin's cement, by 1850 there were still only four works producing Portland cement on the Lower Thames. After 1851 the number on the Thames and Medway increased rapidly with White's Frost works becoming the most important.

The London market was obviously the most important in the country and this was supplied by sailing barges each having a capacity of 80/100 tons. Most of the large manufacturers ran their own fleets of barges with bargeyards and wharves until, in the latter part of the nineteenth century, up to two hundred such craft were in daily use.

By the beginning of the twentieth century, if not before, cement had become a major export commodity and in July 1900 twenty four of the principal firms manufacturing Portland cement amalgamated to form the Associated Portland Cement Manufacturers Ltd.. Since that date APCM has dominated the cement scene, developing products as new markets appear. It has supplied 80% of the cement used in the British sector of the North Sea oilfields, and in addition exports its products to over sixty countries throughout the world. In 1976 about one quarter of all cement in the UK was manufactured on Thameside.

As demand increased the pioneer cement manufacturers rapidly exhausted the quarryable Chalk adjacent to the river. In that location it had the advantage of a minimum thickness of overburden. The solution was to extend quarrying further to the south despite thicker overburden (up to 15 m in places), and some public opposition. The depth to which chalk can be extracted is governed by the level of the water table, which in the Swanscombe area is 2 - 2.5 m OD and consequently workings rarely extend below 3 to 5 m OD. The result has been a steady southward migration of extensive interconnected quarries as shown in Figure 2.2. The scale of Chalk extraction at Barnfield prior to 1912 is clearly shown in Plates 2.2 and 2.3. Figure 2.2 is based on information extracted from eight editions of the Ordnance Survey 1:10,560 and 1:10,000 scale maps published between 1869 and 1974. By the nature of map revision work each stage is probably an under estimate of the true extent of quarrying.

For perhaps 150 years the quarries of the Dartford/Northfleet area have provided unrivalled opportunities for examining the Pleistocene deposits of the area and for collecting archaeological and palaeotological material. Wymer (1968) has catalogued 32 identifiable sites in the area which have yielded archaeological material, and many more have yielded faunal remains. Around the turn of the century one local collector is reputed to have acquired over 80,000 handaxes. One of the reasons why the earlier part of this century produced such rich sites and why artefacts were collected in such numbers was the hand working of the sediments. Steam shovels were used to work the faces, but gravels were then hand-screened providing excellent opportunities for artefact recovery (see Plate 2.1). The development of the study of geology and archaeology in the Swanscombe area is described in Chapters 3 and 4, but it has to be seen against this background of available sections, in a pre-mechanised world.

The reduction in number of cement works due to closures and 'rationalisation' (the Swanscombe works closed in November 1990) and the steady southward movement of the current quarrying area has left behind a landscape of dereliction which is the cause of much concern to the local inhabitants and farmers, and conservation groups. There are limited programmes of reclamation by the cement manufacturers to produce land for agriculture, building and recreational purposes.

A little of the Pleistocene heritage of the Swanscombe area has been preserved for future generations by the generosity of APCM who in 1954 gave the freehold of land at Barnfield Pit to the then Nature Conservancy as a site of outstanding scientific interest. It became Britain's first geological Nature Reserve - the Swanscombe Skull Site NNR and is currently administered by English Nature.

Plate 2.2. Photograph by Smith and Dewey showing N. and N.W. end of Barnfield Pit. Camera situated near TQ 59967459, looking N.W. (c. 295°). See Figure 3.1

Plate 2.3. Photograph by Smith and Dewey showing W. part of pit and overlapping on right (E.) side with Plate 2.2. Camera situated at gravel face near sections 1, 2 and 5 (see Figure 3.1) and looking N.W.

3. AN HISTORICAL PERSPECTIVE ON GEOLOGICAL RESEARCH AT BARNFIELD PIT, SWANSCOMBE

Bernard Conway

INTRODUCTION

This chapter reviews geological research at Barnfield Pit prior to the 1968-1972 excavations led by the late John Waechter of the University of London, Institute of Archaeology.

The first published reference to the Pleistocene deposits at Swanscombe and their contained Palaeolithic artefacts was by F.C.J. Spurrell in 1883; even at this time it was a locality that was already well known to collectors. It was said by Kennard (Oakley 1952) that there was a local tradition that the first handaxes were found at Swanscombe by Harry Lewis a Camberwell shoemaker. In the one hundred and ten years that have elapsed since Spurrell's paper, controlled excavations which have produced geological information have been conducted on only three occasions prior to the 1968-1972 work: in 1912/13 by Smith and Dewey, in 1937 by the Swanscombe Committee of the Royal Anthropological Institute, and in 1955-60 by the Wymers.

Many people have visited the site, collectors and archaeologists have acquired large numbers of artefacts from the deposits and much has been written about them and the site. However, first-hand descriptions of the geology and stratigraphy of Barnfield pit are few and far between and there has been a lamentable lack of differentiation between observation and conjecture. Long before Marston's spectacular discovery of the human skull fragments in 1935-36 archaeologists and geologists were aware of the importance of the site to unravelling the complicated Pleistocene history of the Thames Valley and for establishing the sequence of Palaeolithic industries. Today in order to arrive at some idea of the dispositions and variations of the deposits as seen in former exposures, it is necessary to search national, local and private archives in addition to the published sources. Even then there are many questions left unanswered. When the author first started to research the geological background of the site he was shocked to discover just how little information had been published, and of the contradictory nature of some of that information, on what is arguably one of the most important archaeological sites in Britain. The purpose of this chapter then is to set the record straight by reviewing the primary observations made by previous workers on the geological succession at Barnfield Pit. A more detailed review of the archaeology as described by these workers is presented in the next chapter.

GEOLOGICAL DATA

The local stratigraphic units established by Smith and Dewey in 1912 and 1913 were found to be applicable and useful during the excavations of 1968-72. These names have therefore been inserted in square brackets where necessary in the following summaries to aid clarity and facilitate later discussion.

Dewey 1913 (see Figure 3.1)

The earliest account of the geology and stratigraphy of the Pleistocene deposits of Barnfield Pit was that of Smith and Dewey (1913). Although the report was published under joint authorship it has been

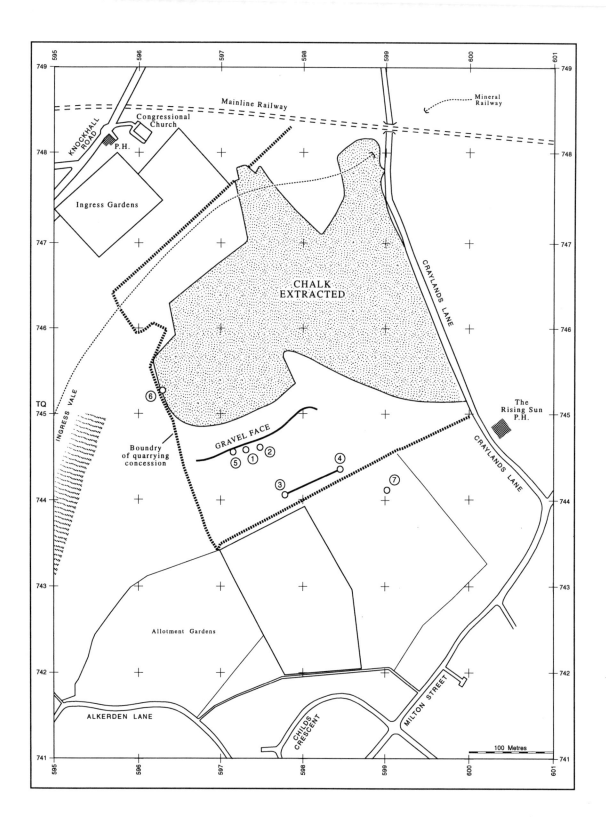

Fig. 3.1. Location of the Smith and Dewey sections and extent of quarrying in 1912 and 1913. See Plates 2.2 and 2.3

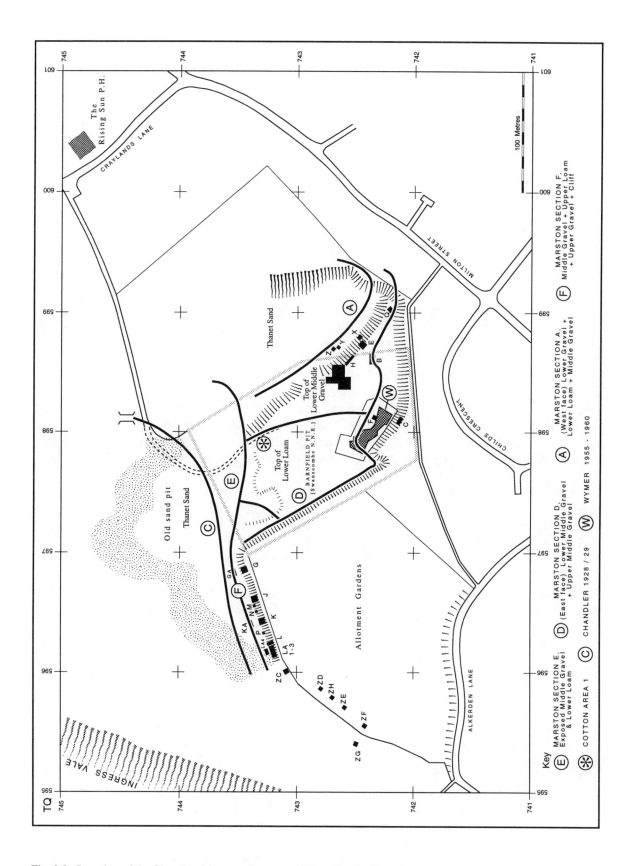

Fig. 3.2. Location of the Chandler, Marston, Cotton and Dines (for the Committee), Paterson (= Marston Section F) and Wymer sections

assumed that the geological contribution was made by Dewey. The account was based on ten days of systematic excavation and examination of extensive sections on the west side of the pit during March and April 1912.

The sections showed 12 to 15 m of sands, gravels and loams resting on a rock-cut bench at about 27.5 m OD. On the south side of the pit, the deposits rested on Thanet Sand but towards the north the gravels overlapped the Thanet Sand and rested on Chalk, due to the general south-westerly dip of the solid formations.

Dewey separated the deposits into five local sub-divisions on the basis of lithology and texture, divisions which he found to persist throughout the pit:

Upper Gravel
Upper Loam
Middle Gravel
Lower Loam
Lower Gravel

The separation of the Middle Gravels into Upper and Lower divisions was made by Dewey in his manuscript notes (Dewey 1912, see below) and appears on annotated photographs, but not in the published report. These two terms were first published by Dines (1938).

Lower Gravel. The Lower Gravels were 1.8 m thick and were composed principally of flint, derived from the Chalk and from the Lower Tertiary beds. In addition there was about 3% of chert from the Hythe Beds of the Lower Greensand, pebbles of white vein quartz, and quartzites of varying colours and textures. The gravels were divisible into three layers, each about 0.6 m thick, on the basis of colour - the lowest being dull red, followed by white and yellow. The colours were due to different states of oxidation of iron. The basal red layer was very coarse and consisted of abraded brown flints and large nodules of flint derived from the Chalk. Mammalian remains were plentiful. The Lower Gravel contained an artefact industry which consisted almost exclusively of thick flakes, the majority of which were found in the bottom red layer.

Lower Loam. The Lower Loam was 0.6 to 1.2 m thick and consisted of fine, purplish brown loam with lenticles of buff-coloured marl, comprising broken shells and pellets of chalk with sand grains. Dewey used the term 'tenacious' to describe the loam, perhaps a reference to the clayey (weathered) surface layer which he did not otherwise record. There were no artefacts or mammalian remains.

Middle Gravel. The [Lower] Middle Gravel consisted of beds of gravel and sand which varied locally, but throughout the pit the base was a bed of gravel 0.6 m thick. On the south side of the pit a further 4.9 m of gravel overlay the basal bed, but on the north side pale yellow current-bedded sands [Upper Middle Gravel] with thin layers of clay replaced the gravel laterally. The total thickness varies from 2.4 to 5.5 m. The gravel consisted almost wholly of flint derived from either the Chalk or Tertiary pebble beds; there were in addition pebbles of white vein quartz, quartzite and limestone, but little Lower Greensand chert. Bifaces and thinning flakes were present in the [Lower] Middle Gravel.

Upper Loam. Dark brown sandy loam without apparent bedding and with spots of manganese dioxide. The upper surface was irregular and it had a thickness of 1.0 to 1.2 m. White patinated ovate bifaces were found in this unit.

Upper Gravel. Stiff brown clay, with a thickness varying from 0.3 to 0.5 m and with gravel concentrated in pockets resting on the irregular surface of the Upper Loam. Most of the pebbles were white-crusted flint with about 3% chert, vein quartz and quartzite.

Dewey had the advantage of being the first geologist to examine and describe the site. He established local sub-divisions in 1912 which, with minor amendments, are widely accepted as valid more than eighty years later. His brief descriptions are clear and unambiguous and contain few of the

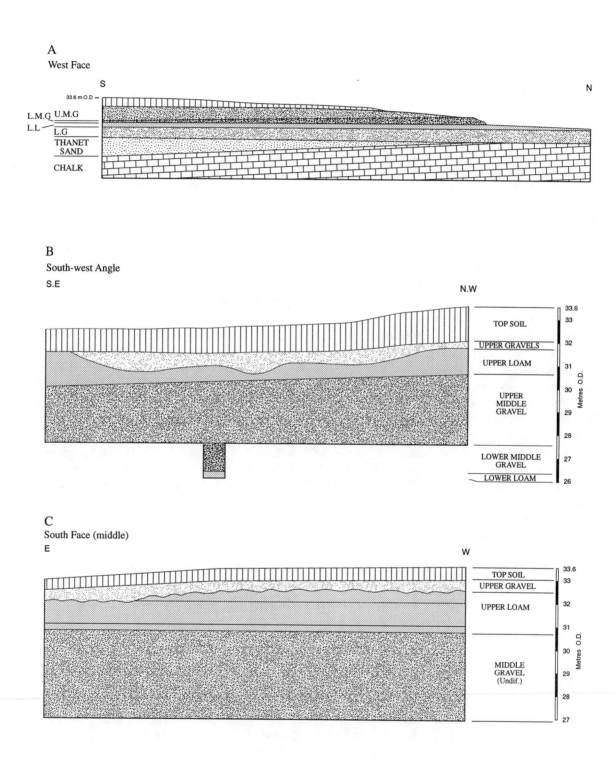

A
West Face

B
South-west Angle

C
South Face (middle)

Fig. 3.3. Smith and Dewey's sections. A is taken from Plate 2.3, and B and C probably form the basis of Smith and Dewey's 1913 figures 6 and 5

contradictions which characterises some later work. Dewey's report, written in collaboration with Smith, is a model of geological clarity within its terms of reference, which were to establish the sequence of implement-bearing deposits. It is puzzling to know why Dewey never divided the Middle Gravel into Upper and Lower in his published account when he certainly did so in the notes he wrote in preparation of that account. Had he done so it is likely that much later confusion could have been avoided, particularly with regard to the Middle Gravel 'channel'. Dewey's descriptions are valuable because they were made at a time when very extensive working faces were available for examination in an area where the landscape has now been largely restored.

Dewey 1912 (see Figures 3.1 and 3.3)

Notes made by Dewey while preparing the published report (see Dewey 1913 above) include annotated photographs of the workings at Barnfield pit. Figure 3.3 is based on three of these photographs which provide additional data that was not presented in the published work. These photos are curated in the British Museum Swanscombe archive.

Figure 3.3A shows the west face of the pit with terrace deposits resting on Thanet Sand and reaching a height of 33.6 m OD at the southern end of the section. Towards the northern end of the face the Thanet Sand thins out and the terrace deposits rest on the Chalk; the Chalk surface shows an apparent low dip to the south.

Figure 3.3B shows a section in the south-west corner of the pit with the Upper Gravel resting on the irregular upper surface of the Upper Loam. Towards the south-east end of the section the Upper Gravel terminates against an increased thickness of Upper Loam. A small excavation in the middle of this section showed 1.2 m of Lower Middle Gravel beneath 3.1 m of Upper Middle Gravel and resting on Lower Loam, the surface of which was at 26.2 m OD. This section is very similar to one of the diagrams published in the report (Smith and Dewey 1914, figure 6). The Upper Gravel and Upper Loam have a combined thickness of about 1.5 m and each shows variations in thickness from 0-3 to 1.2 m. The top soil is shown with a thickness of 1.5 m which is excessive for the area and may include higher beds of loam or sand.

Figure 3.3C shows a section in the middle of the south face of the pit with terrace deposits to a height of 33.6 m OD. The Upper Gravel (0.5 m of dull-yellow gravel) rests on the irregular surface of white sand (0.6 m thick) which thins out towards the eastern end of the section where Upper Gravel rests on Upper Loam. The Upper Loam (0.9 m of yellow-grey loam) is separated from the Middle Gravel by a layer of sand (0.3 m thick). The Middle Gravel (3.7 m thick) is described as a reddish gravel, no current bedded sands are present in this section. This section is very similar to Smith and Dewey (1914, figure 5).

The day report of the excavation for 21st March 1912 used the terms 'upper-middle' and 'lower-middle' gravel although it did not define them. For the first time it is apparent from the diagrams that the former was applied to the current-bedded sands with thin layers of clay and pebbles and the latter term to the horizontally bedded gravel. This differentiation was not made in the published report.

The thickness of the Lower Gravel was uniform throughout the pit at 1.8 m with most of the flakes and cores occurring in the bottom, coarse red, layer. Some artefacts were found in the middle layer, but very few in the top layer. No implements were found in the Lower Loam. The Middle Gravel varied between 3.1 and 5.5 m in thickness but with an average depth of about 4.0 m. Everywhere at the base of the pit, the Lower Middle Gravel was characterised by 0.6 m of gravels. On the south side of the pit there was 4.9 m of gravel above it; on the northern side current-bedded sands replaced the gravel laterally. The Middle Gravel thinned out northwards to about 1.8 m between the Upper and Lower Loams. The Upper Loam thinned out altogether between Barnfield and Collyer's pits.

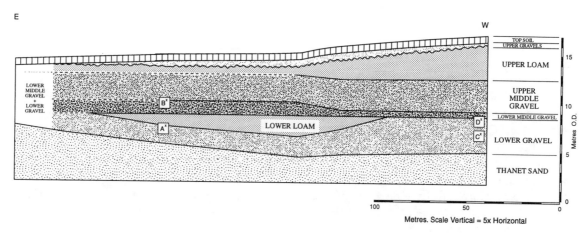

Fig. 3.4. Chandler's 1928-29 section

A

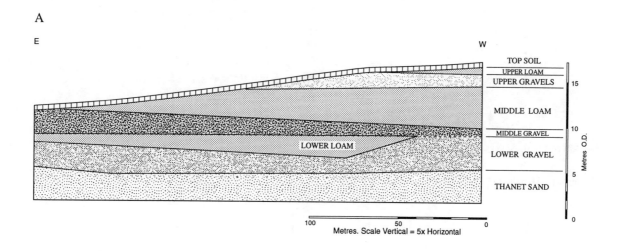

B

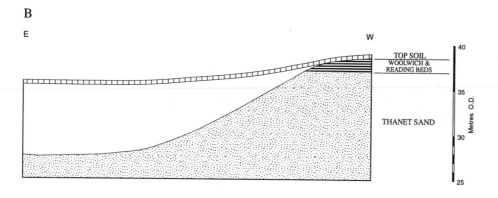

Fig. 3.5. Chandler 1935

15

Dewey 1914

In 1913 Smith and Dewey excavated in Barnfield pit for a further four days to verify sections cut in the previous year and measured new sections in Collyer's pit and New Craylands Lane pit. Little was added to the geological descriptions of the Barnfield deposits beyond variations of thickness in the upper part of the sequence and a dip of about 8° west was observed on the surface of the Lower Middle Gravel at a section in the south-west angle of the pit. Dewey recognized that the Upper Gravel was not a river deposit but that it had 'been washed down from Swanscombe Hill [highest point, 97.6 m OD] where London Clay is dug and the lower Eocene beds are present.'

In Collyer's pit the Upper Gravel and Upper Loam were absent and the section showed 2.1 to 3.1 m of undifferentiated Middle Gravel resting on 0.9 m of Lower Loam overlying the top of the Lower Gravel at the base.

At New Craylands Lane pit 4.3 m of sands and gravels were noted resting on the Chalk surface at 27.5 m OD. These were identified as a 'full development' of the upper part of the Barnfield sequence [Upper Middle Gravel to Upper Gravel].

Chandler 1928/1929 (see Figures 3.2 and 3.4)

Chandler was closely acquainted with the gravel pits of the Swanscombe, Crayford and Dartford areas during the period 1907-1942; between 1921 and 1942 he visited Barnfield pit twenty or thirty times each year (Chandler 1942). His first paper on the Barnfield deposits (Chandler 1928/1929) described the sections exposed in 1928 in the south face of the pit. Figure 3.4 is based on those measured sections which were positioned to take account of differences of ground surface height; the length of the section was given as 256 m. Chandler gave the following brief descriptions of six stratigraphic units:

Lower Gravel. Gravel, coarse at base, with shells and bones in upper part. Thickness 1.8 to 2.2 m.

Lower Loam. Clayey loam. Thickness 0 to 2.4 m.

[Lower] Middle Gravel. Clean gravel, current-bedded and iron-stained in places. Thickness 0.5 to 1.5 m.

[Upper Middle Gravel]. False-bedded clean sand, with pebbles and fine gravel. Thickness 3.1 m.

Upper Loam. Current-bedded, sandy loam. In the middle part of this section the upper part of this bed was described as clayey loam, and the lower part was sandy and bedded. Thickness 3.1 to 3.7 m.

Upper Gravel. Tough clayey gravel, resting on an irregular surface of Upper Loam. Thickness 0.9 to 1.5 m.

Four points on the section are of interest:

A. Position of shell and bone bed at the top of the Lower Gravel.
B. Position of handaxe and flakes at the top of the [Lower] Middle Gravel.
C. Position of abundant *Theodoxus cantianus*.
D. Position of handaxe flakes at the top of undifferentiated gravels.

Chandler was the first worker to recognise the complex nature of the Upper Loam and its relationship to the Upper Middle Gravel, although this is more clearly seen in his later paper (Chandler 1935). The measured profiles enabled the structure of the terrace deposits to be established for the first time.

Dewey 1932

Dewey visited Barnfield pit frequently as the commercial workings progressed. Following his 1912/13 excavations, he published his accumulated observations in 1932. He records that the 'cliff' of Thanet Sand, against which the terrace gravels were banked, was well exposed at the western end of Barnfield Pit in April 1931 when he noted that the Lower Gravel more or less followed the slope of the cliff whereas higher deposits were more horizontally bedded.

Lower Gravel. The colour divisions of the Lower Gravel were not persistent and at the eastern end of the pit disappeared altogether. At its base the gravel consisted of large rounded brown flint cobbles and nodules of flint from the Chalk, some of which still retained chalk in cracks and hollows. He asserted that Clactonian artefacts and mammalian remains were common in the lower part of the red gravel, but the latter were very friable. A tusk of *Palaeoloxodon antiquus* was found measuring 2.0 m in length. Many flint pebbles from Tertiary deposits were present as well as about 3% by weight of chert derived from the Hythe Beds of the Lower Greensand and pebbles of white vein quartz; Bunter Pebble Bed quartzite was also common. The matrix of the gravel consisted of coarse sand with splinters of quartz and flint and some loam. At the base were many boulders of flint and sarsens 'some too heavy for a strong man to lift'. One boulder of puddingstone measured 0.8 m in length. The thickness of the Lower Gravel was 1.8 m.

Lower Loam. Over much of the area of the pit the Lower Loam divided the Lower from the Middle Gravels. It consisted of a purplish-brown loam, often speckled and streaked with manganese dioxide, and localised lenticles of marl comprising shells, pellets of calcium carbonate and sand grains. The marl was penetrated by minute tubules, arising from the decomposition of the rootlets of plants which grew before the overlying Lower Middle Gravel was laid down. Land and freshwater shells were abundant. Thickness 0.6 to 1.2 m. Although he does not describe the weathered nature of the surface of the Lower Loam, Dewey clearly accepted the top as an old land surface. No artefacts were found in this loam.

Middle Gravel. The base of the Middle Gravels consisted of 0.6 m of gravel and it was in this layer that the majority of the Acheulean bifaces were found. Towards the south side of the pit current-bedded sands [Upper Middle Gravel] overlay the basal gravel [Lower Middle Gravels], but increasing amounts of inter-bedded gravel was present towards the north. The gravels were predominantly flint, both rolled Chalk flint and Tertiary pebbles, while chert from the Lower Greensand though present, was not as common as in the Lower Gravel. White quartz, quartzite and limestone also occurred and there was much more sand and fine gravel than in the Lower Gravel. No mammalian remains were found but Acheulean artefacts were common and tended to be concentrated in certain seams which were characterised by being cemented with iron or manganese oxides.

Upper Loam. No shells, flakes or implements found.

Upper Gravel. This bed was a hill-wash rather than a river deposit.

The Boyn Hill terrace showed a total aggradation of about 11.0 m at Swanscombe. The river seemed to have swept laterally, cutting a rock platform at a nearly uniform level of 26.8 m OD for a width of at least 1 km south of the river.

Chandler 1935 (see Figure 3.5)

The considerable changes that took place in the working face of the pit between 1929 and 1934 led Chandler to describing and measuring further sections on which Figure 3.5A is based. It is more difficult to determine the position of this section, but it is somewhere to the south of the 1928/29 section. The length of the section is not given, but it is assumed to be approximately the same as in

Figure 3.4. In this section Chandler recognised another loam bed above the Upper Gravel; the beds he had previously called Upper Loam he now designated Middle Loam.

Lower Gravel. Clayey gravel, unbedded, with large flints. Thickness 1.8 to 2.9 m.

Lower Loam. Sandy and clayey loam. Thickness 0.8 to 2.4 m.

Middle Gravel. Clean, current-bedded sand and small gravel. Thickness 1.5 to 2.4 m.

Middle Loam. Fine-bedded sandy loam in upper part, false-bedded sand and fine gravel below. Thickness 0.6 to 4.6 m.

Upper Gravel. Tough clayey gravel with angular and sub-angular flint and abundant Tertiary pebbles. Thickness 0.9 to 1.2 m.

Upper Loam. Sandy loam. Thickness 0.8 m.

Four points on the section are of interest:

A. The Lower Loam contains a strongly chalky mud showing signs of flow structure.
B. Middle Gravel shows horizontal lines of (?Fe) staining which gives a deceptive appearance of even-bedding.
C. Upper part of Lower Gravel contains freshwater mollusca and mammalian remains.
D. Lower Loam contains numerous *Trocholus hispidus*.

Chandler also records (*ibid*, plate 3A) that the working face at the western end of the pit exposed a section of the channel in which the Barnfield deposits were laid down, this is illustrated in Figure 3.5B. The landward (southern) margin of this channel was seen to be a cliff cut in Thanet Sands overlain by Woolwich and Reading Beds, probably *in situ*, from 36.6 to 38.1 m OD. The Thanet Sand, which floors the channel, slopes down to 27.5 m OD, or rather less. No reference is made to the stratigraphy of the deposits in this marginal area.

Chandler's sections illustrated several features which are important to an understanding of the overall structure of the Barnfield deposits:

1. Recognition for the first time of loams above the Upper Gravel and of an expanded 'Middle' Loam.
2. The lenticular nature of the Lower Loam which was shown to rest in a channel cut into the Lower Gravel.
3. The absence of deep erosional features channelling through the Lower Middle Gravel, Lower Loam and Lower Gravel. This is of particular significance since the observations and measurements were made at a time when the entire southern face of the pit was being worked.

The importance of the last point will be examined in Chapter 4 but it interesting to note that later Chandler (1942) specifically stated that he never saw any evidence for the channel figured by Marston.

Marston 1937a (see Figures 3.2 and 3.6)

Marston first visited Barnfield pit in November 1933 as a collector of Palaeolithic implements and eighteen months later he found the first skull fragment which has attracted attention to the site ever since. At the time of the discovery of the skull bone, June 1935, the area of the pit which was being

A Skull Site

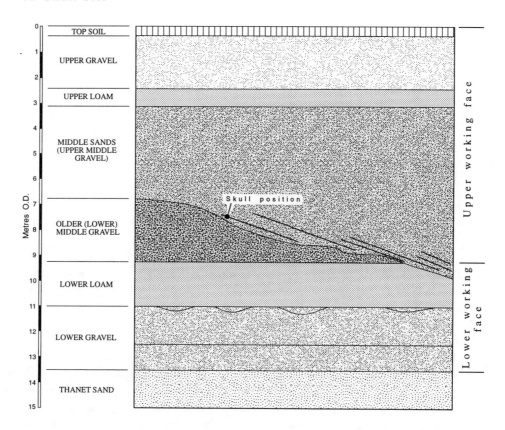

B North-west face

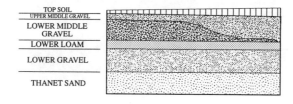

C South Face

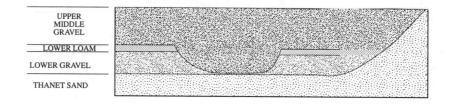

Fig. 3.6. Sections published by Marston in 1937

commercially exploited was the eastern half of the southern face, this was being worked back in a south and south-easterly direction. The western part of the pit was by then disused and unwanted Thanet Sand had been dumped there.

Marston gave an account of his work at Swanscombe to the Royal Anthropological Institute on 12th January 1937 and followed it by a full report published later that year (Marston 1937a). He recorded the following stratigraphic section at the skull site:

Surface soil	
* Stiff brown clay	
Upper Gravels and Upper Loam	about 2.4 m
Yellow Middle Sands	3.7 to 4.3 m
Middle Gravels	3.1 to 3.7 m
Lower Loam	1.2 to 1.8 m
Lower Gravels	1.8 to 2.4 m
Thanet Sand	

* This appears to be Upper Gravel and should be omitted as it is included on the next line.

The thicknesses given show discrepancies when compared with the drawn section (Marston 1937A, figure 5, p 350), reproduced here as Figure 3.6A. Marston's diagram is a composite section, the upper part (above the surface of the Lower Loam) being 30-40 m south of the lower part (below the surface of the Lower Loam).

Marston recognised a phase of erosion and channelling between his Older [Lower] Middle Gravel and his Yellow Middle Sands [Upper Middle Gravel] which he considered to be of major consequence. He represented the channel in his figure 1 (*ibid.*, p 343), but again this is a composite section in which the right-hand half was 40 m north of the left-hand part and orientated at approximately 45° to it. No scale was indicated and the relative thicknesses of the beds shown does not agree with the measurements given above. Figures 3.6 B and 3.6 C are based on Marston's figure 1. Marston described the south face of the old workings where, 'the thick band of the Lower Loam stopped abruptly. It had in effect been eroded or channelled, and still further west the Lower Loam reappeared'. He added that the channel was cut through the Lower Loam and down into the Lower Gravel, 'until the bed of this channel reached almost to the floor level of the Thanet Sand or within 1 foot of it'. However, he stated that he did not establish a connection between this channel and the skull find position because the channel lay outside the confines of the pit.

Lower Gravel. The bottom 0.6 m consisted of a very coarse gravel with very little sand and had a 'rough and tumble appearance', it was covered by a thin layer of brown sticky clay. Clactonian artefacts occurred at one horizon and some flakes showed deep scratches. The upper 1.2 m of the Lower Gravels were finer, well stratified and covered by a shell bed.

Lower Loam. A number of white-patinated Clactonian artefacts were found on the weathered surface of the Lower Loam, together with land shells.

Older [Lower] Middle Gravels. These were more or less horizontally-bedded gravels with an horizon of large stones about 0.6 m above the base.

Middle Gravel Channel Infilling [Upper Middle Gravel]. Oblique seams of red gravel (skull site) with shells occurred in the lower part and were covered by horizontally-bedded muddy gravels and yellow sands with occasional shells.

Upper Loam. Horizontally laminated loam.

Upper Gravel. Stiff brown clay with scattered whitened flints.

B.Conway

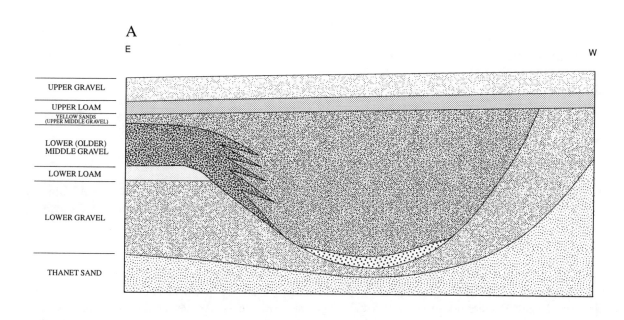

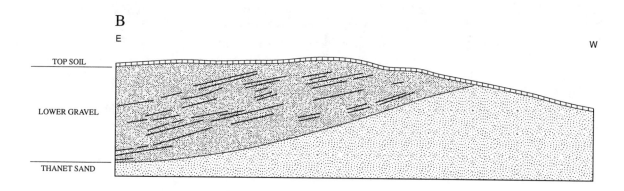

Fig. 3.7. Marston's sections drawn from unpublished paper and photograph in BM archive

21

Marston's principal contribution to the study of the Barnfield deposits was, of course, his discovery in 1935 and 1936 of two human skull fragments associated with Acheulean artefacts. His geological descriptions largely follow Dewey, though with minor first-hand additions. Marston's description of the Lower Loam was the first published reference to the weathered surface of the Loam, though Dewey had earlier implied that the top of the Lower Loam was a land surface. Marston proposed a Middle Gravel erosion stage, with channelling through the Lower Middle Gravel, Lower Loam and Lower Gravel to within 0.3 m of the Thanet Sand on the basis of a mistaken interpretation of finding mixed Acheulean and Clactonian artefacts near the surface of the Thanet Sand (McNabb 1996). He admitted to Chandler and Leach (Chandler 1942) that he had never actually seen the channel. It is very unfortunate that Marston did not differentiate between observation and conjecture when writing his account and preparing his diagrams. The existence of this channel and the consequent necessity of explaining its origin has been given the spurious authority of uncritical repetition by almost everyone writing about the site since 1937.

Marston 1937b (see Figure 3.7)

An unpublished paper by Marston, reproduced in this volume as Appendix II, gives additional geological information on the Lower Gravel and also makes the important point that the Swanscombe deposits show the full channel width of the lower part of the sequence (Lower Gravel and Lower Loam) and that these deposits are not a terrace fragment.

At the base of the Lower Gravel a discontinuous layer of fine gravel, not more than 0.2 m thick, rested on the Thanet Sand and contained small Clactonian artefacts, some of which were patinated white. Marston also recorded part of a tusk of *Palaeoloxodon antiquus* 2.6 m long. The lower part of the main body of the Lower Gravel, the coarse red layer, yielded striated Clactonian flakes; they and the gravel pebbles were usually coated with a tenacious brown clay. Above the red layer the gravels contained a large proportion of flint nodules derived from the Chalk, as well as nodules of chalk. In places the gravels were almost cemented by chalk washout.

Marston devoted a section of this unpublished paper to 'Evidence of the Middle Gravel Erosion Stage'. He observed an excavated exposure which showed current-bedded sands (Upper Middle Gravel) resting on 0.3 m of Lower Middle Gravel which yielded an Acheulean handaxe, overlying Lower Loam. At this point the thickness of the Lower Middle Gravel had been reduced from 3.1-3.7 m to 0.3 m. Unfortunately he offered no similar observed evidence for the existence of the deep channel which he postulated was cut to within 0.3 m of the surface of the Thanet Sand. Figure 3.7A is based on Marston's manuscript diagram. It is interesting to note that the Lower Loam is not shown on the west side of the hypothetical channel (cf. his published diagram and Figure 3.6C).

Figure 3.7B is based on an unpublished photograph of the south face of Barnfield pit taken by Marston in 1934. It shows a margin of the Barnfield terrace deposits resting against a rising slope of Thanet Sand. The photograph has not been annotated but shows apparent bedding traces in the Pleistocene deposits parallel to the Thanet Sand surface. Individual sub-divisions of the deposits cannot be identified, but there is no evidence of channelling.

Marston recognised that the lower part of the sequence (Lower Gravel/Lower Loam) occupied the full width of its own channel and was not part of a truncated Boyn Hill terrace deposit as were higher beds. This is important for the interpretation of the early history of the Lower Thames Valley.

Dines 1938 (see Figures 3.2 and 3.8)

The Swanscombe Committee description of the geology of the Barnfield site (Dines *in* Swanscombe Committee 1938) produced by H.G. Dines with the co-operation of W.B.R. King and K.P. Oakley, relied entirely on the publications of previous workers which they list as Smith and Dewey (1913 and 1914), Chandler (1928/9) and Dewey (1932). But the framework itself was based, with slight modifications, on the work of King and Oakley (1936).

A

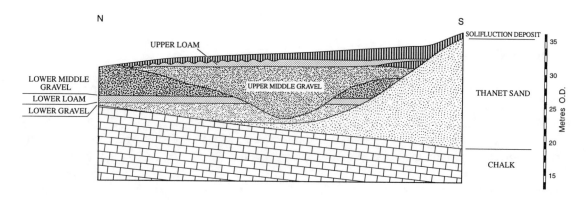

B

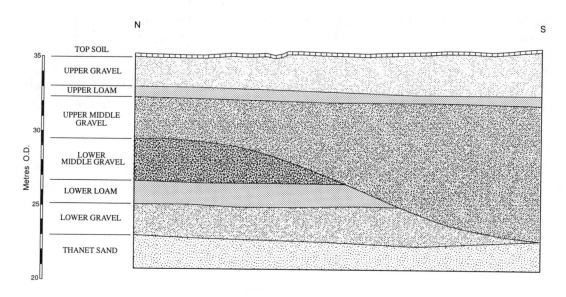

Fig. 3.8. Dines' sections for the Swanscombe Committee 1938

The Committee's view of the structure of the Swanscombe deposits is shown in Figure 3.8A, which is based on Dines's figure 2 (*ibid*), showing only the Barnfield pit section. A generalised section of the deposits exposed in the pit, showing the channelling in the Lower Middle Gravel and underlying deposits is shown in Figure 3.8B, based on Dines's figure 3 (*ibid*). It is a pity that such an eminent group of geologists did not conduct their own independent investigation, particularly in the area of the channel described by Marston.

Figure 3.8A shows a wedge-shaped mass of solifluction material resting on the surface of the Upper Middle Gravel. This was apparently seen at the western end of Barnfield pit adjacent to the Thanet Sand 'cliff'; there is no previous published reference to it, though there is later confirmation (Paterson 1940).

Cotton 1938 (see Figure 3.2)

M.A. Cotton in describing the Swanscombe Committee's excavations in Barnfield pit in June 1937 (Cotton *in* Swanscombe Committee 1938) provides some first-hand geological information regarding the Middle Gravels.

A section excavated some distance to the north-east of the skull site, where the Lower Middle Gravel showed maximum thickness, provided the following:

Upper Middle Gravel. Below the base of the Upper Loam were yellow sands with a thickness of 1.8 m, the lower 0.6 m of which were excavated by hand, but no artefacts were found.

Lower Middle Gravel. Well-stratified layers of coarse gravel and a finer gravel mixed with reddish sand with a thickness of 2.4 m. The gravel yielded bifaces and flakes.

From the above section the [Lower] Middle Gravels were traced south-westwards along the working face towards the skull site.The [Upper Middle Gravel] sands were found to increase in thickness and the horizontally-bedded gravels were cut out by the 'channel', in which false-bedded seams of gravel were deposited. The lowest of these oblique layers contained the skull bones and were covered by sands which transgressed beyond the limits of the channel and over the surface of the adjacent horizontally-bedded gravels.

Paterson 1940 (see Figure 3.2 and 3.9)

Paterson wrote 'The Swanscombe Skull: a Defence' (Paterson 1940) in response to criticisms of the age of the skull (as determined by the Swanscombe Committee 1938) by Vaufrey (1939). Paterson himself was critical of parts of the Committee's report and sought to present a more *accurate* (author's italics) geological account of the deposits of Barnfield Pit. He illustrated this with a generalised section (*ibid*, figure 1 p.167) on which Figure 3.9 is based. The thicknesses given assume that Paterson's diagram is to scale. The total height of the section is given as 12.2 m. On his original section, Paterson indicated individual deposits and disconformities by assigning them numbers. These numbers have been reproduced in the text in brackets and can be related to the unit and sub-unit divisions shown in Figure 3.9.

Lower Gravel. (1), Compact, deep brown gravel with boulders and sub-angular sand grains, most bouldery at base, lying on Thanet Sand. Thickness 0.8 m. (2), Layer carrying large rafts of sand and many boulders; the upper part had been washed and re-sorted. Thickness 1.0 m.

Lower Loam. (3), Shelly loam resting on the uneven surface of the Lower Gravel. Thickness 1.5 m. (4), Surface weathering. No thickness given.

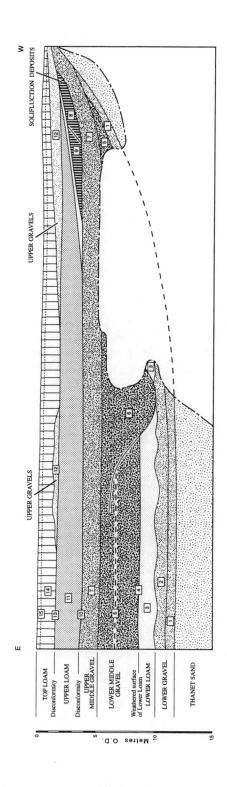

Fig. 3.9. Paterson's section based on Paterson 1937

Lower Middle Gravel. (5), Even-bedded gravels. Thickness 3.5 m. (6), Contemporaneous channel cut through the Lower Loam and with the skull position marked (x). Maximum thickness of Lower Middle Gravel 4.7 m.

Upper Middle Gravel. (7), False-bedded gravels. Thickness maximum 1.5 m.

Solifluction deposits. (8), Raft of Thanet Sand with lustrous brown pebbles and a few sand grains located at the west end of the section. (9), Deep red-brown coarse sand overlain by a thin layer of yellow sand and pebbles banked against (8). (10), disconformity between Upper Middle Gravels and the Upper Loam upon which (8) and (9) rest.

Upper Loam. (11), No description. Thickness 1.7 m.

Upper Gravel. (12), Sandy clayey gravel. Thickness 0.7 m.
(13), Disconformity.

Top Loam. (14), No description. Thickness 1.5 m.
(15), Irregular layer of pebbles. Thickness 0.2 m.

Despite the fact that the 'cliff' of Thanet Sand marking the landward margin of the terrace deposits was exposed for at least four years from 1931, Paterson's diagram is the only published record of the disposition of the beds. The figure is a generalised diagram and it is not possible to say how much of it is conjectural, though it does give the impression of having been sketched on site; the blank areas in the representation of the lower part of the sequence suggest talus. The small area of Lower Loam (3) shown on the west side of the channel is very important to this interpretation. Paterson represents the Middle Gravel channel cutting through the Lower Loam to the surface of the Lower Gravel; he is alone in assigning the channel and its infill to the Lower Middle Gravel. He records solifluction deposits at two levels, in the upper part of the Lower Gravel and on the surface of the Upper Middle Gravel. It would be reassuring to know that these were established from original observations.

Dewey 1959 (see Figure 3.10)

Dewey gave the Stope's memorial Lecture to the Geologists' Association in 1959 with the title 'Palaeolithic deposits of the Thames at Dartford Heath and Swanscombe, North Kent' and it was intended that the text should find a place in the *Proceedings* of the Association. A series of mishaps led to the manuscript being lost for a long period of time until it was found in early 1971. That part of the text concerning Barnfield Pit is largely a re-write of his earlier work (Smith and Dewey 1913; 1914; Dewey 1932), however a piece of data was included which had not previously been published in relationship to the Barnfield site-subsidence of Pleistocene deposits into solution hollows in the Chalk surface.

At a position in about the middle of the north face of the pit (see Figure 3.10) Pleistocene deposits were seen to slope beneath the working face (surface of the Chalk) so that first the Lower Gravel and then the Lower Loam and the Lower Middle Gravel disappeared, but reappeared in reverse order a few yards to the west. Examination had showed that the beds had sunk into a wide, deep solution cavity in the surface of the Chalk. The effect on the terrace deposits of sinking into the solution cavity was that all the lower beds first dipped westwards and then curved upwards with an easterly dip giving rise to a kind of syncline. Another point of interest was that although the three lower divisions of the succession had suffered displacement, the higher divisions passed over the area of disturbance horizontally. In other words the subsidence occurred before the Upper Middle Gravel and Upper Loam were deposited. The length of time between the slumping and the return to horizontal deposition is not known. It is clear however that the beds could not have sunk until the cavity in the Chalk had been dissolved out and that this could not occur until the ground water level in the Chalk fell. Elsewhere in Barnfield Pit other less well exposed solution cavities occurred which locally altered

26

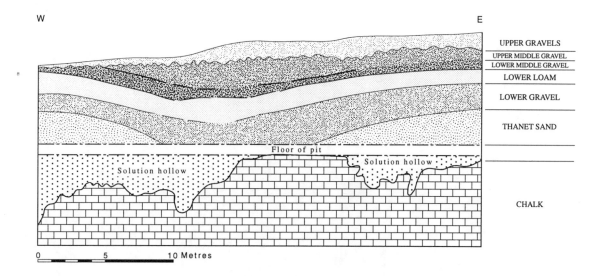

W

E

UPPER GRAVELS
UPPER MIDDLE GRAVEL
LOWER MIDDLE GRAVEL
LOWER LOAM

LOWER GRAVEL

THANET SAND

Floor of pit

Solution hollow

Solution hollow

CHALK

0   5   10 Metres

Fig. 3.10. Dewey's section based on photograph in Dewey 1959

the level of the gravel deposits. Dewey does not give a date for this observation, but it can be fixed with some certainty as 1913 on the basis of an almost identical, and dated, photograph taken by T.W. Reader and published with a description by Dewey (Anon. 1931).

Dewey's recording for the first time of his 1913 observation of disturbance due to collapse into solution hollows has an important bearing on the problem of the Middle Gravel erosion stage and channel. It is significant in this respect that Dewey nowhere mentions seeing a channel on the scale described by Marston when the most extensive sections were available for examination.

Wymer 1964 (see Figure 3.2 and 3.11)

Wymer's report on his excavations at Barnfield Pit in the period 1955-60 provides a description of the Upper Middle Gravels in the area of his own and Marston's discoveries of the skull fragments. His results were published in Ovey (ed) 1964.

Upper Middle Gravel. Unit A, current-bedded sand, with lenticles of fine silt or clay and occasional thin seams of gravel. Thin layer of gravel and some larger flints at base. Thinning flakes in the gravel seams. Thickness 2.4 m. Unit B, current-bedded fine gravel or sand with lenticles of laminated silt and clay (up to 0.15 m thick). Thin layer of coarse gravel with large flints at base. Thickness 0.9 m. Unit C, gravel with large flint cobbles at base, lower part current-bedded, upper part horizontally bedded (including level at which the right parietal bone was found) and with black staining. Thickness 0.9 m.

Lower Middle Gravel. Coarse gravel, resting on surface of Lower Loam. Thickness 0.8 m.

Figure 3.11 is based on part of Wymer's Figure 11 and shows the lower part of the Upper Middle Gravel to be slumped, probably into a solution hollow in the Chalk. A photograph (Wymer's Plate XI) shows micro-faulting associated with this slumping which occurs 27 m south-east of the find position of the right parietal bone.

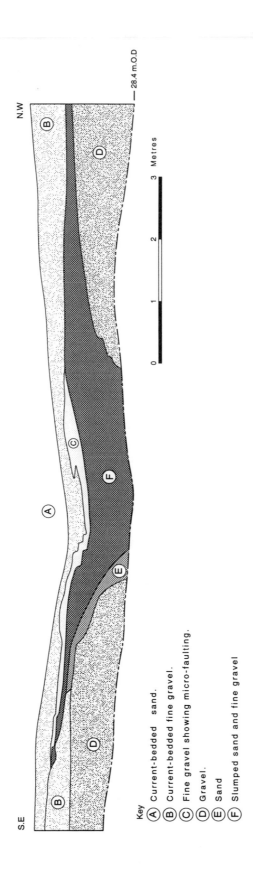

Fig. 3.11. Wymer's section based on Wymer 1964

Wymer's report is of obvious importance as it describes the find position of the right parietal bone, which confirms Marston's account. Also Wymer described slumping of deposits and associated micro-faulting which he suggests might be due to the proximity of a solution hollow in the Chalk. This is of prime importance as, with the exception of Dewey's 1913 observation, this phenomenon has not been recorded at Barnfield before.

SUMMARY

The sum total of the received wisdom of more than fifty years of geological research at Barnfield Pit, Swanscombe, shorn of contradictions, can be summarised as follows.

The deposits of river gravels, sands and loams, at Swanscombe belong to the 'High', '100 foot' or 'Boyn Hill' terrace of the Thames. The sediments were deposited in a wide shallow channel cut in the underlying Chalk and Thanet Sand which was deeper towards its southern bank. The deepest part of the channel is at about 23 m OD; the surface level of the deposits filling the channel is at 30.5 m OD, rising to 33.6 m OD at the southern margin.

The full thickness of the terrace deposits is 12 to 15 m and they have been divided into six local stratigraphic units on the basis of lithology:

Lower Gravel

At the base of the sequence is a medium/coarse, horizontally-bedded sandy gravel with shells, mammalian remains and flint artefacts described in the older literature as Clactonian. Its thickness varies from 0 to 2.9 m. In places the gravel can be divided into three layers based on its colour, red at the bottom followed by white and yellow, but the colour divisions do not persist. An irregular thin layer (0.2 m) of fine gravel rests on the Thanet Sand and contains shells and small sized artefacts some of which are patinated white. The lower 0.6 m of the gravel is coarse, clayey and unbedded with large flints at the base together with a concentration of mammalian remains; artefacts are present, some with striations. The upper 1.2 m of this unit consist of horizontally-bedded medium sandy gravels with chalk pebbles. A lenticular shell bed occurs at the top with some mammalian bones. Artefacts occur throughout.

Lower Loam

A fine, yellow-buff/brown sandy or clayey loam with calcareous concretions and lenticles of shell marl containing abundant land and fresh-water shells; thickness varying from 0 to 2.4 m. The loam is penetrated by tubular root holes and contains scattered shells throughout. The surface of the loam is almost horizontal and is weathered with white patinated artefacts and land shells resting on it. There are no artefacts in the Lower Loam.

Middle Gravels

The Middle Gravels are a composite bed between 4.9 and 6.1 m thick. Horizontally-bedded gravels occupy the full thickness in the northern part of the pit, while to the south the greater part of the gravels is replaced by current-bedded sands.

Lower Middle Gravel

Horizontally-bedded medium/coarse sandy gravel containing scattered shells throughout and with lenses of shelly sand at the base; bifaces occur commonly but no mammalian remains are found. There is a horizon of large flint boulders 0.6 m above the base. Thickness varies from 0.6 to 6.1 m.

Upper Middle Gravel

Pale yellow, current-bedded sands with thin layers of clay, silt and gravel; the thickness varies from 2.4 to 5.5 m. Scattered shells occur throughout but mammalian remains and artefacts are scarce. The upper part of this unit is horizontally-bedded with silt layers and shells. A wedge shaped solifluction mass of sand and pebbles rests on the surface of the Upper Middle Gravel at the western end of the pit.

Upper Loam

Brown horizontally-bedded loam, upper part sandy with an irregular surface, lower part clayey; thickness 1.0 to 1.2 m. No mammalian remains, shells or artefacts occur.

Upper Gravel

Stiff brown clay with variable amounts of gravel which occurs in pockets; thickness 0.3 to 0.7 m. Scattered white patinated bifaces occur. Here and there a yellowish sandy loam (=brickearth) occurs at the top of the gravel.

It is apparent that the length of the descriptions of these units of the Barnfield deposits and the contained detail is directly proportional to the number of artefacts present (or expected to be present) and it also correlates with the height of the beds above the working floors of the pit at the time they were examined!

4. THROUGH THE LOOKING GLASS: AN HISTORICAL PERSPECTIVE ON ARCHAEOLOGICAL RESEARCH AT BARNFIELD PIT, SWANSCOMBE, ca.1900-1964.

John McNabb

INTRODUCTION

The aim of this chapter is to discuss more fully the archaeological interpretations of those workers whose geological observations were described in the last chapter. Readers will find it helpful to have read Chapter 3 and to refer back to the section drawings.

I have tried in this chapter to examine how and why the various students of Barnfield Pit came to hold the views that they did, and to set those views in their broader context.

PRE-SMITH AND DEWEY

In the years leading up to the work of Reginald Smith and Henry Dewey at Barnfield Pit there were several research questions that were being persistently debated. The relationship of human occupation to the ice age; whether or not there had been a number of ice ages; and arising from these two themes, the hotly contested issues that surrounded eoliths. But probably the most pressing research concern in the twelve years between the beginning of the century and the work of Smith and Dewey, was the search for a framework of interpretation that would allow British Palaeolithic studies to be placed in a meaningful chrono-evolutionary scheme.

Even a brief review of the literature on stone tools from this period reveals certain unquestioned assumptions which underlay almost all interpretation. Human evolution was unilinear; the march toward progress was reflected in biface development which was consequently also unilinear and evolutionary in character. Bifaces were therefore repositories of cultural, temporal and developmental information. Dr. A. Sturge in the first Presidential address to the newly formed Prehistoric Society of East Anglia had this advice for geologists studying the fluviatile gravels of the British Pleistocene.

> [geologists]...will be helped by the study of stone implements as much as by topographical and stratigraphical work. These are the true fossils of the gravels, and will, I feel sure, be of as much assistance in forming 'zones' of gravels...

> (Sturge 1908, 14).

In the seminal volume, *Ancient Stone Implements* (Evans, 1897, 2nd edit), Sir John Evans produced a slightly modified classification of stone tools from that first proposed in his brilliant 1859 and 1862 papers published in *Archaeologia* (Evans 1860; 1863). The main points of difference were the recognition of a number of biface types that he believed were made to a specific design format. However, he still considered that the overall division of bifaces was simple, and two fold; 'tongue shaped', and those with a cutting edge all around. Other than a belief that the cruder pointed implements found on higher level gravels were earlier in age than the more refined ovates found lower in the valleys, Evans' work could not be taken as a manual for the subdivision of the Lower Palaeolithic into successive periods using bifaces.

But by the turn of the century such simplistic approaches were no longer acceptable.

Continental colleagues were proposing the kind of progressive unilinear cultural subdivisions, for the Somme valley in France, that were so keenly anticipated in Britain. The expectation of theory, coupled with the lack of consensus about theory for the British data was expressed in the British Museum's guide to its Stone Age exhibitions published in 1902.

> The classification of Palaeolithic implements according to types suggests a relation between form and relative age that cannot be proved till further definite evidence is forthcoming.

> (British Museum Guide 1902, 9).

> A large number of the so-called 'coups-de-poing' may be seen in Cases 107, 108; but no chronological order such as the French scheme implies has yet been established in this country.

> (British Museum Guide 1902, 9).

Reading between the lines, the lack of British results in the face of a wealth of French research was felt by many to be a matter of national honour.

Sturge's opening address to the first Prehistoric Society of East Anglia meeting (Sturge 1908) was less than complementary about the depths to which he though that British Lower Palaeolithic studies had sunk. A committed Francophile, Sturge extolled the virtues of French endeavour, citing the sequences of cultural development that were being established for the whole of the Palaeolithic using Continental evidence.

With this in mind, we should ask why Sturge felt British Middle Pleistocene studies had fallen behind the rest of the world during the first decade of the new century, and where was that great Dreadnought of the British Lower Palaeolithic, Barnfield Pit?

Even a fairly cursory survey of contemporary works dealing with the classification of stone tools during this period reveals that the contribution of Barnfield Pit (which up to the work of Smith and Dewey was universally known as Milton Street) was fairly limited, Evans (1897) mentions the site only once; the 1902 British Museum guide mentions it twice. Both these sources only refer to it in passing. Hinton and Kennard's (1905) seminal work on the relative ages of stone implements in the Thames valley does refer to Swanscombe (although not to Milton Street by name). They describe the prolific nature of the 100' gravels as a source of implements, and assert that almost all are pointed. In a paper on the chronology of the Stone Age delivered in 1909 by Allan Sturge, the pointed implements of the Thames Valley were considered to be earlier than the more refined ovates of Warren Hill in Suffolk.

> To prove the question we ought to show two gravels, one above the other, with the Thames valley types in the lower stratum and the Warren Hill types in the upper. This is difficult to do... I think, however, there is a possibility that we may get the necessary evidence in time.

> (Sturge 1909, 68)

Here Sturge was expressing the details of the chrono-evolutionary sequence that most British scholars confidently expected would be established when the evidence finally came to light. Sturge does not mention Milton Street once.

The Huxley memorial lecture for 1910 was delivered by Boyd Dawkins and dealt with, among other things, the classification of stone tools in the Palaeolithic. Milton Street was mentioned once, in passing, as a prolific source of implements. The substantially rewritten second edition of the British Museum guide to its Stone Age exhibits (1911) only mentions Milton Street, briefly, twice.

It is clear that Milton Street at this time did not hold the special place in the hearts of British prehistorians that it would later assume. Why? The answer to this question provides us with the key to understanding why Sturge felt British Palaeolithic studies lagged behind those on the Continent. The vast majority of the pointed implements at Milton Street came from a single gravel unit. In this respect the site did not differ, substantially, from numerous other gravel sites. Milton street did not demonstrate any evidence of *sequence*. In fact no British site did. Because of its position in the 100' terrace, and the predominance of pointed implements, Milton Street could be slotted into evolutionary classifications, but it was only one site among many that could be so pigeon-holed. It was this lack of a single British site at which the anticipated phases of cultural development could be established that Sturge was bemoaning

The new 1911 British Museum Stone Age guide (*ibid*) was in all probability written by Reginald Smith. The classification adopted by Smith is that of Victor Commont whose extensive researches on artefacts from the terraces of the Somme Valley began to supersede the various systems of classification that had been proposed by other workers (see Hazzledine Warren 1902 for a discussion of the confusing number of different classifications and their inapplicability to Britain). The great appeal of Commont's work was that it precisely conformed to expectations. His system was unilinear, developmental, and stone tools could be used as temporal and cultural zone fossils. The sequence in the Somme did satisfy a time progressive view of culture with the emphasis on development expressed through increasing complexity.

The innate appeal of the classification, the authority of the name Commont, and the prestige of Smith's position in the British Museum undoubtedly contributed to its wide-spread acceptance. For example, in 1912 Chandler and Leach described their finds from the Wansunt Pit at Dartford (Chandler and Leach 1912). The chrono-stratigraphic position of their implements is placed later than those of Milton Street. They quote both the 1911 guide and R. A. Smith personally for help in classifying the artefacts. Now, Milton Street was an important part of the sequence, but its importance was as a reflection of the classification, and not yet because of any outstanding qualities of the site itself. This is clearly demonstrated by an important paper written by R. A. Smith in 1912. It was based on the visit of the Geologists Association to the British Museum Galleries, and in it he describes in much more detail the classification of stone tools and their use as cultural and temporal markers than he did in the more general gallery guide.

> The French classification adopted by the majority of prehistorians in France, and by many also in Germany and other parts of Europe, is here followed with the greater confidence as the progress of research in England tends to confirm it even in minute details...

> (Smith 1912, 137)

Milton Street is not mentioned once.

The Geologists Association visit took place on February 10th 1912, Smith and Dewey began their excavations at Barnfield Pit at the end of March that year. This was the last time that students of the Lower Palaeolithic would be able to ignore Barnfield Pit.

Smith's sub-divisions of the Palaeolithic, as presented in the 1912 paper, are given in Table 4.1.

THE ARCHAEOLOGICAL SIGNIFICANCE OF THE WORK OF SMITH AND DEWEY IN BARNFIELD PIT

The first laurel with which they could be crowned is the insistence on the name Barnfield as opposed to Milton Street. This was the official name of the pit as used by its owners, the Associated Portland Cement Company, who were removing the Pleistocene sands, gravels, and loams in order to quarry chalk for cement making. There were two other pits in the neighbourhood of Barnfield Pit. Colyer's Pit which was also called Milton Street, and New Crayland Lane Pit (occasionally known as Craylands Lane) which also went under the name of Milton Street at times.

Smith and Dewey demonstrated that the stratigraphy that they observed was continuous over the whole of the west and southern faces of Barnfield Pit. The Lower Gravel contained a series of flakes, some retouched, and few cores. Also present were a few elongated and semi-cylindrical flint nodules with flake scars at one end. At the time these were thought to be the characteristic tools of

Name	Assemb. type	Shape	Other defining characteristics
Le Moustier	Flake		Scrapers are dominant tool type unifacial working, Levallois at Baker's Hole.
St. Acheul II	Core tool	Usually oval or heart shaped. Slender, pointed forms (Micoquian) also occur.	Smaller and better worked than before. Micoquian is transitional to Le Moustier.
St. Acheul I	"	Limande is dominant form. Amygdaloid?	Improved flaking, smaller than Chelles. Even/straight edge, twisted edges, cutting edge all around.
Chelles	"	Handaxes, pear-shaped also flat oval	Coarse flaking on all bifaces cortex present on butt, zig-zag edges, Ficrons at St. Acheul, Limandes appear in final phase.
Strepy	"	Cylindrical nodule	Roughly pointed at one end.

Table 4.1. Archaeological sequence as presented by R.A. Smith in 1912 prior to his and Dewey's excavations at Barnfield Pit in the same year. Strepy to St. Acheul II = Drift Period; Le Moustier beginning of succeeding Cave Period. Table compiled from data in table and text of Smith 1912.

Age	Industries with unprepared flakes	Industries with prepared flakes	Industries with bifaces
		Levallois VII	
Wurm		Levallois VI	
	Languedocian	Levallois III-V	Micoquian (= Ach. VI-VII)
Riss			
		Levallois I-II	Acheulian I-V
		Mesvinian	
	Clacton II		
Mindel			
	Clacton I		Chellean (Abbevillian)
Gunz			

Table 4.2. Breuil's Geo-chronological sequence for selected parallel phyla in the European Lower and Middle Palaeolithic (after Breuil 1932).

the Strepy culture. The majority are now known to be the result of natural flaking. The surprise with which the excavators reviewed this material is evident from their report. The lack of bifaces confounded their ability to place a cultural and developmental label on what they had found; this serves as an example of the relationship between expectation and theory that was prevalent at this time.

The Lower Loam was sterile, but the Lower Middle Gravel was rich in pointed bifaces with unworked, or roughly flaked butts, and with sinuous edges. Ovates were few or non-existent. The pointed bifaces were unhesitatingly included within the Chelles culture. At Barnfield Pit the later deposits were less productive. In the report of the first season in 1912 (Smith and Dewey 1913) they hinted that in the current bedded sands [Upper Middle Gravel] there were bifaces that showed advances on the Chelles technique and approached the St. Acheul forms. There were traces of white patination on these ovates. White patinated ovates were reported by the quarrymen from the base of the succeeding Upper Loam. To their frustration the higher units failed to provide unequivocal evidence of more advanced bifaces.

In a resumé (Dewey and Smith 1914) of the first two seasons work carried out in the Swanscombe locality (Smith and Dewey 1913; 1914), the two authors were quite clear that their suggestions of traces of more advanced bifaces in the current bedded sands were accurate. This had been substantiated by finds made in 1913 in the New Craylands Lane Pit, just across the road. Lying on the surface of a current-bedded sand unit, the lateral equivalent of the Upper Middle Gravel in Barnfield Pit, were white patinated ovates of St. Acheul style. They even suggested that the succeeding Le Moustier period was represented in the highest of the three units at New Craylands Lane. The presence of Le Moustier artefacts in the vicinity was demonstrated by a find in the Globe Pit at Greenhithe, from what they took to be a higher stratigraphic unit than any represented in the Barnfield/New Craylands Lane Pits. Also at the Globe Pit was a deposit of Coombe Rock which indicated the initial phase of cold climate after the Thames had cut down from its 100' Terrace level to that of the lower 50' Terrace level. They also investigated Baker's Hole which contained a Levallois industry which they took to indicate Early Le Moustier times.

The first and most obvious importance of this work then, is the identification in a single locality of the stages noted by Commont in the Somme Valley. They were careful to assert that not all the French stages were necessarily present, but that the earliest and the latest certainly were. Thus, on a single terrace the major phases of the Drift period were represented, just as in France, and in their correct stratigraphic order. Britain now had its own St. Acheul, and with it the vindication of the precise model of cultural development that had been anticipated for some time (see above quote from Sturge 1909). The fact that St. Acheul and Barnfield Pit were separated by 120 miles, and that even over this distance the sequence was still valid, leant further support to the model.

The second important result of Smith and Dewey's work was that Barnfield Pit provided an impressive validation for the use of British implements as zone fossils in a sequence that could be demonstrated to have a local as well as international significance. Stratigraphy could be dated by its archaeological content, and implements in particular layers could be used to draw correlations between geographically distinct sites. For example, in discussing the Globe Pit at Greenhithe, Smith and Dewey assert:-

> Though resting on the Thanet Sand, the Pleistocene deposits here correspond to the upper levels at Barnfield, as is proved by the series of implements recovered.

> (Smith and Dewey 1914, 192).

But Smith and Dewey took this concept of zone fossils further, because in order to use bifaces in this way they had to demonstrate that specific implement types were restricted to specific layers. This had been a subject of much controversy (Hazeledine Warren 1902). In their 1914 resumé, they discuss opinions that particular layers are found with an assortment of biface types.

> This is contradicted by the results of our excavations; for it has been shown that the older deposits contain implements or flakes of marked character without any admixture of other forms.

> (Dewey and Smith 1914, 96)

Not only had Barnfield Pit vindicated their expectations in providing a framework within which to chart the progress of human evolution, it had also provided them with a powerful analytical tool that could date sites both geologically and culturally.

At first glance it is difficult to see how such concepts were maintained. The plates that they publish show the presence of pieces that would now be described as ovates in and amongst Chelles forms. The more ovate looking are often described as transitional or latest forms. It is likely that many criteria were employed in assessing the cultural status of a biface. Many were subjective criteria such as degree of technical refinement, how straight the sides were, where the point of maximum width in relation to the point and butt was, or even size (small = late) etc. As far as the importance of biface shape is concerned, up to about 1914 even Smith and Dewey on occasion contradict themselves about its significance. Certainly in many of the earlier classifications people such as Evans (1897) were far less certain about the importance of this variable. It is possible that the work of Smith and Dewey at Barnfield finally served to fix biface shape, in the minds of British Pleistocene archaeologists, as reflecting something that had been of great importance to the Palaeolithic knappers.

CHANDLER AND THE LATE 1920s AND EARLY 1930s

By the time Chandler published the results of his researches, the theoretical background of Lower Palaeolithic archaeology had changed considerably since the days of Smith and Dewey. From the First World War onwards, unilinear cultural evolutionary theory, within which the work of Smith and Dewey was embedded, had given way to diffusionism as the major explanation for culture change at least in mainstream prehistory. Since the 1920s did not see any major new investigations at Barnfield Pit, diffusionism does not really figure much in the contemporary literature on Swanscombe.

The 1920s saw the gradual adoption of an interpretation of culture change seen through a framework called parallel phyla. This theory, pioneered in France by people like Perony (see Sackett 1981), and in Britain by Hazzledine Warren (1923, 1926), held that different and independently evolving contemporary lineages of stone tool using peoples could exist side by side. On occasion they could hybridise to produce new lineages. Stone tools were considered to be the calling cards of individual cultures, with each lineage or phylum expressing its own individuality through distinctive tools. This view of tools was known as the type fossil approach, diagnostic pieces being regarded as *fossile directeurs*. Since certain attributes of these type fossils changed, or evolved, over time, they were capable of reflecting each developmental stage in the history of an evolving phylum. Part of the appeal of this approach may have been that the old concept of time progressive cultural evolution remained embodied within the new explanations of culture change, but just expressed in a different way.

The work of Chandler is to be seen against this background. His work comprises five short articles (1928/29; 1931a; 1931b; 1932; 1935), two of which deal with Rickson's Pit, but can not be divorced from the work on Barnfield Pit. Their importance as a body is that in the eight years that they span, they chart the progress of the Clactonian, a non-biface assemblage type first described by Hazzledine Warren in 1922 (Warren 1922; 1926), from its humble beginnings on the coast of Essex, to international stardom. This meteoric rise was a reflection of two things; the ease with which the Clactonian as a concept fitted into the prevailing theoretical model (parallel phyla), combined with the prestige of the Abbé Breuil. By the late 1920s and early 1930s Breuil had acquired a formidable reputation as a prehistorian. He was responsible for taking the locally applied researches of Warren and Chandler and setting them in the broader European context by inserting the Clactonian within a distinct and geographically widespread non-biface phylum. Chandler's role in all this is rather a modest one. He was the first person to give the flintwork found by Smith and Dewey in the Lower Gravel a cultural label, and in so doing was the first person to formally recognise the Clactonian in the Lower Thames Valley.

Taking Chandler's work as a whole it embodies all the features that would characterise as well as curse the Clactonian in later decades; wide flaking angles, plain flake butts, and a minimum of retouch. Also present were intentionally manufactured chopping tools (in this Chandler and Warren differed from Breuil who believed that chopping tools were cores and that the Clactonian was a flake based assemblage type). The tools were capable of subdivision into eight separate classes, among which were chopping tools (five sub-types), proto-handaxes, Strepy points, and even an early description of a flaked flake which was thought to be an atypical Levallois core! Implicit in his work is the concept that morphology can be equated with tool type, and that individual artefacts were deliberate target forms. This principle was endemic to the thinking of all researchers of this period (see below).

Within the Lower Gravel Chandler identified two phases of occupation. The earliest phase, the so-called derived series, contained flakes and cores that he believed dated to the interglacial preceding the one responsible for the deposition of the Lower Gravel. As the name implied, the large and glacially striated flakes and cores that formed the derived series had been re-worked into the later Lower Gravel. The contemporary series was represented by flakes and cores which were coeval with the Lower Gravel.

The influence of Breuil is clear in the development of Chandler's ideas. Initially, Chandler (1928/29) described the contemporary series as Clactonian, but hesitated to label the derived series at all, although he argued that there was no genuine technological difference between the two. Furthermore he hinted at some similarities between certain of the proto-bifaces and proper Acheulian bifaces. However, by 1930 (Chandler 1931A), he was clear that any St. Acheul affinities were fortuitous, and that the makers of the derived series demonstrated cruder technical abilities. This was a reflection of Chandler fitting his ideas into the growing Breuil world view (the reworked pre-glacial character of the derived series indicated its affinities with Breuil's Clactonian I, see Table 4.2). It was also an indication of the ever increasing influence of Breuil on British Lower Palaeolithic interpretation during the 1930s (see below).

MARSTON, THE SWANSCOMBE COMMITTEE, PATERSON, ASHLEY-MONTAGU AND THE 1930s AND 1940s

For Barnfield Pit the 1920s and 1940s were slow decades. But by comparison, the 1930s were a golden age, crowned by Marston's discovery of the first portion of the Swanscombe skull, and the publication of the report of the Swanscombe Committee in 1938.

One of the most significant developments in mainstream Prehistory during the 1930s was the widespread acceptance of new concepts of what an archaeological culture was, and how individual cultures could be recognised in the archaeological record (see Trigger 1989, especially Chapter 5). These views were pioneered by people such as Kossina, and more especially Gordon Childe, whose works had a wider audience in the English-speaking world. Out of the new understanding of culture arose a new understanding of the kind of history archaeologists were trying to write. This became known as the culture historical approach. Although the impact of this was not as deeply felt by students of the Lower Palaeolithic as it was by those of later Prehistory, the influence of the new concepts of culture did, nevertheless, filter down. Sackett (1981), in discussing contemporary developments in the Palaeolithic of France, asserts that French scholars of this time deferred the writing of culture histories to some future date, and concentrated instead on the establishment of local and regional sequences. While British students were certainly as pre-occupied with establishing regional sequences as their French colleagues were, reading the works of Oakley, Paterson, and Marston, one gets a very strong impression that they did feel that they were writing culture history. In this sense the culture historical approach complemented the parallel phyla approach. Parallel phyla charted the shifting fortunes of culture change and culture development.

The 1930s opened with an important paper by Breuil (1932) setting Swanscombe and the British sequence in its wider European context. This paper had a big impact on British systematics; for example all the major articles on Swanscombe from this period either adopted, adapted, or at least referred to the Breuil framework. The framework is given in Table 4.2. Breuil was not the first to apply the type fossil approach to British Lower Palaeolithic studies (for example Warren in 1926 and 1933 used biface shape to suggest a sub-division of the geological sequence), but he was probably the most influential. His standing as an international scholar would have ensured a primary position for any framework that he suggested, and his pan-European developmental sequence lacked the parochial flavour of those of scholars such as Warren; with the use of type fossils his work ensured that both local and regional sequences could be placed within a much broader perspective. Another important implication of Breuil's work was his application of the Penk and Bruckner (1909) four glacial/three interglacial framework (see Table 4.2) as a background for his archaeological successions. The Penk and Bruckner framework became integral to British Lower Palaeolithic studies throughout the 1930s and 1940s.

But all golden ages have a price; trowel away beneath the surface and you often uncover a different picture. Even a casual glance through journals of this period reveals a great number of papers in which fundamental disagreements between individual scholars combined to prevent the emergence of a consensus of opinion on almost every aspect of Pleistocene research. In this respect Swanscombe provides a useful illustration of just how far away a common understanding of the Pleistocene, and how to study it was. The reasons for this state of affairs are complex but they operate on two levels. The first, briefly outlined below, represented differences of individual scholarly opinion and approach. These can be grouped under the heading of operational difficulties. The second level of explanation represents much deeper and more fundamental difficulties with the theoretical framework itself. These are described in a later section.

Operational difficulties

Although these are discussed as individual points, they are in reality interwoven themes which acted on each other to influence the direction interpretations took.

1. A lack of consensus on the applications of archaeological terminology. Different authors were using the same terms to mean different things. This was particularly noticeable in the usage of such labels as Acheulian and Chellean (Hazzledine Warren 1924; 1926; 1933). Another example is Burchell and Reid Moir's (1933) conflation of the terms Levallois and Mousterian, compared to Breuil's (1932) very different usage. The situation became so bad that Dewey (1930) advocated the abandonment of the terminology that he and Smith had originally established.

2. A symptom of the above was the use by some authors of technological features, such as faceted butts (=Levallois), or thick flakes (=Clactonian), to define an archaeological culture, as well as using the more traditional cultural signatures such as the presence or absence of diagnostic type fossils. An example of this is Marston using deep 'biting' flake scars on bifaces to argue that they were Abbevillian (Marston 1937A; and see below).

3. At the root of most of the archaeological problems was the fact that the identification of type fossils was, essentially, a very subjective business, made so by a lack of adequate operational definitions. For example Breuil based his classifications on:-

> ...individual pieces, even single flakes. How this was done was never made entirely clear; indeed it was part of his mystique.

> (Collins 1986, 36)

> It (the principle of the type fossil) was applied simply to whatever one considered to be diagnostic for purposes of space time-classification and its usage consequently varied from one researcher to the next depending on the tasks that happened to engross him.

> (Sackett 1981, 89)

Not only could individual workers not securely identify different examples of the same type fossil, but different workers had different ideas on what attributes were significant in a type fossil. This explains the differences of opinion between those who considered the bifaces from the Upper Loam as being Middle Acheulian (Hawkes 1938; see below), and those who considered them to be Late or Upper Acheulian (King and Oakley 1936; Paterson 1940; see below). Another example of this is Paterson's (1940) insistence that particular types of core were the diagnostic type fossil for High Lodge as opposed to the scrapers cited by everyone else (see below). An important implication of all this difficulty was that;

4. Stratigraphy was intimately tied to tool typologies and to sequences of typological development that all too often influenced the chrono-stratigraphic placement of a sedimentary layer or unit. So, for example, a Riss-Wurm interglacial deposit would automatically infer a Late Acheulian/Middle Levallois age and vice versa. A good example of this is the dating of the Swanscombe skull by the artefacts with which it was associated. The closest artefact to it was an Acheulian I biface, but not far away were Acheulian III bifaces. Since a more primitive biface can be derived into a later deposit containing a more advanced one, but not the other way round the age of the skull was therefore set at Acheulian III, or early Middle Acheulian. This implied a Mindel-Riss age (see below).

The degree to which these operational difficulties plagued the subject is quite clearly indicated in the following extract which was a reply given to a paper read at the Geologists Association entitled 'Pleistocene Chronology' (Bull 1942).

> It is to be hoped that Mr Bull's excellent summary of Pleistocene events will help to lessen the breach, which still to some extent exists between geologists and archaeologists; for some of the former persistently ignore palaeoliths, while archaeologists have caused so much confusion by frequently altering the names of the industries that few geologists have kept pace with them.
>
> (Bury 1942, 20).

The paper by Bull (*ibid*) is interesting in this context. The paper itself, the character of the seventeen replies (many by eminent students of the Lower Palaeolithic such as Chandler, Oakley, Leach etc.), and Bull's own reply illustrate just how deeply divided a house Pleistocene research really was.

It is against this general background that we may now examine the views of Marston, the Swanscombe Committee, Paterson and Ashley-Montague. They are grouped together because they all fall under the umbrella of a common belief in parallel phyla, a common understanding of culture, and the use of the type fossil approach. (In the case of Ashley-Montague the latter has had to be assumed.)

MARSTON

Alvan T. Marston was a dentist from Clapham. He began to visit Barnfield Pit in 1933, collecting artefacts and making geological and stratigraphic observations. His work was rewarded with the finding of an occipital bone in 1935, which refitted to a left parietal bone discovered the following year. The Royal Anthropological Institute decided to initiate, at Marston's request, an official investigation at Barnfield Pit. Marston's own publication (1937A) appeared in advance of the official report which was published the following year.

What follows is a distillation of Marston's views based upon his 1937 paper, a slightly later unpublished paper which is reproduced as Appendix II in this volume, and archival material in the British Museum. His archaeological observations can be divided into two groups.

1. Pre-Middle Gravel channel phase

In the 1937A paper the Lower Gravel was divided up into three sub-units. The basal sub-unit contained what he called a small Clactonian Industry, characterised by flakes which were usually 5 cm or less in length. The middle sub-unit contained ordinary sized Clactonian artefacts characterised by a greenish patination, as well as Strepy type artefacts. The archaeology in this sub-unit occurred in a single horizon which was considered to be a soliflucted deposit because of poor bedding and striations on the artefacts; it was sealed by a thin clay layer. The third and highest sub-unit of the Lower Gravel contained only Clactonian artefacts, which were large and chocolate brown in colour.

In the un-published paper Marston only divided the Lower Gravel into two sub-units. The description of the lowest one was the same as in the 1937 paper. The small Clactonian was postulated to have come from a nearby working floor. This lower most sub-unit was not present everywhere in the pit, but was locally replaced by the succeeding sub-unit. The basal portion of this succeeding unit was characterised by solifluction. This solifluction effectively divided the Lower Gravel into two temperate and temporally distinct phases. In the higher portion of the second sub-unit, above the solifluction, Marston identified fluvial re-working of the gravels. Within this horizon were Strepy core tools and Clactonian flakes and core tools.

The Lower Gravel was capped by a shell bed which was overlain by the Lower Loam representing the end of the first phase of terrace building at the site. At the top of the Loam, Marston claimed that a land surface developed identified by the presence of white patinated Clactonian artefacts which had been exposed to sub-aerial weathering. Although this represented a break in the sequence, Marston felt it was not as significant a hiatus as that represented by the channel he identified in the succeeding Middle Gravels.

In the 1937 paper, the Middle Gravels were divided into the Older Middle Gravel [=LMG], which were followed by the cutting of a major channel (the Middle Gravel erosion stage), which was then infilled by later deposits (=UMG and succeeding units). In the Older Middle Gravel to the east of the point where the channel was located Marston claimed to find evidence for Abbevillian artefacts. After a phase of uplift the top of the Older Middle Gravel became a land surface on which Acheulian occupation occurred. On the basis of the flakes found at this level Marston argued that the Clactonian was still present at this stage, but the Abbevillian had by now been replaced by the Acheulian. In the unpublished paper he suggested that Acheulian bifaces were found in the upper part of the Older Middle Gravel, as well as on its surface, but maintained his earlier belief that the Abbevillian was not present in the upper part of the unit (see below).

2. The cutting of the channel and the deposits that infilled and overlay it

When the river began to cut down into the underlying deposits (MG erosion stage cutting through LMG and below) in this new phase of fluvial activity, it left a series of beaches at its margin. The first such was the deposit in which the skull was discovered. The archaeology associated with it was Acheulian. Marston's 1937 paper makes it clear that at least some of these bifaces were typed by the Abbé Breuil himself. Bifaces of Acheulian I and III were present in association with the skull, and the remains were therefore equated with Acheulian III. The typological identification of the bifaces was critical, since this was considered the only reliable means of establishing the age of the skull itself. The Clactonian had by now disappeared.

The channel was infilled with a series of gravels and sands [=UMG], and then overlain by the Upper Loam. On the surface of this later unit were white patinated bifaces and two small *in-situ* working floors, one of which contained thinning flakes, and the other refitting material. Although no stage or phyletic associations were suggested, the bifaces were not considered as late as those from Rickson's Pit.

Marston initially identified the channel on the basis that the gravels in the Older Middle Gravel were laterally replaced, in the vicinity of the channel, by yellow sands and finer sediments. Towards the top of the section in this same locality were a series of oblique reddish gravel lenses. The downward trend of these suggested a channel margin. Unfortunately, only a small portion of this feature was visible in the corner of the working face of the quarry. The majority of what he interpreted as a channel lay beyond the limit of the quarry face. As Conway demonstrates in the preceding chapter, Marston allowed his belief in the channel to colour his interpretations of the stratigraphy that was present in order to establish a succession he never actually saw but firmly (and honestly) believed to be genuine. Marston therefore used the archaeology of the Middle Gravels to provide extra support for the identification of the channel. In the 1937 paper his identification of Abbevillian to the east of the channel's location, but only more advanced Acheulian to the west of it, is to be understood in this light. The presence of Acheulian bifaces from the infill of the channel reinforced his belief that the deposits to the west of the feature were much later in time than those to the east of it. This is a good example of many of the operational difficulties described earlier acting together to influence interpretation and even observation.

But this interpretation was not without its difficulties. Conventional thinking would have required Abbevillian artefacts (considered to be pre-Mindel and therefore derived from older deposits, see Table 4.2) to be very rolled, but many were actually in fresh condition. Marston resolved this by arguing that condition was a poor criterion of age, and suggested that knapping technique was a much better one. The crudity of the Abbevillian pieces was a result of their having been made by swinging against an anvil, hence deep randomly orientated flake scars. These bifaces lacked the shallow herring-bone patterned flake scars that resulted from the use of a soft hammer by Acheulian knappers.

THE SWANSCOMBE COMMITTEE

The names of the officers of the Swanscombe Committee read like entries from *Who's Who*; Oakley, Dines, Hinton, King, Hawkes, Kennard etc. Much of the authority of the report is a reflection of the prestige and position of each of its contributors. They were the establishment. The Report of the Swanscombe Committee was the official party line.

The geological background was set against the work of King and Oakley (1936) who produced a synthesised geological and archaeological stratigraphic history of the Lower Thames Valley. In keeping with the spirit of the times, these authors used stone tools as chrono-stratigraphic type fossils for the subdivision of the various units discussed. The theory was an attempt to validate contemporary views on stone tools as cultural and geo-chronological markers. Table 4.3 outlines the main phases of the model as it applied to Swanscombe in 1936 before the Committee's report was published. In the 1938 report the geology remained unchanged, but some amendments were made to the archaeological sequence.

The archaeology was mostly written by Hawkes with the aid of Oakley and Hazzledine Warren. The influence of Breuil is very evident; the typological characterisation of bifaces follows his system, as does the overall presentation of developmental phases within individual cultural phyla. But there is also a clearly local flavour to the conclusions of the Committee. The work of Smith and Dewey, and Chandler, sought to fit the Swanscombe data in the wider (usually French) context. The Committee took the commonly accepted theoretical background of the day (Breuil) at face value, but attempted to adapt it to the local evidence. This is in part a reflection of the work and growing influence of Kenneth Oakley, who with Mary Leakey in 1934, worked at Jaywick Sands, Clacton (Oakley and Leaky 1937). They published a typological and developmental sequence for the Clactonian based upon their researches at Jaywick Sands which was entirely local in origin and character. This is presented in Table 4.4. The conclusions of the Swanscombe Committee were therefore embedded in Breuil's work, as well as the sequences proposed by Oakley working with King and with Leakey. When combined, this represented a powerful home grown theoretical model; the first synthesised archaeological and geological work on this scale since that of Hinton and Kennard in 1905. This was the added ingredient of localised Anglo-Saxon flesh to the bones of French interpretation. The conclusions of the Committee are presented in Table 4.5.

Age	Stage No.	Stage name	Swanscombe unit	Archaeology
	XI	Taplow		
Riss	X	Baker's Hole Main Combe Rock	Upper Gravel	
	IX	Pre-Combe Rock Erosion stage	Upper Loam	Late Acheulian Early Levallois
	VIII	Middle Barnfield (late Boyn Hill)	Middle Gravels	Early Levallois Mid. Acheulian Clacton III
	(VI-VII)	Cutting/filling of Clacton channel	Hiatus = Weathered surface of Lower Loam	Clactonian II (late IIb or III?
	V	Lower Barnfield (early Boyn Hill)	Lower Loams Lower Gravels	Contemp. Cl. II Derived Cl. I
	IV	Pre-Boyn Hill erosion stage		
Mindel	III	Great Eastern		

Table 4.3. Early phases of King and Oakley's model of the Lower Thames Valley as it refers to Swanscombe. (Age has been inferred from other sources).

In the following table, partly based on Breuil (1932, 127), approximately contemporaneous cultures are shown on the same line:

-	'Cave Mousterian'	Levallois VI-VII	-
Acheulian VI-VII	Clactonian IV	Levallois III-V	Tayacian II and Crayfordian
Acheuliuan III-V	Clactonian III	Levalloisian I-II	Tayacian I
Acheulian III (France only)	Clactonian IIb	Proto-Levallosian	
-			
Acheulian II	Clactonian IIa	-	-
Acheulian I-II	Clactonian I	-	-
Abbevillian	Clactonian I?	-	-

Table 4.4. Correlation between different British Palaeolithic Industries as quoted by Oakley and Leakey (1937,242).

Age	Somme archaeological sequence as reported by Committee in 1938	Swanscombe unit	Archaeology	King and Oakley stage
Wurm				
	Final Acheul. (VI-VII) contemporary with Mid. Lev. (III-V)			
Riss		Upper Gravel		
	Mid. Ach. (III-V) contemporary with Early Lev. (I-II)	Upper Loam	Mid. Ach.	IX
		U.M.G.	Mid. Ach.	VIII
		Channel	Mid. Ach.	VIII
		L.M.G.	Mid. Ach. + Cl. Iib/III	VIII
		Weath. L.L.	Cl Iib?	VI+VII
		Lower Loam		V
		Lower Gravel	Cl. II Contemp. Cl. I derived	V
Mindel				

Table 4.5. Oakley's reconstruction of the context of the Swanscombe deposits (drawn from the 1938 Committee report).

Archaeologically the Lower Gravel and Lower Loam was Clactonian. The Strepy elements were seen as either cores or as integral parts of an otherwise flake orientated Clactonian culture. Marston's small Clactonian was retained. Differences in size and condition in the remaining overlying Clactonian were considered to be a result of raw material differences as much as tradition. Following Breuil, they assigned all the Lower Gravel to the Clactonian II stage of his sequence, apart from occasional large and striated (derived) pieces which were assigned to the earlier Clactonian I phase. Following Oakley and Leakey (1937), and Warren (1932), the Lower Gravel was assigned to a new subdivision within phase II, phase Iia. The type assemblage at Clacton was considered to be typologically more advanced and was assigned to phase Iib. In keeping with the time dependant nature of the parallel phyla, the flintwork from the land surface at the top of the Lower Loam was thought to show advances on that from the gravels below, its flakes possessing more 'resolved' retouch. This concept was never clearly defined but seems to imply a more invasive and regular character to the retouch, and the covering of a greater length of the flake edge which in turn imparted a more definite morphology to the flake tool.

The Lower Middle Gravel was characterised as being Acheulian. The differences in style and technique between individual bifaces were a reflection of the natural range of finishes present in any Acheulian assemblage. The cruder pieces which showed little or no evidence of thinning or shaping were rough-outs and unfinished bifaces, not Abbevillian. Hawkes noted that the early Acheulian of Breuil's system (I and II) was not present at Swanscombe, so it would be unlikely that an even earlier contemporary Abbevillian would also be present. The industry of the Lower Middle Gravel was assigned to the early Middle Acheulian of Breuil (Acheulian III). Occasional Clactonian scrapers (Clactonian III) were also noted to be present in this unit.

The skull layer represented a gravel bank on the land surface at the top of the Lower Middle Gravel, and was isolated as the river began to cut down and form the channel that Marston had identified cut into the Lower Middle Gravel. Hawkes assigned these bifaces to the Acheulian III phase as well. Any flakes and simple flake tools present were equated with the Acheulian. This provides an interesting sidelight on the use of type fossils within the parallel phyla approach. Clactonian III was identified by the presence of scrapers (such as those from High Lodge), since this was the diagnostic type fossil of this phyletic stage. Other flake tools could be accommodated within the expanding perception of the Acheulian (see Harper Kelly 1937, for a contemporary discussion of flake tools in biface assemblages). However, a well made scraper in a deposit that was contemporary with Acheulian III bifaces had, by definition, to be Clactonian III.

The infill of the channel and the yellow sands which formed the Upper Middle Gravel was mostly sterile, although what was present was identified as Acheulian III. Hawkes also concluded that there was no Levallois present in the Middle Gravels or in any of the higher units of the Barnfield sequence. Claims had been made for such a presence by Oakley and Leakey (1935).

The main body of the Upper Loam was sterile, but occupation was present on the surface of the Upper Loam. Hawkes noted that the bifaces here were slightly more advanced than those below, but still fell within the Middle Acheulian range. More advanced sub-cordates and ovates were reputed from the pit but were never found *in situ* and Hawkes suggested that they might have belonged to a later channel that post-dated the Upper Loam.

M. A. Cotton also excavated in the Lower Middle Gravel for the Committee, and her work was published in the final report (1938). This work has not been described here because her conclusions wholly supported those of the Committee, as well as Hawkes' overall interpretation of the archaeological sequence from the pit.

Oakley placed the archaeology of the Pit in its wider context (see Table 4.5). The Final Acheulian (VI-VII) was contemporary with Middle Levalloisian material in France. This was dated to the Riss-Wurm interglacial. At the New Craylands Lane Pit was an assemblage of Middle Acheulian twisted ovates. This same tool type occurred with primitive Levallois in the local Upper Loam at Rickson's Pit. By implication therefore, Middle Acheulian and primitive/Early Levalloisian were contemporary phyletic stages. In the underlying local Middle Gravels at Rickson's Pit were Middle Acheulian bifaces that were, typologically, slightly later than those from Barnfield Pit. The Lower and Upper Middle Gravels, including the skull horizon, were therefore placed in an early Middle Acheulian bracket which was dated to the Mindel-Riss interglacial. This reinforced the Mindel-Riss date given to the skull horizon by Breuil. Further support for this date was found in the faunal and sediment mineralogy parallels between Swanscombe and Clacton, and in the fact that Boyn Hill terrace gravels sat on top of the Chalky Boulder Clay/ Great Eastern glacial till at Hornchurch (see Tables 4.3 and 4.5). In 1938, the most important method of dating a site was quite clearly tool typology.

In 1939 Oakley led a Geologists Association field meeting to Barnfield Pit (Oakley 1939). The report of that meeting represents a succinct precis of the Swanscombe Committee's report, and Marston's objections to it. It also emphasises a point not elaborated on in the report. In the King and Oakley model of the Lower Thames Valley (see Tables 4.3 and 4.5) the only major down cutting episode prior to the lowering of the base level which would initiate the 50' terrace, was the inter-Boyn Hill erosion stage (VI) which formed the Little Thurrock/Clacton channel. Within this overall framework there was no room for the major hiatus and terrace aggradation that Marston believed was represented by his channel. The short 1939 paper deals with this difference. The opinion of the Committee was that Marston's channel represented a localised scouring event. As braided rivers moved across their flood plains they cut successive adjacent channels, filled them, and then migrated elsewhere. In such a scenario the feature that Marston saw could easily be incorporated into the succeeding Middle Barnfield stage (VIII) of the King and Oakley model, without upsetting the general model in any way. The Committee's identification of all the archaeology from the Middle Gravels as being Middle Acheulian ensured that a significant hiatus, one long enough to accomodate Marston's view of the channel, never occurred. Once again, typology had set the agenda for stratigraphic interpretation.

PATERSON

Taken at face value, Paterson's criticisms of the work of the Committee were a response to initial criticisms by Vaufrey on the age of the Swanscombe skull. Vaufrey suggested that it was Riss-Wurm in age on the basis of typology, stratigraphy and fauna. Paterson demonstrated that the skull was associated with Middle Acheulian bifaces and reinforced the Committee's interpretation of a Mindel-Riss age (see Table 4.6).

Age	Glaciation number	Stage name	Swanscombe unit	Archaeology
A fifth cold phase	?	?	Pebble layer within top loam (15)	
			A top loam (14)	
			------(13)------	
Wurm	3	X Little Eastern or Hunstanton	Upper Gravel (12)	
		IX	Upper Loam (11)	Upper Acheulian (=Elveden)
Riss	2	Great eastern	Solifluc.(8)/(9)?	
			------(10)------	
		VIII	U.M.G. (7)	Mid. Ach.
		VIII	Channel (6)	Mid. Ach.
		VIII	L.M.G. (5)	Mid. Ach. + Cl.
		VI	Weath. L.L. (4)	Barn. Cl. - D/C?
		V	Lower Loam (3)	
		V	L.G. (rewrk) (2)	Barn. Cl.
		V	L.G. (solif) (2)	phases - C
		V	L.G. (base) (1)	- B
Mindel	1	Norwich Brickearth		

Table 4.6. Paterson's interpretation of the stratigraphic and archaeological sequence at Barnfield Pit. Numerals in parenthesis = Paterson stages (see Chapter 3 and Figure 3.8). Roman numerals = King and Oakley 1936 stage numbers (see Table 4.3).

However, on the question of the cultural position and age of the bifaces from the Upper Loam, Paterson supported Vaufrey and asserted that they should be equated with a Late or Upper Acheulian age bracket. He argued that the bifaces from the Upper Loam were in fact identical to those from Rickson's Pit which were associated with Middle Levallois flintworking (and therefore the equivalent of the Upper Acheulian phyletic stage). Paterson therefore argued that this demonstrated a similar age for the bifaces in the Upper Loam at Barnfield Pit. But this created a problem since conventional wisdom required that the contemporary Upper Acheulian/Middle Levallois phyletic stages be dated to the Riss-Wurm interglacial period (see Tables 4.3, 4.4, 4.5). The Committee had determined that the last cold stage present in Barnfield Pit was the Upper Gravel right at the top of the sequence. These they dated to the Riss glaciation, thus leaving no room for the later climatic phases suggested by

Paterson. His ingenious resolution of this paradox is described below in its proper stratigraphic context.

As Table 4.6 shows, Paterson's (1940) reworking of the Barnfield sequence is very different from that of the Committee. The numbers in parenthesis refer to Paterson's stages as presented in Chapter 3 (see also Figure 3.8). His two fold division of the Lower Gravel with an upper solifluited sub-unit whose upper portions had been fluvially re-worked, is drawn from Marston (see above and Appendix II). The solifluction in the Lower Gravel marks the beginning of the downcutting that resulted, as Paterson believed, in the Clacton channel. Paterson relegated the weathered horizon at the top of the Lower Loam (a marsh deposit that aggraded during the wetter solifluction period) to a drier phase that occurred during the Clacton channel's infilling. Paterson did not support the links suggested between the flake tools from the top of the Loam and those from High Lodge, as tentatively suggested by Hawkes. He asserted that the true culturally diagnostic artefacts from the latter site were specific core forms, and since the loams lacked these, the assemblage from the top of the Lower Loam, and Clactonian III were different. As noted above, Paterson supported the identification of the Middle Gravels as being Middle Acheulian in age. He also indicated that he thought the channel identified by Marston was stratigraphically associated with the Lower Middle Gravel. This observation is never commented on by other authors.

Paterson resolved the chrono-stratigraphic and typological contradiction raised by the re-interpretation of the bifaces from the Upper Loam by cleverly exploiting a contradiction in the Committee's own data. On page 25 of the Committee's report (1938; not page 26 as Paterson asserts), the Upper Middle Gravel is said to pass conformably into the Upper Loam. On page 27 and Figure 2 of the report a mass of solifluction is shown to lie on the surface of the Upper Middle Gravel, and that the Upper Loam is banked up against this wedge. Paterson therefore suggested that there was a previously unrecognised glacial erosion phase between the Middle Gravels and the Upper Loam. By inserting a cold period between these two units, he shunted the glacially generated Upper Gravel up the framework, so that they became a Wurm equivalent deposit and the newly identified cold stage therefore dated to the Riss glaciation. Any artefacts in the intervening unit automatically became Riss-Wurm in age. Thus typology and stratigraphy were reconciled.

Paterson occupies an unusual place in the history of Swanscombe and the British Lower Palaeolithic. As a single body of work his models of cultural development integrated geology, climate, stratigraphy, archaeology, and even philosophy (Paterson 1940). Yet, like his observations on Swanscombe, his work was largely ignored by his contemporaries and almost never quoted. Perhaps his highly critical views of the Committee's work, and consequently the establishment, has something to do with this (he even criticised the use of the Penk and Bruckner framework on the basis that it was relevant only to local Alpine events). His work is a good illustration of just how deep the differences between some scholars of this period really were, while at the same time being firmly rooted in the common assumptions of the period (see below).

ASHLEY-MONTAGU

Excavations were conducted by Ashley-Montagu between the end of May and September 1948. Beyond two brief notes (1948; 1949), the material remains unpublished. The flintwork is curated in the British Museum, although no notebooks or archival material are known to exist. He confined his excavations to the Middle Gravels, and one gets the impression that he was hominid hunting. Ashley-Montagu supported the conclusions of the Committee, and confirmed that the Middle Gravels were Middle Acheulian, although he did recover a single Early Acheulian biface. He also supported a Mindel-Riss date.

SOME OBSERVATIONS ON THE THEORETICAL BACKGROUND OF BRITISH LOWER PALAEOLITHIC FRAMEWORKS DURING THE MIDDLE OF THE 20th CENTURY

The remarks made in this section apply to the interpretations made by scholars during the thirty year period, beginning in 1920, during which parallel phyla and type fossils were the mainstay of all interpretation. Since all thinking on the Lower Palaeolithic was so deeply rooted in the concepts of parallel phyla and type fossils, we should ask why they were such persuasive beliefs? There are three reasons.

1. Belief in the time dependant progressive nature of cultural development, which was seen as a progression through a series of stages, each one an advancement on its predecessor.

2. Tool morphology was believed to be a result of deliberate design, and each artefact that was knapped was an intended target form. Consequently the stages of a developing phyla could be identified with particular diagnostic tool types. Typical of both of these views are Marston's opinions on the Abbevillian in the Middle Gravels.

3. This led to what Sackett (1982) has described as an organic view of culture. As a culture grew so its artefacts and type fossils grew with it. This is very apparent from the preceding sections describing work on Swanscombe.

When taken together, and combined with the unquestioned belief that stone tools could be used to date a geological layer (a belief that was itself a result of the acceptance of the above three points), these beliefs became self perpetuating and self validating. In effect these common assumptions acted as a 'conceptual lock'. No new theories could be formulated without reference to the lock, and none would be taken seriously that did not conform to it. The lock served to funnel any potential interpretation and allowed theory building only so much latitude within which to explore new ideas. For example, Paterson's framework of interpretation was very different from that of the orthodoxy of the Committee, yet like the Committee's it is both a product of and a reflection of the lock.

But how could such an intellectual vice have become so endemic to all Palaeolithic theory building. At a more visceral level than the three points outlined above lay a much more deeply rooted belief that underpinned the thinking of almost all the natural and social sciences of this period. This was the belief in the 'ladder of progress'. One of the legacies of Darwin's work was to infuse into all scientific thinking the necessity of seeing any change that occurred over time as being inherently progressive. This suited the embedded cultural, social and economic prejudices of the late Victorian and Edwardian eras. Although by the beginning of the third decade of the 20th century paradigms had shifted dramatically, the deeply seated belief in the progressive nature of change over time, and especially the steady march of progress toward increasing complexity had not changed. This last point is extremely important since it explains how and why the type fossil approach and all that it implied, could come to occupy such a pivotal role in structuring interpretation. It is also important because it forges a link between Smith and Dewey and later students of Barnfield Pit. The time progressive nature of development, expressed archaeologically through increasing complexity in material culture, was one of the unconscious assumptions common to both eras.

THE 1950s

During this decade there was only one excavation carried out in the Barnfield pit, this was by Wymer (*in* Ovey (ed) 1964). It was conducted against a theoretical background that was undergoing considerable change. While the conceptual lock still held prehistorians in a theoretical vice, cultural interpretation had simply devolved into a constant rehashing of the same old viewpoints, but just expressed in slightly different ways. Few scholars during the 30s and 40s doubted that the type of framework being applied to the data was sound, it was just the fine tuning that needed adjusting (for example the differences between Paterson and Oakley).

Glaciation	Core	Cultures	Flake	
Wurm 3				
Wurm 2				
			Lev. VII	Mousterian
			Lev. VI	Mousterian
Wurm 1				
	Acheulian VII		Lev. V	Mousterian
		Clactonian III?		
		High Lodge		
	Acheulian VI		Lev. IV	
			Lev. III	
Riss 2	Acheulian V			
	Acheulian IV			
			Lev. II	
Riss 1			Lev. I	
		Clactonian IIb		
		Clactonian IIa		
	Acheulian III			
Mindel 2				
	Acheulian II			
Mindel 1				
	Acheulian I			
	Abbevillian	Clactonian I		
Gunz 2				

Table 4.7. The early to middle 1950s view of parallel phyla and cultural development as based on European evidence - after Watson 1956, Table 1.

But this circle was gradually broken during the 1950s. Increasingly, dissatisfaction with one of the cornerstones of the culture historical approach, type fossils, inevitably led to the questioning of the kind of archaeological interpretations built around them. In France, F. Bordes (Bordes and Bourgon 1951; Bordes 1950A) was developing an analytical system that characterised an assemblage by taking into account all the retouched tools present, not just single apparently culturally diagnostic pieces. Acceptance of this kind of approach rendered the concept of the type fossil redundant. There was a domino effect. If type fossils did not genuinely characterise the assemblages within which they occurred, then they could not be used as identity tags for the recognition of individual cultures, or in recognising similar but geographically distinct cultural groups.

> ...it is doubtful if the seven stages of Acheulian recognised in the Somme are precisely applicable to the sequences found in other parts of N.W. Europe, so for the present it is perhaps wiser to describe the industry of Swanscombe Man as Middle Acheulian.

> (Oakley 1952, 285)

Remove the concept of these artefacts from the cultural equation and the ability to date an assemblage was also removed. On this point McBurney was able to express more fundamental concerns.

> After some twenty years of trial it is, however, probably fair to say that few investigators would care to rely on the wide validity of the distinctions proposed by Breuil, as a criterion of date. Indeed the whole question of the recognition of typological development of handaxes seems to have relapsed into extreme uncertainty.

> (West and McBurney 1955, 145)

At a deeper level it also removed the 'hard' evidence for successive development within cultural lineages. During the 50s many students of the period began to speak in terms of an Early, Middle and Late Acheulian without any reference to internal development within each phase. Not surprisingly therefore the principle of independently evolving but contemporary cultural phyla also succumbed to the winds of change.

Advances in analytical techniques in both dating and geology were showing that stone tool based chrono-stratigraphies, as applied to parallel phyla, were unrealistic when compared to those successions developed from the study of litho-stratigraphy (see especially Zeuner 1955; Bordes 1950B). New discoveries at Olduvai Gorge (Leakey 1951) demonstrated simple non-biface industries stratified beneath Acheulian ones, there was no evidence of any genuine contemporaneity between different cultural groups. Leakey argued for a 'slow and gradual evolution' from the Oldowan to the Acheulian and dated the initial Acheulian phases to an equivalent of the early Mindel. The implication of this was that the underlying beds with their Oldowan assemblages were much earlier again. The strength of Leakey's argument lay in this typological development being demonstrated at one site. Elsewhere in Africa the pattern of non-biface industries evolving into biface ones was consistently repeated (Waechter 1952). Africa was becoming increasingly considered as the centre of the cultural and biological evolution of early humans. This was a view made all the more convincing by the virtual absence of such a pattern in Europe (McBurney 1953; the lack of any mention of the Clactonian and the Swanscombe Lower Gravel here is puzzling, Warren had already published his definitive interpretation in 1951). Furthermore Leakey ascribed a high antiquity to the unbroken Olduvai sequence (see above; the Oldowan phase was, by definition, pre-Mindel). The concept of a pre-Acheulian Abbevillian phase developing into an Early Acheulian in Europe and France especially was difficult to envisage (see quote by Bordes below).

But not all scholars were willing to abandon the comfort of previous interpretations so readily. The British Museum's *Flint Implements* (Watson 1949 1st edit.; 1956 2nd edit.) filled the gap left by the now antiquated guide of R.A. Smith (1926). Watson's chronological framework is presented in Table 4.7, and the influence of Breuil's classifications of stone tool development, embedded within the framework of parallel phyla, is still very evident. In France, even Bordes, at the forefront of the move away from Breuil and all that his method implied could not quite abandon the concept of cultural development and the march of progress toward increasing complexity.

> It seems to us that this new point of view has the advantage of putting the French Acheulian out of the position of a freak, and giving it an evolution more like that known elsewhere in the world...two years ago I had a very pleasant trip in the Somme valley with Professor Henry Breuil which was very instructive for me, but neither of us changed our respective opinions very much.

> (Bordes 1956, 5)

Bordes' paper is instructive. He reinterprets the Somme sequence giving stratigraphic succession and sedimentology the primary roles in structuring chronology. The cultural succession revealed brought into focus the degree of difference between this 'new' palaeo-archaeology and that of Breuil and the old culture historical approach, but it was still a developmentally progressive sequence though. In Britain, despite dissatisfaction with the type fossil approach, the King and Oakley (1936) model, as used by the Swanscombe Committee, was still being referred to as a model for dating Lower Thames Valley sediments until the early 1960s (Ovey (ed.) 1964).

In some respects the persistence of belief in development as expressed through increasing complexity (for example Bordes; the succession of Early-Middle-Late Acheulian; and especially Leakey at Olduvai) echoed the earlier linear evolutionary sequences of Smith and Dewey. It can perhaps be best understood in terms of the strength of the ingrained 'social Darwinism' that had helped to structure much of the thinking in the social sciences and the humanities during the twentieth century. Although major shifts in theory building occurred during the first sixty years of this century, this theme was central to all of them.

When Wymer began excavating in the Barnfield pit it was, to some extent, within a theoretical melting pot.

WYMER

Although the full scale Wymer excavations began in 1955 he had been conducting intermittent investigations in the pit since 1950. His excavations were mostly confined to the Upper Middle Gravel, and the results of the five year project were published in 1964 (*in* Ovey *ibid*). Theoretically his published analysis reflects his views for the early 1960s, but is here taken as being representative of the last part of the preceding decade as well.

He sub-divided the Upper Middle Gravel into five basic sub-units (A-E), although not all were present through-out the pit, and sub-unit D eventually proved to be part of C. Archaeologically, he treated the artefacts from all the sub-units as part of the same phenomenon, on the basis that as the stream that deposited the Upper Middle Gravel cut, filled, and re-cut channels, artefacts would be constantly swept off adjacent landsurfaces into the shifting stream, and then be re-exposed and then entrained into the stream once more during the next episode of channelling. Since it was impossible to separate artefacts on the basis of condition they were all considered contemporary on a unit basis.

There is one feature of Wymer's work that was never really expanded on by other students, this was the range of variation in biface shape, overall morphology, and finish present on the bifaces. This has important implications for biface studies. It meant that at this site the Palaeolithic knappers did not have a fixed concept of shape in their heads when they sat down to make serviceable tools. Wymer explained the variation in terms of differing abilities of the knappers, function and raw material, and asserted that typological characterisation of the bifaces was impossible. In the preceding decade this would have been almost unthinkable.

Wymer defended the identification of the Middle Gravel as Middle Acheulian, but did not accept the identification of the material from the Upper Loam as being the same. The presence of tranchet finishes, S twists, and a preference for cordiform shapes suggested to him a more advanced phase of the Acheulian culture, although he resisted the temptation to label it. Wymer also disputed another fundamental tenet of the *ancien regime*. He asserted that there was no real technological difference between the Clactonian from Swanscombe and the supposedly more advanced facies at Clacton. The concept of a Clactonian III was dismissed as rubbish.

In summing up, Wymer asserted that three assemblage types were present at Swanscombe. The Clactonian, which was always stratified beneath, and therefore earlier than the Acheulian, and two variants of the Acheulian. The stratigraphically higher one showed more advanced technological features. Since no Early Acheulian was proved from Britain at that time, and the Acheulian appeared to directly replace the Clactonian rather than develop side by side with it, Wymer's views can be seen to reflect the changing opinions on the nature of cultural development that were taking place during the 1950s. In the report published in 1964, the scenario offered leaves no room for the concept of parallel phyla. But it is interesting to note that it was still the *succession* of assemblages at Swanscombe that was proving the decisive factor in structuring interpretation.

In 1961 Wymer published the results of his researches into the deposits and archaeology of the Caversham channel (Wymer 1961). This was a seminal paper. He presented a typological framework, backed by stratigraphic observation from sections, for the Thames Valley. This paper, and its suggested framework, was the forerunner of later works (especially Wymer 1968). For the first time the grounds for differentiating between Early (a typological presence only), Middle and Late Acheulian tools were clearly stated. The legacy of earlier decades is still apparent however since it was the biface that was still the lynch pin of the system. The system itself was generated on local data, and applied to a local regional sequence alone. Barnfield Pit was a key site in the establishment of this sequence.

By and large, this was the state of affairs when John Waechter began the excavations in 1968 which are described in this volume.

CONCLUSIONS

The work of Smith and Dewey provided a much needed framework with which to structure the growing mass of archaeological data that was accumulating in the first decade of the century. The fact that at Barnfield Pit several assemblages occurred in stratified contexts assured the site's importance in testing models of cultural development. The progress from apparently simple to more complex suited several theoretical models during the century and established the Barnfield pit as both the weather vane of interpretation as well as its yardstick. Modern theoretical work, as well as a more comprehensive understanding of the Lower Palaeolithic settlement of Britain, has demonstrated that the sequence of assemblages at Barnfield Pit is only of local significance, and can not now be viewed as time progressive.

No generation can be truly aware of all the forces which shape its direction. Those students of Barnfield Pit whose work has been discussed in these two chapters were products of their times, and their overall interpretations of what they saw and described reflect both the conscious and unconscious influences that acted upon them. Perhaps then the most enduring legacy of Barnfield Pit will prove to be as a reflecting mirror for a disciplines growing pains; a window on archaeologists as much as the practice of archaeology and like the practitioners of past generations we must consider that 'for now we see through a glass darkly...'.

5. THE HISTORY OF THE 1968-1972 EXCAVATIONS

John McNabb and Nick Ashton

INTRODUCTION

This chapter will describe the development of the Waechter excavations in Barnfield Pit over the five year period during which the site was dug. As such, it forms the basis for the faunal and archaeological finds reported in Chapters 9 to 11, 13 and 16. The divisions between the Lower Gravel units, midden and Lower Loam units are listed in Table 5.1 and explained below. The divisions derive from the stratigraphic observations made during the excavation. The data for this chapter has been drawn from a number of different sources. These include the published interim reports (Waechter and Conway 1968; Waechter *et al.* 1969; Waechter *et al.* 1970; Waechter *et al.* 1971), unpublished field notes and section data from Conway, Waechter's unpublished field notes, the site/trench notebooks, and contemporary colour slides. All this material is held in the excavation archive at the British Museum.

Lower Middle Gravel
Weathered Surface of Lower Loam/Surface of Lower Loam
Lower Loam, main body within which occur:
    Knapping floor (B3/C3)
    Shelly Sand (B3)/ Pebble Complex (B2)
Base of Lower Loam
Lower Loam/Lower Gravel junction (LL/LG)
Midden
Lower Gravel (1)
Lower Gravel (2)
Lower Gravel (3)
Lower Gravel (4)/Lower Gravel solifluction

Table 5.1. List of stratigraphic units adopted during excavation and used as the basis for the faunal and archaeological analyses.

Heights in relation to sea level for various features and levels within the limits of the main area have been extrapolated from a survey conducted by J. R. Hallam, of the British Geological Survey, which was carried out in 1972. All orientations quoted in this chapter refer to grid north. The orientations published by Waechter in the interim reports (particularly 1970) should be treated with some caution. A considerable amount of detail has been included that may be considered unnecessary, but the information presented here should allow the collections curated in the British Museum to be more effectively used, without necessarily having to negotiate a patchy and often confusing archive. At the end of the description of each year of the excavation, a reconstruction is presented of how the main area looked at the end of the season.

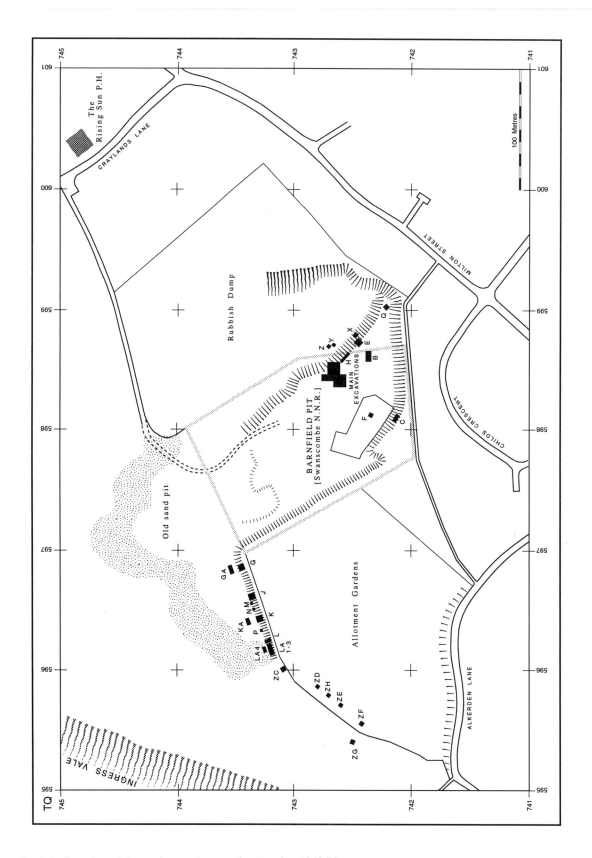

Fig. 5.1. Location of the sections and excavation trenches 1968-72

Year	1968	1968	1969	1970	1971	Current interpretation
Trench	AE	A	A/A1	A2	A3	
Spits measured from	Ground surface = c.27 m OD	Ground surface = c.27 m OD	Top of L.G. = c.25 m OD	27.73m OD or top of L.G.	Top of L.G.	

26.00m OD...

Humus

2B 50-60

2B 1.45-1.65

25.00m OD = top of LG_____

			0-25	0-20	0-40	
		3 2.00-2.20		[= spit 1 = unit(1)]	unit (1)	unit (1)
		3 2.20-2.40	25-50	2.6-3.0 or 20-40		
				[= spit 2 = unit(1)]		
		3 2.40-2.60				
		3 2.45-2.60	50-70	3.0- or 40-60		
		3 2.60-2.80		[= spit 3 = unit(2)]	unit (2)	unit (2)
		3 2.80-3.00				
	2.5-3.1		90-110			

24.00m OD_____

		3 .00-3.20				
		3 .20-3.40	110-130	3.62-3.97		
	3.1-3.8	3 .40-3.50/55	130-150	[= spit 4 = unit (3)]	unit (3)	unit (3)
			150-170			
		3 .55-3.65				
		3 .65-	- Base	3.97-4.47		
			of L.G.	[= spit 5 = unit (4)]	unit (4)	unit (4)

23.00m OD...

		3 .8-4.2		top of mess		
				4.47-		
				[= spit 6 = unit (4)]		

22.60m OD = Thanet Sand...

Table 5.2. Relationship between the excavation spits for each trench and year, with units (1) - (4) used for the analysis of the artefacts (see Chapter 16).

THE 1968 SEASON

Three trenches were opened in 1968 (see Figure 5.1; Waechter and Conway 1968, figure on p. 56). The largest of the three, trench A (later to be expanded into the main area, see Figure 5.2), was dug into a bluff running south-east to north-west across the south-western corner of Barnfield Pit, and near the eastern boundary of the conservancy area. The bluff marks the western most limit of gravel extraction (here being the Lower Gravel) in this part of the pit. It represents a 4 m drop from a platform of *in situ* Lower Loam (which at least in the vicinity of the main area is overlain, locally, by patches of up to 1 m of Lower Middle Gravel), to a thin veneer of Lower Gravel to the east. This remnant of Lower Gravel is never more than 30 cm thick, and overlies Thanet Sand. Eastwards again, the Pleistocene sands and gravels have been completely worked out.

Trench A was situated on the site of an earlier section cut by Kerney (1971) in 1967. In the

1968 interim report Waechter gives the dimensions of trench A as being 5 x 4 m. This is probably the size of the trench as originally laid out, prior to digging. Sections from Conway's field notebooks, drawn after trench A had been dug, show the long axis of the trench (NE - SW) to be 5.2 m long, and the short axis (NW - SW) as being 3.4 m long. Contemporary photographs indicate that the form of the trench was an open ended box (see Figures 5.2 and 5.3a), the open side (NE) aligned with the line of the bluff. This is illustrated in Waechter's 1968 interim report (plate 1 (top), camera pointing south-west).

Unit	Layer	Spit
Lower Loam B, E ext.	1	surface L.L.
"	1	1-40
"	1	40-60
"	1	60-70
"	1	70-80
"	1	80-90*
"	1	90-100*
"	1	100-110*
"	1	110-120
"		120-130
Baulk removal		Base LMG-130
Lower Loam/Lower Gravel	3	
Light brown gravels	3	
Lower Gravel	4	

* marked red and grey gravel

Table 5.3. Spits and heights below datum for trench B, 1968.

At the Lower Loam/Lower Gravel junction, at 1.65 m below ground surface (25.35 m OD in the south western corner of the trench), the excavators identified a horizon characterised by mega-fauna and shells (Waechter and Conway 1968, plate 1, bottom right). This was the midden horizon of succeeding seasons, which in 1968 had yet to be recognised as such. Furthermore, during this first season the midden was believed to be associated with the base of the Lower Loam, but by 1970 it was recognised to be part of the top most level of the Lower Gravel. The midden was restricted to the south-western half of the trench, and the photograph in plate 1 of the 1968 interim shows the midden in the background having been completely excavated.

Whereas the Lower Loam was excavated over the whole of the trench, the digging of the Lower Gravel was restricted to a sondage in the north-eastern half of the trench (called AE). Its position has been reconstructed using Conway's unpublished section drawings and contemporary photographs (see Figure 5.3a; the upper part of AE is shown in the 1968 interim, plate 1, top). Thanet Sand was reached at 2.38 m below the Lower Loam/Lower Gravel junction (22.75 m OD).

The notebook for trench A and the field notes made by Waechter indicate that three stratigraphic subdivisions were identified for the purposes of excavation. Layer 1 represented humus and backfill, layers 2 and 2B were the Lower Loam (including the midden), and layer 3 was the Lower Gravel. The Loam was excavated in spits, usually of 10 cm depth, although the spit depths recorded on the artefacts suggested that spit intervals could vary. The Lower Gravel was dug, for the most part, in spits of 20 cm. Unfortunately, the markings on the artefacts and the information in the trench A notebook do not always tally, but the information given in Table 5.2 is based on the artefact markings.

The other two cuttings made in 1968 were trenches B and C (see Figure 5.1). Trench B was 30 m to the south of A. The long axis of B was laid out in an east-west direction, in order to intersect at right angles the direction of the Lower Gravel channel, and aligned to grid north. An area of 8 x 4 m was cleared to the top of the Lower Loam through 0.45 - 0.75 m of backfill and Lower Middle Gravel. A 2 x 2 m area was then laid out, 1 m in from the north, west, and south edges of the cleared

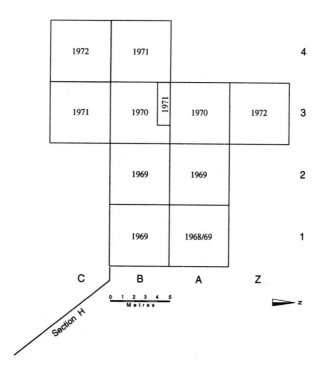

Fig. 5.2. Plan of excavation squares A1 to C4

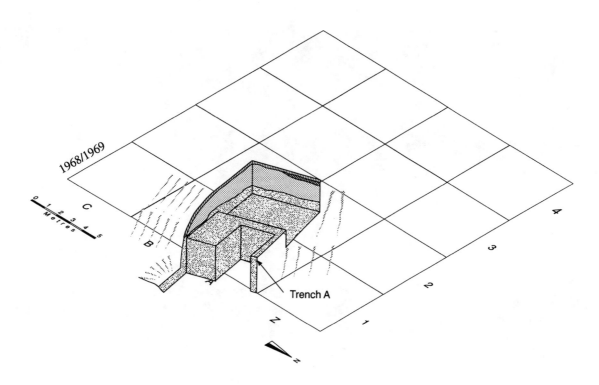

Fig. 5.3a. Isometric plan of excavation in 1968

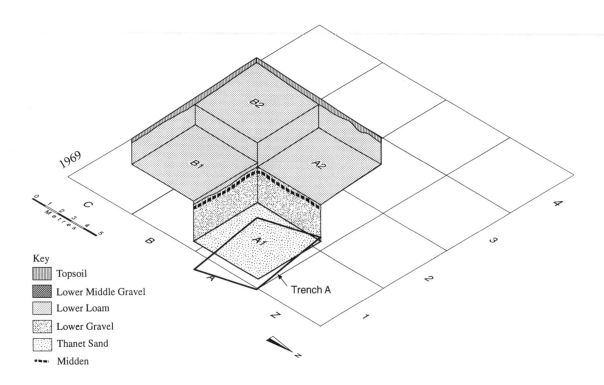

Fig. 5.3b. Isometric Plan of excavation in 1969

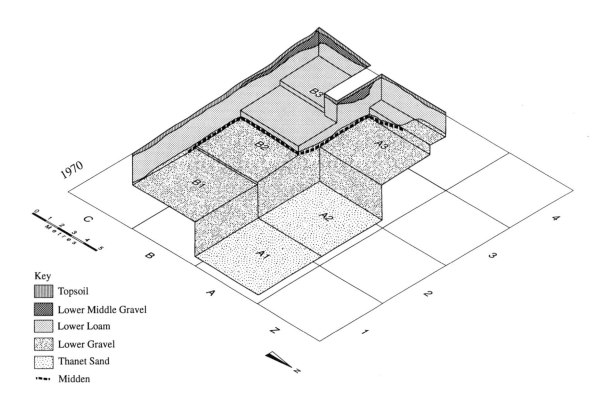

Fig. 5.3c. Isometric plan of excavation in 1970

58

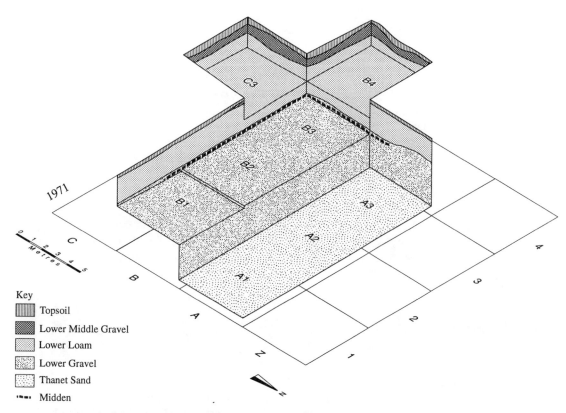

Key
Topsoil
Lower Middle Gravel
Lower Loam
Lower Gravel
Thanet Sand
Midden

Fig. 5.3d. Isometric plan of excavation in 1971

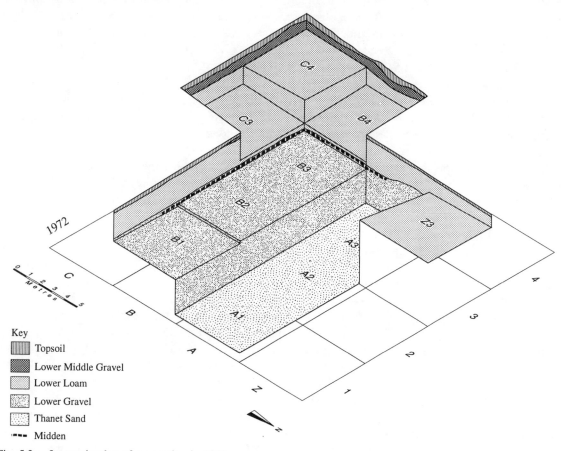

Key
Topsoil
Lower Middle Gravel
Lower Loam
Lower Gravel
Thanet Sand
Midden

Fig. 5.3e. Isometric plan of excavation in 1972

area. This was excavated to 3.0 m below the original ground surface (27.37 m OD in the north-west corner), exposing between 40 and 60 cm of Lower Gravel at the base. The artefacts from B are marked 'B, E, ext.', which refers to this sondage, and they were excavated in spits. No notebook for this trench has survived, but the spit depths are recorded on the flints (Table 5.3). As can be seen from the table the layer numbering for B was different from that used in A (see Table 5.2), since the whole of the Lower Loam is included in layer 1. The absence of a layer 2 may suggest that some material is missing from this trench.

Trench C was situated 70 m to the south-west of trench A (see Figure 5.1) and was orientated south-east to north-west. A ground plan of Waechter's, dated to 1968, gives the dimensions of the trench as being just over 3.6 m (SW - NE) by 4.55 m (SE - NW). This was probably the size of the trench as originally laid out. Contemporary photographs indicate that only a section was cut at this locality in 1968. Conway's field notes indicate that the south-west section was just over 2.6 m in length at ground surface narrowing down to 1.20 m at the base. Trench C exposed 2.10 m of Upper Middle Gravel overlying 1.30 m of Lower Middle Gravel, in turn overlying 18 cm of Lower Loam at the base. The ground surface here was at 30.50 m OD and the Lower Loam/Lower Gravel junction was at 26.98 m OD. Unfortunately none of the artefacts can be related to the section.

THE 1969 SEASON

The frequency of artefacts and bone from trench A, and the possibility of the midden horizon continuing to the west and to the south-west of this trench, largely determined the excavation strategy for the season. The first task was to bulldoze away a large mound of spoil to the south-west of the 1968 trench. Waechter's notes suggest this was the dump for the excavations of Ashley Montagu in 1948 and possibly the Wymer's in the 1950s (see Waechter and Conway 1968, plan, p. 68). Sixteen 5 x 5 m squares were laid out in a 4 x 4 m grid. The alignment of the grid was the same as that of the 1968 trench B, and as such the main area layout was designed to give a cross-section across the Pleistocene channel (Figures 5.1, 5.2 and 5.3b; Waechter *et al.* 1969, 86).

The 1969 season concentrated mostly on excavating the Lower Loam due to the possibility of finding *in situ* occupation floors, as suggested by the desiccation/weathered horizons discovered in the Loam in trench B. Whereas in 1968 the trenches were dug using the spit technique, in 1969 a three dimensional recording system was adopted, which was also used in subsequent seasons in the Lower Loam. The x coordinate was measured from the west face of the square, the y coordinate from the south face, and depth (z) was recorded from a datum of fixed height. In 1969 the datum was 27.13 m OD (89'), although in subsequent seasons a datum of 27.43 m OD (90') was also used. However, the survey of the pit, by Hallam in 1972, concluded that Waechter's datums were 30 cm too low. The real datums are, therefore, 27.43 and 27.73 m OD and the site notebooks have been amended accordingly. Table 5.4 summarises which squares were dug in which years, and to which datums the various finds within those squares relate.

Three squares (A2, B1 and B2) within the main area grid were opened during 1969 (see Figures 5.2 and 5.3b). The Lower Loam in A2 was completely excavated down to the midden level, which was found to continue westwards into this square from A/A1. A plan of the midden was published in the 1969 interim, where the left-hand edge represents the northern edge of the trench. Plate 26 (Waechter *et al.* 1969) is a photograph of the main faunal elements found on the floor, the bottom margin of the photograph representing north. When the midden was dug, the excavators discovered a second bone level directly beneath the first. The published plan of the 1969 midden only shows the material from the upper level. The lower level was recorded in the A2 notebook. Both midden levels were considered to be part of the same depositional feature. Excavation in trench A2 stopped just below the second midden level. The photograph in plate 27 of the 1969 interim depicts A2 at this stage of the excavation with the camera pointing due west.

The other two squares, opened in 1969, were B1 and B2 to the south of the A trenches (see

Figures 5.2 and 5.3b). B2 was only taken down about 0.5 m to expose the surface of the Lower loam which had been covered with quarry rubble. The Lower Loam in B1 was excavated to within 0.30 to 0.50 m of the level of the midden in the A trenches, although the sections in the old trench A indicated that the midden horizon did not extend under the Loam in B1. A full description of the excavation rational and methodology applied to the digging of the Lower loam and the midden in the 1969 season is given by Newcomer (Waechter *et al.* 1969).

The only excavating that occurred in the Lower Gravel in the main area in 1969 was that associated with cutting back the faces of the old trench A in order to align it with the new grid. The majority of A now formed square A1 (Figure 5.3b). The north-west face of A was cut back until it formed a continuous east-west line with the north face of A2. Artefacts found during this phase of excavations in trench A were not recorded three dimensionally, but used the spit system (Table 5.2).

Trench	Units	Year	Datum	Exc.Nos.
A2	LL + Mid.	1969	27.43	1-224
A3	LL + Mid.	1970	27.73	1-112
A3	Mid. + top LG	1971	27.73	113-122
B1	LL	1969	27.43	1-61
B1	LL + top LG	1970	27.73	62-145
B2	LL + Mid	1970	27.43	1-98
B2	Mid.	1971	27.73	99-124
B3	LL	1970	27.73	1-32
B3	LL + Mid.	1971	27.73	33-80
B4	LL	1971	27.43	1-67
B4	LL	1972	27.73	68-113
C3	LL	1971	27.43	1-113?
C3	LL	1972	27.43	114?-124
C4	LMG	1972	27.73	1-2
Z3	LL	1972	27.73	1-19

Table 5.4. The datums for each grid square and each year of excavation for three dimensional recording in the Lower Loam, midden and top of the Lower Gravel.

Outside the main area a number of other trenches were opened during this season. The most important was trench E situated 32 m to the south-east from square A1 (see Figure 5.1). The trench was cut into the same bluff line as the 1968 trench A. Waechter asserts in the 1969 interim that the trench was 2 x 2 m, but the 1969 ground plan suggests it was 5 x 5 m. Handwritten notes, explaining the recording system, also indicate that the trench was wider than suggested in the interim. These notes identify two phases of excavating in trench E during 1969. Finds E1 - E9 are marked 'Sc69', but finds E1/1 - E1/3 are marked 'Sc69, rapid dig'. Slides taken in 1969 suggest that a fairly wide section was originally marked out, only the top part of which was cleaned along the whole exposed face. Excavation through the depth of the Lower Loam was confined to a smaller area adjacent to the north-west edge of the cutting. This may be the 2 x 2 m area described by Waechter. The artefacts were three dimensionally recorded with the x coordinates taken from the south-east face of the trench and the y coordinates from a step on the south-west face. When part of the step was removed, any artefacts recovered from within the step were given a negative y coordinate. The datum used for this trench was 27.73 m OD and the surface of the Lower Loam in the south-west face was at 26.16 m OD. The most interesting finds in trench E in 1969, were two footprints, preserved on a buried landsurface, one of which was provisionally identified in the notes as a deer print (E5). The other one (E6) is marked '?sapiens'. These footprints are more fully discussed in Chapter 13.

Trench F was laid out 52 m to the south-west of square A1, but was not excavated during 1969. Three geological test pits (about 2 x 2 m) were dug during this season, X, Y, and Z. All of them were situated in the thin veneer of Lower Gravel to the east of the Lower Loam/Lower Gravel bluff, with trench X 2 m to the north-east of trench E, and trenches Y and Z about 12 m to east of square A1 (see Figure 5.1). They were cut in order to examine the nature of the lower part of the Lower Gravel base, and their relationship with the underlying Thanet Sand.

THE 1970 SEASON

The main aims of this season were to explore further the extent of the midden in the main area by opening two new trenches, A3 and B3 (see Figures 5.1, 5.2 and 5.3c), as well as to finish off those squares which had been opened but only partly dug in 1969.

Square A2 at the close of the previous season had been left with the surface of the Lower Gravel exposed beneath the lower midden. During this season the Gravels in A2 were taken down to the surface of the Thanet Sand. It was dug in six spits which it appears, from the markings on the flint, probably correspond to four geological units (see Table 5.2). The lowest unit (4) is probably equivalent to Conway's base level (1970 figure 11, L.G. layers 1A - 1C). The division between (2) and (3) could therefore be the pupchen horizon that divides the Gravel in half (Conway's layer 4, the only layer in the body of the Lower Gravel with chalk pebbles). The flints are also marked with heights below datum. In some cases the datum was 27.73 m OD, while in others they were measured from the top of the Lower Gravel (see Table 5.2).

To extend the midden to the west, square A3 was opened. On the published plan of the A3 midden, grid north is represented by the left-hand edge of the diagram (Waechter *et al.* 1970). The eastern edge, where the core and flint block (1 and 2) are situated, represents the A3/A2 junction. Not all of the midden in this square was dug, and a step 1.0 m wide and 0.59 m high was left on the west side of the square.

Square B1 had been left with approximately 30 - 50 cm of unexcavated deposit overlying the level of the midden, although as the sections for trench A 1968, and A2 1969 indicated, the midden itself did not extend under B1. Excavation confirmed this. The Lower Loam passed into the Lower Gravel via a zone of mixed Loam and Gravel. The interim reports and the notebooks indicate that approximately 20 cm of the Lower Gravel was excavated. This material, unlike the Lower Gravel in the A trenches, was three dimensionally recorded.

Square B2 was situated to the south of A2, and was excavated to just below the midden horizon during this season. Excavation confirmed the presence of the midden in this square (see Waechter *et al.* 1970, figure 4 and plate 1 - photo from south-east). Although Waechter gives the average height of the midden as 24.64 m OD (Waechter *et al.* 1970, figure 1), this was based on the initial survey, and a more accurate height is about 25.00 m (based on Hallam's survey and section drawings). The whole of the midden in square B2 could not be excavated this season and a 1.50 m wide and 0.71 m high step was left in the western half of the square (Waechter *et al.* 1970, figure 1).

Square B3, to the south of A3, was excavated through part of the Lower Loam, although a 1 m wide baulk was left on the north side, at the A3/B3 junction which was 3.5 m in length from the west face (Figure 5.2c). At just over 1 m depth in the Lower Loam, discrete scatters of flint debitage were encountered, described as the 'knapping floor' (see Chapter 16). They consisted of a series of 'complexes' and were distinct from the midden (which Waechter also called the floor in his interim reports).

Regrettably there is some difficulty in fixing the exact positions of complexes 19 and 20. The position of 19, which was never recorded in the B3 notebook, can be reconstructed from a ground plot of x and y coordinates, presumably made by Waechter. On this plot, 20 appears to the north of 19, and not to the east of it as the coordinates in the notebook for 20 suggest. If the coordinates in the notebook for 20 were correct, then it would have been unnecessary to remove part of the A3/B3 baulk, undertaken to expose the whole of complex 20. The discrepancy is resolved if it is assumed that the coordinates for this complex were accidentally reversed when entered into the notebook. The position of the complex would then be consistent with its position as described in the text of the 1970 interim. Two photographs of complexes 19 and 20 are presented in the 1970 interim. In plate 2a of complex 19 the right hand side of the frame is to the north. Complex 20 is shown in plate 2b, where the top of the photo is north and the east end of the baulk is shown on the left.

Square B3 was not excavated down to the midden level because of the need to concentrate on the knapping floor. Excavation in the western half of the trench stopped at about 26 m OD, some 20 cm below the knapping floor. The eastern half of the trench was excavated down a further 35 cm to form a level platform with the surface of the step left in the western part of the adjacent square B2. This stage of the excavation is illustrated in plates 1 and 3 of the 1970 interim which relate to the reconstruction in Figure 5.3c.

Trench E was formally extended to 5 x 5 m during 1970. The handwritten notes accompanying E indicate no change in the recording system from the previous year. The full depth of the Lower Loam was not excavated. Further foot prints were identified within the Loam in E at approximately 26.00 m OD (see Chapter 13).

Trench F, which had been laid out in 1969 was extended to 1 x 4 m, during this season (see Figure 5.1). The purpose of this trench was to examine the nature of the Lower Middle Gravel/Lower Loam interface.

Trench G/GA was cut to examine the full Barnfield sequence (see Figure 5.1). It was located at the eastern end of a cliff face below the Alkerden Lane allotments. This is the site of Marston's section F. The section was 5.0 m wide and 11.10 m high, with the top of the section at 34.46 m OD. The base of the section penetrated 0.7 m of Thanet Sand.

A further section L was cut at the western edge of the cliff and showed the full sequence of deposits from the Upper Gravel to the base of the Lower Gravel (see Figure 5.1). The Thanet Sand surface was at 21.80 m OD.

The data and significance of the cliff sections are discussed in Chapter 6.

THE 1971 SEASON

The main aim of the 1971 season was to explore the possibility of the Lower Loam knapping floor continuing to the south of square B3 (ie into C3), and to the west (into B4), since no evidence of its existence to the north or to the east had been identified during the excavation of squares A3 and B2 (see Figures 5.1, 5.2 and 5.3d). Furthermore, the midden, only partially exposed in squares A3 and B2 in the previous season, needed excavating in the western portion of both these trenches. Also, the southern section of A3 indicated that the midden was present under the Loam of B3. Just under 1 m of unexcavated Lower Loam remained to be dug out of B3 in order to expose the midden.

The 1 m wide step in the west of A3 was removed which extended the midden horizon to the western edge of the trench. The interim seems to imply that although the deposit may have continued to the west, the number of finds was falling off in this direction. As with A2, a second level of the midden was identified below the first, but unfortunately, apart from a small number of contemporary slides, no records of this horizon remain. As with the other A trenches, the underlying Lower Gravel was excavated down to the Thanet Sand surface which in this trench was approximately 4.50 m below the ground surface in the north-west corner. The Lower Gravel was dug in spits, but unlike A2 no attempt was made to tie the spits down to specific heights below datum (see Table 5.2). Apart from two 20 cm spits at the beginning of the sequence, the four unit division made in 1970, (1) - (4), was used as the basis for each spit in 1971.

The step in the western portion of square B2 was also removed in order to expose the remainder of the midden, which continued to the western edge of the trench.

The step in the western portion of B3, left at the end of the 1970 season, was at 26.00 m OD. Waechter's interim (Waechter *et al.* 1971) for this season indicates that at this level a second potential knapping floor may have existed. This was based on the condition of at least one mint flake found at this level. Refitting has however demonstrated that this flake (P1989.1-3.1261) actually refits onto material from the higher 1970 floor indicating that there is no second level at this depth (see Chapter 16 for a discussion of the implications).

Below the knapping horizon, in the lower half of the Loam in B3 at 25.80 m OD, an extensive land surface was excavated which was characterised by fine sandy gravel overlying a shell rich horizon of bedded sands. The horizon was only 20 cm at its thickest, but covered a surface area of 20 m^2. When the shelly sand was removed the base of the horizon was seen to be irregular, with a series of shallow depressions, tentatively interpreted as animal footprints modified by water. On steeper parts of the sloping land surface rain water runnels were also tentatively identified (Waechter *et al.* 1971, plate 29). The midden was richer in B3 than in B2, but like B2 no second midden horizon was present. There is no indication of the midden dying out westwards in the B trenches.

Square B4 was opened in order to trace the knapping floor westwards. It was excavated to 20 cm below the knapping floor level, but no evidence of the floor was found (see Chapter 16).

Plate 27 of the 1971 interim (Waechter *et al.* 1971) illustrates the relationship between A3, B3 and B4 just prior to backfilling.

Trench C3, located to the south of B3, was excavated to examine whether the knapping floor continued in this direction. An antler and skull of a fallow deer (#63 and #64, Waechter *et al.* 1971, plate 30), two pebbles (P1989.1-3.1181-2) and two fresh flakes (P1989.1-3.1179-80, Waechter *et al.* 1971, 75-6; see Figures 1.2 and 2.1) were found between 26.05 and 25.83 m OD and up to 8 m to the south of the scatters in B3. Although the heights are slightly lower than the scatters in B3, over a distance of several metres the difference is negligible. As yet there is no refitting between the two squares.

Trench Q (see Figure 5.1) was cut in the south face of Barnfield Pit below the houses on Milton Street. It was 3.3 m deep and 0.75 m wide. It was cut in order to examine the nature of the Lower Loam and its junction with the gravels above and below. The height of the Lower Loam surface was at 26.70 m OD.

Trench H was cut on the same bluff line as trench A 1968 and trench E (see Figure 5.1). It was 9.3 m long, and its purpose was to further investigate the relationship between the Lower Loam/Lower Gravel interface. It was 2.0 m at its deepest, and penetrated 0.5 m into the top of the Lower Gravel. The midden of the main area was absent, thus confirming the evidence of trench A and trench B1 that this feature did not extend to the south-east. The ground surface at the south-western end of the section was at 26.02 m OD.

Six further trenches were cut during this season, all in the east-west cliff line below the Alkerden Lane allotments, and to the west of trench G which was cut in 1970 (see Figure 5.1). These trenches, J, K, L, M, N, and P were, like G, designed to explore more of the relationship between various units in the upper part of the Barnfield Pit sequence (see Chapter 6).

THE 1972 SEASON

Unfortunately, no interim for this, the final season of the Barnfield excavations was ever published, and consequently the amount of information available is limited. Squares C3 and B4 were continued, both reaching an average of 25.20 m OD at the end of the season. Neither square reached the base of the Lower loam.

A new square, Z3, which was situated directly north of A3 (see Figure 5.3e), was opened in order to examine the Lower Loam. The square was started later in the season and only reached a level of 25.80 m OD (see table 4). The notebook for the square indicates that the western half of the square, which is deeper than the eastern half, was taken down as a single block.

The main focus of activity within the main area in 1972 was the excavation of the second of the two new squares to be opened that season, C4. At the junction of the Lower Middle Gravel with the underlying Lower Loam a land surface was discovered (26.80 m OD), retaining a large number of animal foot prints. This surface is discussed fully in Chapter 13.

1972-1994

The excavations finished in 1972, since when the pit has ceased to be a commercial tip. The whole site is now maintained as a nature reserve with the skull area (NNR) preserved as an SSSI. Since the 1968-72 excavations, geological sections have been exposed on four occasions: in 1977 for a field visit by INQUA (Conway and Waechter 1977); in 1982 by Bridgland for the NCC as part of the Geological Conservation Review (Bridgland *et al.* 1985) (sections reopened in 1986); in 1985 to celebrate the fiftieth anniversary of the discovery of the first skull piece (Duff 1985); and in 1995 for a field visit by the QRA (Ashton *et al.* 1995).

Plate 5.1. View of the 1968-72 excavations. The main area looking west

6. THE GEOLOGY OUTSIDE THE NATIONAL NATURE RESERVE, 1968-72

Bernard Conway

The primary purpose of the 1968-72 excavations was an examination of the lower part of the sequence of Pleistocene deposits within the National Nature Reserve at Barnfield Pit (Lower Gravel and Lower Loam) in the NNR. However the opportunity was taken to clear temporary sections of higher parts of the sequence in old workings outside the NNR.

When the excavations commenced in 1968 a much overgrown area of old quarry workings extended north-westwards of the NNR, the 'Old Sand Pit' shown in Figure 5.1. These old workings had an area of about 2 ha and were the last manifestation of the large chalk quarry which in the early part of this century extended a further 400 m northwards to the railway line (see Figures 3.1 and Plates 2.2 and 2.3). Commercial exploitation ceased in the late 1930s and subsequently the chalk quarry was largely backfilled with Thanet Sand over burden from other chalk workings in the Swanscombe area. In 1968 the south face of the Old Sand Pit, much degraded and partially vegetated rose 7 to 9 m above the back-filled floor of the pit and only the Upper Gravel and the upper part of the Upper Loam were visible in the weathered face. The south face of this pit provided all that remained of the once extensive Pleistocene sections. In 1974 the Old Sand Pit was backfilled with Thanet Sand as part of a programme of re-instating the landscape.

In order to obtain geological data against which to assess the work of Chandler, Marston, Dines and Paterson (see Chapters 3 and 4) it was decided to cut sections in the southern face of the old workings and in the floor of the pit. The complicating factor was that as a consequence of the backfilled chalk workings only a narrow strip, less than 10 m in width from the foot of the face, was available for examination. Financial, labour and safety considerations made it impossible to clear the entire face and expose a section to the top of the Thanet Sand. The compromise was to make a series of thirteen cuttings, up to 5 m in width, spread over a horizontal distance of 105 m in an ENE-WSW direction. These were supplemented by six exploratory pits, cut from original ground surface, extending a further 90 m in a NE-SW direction. It should be emphasized that all the sections were cut and examined as plane faces and not, as those inside the NNR area (Chapter 7), in three dimensions.

Due to the unconsolidated nature of most of the deposits, and the difficulty of supporting 'one-sided' excavations of much more than 2 m in height, sections remained open for only a week or two, and in one instance for little over an hour. Despite this limitation sufficient data was recorded to re-enforce the opinion expressed earlier (Chapter 3) that during the thirty years from 1900 to 1930 when the pit was being very extensively worked commercially and when hundreds of metres of section were available for examination very little of the true nature and structure of the deposits was seen or recorded.

In the descriptions of each section that are given at the end of this chapter, the sections are treated in geographic sequence from east to west and in stratigraphic sequence from top to bottom. The Ordnance Datum heights given are based on levelling carried out by Mr J R Hallam and are the result of two circuits which produced a maximum closure error of 0.01 m.

The deposits exposed in the sections cut in the Old Sand Pit were, with one notable exception, found to be assignable to the sequence established and described by Smith and Dewey (1913 and 1914). The existing terminology is therefore retained for the local stratigraphic units. The exception to this is the recognition of a previously undescribed bed, occurring between the top of the Upper Middle Gravel and the bottom of the Upper Loam, and for which the new stratigraphic unit name 'Upper Sand' is proposed. The Pleistocene sequence at Barnfield Pit, as illustrated by the sections on the south face of the Old Sand Pit, is shown in Figure 6.1, and the positions of the sections shown in Figure 5.1.

Section G/GA (Figure 6.2) presents what over the years has come to be regarded as the 'typical' Swanscombe profile; all Smith and Dewey's stratigraphic units are present in the relationships

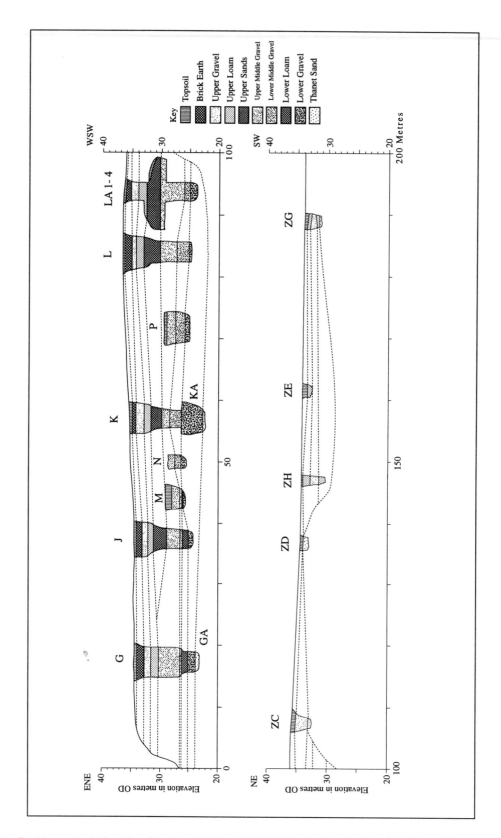

Fig. 6.1. Position and relationship of sections G/GA to ZC/ZJ (Alkerden Lane). See also Figure 5.1

and thickness ranges that they indicated. However, to the west of section G/GA the sequence is seen to change; the Lower Loam thins out and disappears between sections M and N and the new unit, the Upper Sand, appears between the Upper Middle Gravel and the Upper Loam to the west of section J.

The stratigraphic relationships and depositional history of these sediments are described below in chronological order.

LOWER GRAVEL

All the sections cut in the south face of the Old Sand Pit show the Lower Gravel to rest on Thanet Sand. The base of the Lower Gravel is a sharp erosional boundary (E1, see Chapter 8) frequently marked by a lag deposit of large flint cobbles, some of which have been impressed into the top of the Thanet Sand as a result of overburden loading. The boundary is also occasionally marked by a few ml of soft brown clay (see also Chapter 7). In section G/GA (Figure 6.2) the surface of the Thanet Sand is at an elevation of 23.89 m OD; to the west it slopes down gently at about 2-2.5 degrees to 21.80 m OD in section L (Figure 6.6). Further to the west it rises about 5 degrees to 22.74 m OD in section LA4 (Figure 6.7) and then steeply at about 40 degrees to section ZC where its elevation is 33.25 m OD. To the south-west of section ZC for a distance of about 90 m the top of the Thanet Sand is almost horizontal at between 33.59 and 33.84 m OD and includes scattered pebbles and some clay. This may represent the basal few centimetres of the Woolwich and Reading Beds or it may be cryoturbation disturbed Thanet Sand.

The Lower Gravel varies in thickness from 1.05 to 3.45 m and comprises, sometimes indistinctly, horizontally-bedded medium/coarse flint gravel with a sand matrix. Where the Lower Loam overlies the Lower Gravel, eg. in section G/GA, the upper part of the Lower Gravel is a white sand with well-preserved shells exhibiting little decalcification. Where the Lower Loam is not present the top of the Lower Gravel is marked in some places by up to 15 cm of iron oxide cementation of the gravel surface and/or with some clay in the matrix. The deposition of secondary iron oxides, as clast skins and as matrix cement, occurs concordantly with the bedding but is not horizontally continuous for more than a few metres at a time.

The Lower Gravel in the Old Sand Pit sections cannot be sub-divided on textural grounds, though generally it is coarser and with less matrix in the lower part. Throughout the sections the Lower Gravel yielded little vertebrate faunal material - a milk tooth of *Palaeoloxodon antiquus* towards the base of section LA4, and elsewhere indeterminate rolled bone and antler fragments. Occasional rolled flakes occurred throughout the full thickness The scattered molluscan remains are discussed in Chapter 8.

The surface of the Lower Gravel undulates slightly by about 0.8 m and ranges in elevation from 25.09 to 25.90 m OD, it is most clearly seen as a sharp erosional boundary in those sections where it is overlaid by the Lower Loam.

LOWER LOAM

The Lower Loam was found to be restricted to the eastern end of the south face of the Old Sand Pit, to section G/GA, J and M (Figures 6.2, 6.3), where its thickness reduced from 1.40 m (G/GA) to 0.10 m (M) over a horizontal distance of c.25 m. The junction of the Lower Loam with the Lower Gravel is a sharp erosional boundary, the lower part of the Lower Loam does not contain any gravel clasts. The lower part of the Lower Loam in sections G/GA and J comprises horizontally-bedded yellowish brown clayey sands with several thin lenses, 3 to 4 cm thick, of white shell sand of limited horizontal extent - about 1 m or so. This was overlaid by 0.2 to 0.5 m of brown silty clay with some sand which

Trench G - GA

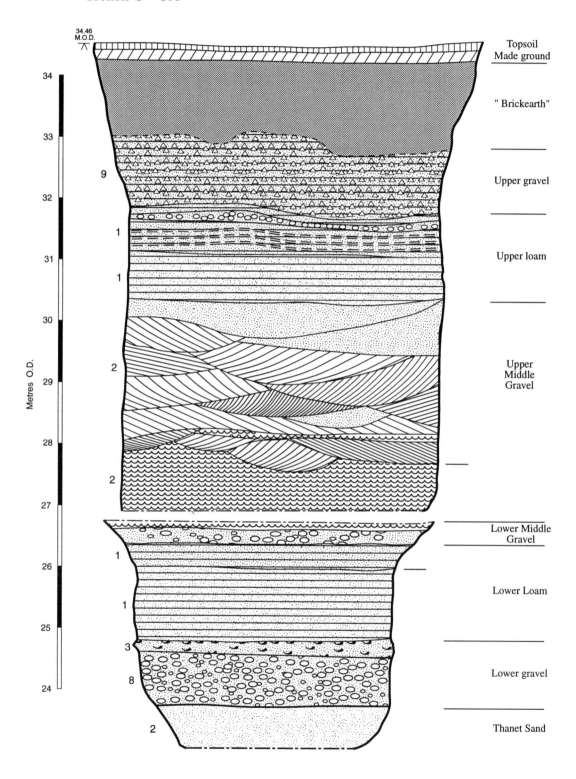

Fig. 6.2. Section G-GA (see opposite page for description)

SECTION G. Nat. Grid Ref TQ 59685 74344_

From	To	Thick		OD Ht.
GS	0.10	0.10	TOPSOIL	34.46
0.10	0.30	0.20	MADE GROUND	
				34.16
0.30	1.60	1.30	'BRICKEARTH'.Yellowish brown (10YR 5/2) loose clayey silt with scattered flint pebbles; pebbles increase in frequency below 1.00 m. Lower boundary irregular and indistinct.	
				32.86
1.60	2.70	1.10	UPPER GRAVEL. Light brown (5YR 5/6) fine/medium gravel in a hard sandy clay matrix with scattered cobbles. Clasts predominantly of flint from the Chalk, but include well rounded pebbles derived from Tertiary deposits; many clasts show thermal fractures. Biface at 2.60 m. Lower boundary is sharp and undulating and shows a few cm of hard shaly silty clay with poorly developed listric surfaces.	
				31.76
2.70	3.65	0.95	UPPER LOAM. Light brown (5YR 5/6) indistinctly ripple-bedded hard clayey sand with irregular and discontinuous bands of light grey (N7) clay up to 5 cm thick. A band of fine/medium flint gravel at 2.80 to 2.90 m and greyish orange (10YR 7/4) medium sand at 3.45 to 3.60 m.	
				30.81
3.65	4.25	0.60	UPPER LOAM. Light brown (5YR 5/6) horizontally-bedded clayey medium/coarse sand with patches of fine gravel.	
				30.21
4.25	6.70	2.45	UPPER MIDDLE GRAVEL. Multi-coloured (yellows, oranges and browns) trough cross-bedded fine/medium sand with occasional bands and wisps of silty clay and fine gravel. Handaxe finishing flake at 4.90 m.	
				27.76
6.70	7.75	1.05	UPPER MIDDLE GRAVEL. Greyish orange (10YR 7/40) ripple-bedded medium sand with well-developed micro-faulting with throws of up to 12 cm. Dark yellowish brown (10YR 4/2) clayey silt occupies bedding and fault planes.	
				26.71
7.75	8.00	0.25	LOWER MIDDLE GRAVEL. Dark yellowish orange (10YR 6/6) horizontally-bedded medium/coarse sandy gravel with flint cobbles at base and scattered clay casts.	
				26.46
8.00	8.40	0.40	LOWER LOAM. Light brown (5YR 5/6) soft sandy clay with some impressed gravel in top 10 cm. Two cores 8.00 to 8.10 m.	
				26.06

SECTION GA. Nat Grid Ref. TQ 59685 74354

From	To	Thick		OD Ht.
0	0.40	0.40	MADE GROUND	26.99
				26.59
0.40	0.80	0.40	LOWER LOAM. Light brown (5YR 5/6) soft sandy clay with scattered flint pebbles and carbon crumbs.	
				26.19
0.80	2.00	1.20	LOWER LOAM. Moderate yellowish brown (10YR 5/4) clayey fine/medium sand with thin lenses of white shell sand, and scattered flint pebbles.	
				24.99
2.00	2.20	0.20	LOWER GRAVEL. White fine/medium shell sand.	
				24.79
2.20	3.10	0.90	LOWER GRAVEL. Light brown (5YR 5/6) horizontally-bedded medium/coarse sandy gravel; some clay in matrix below 2.70 m.	
				23.89
3.10	3.80	0.70	THANET SAND.	
				23.19

The floor of the pit, at the foot of section G coincided with the top of the Lower Middle Gravel; a small pit was cut at the foot of the face to a depth of 0.70 m to establish the thickness of this bed. The sequence was continued downwards in section GA, a pit cut about 10 m north of the foot of the face of section G, in the floor of the pit.

Trench J

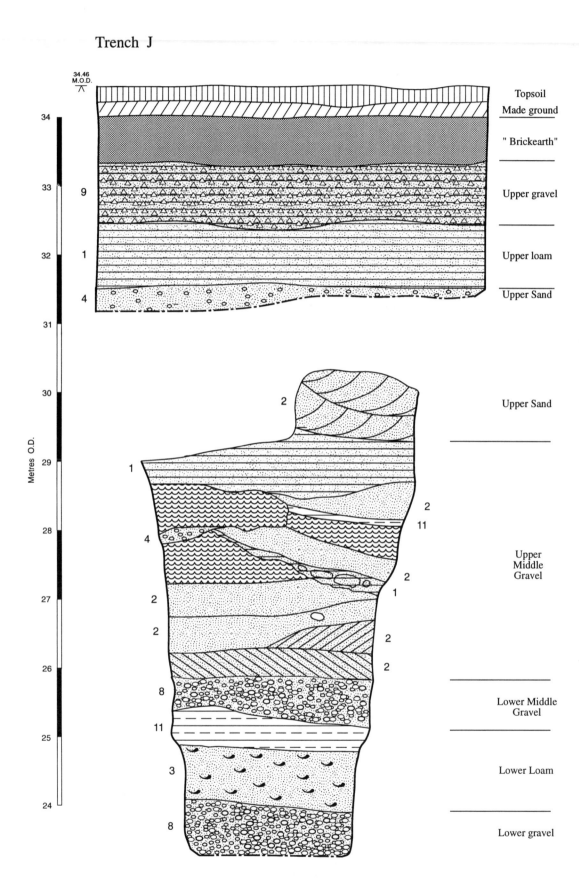

Fig. 6.3. Section J (see opposite page for description)

B.Conway

SECTION J. Nat. Grid Ref. TQ 59662 74335.

From	To	Thick		OD Ht.
GS	0.20	0.20	TOPSOIL	34.46
0.20	0.40	0.20	MADE GROUND	34.06
0.40	1.10	0.70	'BRICKEARTH'. Yellowish brown (10yr 5/2) loose clayey silt with scattered flint pebbles; the number of pebbles increases below 0.90 m. Lower boundary irregular and indistinct. Fragments of broken and crushed bone down to 0.60 m.	
				33.36
1.10	2.00	0.90	UPPER GRAVEL. Light brown (5YR 5/6) fine /medium gravel in a hard sandy clay matrix with scattered flint cobbles. Lower boundary sharp undulating.	
				32.46
2.00	2.90	0.90	UPPER LOAM. Light brown (5YR 5/6) hard clayey sand with irregular and discontinuous bands of light grey (N7) clay up to 5 cm. thick.	
				31.56
2.90	3.25/3.40	0.35/0.50	UPPER SAND. Greyish yellow (5YR 8/4) planar fine/medium sand with scattered small white flint pebbles.	
3.25	3.50	0.25	GAP	
3.50/3.40	4.50	1.00/1.10	UPPER SAND. Brownish grey (5YR 4/1) trough cross-bedded sand. Biface thinning flake at 4.50 m.	
				29.96
4.50	5.20	0.70	UPPER SAND. Light brown (5YR 5/6) even-bedded sandy clay with scattered fine gravel and carbon crumbs on bedding planes.	
				29.26
5.20	7.00	1.80	UPPER MIDDLE GRAVEL. Multi-coloured yellows, oranges, browns and greys) ripple-bedded fine/medium sands and silty clays. This bed is cut by a low angle fault, inclined c.64 degrees from the vertical; slump structures are present.	
				27.46
7.00	7.90	0.90	UPPER MIDDLE GRAVEL. Light brownish grey (5YR 6/1) sandy clay; yellowish brown (10YR6/2) planar cross-bedded medium/coarse sand with scattered flint pebbles.	
				26.56
7.90	8.30/8.60	0.40/0.70	LOWER MIDDLE GRAVEL. Moderate yellowish brown, horizontally-bedded medium/coarse sandy gravel with flint cobbles at the base. Some FE cementation in top 10 cm.	
				26.16/ 25.86
8.30/8.60	8.80	0.50/0.20	LOWER LOAM. Light brown (5YR 5/6) silty clay with light grey (N6) mottles.	
				25.66
8.80	9.60	0.80	LOWER LOAM. Moderate yellowish brown (10YR 5/4) horizontally-bedded clayey sand with lenses of white shell sand and scattered flint pebbles.	
				24.86
9.60	10.40	0.80	LOWER GRAVEL. Moderate reddish brown (10R 4/6) horizontally-bedded medium/coarse sandy gravel.	
				24.06

Use of a hand-auger and sampling tube from the base of this section established the presence of the Thanet Sand at a depth of 1.00 m, ie at an elevation of 23.06 m OD.

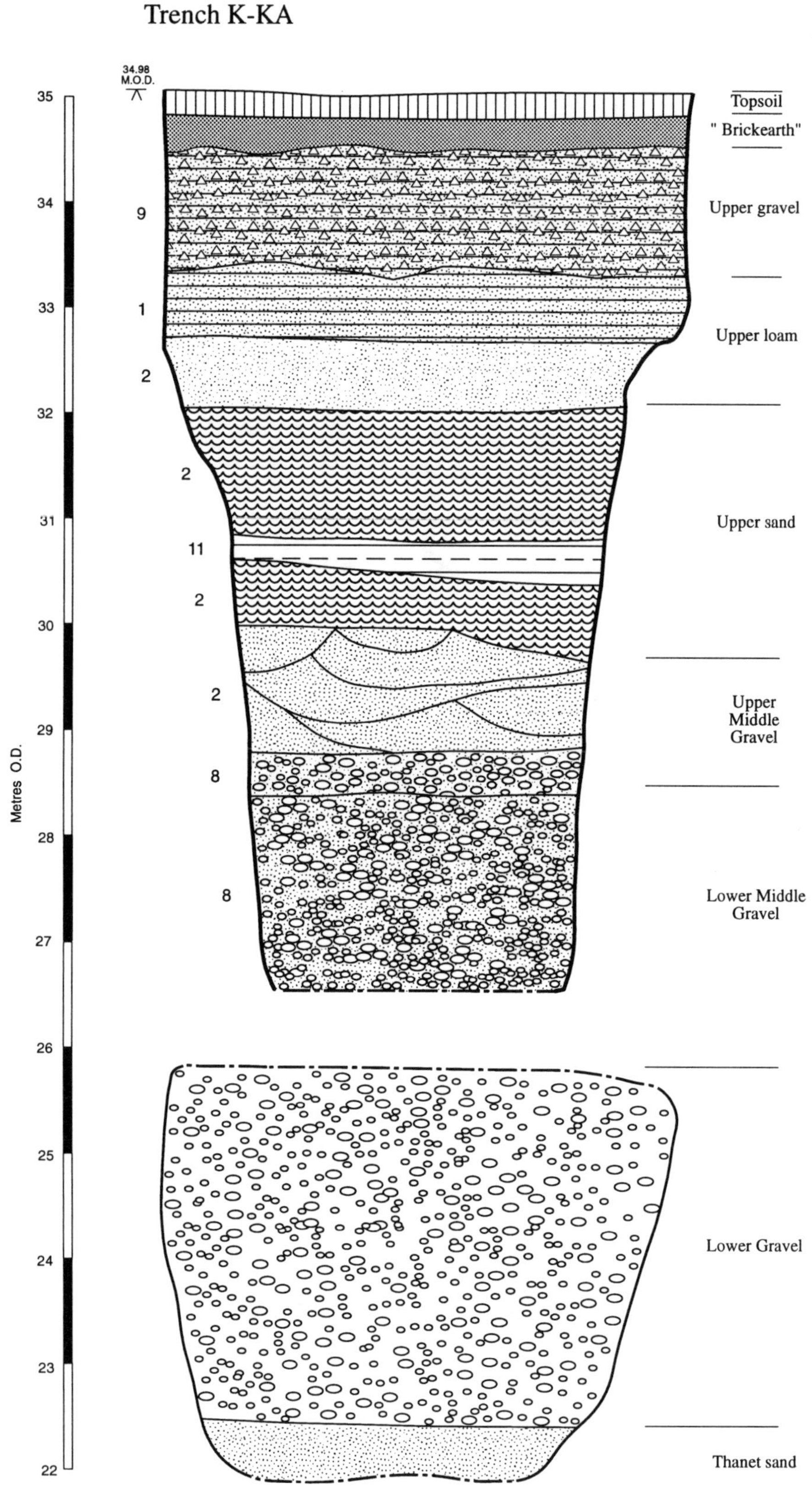

Trench K-KA

Fig. 6.4. Section K (see opposite page for description)

B.Conway

From	To	Thick		OD Ht.
GS	0.20	0.20	TOPSOIL	34.98
				34.78
0.20	0.60	0.40	'BRICKEARTH'.Yellowish brown (10YR 5/2) loose clayey silt with scattered flint pebbles. Lower boundary irregular and indistinct.	
				34.38
0.60	1.70	1.10	UPPER GRAVEL. Light brown (5YR 5/6) medium gravel in hard sandy clay matrix with scattered flint cobbles.	
				33.28
1.70	2.30	0.60	UPPER LOAM. Light brown (5YR 5/6) horizontally-bedded hard very clayey sand with irregular and discontinuous bands of light grey (N7) clay up to 5 cm thick.	
				32.68
2.30	3.00	0.70	UPPER LOAM. Light brown (5YR 5/6) horizontally-bedded coherent medium/coarse sand with scattered flint pebbles.	
				31.98
3.00	4.20	1.20	UPPER SAND. Pale orange (10YR 8/4) ripple-bedded medium/coarse sand with wisps and strings of silty clay delineating bedding.	
				30.78
4.20	4.40/4.60	0.20/0.40	UPPER SAND. Moderate brown (5YR 4/4) horizontally-bedded silty clay with sand partings and carbon crumbs.	
				30.58/ 30.38
4.40/4.60	5.10/5.40	0.70/0.80	UPPER SAND. Pale orange (10YR 8/4) medium/coarse ripple-bedded sand with wisps and strings of silty clay delineating bedding.	
				29.78/ 29.68
5.10/5.40	6.25	1.15/0.85	UPPER MIDDLE GRAVEL. Multi-coloured (yellows, oranges and browns) trough cross-bedded medium/coarse sands with thin layers of clay and fine gravel. Handaxe finishing flakes at 5.80 m.	
				28.83/ 28.63
6.25	6.60	0.35	UPPER MIDDLE GRAVEL. Light brown (5YR 5/6) indistinctly planar cross-bedded medium/coarse sandy gravel.	
				28.48
6.60	8.40	1.80	LOWER MIDDLE GRAVEL. Greyish orange (10YR 7/4) horizontally-bedded medium/coarse very sandy gravel with scattered flint cobbles.	
				26.68

From	To	Thick		OD Ht.
0	3.00	3.00	MADE GROUND	26.68
				23.68
3.00	4.30	1.30	LOWER GRAVEL. Greyish orange (10YR 7/4) horizontally-bedded medium/coarse sandy gravel with scattered flint cobbles. Flakes at 4.00 m.	
				22.38
4.30	4.60	0.30	THANET SAND	
				22.08

showed grey reduction mottles in places. Vertebrate faunal material was scarce and consisted of only a few indeterminate broken pieces of bone and antler. Archaeological material was more plentiful - scattered slightly rolled flakes occurred throughout the body of the Lower Loam and surface clay layer. The molluscs are discussed in Chapter 8.

The top of the Lower Loam is a sharp erosional boundary with a few flint clasts impressed from the Lower Middle Gravel above as a result of overburden loading. The surface shows irregularities of up to 0.3 m in amplitude and varies in elevation from 26.56 to 26.00 m OD over a horizontal distance of about 25 m. The Lower Loam was deposited in a shallow channel cut into the top of the Lower Gravel; these sections show the western margin of that channel (cf. Chandler's 1928 section illustrated in Figure 3.4). The erosional surface which truncates the top of the Lower Loam is continuous with that cutting the top of the Lower Gravel where the Lower Loam is not present. It is an undulating surface ranging in elevation between 25.1 and 26.5 m OD.

LOWER MIDDLE GRAVEL

The Lower Middle Gravel was found in all the sections in the Old Sand Pit sections and rests on either Lower Loam or on Lower Gravel. This lower boundary is an undulating erosional surface with an elevation ranging from 26.56 m OD at the eastern end of the face to 25.25 at the western end, a general fall of 1.31 m over a horizontal distance of 75 m which terminates at the Thanet Sand cliff.

This unit shows marked changes of thickness, from 0.2 to 2.3 m the thickness increasing generally westwards. The Lower Middle Gravel consists of yellowish brown, horizontally-bedded, medium/coarse sandy/very sandy gravels with a lag deposit of large flint cobbles and scattered clay clasts at the base. At its thickest point, in section N, the lower part consists of a pebbly silty sand. The only vertebrate remains recovered was a worn and poorly preserved horn core of *Bos*; the scanty shell data is reviewed in Chapter 8. Archaeological material was rather more abundant and comprised scattered, slightly rolled, biface thinning flakes throughout the thickness of the gravel together with three pointed bifaces.

The upper boundary of the Lower Middle Gravel is a broadly undulating erosional surface with an elevation of 26.71 m OD at the eastern end of the face, section G (Figure 6.2), rising to at least 28.40 m OD in the middle, sections N and K (Figure 6.4) and falling at the western end to 26.44 m OD in section LA4 (Figure 6.7). The top 10 cm or so of the gravel shows variable iron oxide cementation of the sand matrix. The boundary is sharp and shows no lateral passage into the Upper Middle Gravel sands above.

UPPER MIDDLE GRAVEL

The Upper Middle Gravel occurs in all the Old Sand Pit sections and is texturally very variable in marked contrast to the Lower Middle Gravel. It consists in the main of multi-coloured cross-bedded sands with subordinate pebble horizons, gravels and silty clays; in section G (Figure 6.2) the lower part consists of ripple-bedded sands. The Upper Middle Gravel varies in thickness from 1.60 to 3.90 m and ranges in elevation from 29.45 to 30.54 m OD.

In section G the ripple-bedded sands, in the lower part of the Upper Middle Gravel, show the extensive development of small scale, mostly reverse, faults, (Figure 6.5). The throws on individual faults are variable up to 12 cm and disturbance appears to be almost confined to the ripple-bedded sand, though one or two faults do extend c.0.5 m into the cross-bedded sands above. The faulting appears to be the result of cambering associated with a sag structure. Extension of faults into the Lower Middle Gravel below could not be traced. On the western side of section G fine silty clay

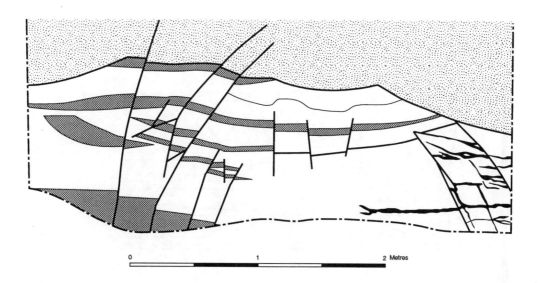

Fig. 6.5. The lower part of the Upper Middle Gravel in Section G showing small scale faults

occupies bedding, fault and fracture planes - probably the result of injection due to complex hydrostatic conditions associated with tension in the shoulder area of a sag. Some of the fault movements were rejuvenations which took place after deposition of the cross-bedded sands. Similar micro-faulting was observed by Wymer (1964; see Figure 3.10), in the vicinity of the find positions of the skull bones; where it was seen to be associated with a similar (or ? the same) sag or slump feature.

The Upper Middle Gravel in section J presents a degree of structural complexity not seen elsewhere in this bed (Figure 6.3). A sequence of even-bedded and ripple-bedded sands were subjected to erosion and slumping or thrusting. The sole of what is taken to be a thrust mass shows a zone of sandy clay clasts of boulder size in a remoulded clay matrix. A detached "raft" of ripple-bedded sand, with discrete boundaries, overlies the intersection of the thrust plane with the eroded top of the Upper Middle Gravel. These structures appear to result from "pushing" from the west, but the cause of the movement is not clear.

Towards the western end of the Old Sand Pit face the top 15-20 cm of the Upper Middle Gravel show disturbance and contortions which are attributable to cryoturbation, beneath a solifluction clay at the base of the Upper Sand.

UPPER SAND

This is a new stratigraphic unit to the Swanscombe sequence which can be clearly distinguished on structural and textural criteria. It consists predominantly of ripple-bedded sands with scattered pebbles, some planar cross-bedded sands, and with wisps and thin bands of clay. The thickness varies from 2.00 to 2.90 m.

At the western end of the face, sections LA1-4 (Figure 6.7), the upper part of the ripple-bedded sands include regularly spaced, thin horizontal bands 2-5 cm thick, of sandy clay which are cut (LA1) by well-developed ice wedge casts 10-30 cm in depth; the ice wedge casts rarely cut more than one clay band. At the base of the Upper Sand (LA1, LA2, LA3) ripple-bedded sands rest on a

Trench L

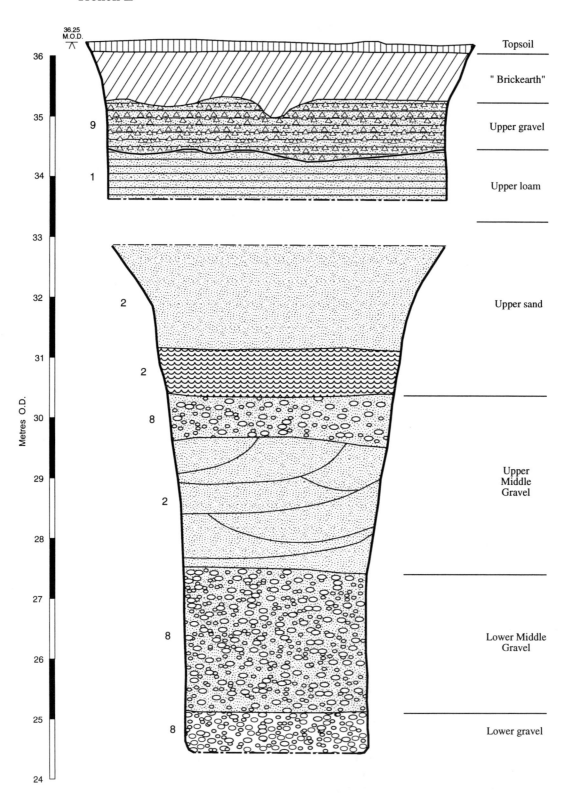

Fig. 6.6. Section L (see opposite page for description)

B.Conway

<u>SECTION L</u>. Nat. Grid Ref. TQ 59628 74322

<u>From</u>	<u>To</u>	<u>Thick</u>		<u>OD Ht.</u>
GS	0.20	0.20	TOPSOIL	36.25
				36.05
0.20	1.00	0.80	'BRICKEARTH'. Yellowish brown (10YR 5/2) loose clayey sandy silt with scattered flint pebbles in upper part. Below 0.50 m many flint pebbles in loose silty sand. Neolithic flakes at 0.30 m.	
				35.25
1.00	1.90	0.90	UPPER GRAVEL. Light brown (5YR 5/6) medium coarse gravel in a hard sandy clay matrix with scattered flint cobbles.	
				34.35
1.90	2.60/3.00	0.70/1.10	UPPER LOAM. Light brown (5YR 5/6) horizontally-bedded firm clayey sand with irregular and discontinuous bands of light grey (N7) clay up to 5 cm thick.	
				33.65
2.60	3.40	0.80	GAP	(33.25)
				32.85
3.40/3.00	5.10	1.70/2.10	UPPER SAND. Dark yellowish orange (10YR 6/3) horizontally-bedded fine/medium sand.	
				31.15
5.10	5.90	0.80	UPPER SAND. Pale orange (10YR 8/4) ripple-bedded fine/medium sand with wisps of silty clay delineating bedding.	
				30.35
5.90	6.60	0.70	UPPER MIDDLE GRAVEL. Greyish orange (10YR indistinctly planar cross-bedded fine/medium sand with thin layers of fine gravel.	
				29.65
6.60	8.70/8.80	2.10/2.20	UPPER MIDDLE GRAVEL. Greyish orange (10YR 7/4) trough cross-bedded fine/medium sand with thin layers of fine gravel and coarse sand.	
				27.55/ 27.45
8.70/8.80	11.00	2.30/2.20	LOWER MIDDLE GRAVEL. Greyish orange (10YR 7/4) horizontally-bedded medium sandy gravel.	
				25.25
11.00	11.70	0.70	LOWER GRAVEL. Light brown (5YR 5/6) horizontally-bedded medium gravel with a little sand. Worn flake at 11.20 m.	
				24.55

Use of a handauger and sampling tube from the base of this section established the presence of the Thanet Sand at a depth of 2.75 m, ie at an elevation of 21.80 m OD.

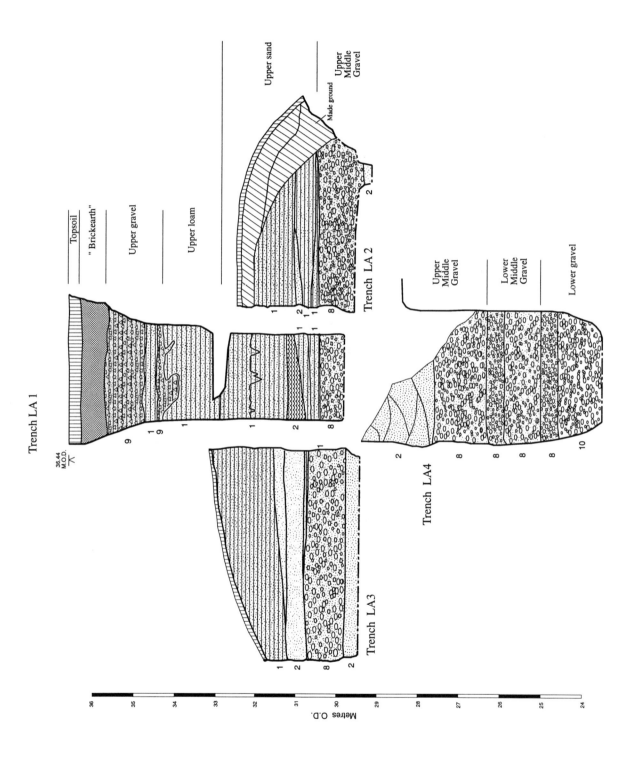

Fig. 6.7. Section LA1 - LA4 (see next two pages for description)

SECTION LA1.   Nat. Grid Ref. TQ 59620 74320

From	To	Thick		OD Ht.
GS	0.30	0.30	TOPSOIL	36.44
				36.14
0.30	0.90	0.60	'BRICKEARTH. Yellowish brown (10YR 5/2) loose silty sand with scattered pebbles.	
				35.54
0.90	1.85	0.95	UPPER GRAVEL. Moderate yellowish brown (10YR 5/4) medium/ coarse gravel in a firm/hard sandy clay matrix with light grey (N7) mottles.	
				34.59
1.85	2.15	0.30	UPPER GRAVEL. Light brown (5YR 5/6) firm clayey fine/medium sand with light grey (N7) mottles.	
				34.29
2.15	2.25/2.70	0.10/0.55	UPPER GRAVEL. Moderate yellowish brown (10YR 5/4) medium/ coarse gravel in a firm/hard sandy clay matrix. Lower boundary sharp and irregular, clayey gravel occupies ice-wedge structures in bed below.	
				34.19/
				33.74
2.25/2.70	3.70	1.45/1.00	UPPER LOAM. Moderate yellowish brown (10YR 5/4) horizontally-bedded firm sandy clay with thin bands of greyish orange (10YR 7/4) medium sand up to 5 cm thick, irregular and discontinuous. Scattered carbon crumbs on bedding planes.	
				32.74.
3.70	5.30	1.60	UPPER SAND. Light brown (5YR 5/6) to dark yellowish orange (10YR 6/6) horizontally-bedded soft/firm clayey fine/medium sand with thin layers of soft pale yellowish brown (10YR 6/2) sandy clay, 2 to 5 cm thick. Ice-wedge casts 4.35 to 4.90 m.	
				31.14
5.30	5.45/5.80	0.15/0.50	UPPER SAND. Pale yellowish orange (10YR 8/6) tipple bedded fine sand with bedding delineated by wisps of dark yellowish brown (10YR 4/2) clayey sand. Lower part of this bed shows indistinct planar cross-bedding.	
				30.99/
				30.64
5.45/5.80	5.95	0.50/0.15	UPPER SAND. Medium bluish grey (5B 5/1) firm sandy clay with moderate brown (5YR 4/4) mottles and flint pebbles.	
				30.49
5.95	6.05	0.10	UPPER MIDDLE GRAVEL. Dark yellowish brown (10YR 4/2) soft sandy clay with lenses and irregular patches of dark yellowish orange (10YR 6/6) medium sand. Hand-axe finishing flakes at 5.85 m.	
				30.39
6.05	6.70	0.65	UPPER MIDDLE GRAVEL. Pale greyish orange (10YR 8/4) loose very sandy medium gravel with lenses of medium/coarse sand.	
				29.74

SECTION LA2. Nat. Grid Ref. TQ 59616 74319

From	To	Thick		OD Ht.
0	0.10	0.10	SOIL	32.49
				32.39
0.10	0.40	0.30	MADE GROUND. Also covers slip material from face above.	
				32.09
0.40	1.50	1.10	UPPER SAND. Light brown (5YR 5/6) clayey fine/medium sand with thin bands of pale yellowish brown (10YR 6/2) firm silty clay 2 to 5 cm thick.	
				30.99
1.50	1.50/1.65	0/0.15	UPPER SAND. Pale orange (10YR 7/2) ripple-bedded fine/medium sand with bedding delineated by wisps of silty clay.	
				30.99/
				30.84
1.50/1.65	1.85	0.20/0.45	UPPER SAND. Medium bluish grey (5B 5/1) firm sandy clay with moderate brown (5YR 4/4) mottles and flint pebbles. Upper surface with pockets of moderate yellowish brown (10YR 5/4) medium coarse sand.	

Section LA2 cont...

From	To	Thick		OD Ht.
				30.64/
				30.54
1.85/1.95	2.00	0.05/0.15	UPPER MIDDLE GRAVEL. Moderate yellowish brown (10YR 5/4) contorted soft clayey laminated medium sand. At base pale orange (10YR 8/4) fine sand filling irregularities in surface of bed below.	
				30.49
2.00	3.00	1.00	UPPER MIDDLE GRAVEL. Very pale orange (10YR 8/2) very sandy medium gravel.	
				29.49
3.00	3.20	0.20	UPPER MIDDLE GRAVEL. White trough cross-bedded medium/ coarse sand.	
				29.29

SECTION LA3 Nat. Grid Ref. TQ 59623 74321

From	To	Thick		OD Ht.
0	0.10	0.10	SOIL	33.24
				33.14
0.10	1.80/2.00	1.70/1.90	UPPER SAND. Light brown 5YR 5/6) clayey sand with thin bands of pale yellowish brown (10YR 6/2) firm silty clay 2 to 5 cm thick. Bedding much contorted 1.20 to 1.80 m. Lower boundary sharp and irregular.	
				31.44/
				31.24
1.80/2.00	2.00	0/0.20	UPPER SAND. Very pale orange (10YR 8/2) medium sand with irregular band up to 5 cm thick of pale yellowish brown (10YR 6/2) silty clay.	
				31.24
2.00	2.60/2.50	0.60/0.50	UPPER SAND. Pale orange (10YR 7/2) ripple-bedded fine/medium sand with lens of planar cross-bedded sand.	
				30.74/
				30.64
2.60/2.50	2.60	0/0.10	UPPER SAND. Medium bluish grey (5B 5/1) firm sandy clay with moderate brown (5YR 4/4) mottles and scattered flint pebbles.	
				30.64
2.60	3.50	0.90	UPPER MIDDLE GRAVEL. Very pale orange (10YR 8/2) medium very sandy gravel with thin lenses of Fe cementation.	
				29.74
3.50	3.90	0.40	UPPER MIDDLE GRAVEL. White trough cross-bedded medium coarse sand.	
				29.34

SECTION LA4. Nat. Grid Ref. TQ 59619 74325

From	To	Thick		OD Ht.
				29.74
0	2.00	2.00	UPPER MIDDLE GRAVEL. Pale greyish orange (10YR 8/4) trough cross-bedded fine/medium sand with dark yellowish brown (10YR 4/2) sandy clay delineating bedding.	
				27.74
2.00	3.30	1.30	UPPER MIDDLE GRAVEL. Greyish orange (10YR 7/4) planar cross-bedded very sandy medium gravel. 2.60 to 2.70 m fine/medium sand.	
				26.44
3.30	3.80	0.50	LOWER MIDDLE GRAVEL. Moderate brown (5YR 4/4) horizontally-bedded coarse sandy gravel.	
				25.94
3.80	4.70	0.90	LOWER MIDDLE GRAVEL. Pale orange (10YR 8/4) horizontally-bedded medium/coarse sandy gravel with flint cobbles at base.	
				25.04
4.70	5.10	0.40	LOWER GRAVEL. Moderate brown (5YR 4/4) horizontally-bedded coarse sandy gravel.	
				24.64
5.10	6.15	1.05	LOWER GRAVEL. Pale yellowish brown (10YR 6/2) horizontally-bedded medium/coarse gravel with some sand and flint cobbles at base. Some clayey silt present as films on clasts.	
				23.59

Use of handauger and sampling tube from the base of this section established the presence of the Thanet Sand at a depth of 0.85 m, ie at an elevation of 22.74 m OD.

bluish grey pebbly sandy clay, 0.50 m thick, which rapidly reduces in thickness to 0 in a horizontal distance of c.9 m. This clay is associated with disturbance of the Upper Middle Gravel immediately below to a depth of c.20 cm and is interpreted as a solifluction deposit which moved from west to east.

The Upper Sand appears to rest in a channel c.80 m wide cut into the top of the Upper Middle Gravel, and its surface ranges in elevation from 31.56 to 33.25 m OD.

UPPER LOAM

The Upper Loam occurs in all the sections cut in the south face of the Old Sand Pit and consists predominantly of brown, horizontally-bedded clayey sand/sandy clay with thin, irregular and discontinuous bands of grey clay, up to 5 cm in thickness, in the upper part and scattered flint pebbles and patches of gravel. The clayey sands show localised patches of carbon crumbs on bedding planes. In section G (Figure 6.2) the Upper Loam comprises clayey sands, but the clay content increases westwards. The discontinuity and disturbance of the thin clay bands may be the result of cryoturbation, though the surrounding sands show no marked complementary structures.

The thickness of the Upper Loam varies from 0.90 to 1.40 m and its surface reaches a maximum elevation of 34.35 m OD. In section LA1 (Figure 6.7) the surface is penetrated by ice wedge casts to a depth of 0.40 m. The Upper Loam has yielded no faunal material but archaeological material is present in the form of a scatter of biface thinning flakes in a very sharp condition in the top 20 cm.

UPPER GRAVEL

The Upper Gravel occurs in all the sections in the south face of the Old Sand Pit and varies in thickness from 0.90 to 1.65 m. It consists of fine/medium gravel in a hard sandy clay matrix with scattered flint cobbles. The clasts are predominantly of flint from the Chalk, which in places show a tendency to be clustered in 'nests', but also include c.30 % of well-rounded pebbles derived from Tertiary deposits; many clasts show thermal fractures. A thin layer of crushed chalk, incorporated in the Upper Gravel, was seen in foundation trenches for building construction on the north side of Gilbert Close, c.50 m west of the NNR (trench ZJ). The base of the bed is a sharp, undulating erosion surface and in places is marked by a few cm of hard shaly clay with listric surfaces poorly developed, this is interpreted as a shear surface. In section LA1 the Upper Gravel contains a 'raft' of brown clayey sand 30 cm in thickness and at least 3 m in horizontal extent which has the appearance of Upper Loam material. The same section shows two ice-wedge structures, filled with gravel in a clay matrix, extending from the base of the Upper Gravel into the Upper Loam to a depth of 0.40 m (Figure 6.7). Both ice-wedge casts are inclined at c.60 degrees from the vertical in an easterly direction and the adjacent part of the Upper Loam shows disturbance and complementary structures.

The Upper Gravel, as has long been recognised, is a solifluction deposit and the marked asymmetry of the ice-wedge casts is the result of drag caused by movement of the clayey gravel from west to east over the surface of the Upper Loam, during which Upper Loam material was incorporated in the solifluction material. The top of the Upper Gravel in section G is at an elevation of 32.56 m OD and it rises westwards to 35.54 m OD in section LA1.

BRICKEARTH

In all the sections cut in the south face of the Old Sand Pit the Upper Gravel passes upwards into a loose clayey silt with scattered flint pebbles which was labelled 'Brickearth'. The number of clasts decreases upwards and the junction between the Upper Gravel and the Brickearth has been taken at the point at which the matrix ceases to be coherent. It seems probable that the 'brickearth' is the deeply weathered surface of the Upper Gravel, where it is not overlain by higher deposits. The thickness of this loose deposit ranges from 0.40 to 1.10 m and the elevation of the top rises westwards from 33.66 m to 36.14 m OD.

The brickearth has yielded mammalian faunal material in the form of indeterminate crushed and broken bone fragments. The molluscan fauna is reviewed in Chapter 8. Several small scatters of Neolithic flakes were also found which, together with the mollusca, are clearly intrusive.

HIGHER LOAM

In the area to the south-west of the Old Sand Pit, two exploratory pits, ZG and ZH, showed 0.60 to 1.50 m of horizontally bedded clayey sand with scattered flint pebbles resting on Upper Gravel. This loam has yielded a small scatter of biface thinning flakes in very sharp condition.

The sections described above permit a profile of the Pleistocene deposits in the Old Sand Pit to be drawn with some confidence, this is presented in Figure 6.1. This demonstrates quite clearly that the Barnfield Pit sequence occurs near the southern and landward margin of the deposits mapped by the Geological Survey as 'Boyn Hill Terrace'. The deposits rest throughout on an eroded surface of Thanet Sand, though early descriptions (Smith and Dewey 1913) indicate that c.150 m to the north of the 1968/1972 sections Pleistocene deposits rested directly on a Chalk surface. The proximity of the Bullhead bed, at the base of the Thanet Sand at its junction with the Chalk, provided a source of large flint boulders particular to the gravels in the lower part of the sequence. Other immediately local sources of material are suggested by the presence of Chalk clasts in the Lower Gravel indicating active erosion of chalk rock, and the adjacency of outcrops of Woolwich and Reading beds as a source of the well rounded flint pebbles which form a significant proportion of the gravel clasts.

The Thanet sand bench on which the Pleistocene deposits were laid down has the apparent form of an asymmetric channel sloping gently downwards in a WSW direction to its lowest point at 21.80 m OD and then rising rapidly to 33.25 m OD at the southern margin of the deposits. The steep rise of in excess of 10 m over a horizontal distance of c.12 m is the 'cliff' feature illustrated by Chandler (1935; see also Figure 3.5B) and Marston (1937b; see also Figure 3.7B). It was also represented by Paterson at the western end of his section (1940; see also Figures 3.7B and 3.9).

B.Conway

SECTION M. Nat. Grid Ref. TQ 59656 74338

From	To	Thick		OD Ht.
				29.30
0	0.80	0.80	MADE GROUND. A mixture of Thanet Sand a gravel showing apparent 'bedding' dips of 40 degrees North.	
				28.50
0.80	1.90	1.10	UPPER MIDDLE GRAVEL. Dark yellowish orange (10YR 6/6) trough cross-bedded fine/medium sand.	
				27.40
1.90	2.30	0.40	UPPER MIDDLE GRAVEL. Pale orange (10YR 8/2) trough cross-bedded fine/medium sand with some fine gravel.	
				27.00
2.30	3.30	1.00	LOWER MIDDLE GRAVEL. Greyish orange (10YR 7/4) medium/coarse sandy gravel with scattered flint.	
				26.00
3.30	3.40	0.10	LOWER LOAM. Light brown (5YR 5/6) firm sandy clay.	
				25.90
3.40	3.90	0.50	LOWER GRAVEL. Light brown (5YR 5/6) medium/coarse sandy gravel. Heavily worn flake at 3.65 m.	
				25.40

This section is obviously very close to the edge of the infilled chalk quarry, as evidenced by the high angle of apparent dip on the tip surfaces in the made ground material.

SECTION N. Nat. Grid Ref. TQ 59650 74335

From	To	Thick		OD Ht.
0	1.10	1.10	MADE GROUND	29.00
				27.90
1.10	2.00	0.90	LOWER MIDDLE GRAVEL. Greyish orange (10YR 7/4) horizontally-bedded medium/coarse sandy gravel. Handaxe finishing flake at 2.00 m.	
				27.00
2.00	2.70	0.70	LOWER MIDDLE GRAVEL. Moderate yellowish brown (10YR 5/4) silty fine sand with flint pebbles.	
				26.30
2.70	3.10	0.40	LOWER MIDDLE GRAVEL. White horizontally-bedded fine/medium sand.	
				25.90
3.10	3.70	0.60	LOWER GRAVEL. Light brown (5YR 5/6) horizontally-bedded very sandy medium/coarse gravel. Patchy Fe cementation 3.10 to 3.17 m.	
				25.30

Sections M and N were cut after the main series of sections in the south face of the Old Sand Pit when it was found that the Lower Loam had 'disappeared' between sections J and K.

SECTION P. Nat. Grid Ref. TQ 59634 74327

From	To	Thick		OD Ht.
0	1.80	1.80	MADE GROUND	29.40
				27.60
1.80	2.80	1.00	LOWER MIDDLE GRAVEL. Greyish orange (10YR 7/4) horizontally-bedded very sandy medium gravel.	
				26.60
2.80	3.50	0.70	LOWER MIDDLE GRAVEL. Pale orange (10YR 8/4) horizontally-bedded very sandy medium gravel.	
				25.90
3.50	4.50	1.00	LOWER GRAVEL. Light brown (5YR 5/6) horizontally-bedded medium/coarse sandy gravel. Rolled flakes at 4.00 and 4.30 m.	
				24.90

SECTION ZC. Nat. Grid Ref. TQ 59603 74309

GS	0.35	0.35	TOPSOIL	35.40
				35.05
0.35	0.95	0.60	MADE GROUND	34.45
0.95	2.15	1.20	UPPER GRAVEL. Moderate brown (5YR 4/4) medium coarse gravel in firm/hand sandy clay matrix with some wisps of crushed chalk.	
				33.25
2.15	3.00	0.85	THANET SAND. Moderate yellowish brown (10YR 5/4) coherent silty fine sand. Irregular wisps of light brown (5YR 5/6) clay 2.15 to 2.45 m.	
				32.40

SECTION ZD. Nat. Grid Ref. TQ 59589 74278

GS	0.35	0.35	TOPSOIL.	34.19
				33.84
0.35	1.10	0.75	THANET SAND. Moderate yellowish brown (10YR 5/4) soft silty fine sand. Irregular wisps of light brown (5YR 5/6) clay 0.35 to 0.65 m.	
				33.09

SECTION ZE. Nat. Grid Ref. TQ 59574 74258

GS	0.60	0.60	TOPSOIL.	34.49
				33.89
0.60	0.90	0.30	MADE GROUND.	
				33.59
0.90	1.50	0.60	HIGHER LOAM. Light brown (5yr 5/6) firm clayey silty medium sand.	
				32.99

SECTION ZF Nat. Grid Ref. TQ 59558 74239

From	To	Thick		OD Ht.
GS	0.25	0.25	TOPSOIL	34.89
				34.64
0.25	1.05	0.80	Dark yellowish brown (10YR 4/2) hard silty clay with scattered flint pebbles.	
				33.84
1.05	1.40	0.35	HIGHER LOAM. Light brown (5YR 5/6) soft/firm clayey fine sand.	
				33.49

SECTION ZG. Nat. Grid Ref. TQ 59542 74246

GS	0.20	0.20	TOPSOIL	33.99
				33.79
0.20	0.80	0.60	HIGHER LOAM. Moderate yellowish brown (10YR 5/4) clayey sand with light grey (N7) mottles.	
				33.19
0.80	1.60/1.80	0.80/1.00	UPPER GRAVEL. Dark yellowish brown (10YR 4/2) medium/coarse gravel in soft/firm sandy clay matrix.	
				32.39/
				32.19
1.60/1.80	2.50	0.70/0.90	UPPER LOAM. Pale yellowish brown (10YR 6/2) firm clayey sand with scattered flint pebbles. Medium/coarse gravel with handaxe finishing flakes 1.70 to 1.80 m.	
				31.49
2.50	2.80	0.30	THANET SAND.	
				31.19

SECTION ZH. Nat. Grid Ref. TQ 59580 74269

GS	0.20	0.20	TOPSOIL.	34.34
				34.14
0.20	1.70/1.50	1.30/1.50	HIGHER LOAM. Moderate yellowish brown (10YR 5/4) clayey sand with scattered flint pebbles. Handaxe finishing flake at 1.40 m.	
				32.84/
				32.64
1.70/1.50	3.00	1.50/1.30	UPPER GRAVEL. Dark yellowish brown (10YR 4/2) medium/coarse gravel in soft sandy clay matrix. Handaxe finishing flakes at 2.20 m.	
				31.34
3.00	4.00	1.00	UPPER LOAM. Pale yellowish brown (10YR 6/2) clayey sand. Handaxe finishing flakes 3.00 to 3.03 m.	
				30.34

SECTION ZJ. Nat. Grid Ref. From TQ 59682 74224 to 59702 74243

GS	0.15/0.25	0.15/0.25	TOPSOIL.
0.15/0.25	0.70	0.55/0.45	UPPER GRAVEL. Dark yellowish brown (10YR 4/2) soft/firm sandy clay with greenish grey (5YR 6/1) mottles and scattered flint pebbles. Thin layers of crushed chalk fragments at 0.50 m
0.70	0.90	0.20	UPPER LOAM. Moderate yellowish brown (10YR 5/4) firm clayey sand with scattered flint pebbles.

This section was measured in 1971 on a building site on the north side of Gilbert Close, c.50 m west of the NNR where a temporary exposure was seen in a foundation trench 20 m long in ENE to WSW direction.

7. THE GEOLOGY INSIDE THE NATIONAL NATURE RESERVE, 1968-72

Bernard Conway

INTRODUCTION

The archaeological excavation which commenced in 1968 inside the National Nature Reserve was primarily intended to investigate the deposits of the lower part of the Barnfield Pit sequence. Over the period of five seasons, ten five metre squares were cut in the floor of the south-eastern part of the NNR centred on National Grid Reference TQ 559845 174265 (see Figure 5.1). This became known as the 'main area'. Excavation started at a low north-west/south-east oriented bluff on the eastern side of the NNR. This bluff was cut in the late 1930s to accommodate a railway track used to transport gravel to the washing plant. It effectively separates the greater part of the site to the west (the final working floor of the pit prior to the cessation of commercial activity in 1939 where aggregate extraction stopped at or just above the surface of the Lower Loam), from the area to the east which is 2 to 2.5 m lower and where gravel had been removed almost to the top of the Thanet Sand.

The main area of the NNR was therefore perceived to retain the full thickness of the Lower Gravel and Lower Loam resting on Thanet Sand and overlain by up to a metre of Lower Middle Gravel (Oakley 1964, figure 5). The marginal area to the east of the bluff was thought to have up to half a metre of Lower Gravel resting on Thanet Sand. Grassed mounds in the southern part of the NNR were debris dumped from excavations made in the 1940s and 50s. These are still visible today.

Excavation logistics dictated that work started at the bluff with square A (re-numbered A1 in the 1969 season) and proceeded in a westerly direction, cutting into the abandoned working floor of the pit. The A-series of squares (1-3) were cut down to the top of the Thanet Sand and showed the full thickness of the Lower Gravel and Lower Loam overlain in places by a thin remnant the Lower Middle Gravel and some quarrying debris. The B-series of squares (1-4), on the south side of the A-series, were cut down to the top of the Lower Gravel and showed the full thickness of the Lower Loam. Squares C3 and Z3 were cut down into the Lower Loam and square C4 only reached the surface of the Lower Loam. The face of the bluff was cut back from the south-eastern corner of square B1 for a distance of 10 m in a south-easterly direction and recorded as section H. It showed the full thickness of the Lower Loam resting on Lower Gravel.

In addition eight small inspection pits were dug on south-east and south-west lines from the south-east end of section H at intervals up to 50 m from the main excavation area. This enabled the nature and extent of the surviving deposits to be established. Finally the lower part of the degraded west face of Barnfield Pit (abandoned in 1939) was cut and cleaned, near to the south-western corner of the NNR and recorded as Section C. This revealed 4 m of the upper part of the Barnfield sequence resting on Lower Loam.

Section C and square A3 were re-opened in 1977 for a visit by INQUA and a classification of the full sequence described (Conway and Waechter 1977; a modified version of this is presented in Figure 8.1) The deposits were divided into three stages, the lower two (I and II) of predominantly temperate fluviatile origin and the upper (III) of mainly cool or cold terrestrial origin. Deposits of the first fluviatile stage occupy a shallow channel about 500 m wide cut in the underlying Thanet Sand and Chalk. Stage II deposits are more extensive, overlapping those of Stage I. The terrestrial deposits of Stage III overlap those of Stage II at the south-western, landward, margin of the terrace and thin in a north-easterly direction

The principal concern of the 1968-72 excavations in the main area was with the Stage I deposits which were sub-divided as follows:

Ie. Surface Layer of Lower Loam
Id. Main body of Lower Loam
Ic. Midden Level, top Lower Gravel
Ib. Main body of Lower Gravel
Ia. Basal Gravel, Lower Gravel

The full thickness of Stage I deposits is shown in Plates 7.1 and 7.2.

The descriptions that follow refer only to the deposits examined in the excavations in the main area, and those test pits and sections in the NNR which were dug to clarify stratigraphic relationships relevant to the main area. Individual unit descriptions are given in Table 7.1. These are illustrated in the section drawings in Figures 7.2; 7.3; 7.4; 7.6; 7.9; and 7.10. Readers will find it helpful to familiarise themselves with these sections in conjunction with Table 7.1 first.

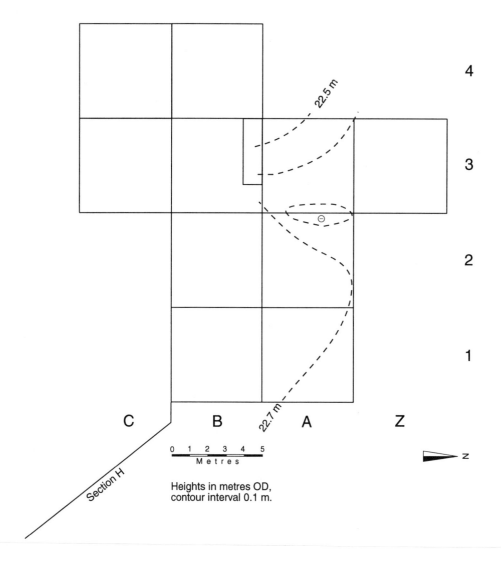

Fig. 7.1. Contour plan of the surface of the Thanet Sand in squares A1 to C4

B.Conway

LOWER MIDDLE GRAVEL, Stage Iia

3.   Moderate yellowish brown (10YR 5/4) medium/coarse sand with some medium gravel.

2A.   Dark yellowish brown (10YR 5/6) medium/coarse sandy gravel.

2.   Pale orange (10YR 7/2) medium/coarse sandy gravel with scattered flint cobbles at base; sandy patches with abundant shells, particularly *Unio*.

1.   Dark yellowish orange (10YR 6/6) coarse sand with pebbles.

SURFACE LAYER OF LOWER LOAM, Stage Ie

4.   Moderate brown (5YR 4/4) to light brown (5YR 5/6) silty clay with some sand and scattered pebbles; shells and shell debris together with localised concentrations of crushed and broken bone and antler, and teeth. Footprints.

MAIN BODY OF LOWER LOAM, Stage Id

4A.   Moderate brown (5YR 4/4) clayey loam with some sand in lower part and an horizon of desiccation pellets.

3.   Yellowish orange (10YR 7/6) to moderate yellowish brown (10YR 5/4) fine/medium silty sand with shell debris and shell sand lenses.

2.   Dark yellowish orange (10YR 6/6) to moderate yellowish brown (10YR 5/4) clayey silty sand with shells, shell debris and nodular calcareous concretions.

1D.   Pale yellowish orange (10YR 8/6) sandy silty clay with scattered pebbles.

1C.   Pale yellowish brown (10YR 6/2) sandy silty clay with contorted wisps of greyish brown (5YR 3/2) clay.

1B.   Greyish brown (5YR 3/2) clayey silt.

1A.   Moderate yellowish brown (10YR 5/4) fine/medium silty sand with shell debris and lenses of white shell sand.

1.   Pale yellowish brown (10YR 6/2) silty sand with pebbles.

MIDDEN COMPLEX, Stage Ic

8B.   Greyish orange (10YR 7/4) fine/medium sand with some fine gravel and shell debris.

8A.   Greyish orange (10YR 7/4) medium sandy gravel with shells.

7E.   Pale orange (10YR 7/2) medium sand with small pebbles, shells abundant, including large numbers of *Potomida*.
           The main bone horizon occurs at the base of this bed.

7D.   Greyish orange (10YR 7/4) silty medium sand with scattered pebbles, shells and bone fragments.

7C.   Dark yellowish orange (10YR 6/6) medium gravel in silty sand matrix with shells, poorly sorted. Also includes a layer of fine gravel, thin lenses of sandy clay with pebbles and patches of limonite-cemented sand and gravel.

7B.   Greyish orange (10YR 7/4) silty fine sand with scattered pebbles and shell debris.

7A.   Dark yellowish orange (10YR 6/6) medium gravel in silty fine sand matrix with shell debris, bone fragments and clay clasts.

MAIN BODY OF LOWER GRAVEL, Stage Ib

6.   Pale yellowish brown (10YR 6/2) loose sand with pebbles, poorly sorted.

5B.   Greyish orange (10YR 7/4) loose medium sand with fine/medium gravel.

5A.   Dark yellowish orange (10YR 6/6) loose silty sand with some fine gravel and shell debris.

5.   Greyish orange (10YR 7/4) loose sandy medium/coarse gravel, horizontally-bedded and with scattered shells.

4A.   Pale yellowish brown (10YR 6/2) loose sand with fine gravel, current bedded. Shells.

4.   Moderate yellowish brown (10YR 5/4) to dark yellowish orange (10YR 6/6) compact fine sandy gravel with chalk and clay

clasts.

3A.   Dark yellowish orange (10YR 6/6) compact medium sandy gravel.

3.   Pale yellowish brown (10YR 6/2) to pale orange (10YR 8/2) loose medium sandy gravel with scattered shells, horizontally-bedded.

2A.   Greyish orange (10YR 7/4) horizontally-bedded medium sand.

2.   Light brown (5YR 5/6) to dark yellowish orange (10YR 6/6) horizontally-bedded medium/coarse sandy gravel.

1C.   Greyish orange (10YR 7/4) loose medium sand with some silt and pebbles, scattered crumbs of chalk.

BASAL GRAVEL, Stage Ia

1B.   Moderate yellowish brown (10YR 5/4) medium sandy gravel with some silt, poorly sorted. Large flint boulders occur at the base of both 1A and 1B, resting on and embedded in a thin layer of light brown (5YR 5/6) sandy clay.

1A.   Dark yellowish orange (10YR 6/6) medium coarse gravel in a sandy clay matrix, poorly sorted. Passes laterally into 1B.

THANET SAND (Eocene)

Table 7.1. Notes on the lithology of sections in the A-B-C series of squares, Figures 7.2 to 7.5.

KEY

TOP SOIL	CROSS BEDDED SAND	F/M GRAVEL IN SANDY-CLAY MATRIX
MADE GROUND	RIPPLE BEDDED SAND	GRAVEL
" BRICK EARTH "		SILTY GRAVEL
SAND	CLAYEY LOAM	SANDY GRAVEL
SHELLY SAND		
PEBBLY SAND	SILTY CLAYS	
SILTY SAND	SANDS + SILTY CLAYS	
SANDY CLAY		

LOWER GRAVEL (Stage I a-c)

The full thickness of the Lower Gravel was seen only in the three A-series squares where it ranged from 2.05 m at the eastern side of A1 to 2.95 m at the western side of A3, a distance of 14 m. On lithological and structural criteria three sub-divisions were recognised: Basal Gravel (Ia) resting on Thanet Sand, the main body of the Lower Gravel (Ib), and the Midden level (Ic). The Thanet Sand surface on which the Lower Gravel rests (Figure 7.1 and Plate 7.1) was at an elevation of 22.4 m OD on the eastern side of square A1 and 22.75 m OD on the western side of A3 (Plate 7.2) a fall of 0.35 m over a horizontal distance of 14 m, an apparent dip of barely 1 degree south-west.

Basal Gravel - Stage Ia (Units IA - IC on Table 7.1; Figures 7.2-7.4)

The Basal Gravel varies in thickness from 0 to 0.5 m and occurs as low, discontinuous hummocks of poorly sorted, unbedded flint gravel in a firm brown sandy clay matrix. Well-rounded black flint pebbles, derived from the Woolwich and Blackheath Beds (Eocene) and showing thermal fractures, form 15-20 % of the gravel and occur in irregular patches. Hard, rounded clay clasts (? London Clay) are also present. The gravel contains wisps and thin lenses of white-patinated fine gravel which yielded small struck flakes in a slightly abraded condition. A lens of cross-bedded coarse sand at the top of the Basal Gravel also yielded flakes and was overlain by several centimetres of limonite-cemented fine gravel. At the base of the Basal Gravel flint boulders, up to 30 x 20 x 15 cm, representing channel lag material, rest on and in the Thanet Sand surface, which over much of its exposure was marked by the presence of a thin layer (2 cm) of soft brown silty clay containing scattered flint pebbles of fine gravel grade. Where this clay layer was absent the top of the Thanet Sand was disturbed to a depth of 5-6 cm and contained scattered small flint pebbles and rounded clay clasts. The flint boulders intruded to a maximum depth of 10 cm into the Thanet Sand.

Where the Basal Gravel is absent the bottom 0.5 to 0.7 m of the main body of the succeeding Lower Gravel (Stage Ib) comprises a medium/coarse sandy gravel with an appreciable (8-10%) silt content and many of the flint pebbles have an orange or brown clay coating. A lag deposit of flint boulders rested on and were embedded in the surface of the Thanet Sand. Large abraded struck flakes were found, frequently heavily encrusted with concretionary calcium carbonate. The mollusc fauna from this unit included worn fragments of a large bivalve shell (? *Potomida*).

Three of the small exploratory pits, X, Y and Z (see Figure 5.1), confirmed the presence, nature and thickness of the Basal Gravel for a distance of 25 m south-east of square B1.

Lower Gravel - Stage Ib (Units 2 - 6 on Table 7.1; Figures 7.2-7.4; 7.6 and 7.9)

The full development of the main body of the Lower Gravel ranges from 2.05 to 2.95 m in thickness. It comprises loose, horizontally-bedded sandy medium/coarse flint gravel with shells and shell debris. Overall the bed fines upwards to sands and fine gravel in the upper part. Stage Ib gravels were divided into two parts of more or less equal thickness by a 10 to 30 cm band of chalk and clay clasts in a sand matrix with some fine gravel (unit 4 Table 7.1, Figures 7.2 - 7.4). Shell material is scattered throughout the Lower Gravel, above the chalk clast horizon it is well-preserved, below it is fragmentary and partially decalcified.

The gravels below the chalk clast horizon showed several discontinuous bands of iron staining, 10 to 15 cm in thickness, which were concordant with the horizontal bedding. The base of the Lower Gravel is marked by a lag deposit of flint cobbles and boulders resting on the Basal Gravel (Ia) or on, or intruding into, the Thanet Sand. Above the chalk clast horizon the horizontally-bedded medium sandy gravels grade upwards into pebble sands with shell debris and bands of loose silty sand 10 to 15 cm in thickness. This level yielded a number of derived fossils, including a Jurassic *Gryphaea* and several partially decalcified chalk belemnites.

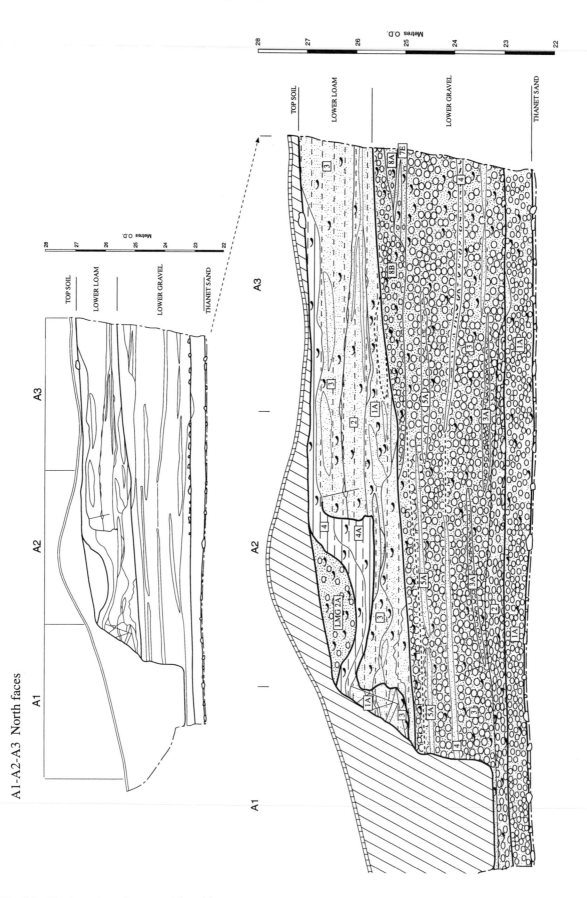

Fig. 7.2. North section of squares A1 to A3

A1-A2-A3. South Faces. Part 1.

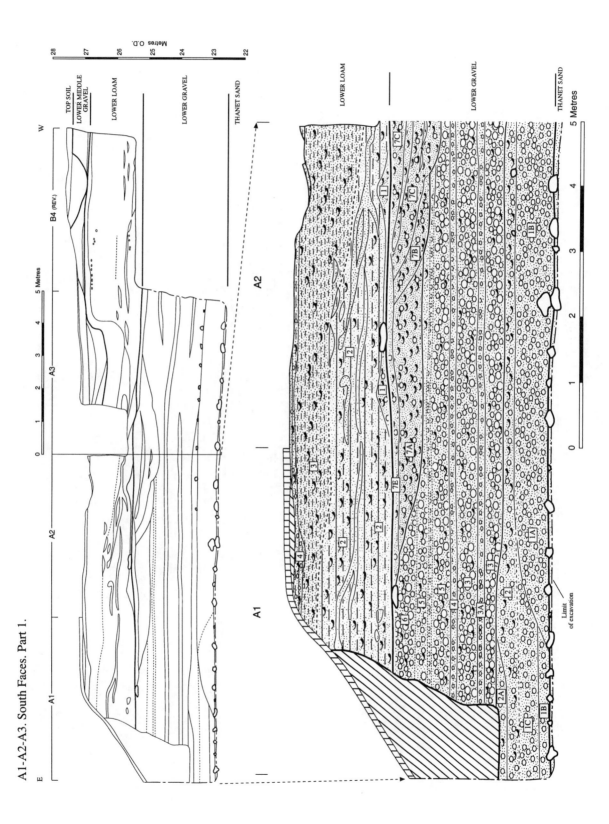

Fig. 7.3a. South sections of Squares A1 to A2 (continued in Figure 7.3b)

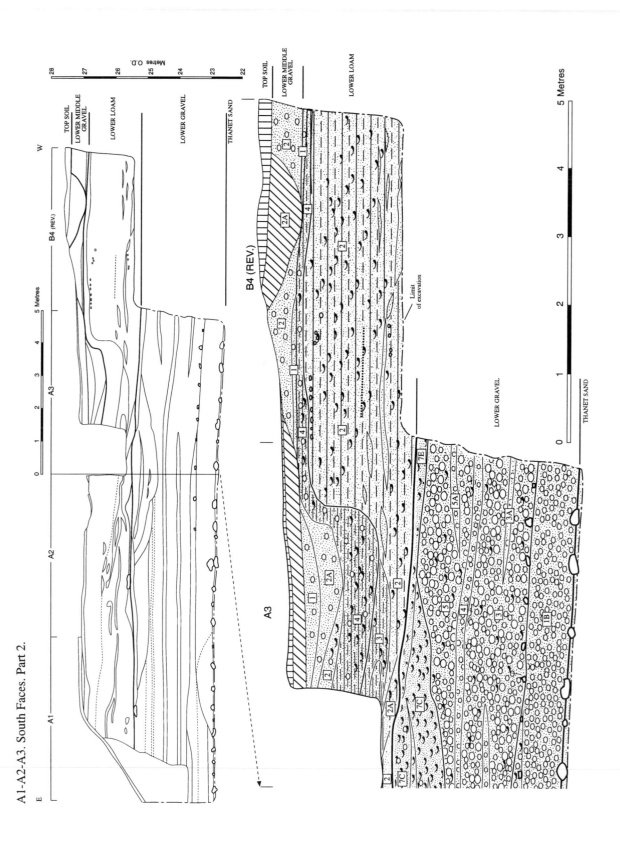

Fig. 7.3b. South sections of Square A3 and reversed section of Square B4 (continued from Figure 7.3a)

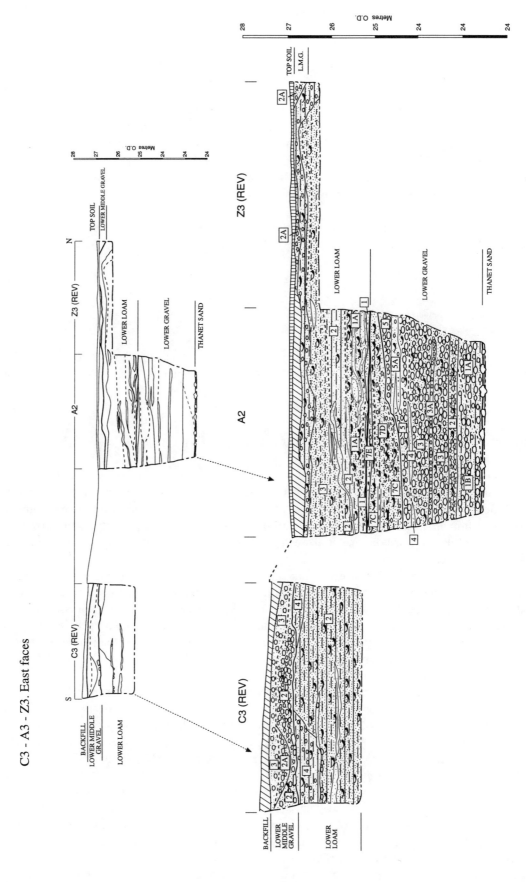

Fig. 7.4. East sections of Squares C3 (reversed), Square A2 and Square Z3 (reversed)

The clasts in the chalk pebble horizon comprise 60% chalk and 25% London Clay, the remainder being flint; individual clasts range in size up to 15 x 10 x 4 cm. The surfaces of the chalk clasts were usually found to be 'armoured' with impressed coarse sand and to have concave facets on them, the result of contact with flint pebbles during compaction of the sediments. Some chalk clasts showed cracks radiating from the concave facets caused by point-loading during compaction. The London Clay clasts appeared to be worn, joint-bounded blocks, with sand-filled shrinkage cracks on their surfaces. The clay clasts yielded a shark tooth, *Odontaspis*, and several fragmentary gastropods.

The upper surface of the main body of the Lower Gravel is an erosional surface cutting horizontal bedding (Figure 7.5). Within the main area this was seen as a shallow channel c. 10 m wide, apparently trending NW - SE and with a maximum depth of 0.8 m. This channel was cut in two stages and in-filled with lenticular beds of medium/fine gravel and sand containing much shell material and bone at two levels towards the top. The channel in-fill material has been distinguished as the Midden level (Stage Ic).

Much of the shell material from stage Ib deposits was found to be fragmentary and partially de-calcified, above the chalk clast horizon the following were identified:

> *Lymnaea peregra*, Muller
> *Bithynia* sp. (opercula)
> *Pisidium amnicum*, Muller
> *Pisidium* sp. (small)
> *Potomida littoralis*, Cuvier

Abraded flakes and cores occurred throughout the gravels of stage Ib, those below the chalk clast horizon occasionally of large size, frequently partially or completely encrusted with concretionary calcium carbonate.

Midden Level - Stage Ic (Units 7A - 8B on Table 7.1; Figures 7.2-7.4; and 7.9)

The channel containing the midden deposits was seen in the west face of square A2, the south faces of A1-3 and the north face of A3, where it cut the horizontal bedding of the main body of the Lower Gravel. Section H (see Figure 7.6) south-east of square B1, cut into the bluff on the east side of the main excavation area, showed the erosional surface at the top of the main body of the Lower Gravel but no channel deposits or bone material were present. The erosion surface is irregular with apparent dips of 2 or 3 degrees south-east.

The channel infill, with a maximum thickness of 0.8 m comprised indistinctly-bedded dark yellowish orange fine/medium gravels in a shelly, silty sand matrix which passed laterally into shelly sand with scattered pebbles and bone fragments. There were several thin horizons of limonite cementation. The infill material was capped by a layer of loose shelly sand with pebbles, 10 cm thick. In and on the base of this shelly sand a concentration of well-preserved mammalian bone material was found (referred to as the midden) together with rolled flakes and cores. About 50 m^2 of the main bone horizon were exposed (see Figure 7.7).

The larger mammalian material recovered from the midden is described in Chapter 11. Where the capping shelly sand horizon thickens to 15 cm a second level of bone material was found at the base. Archival material in the B.M. indicates that these two levels were only present in the A trenches (labelled upper and lower floors). Some bone material was also found beyond the limit of the channel, including the skull of *Stephanorhinus hemitoechus* (minus teeth; NHM. No. M43937), resting on the eroded surface of the main body of the Lower Gravel.

Shells and shell debris occur abundantly throughout the channel deposits, and of particular note are the large numbers of the fresh-water mussel *Potomida littoralis*, Cuvier, both as individual valves and as joined pairs. Some of the valves show a calcareous encrustation on the posterior part of the shell and since in life this species is normally buried anterior end down in the stream bed, the encrustation would appear to be of primary origin. Other shells and pebbles are also frequently encrusted the origin of which may be associated with the activity of calcareous algae, eg. *Chara* the oogonia of which occur throughout the shelly sands.

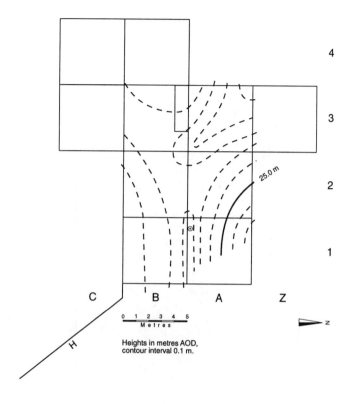

Fig. 7.5. Contour plan of the surface of the Lower Gravel in Squares A1 to C4

The occurrence of *P. littoralis* appears to be concentrated in the pale sand capping the bone horizon, but scattered examples are found throughout the channel deposits. Shell material from the channel deposits yielded the following species:

Bithynia tentaculata, Linne	16
Lymnaea peregra, Muller	16
Ancylus fluviatilis, Muller	8
Sphaerium corneum, Linne	14
Pisidium sp. (small)	39
P. amnicum, Muller	1
Vallonia pulchella, Muller	2
Hygromia hispida, Linne	4

(Aquatic species 94%, terrestrial species 6%)

The upper surface of the midden channel fill is a slightly undulating stratigraphic break (Figure 7.7) which is followed by the Lower Loam (Stage Id). Two large flint boulders were found resting on this surface, one, in the middle of the south face of square A2, was associated with several struck flakes and bone fragments. The larger of the flint boulders measured 35 x 25 x 15 cm.

LOWER LOAM (Stage Id and Ie)

The Lower Loam was exposed in all the excavated squares within the NNR and also in section H. Two sub-divisions were recognised, the main body of the Lower Loam (Id) and the discontinuous Surface

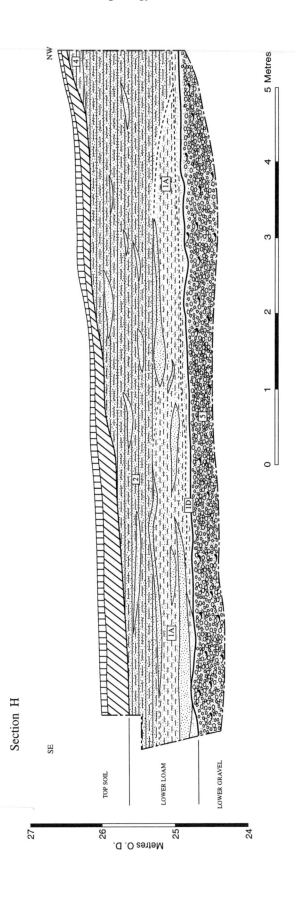

Fig. 7.6. Section H adjacent to Square B1 (see Figure 7.1)

B.Conway

Layer (Ie). The Lower Loam rests on the eroded surface of the Lower Gravel, stage Ic, in squares A2 and A3, and stage Ib elsewhere. In the north face of square A1 this erosion surface had an elevation of 24.75 m OD and at the western end of A3 25.6 m OD, suggesting an apparent dip of 5 degrees to the east. However, when the erosion surface elevations were contoured over the A and B series of squares, Figure 7.5, a somewhat different picture emerged. A slight east-west ridge, 0.3 to 0.5 m high, between B1-B2 and A1-A2 turns north-eastward in A3 and the true slope dips off this ridge (N to NNE in A1 and A2, S to SSW in B1 and B2 and SW to SSE in B3).

The maximum thickness of the Lower Loam was found to be 2.05 m in squares A3 and B3, where both sub-divisions were found. The top of the Lower Loam is an erosional surface, in squares A3 and B3 this was cut into stage Ie deposits, elsewhere into Id material.

Lower Loam - Stage Id (Units 1 - 4A on Table 7.1; Figures 7.2-7.4; 7.6; and 7.9)

The main body of the Lower Loam comprises predominantly sandy and silty loams in bodies with an overall lenticular structure. Thin lenses of white shell sand, representing the infill of shallow stream

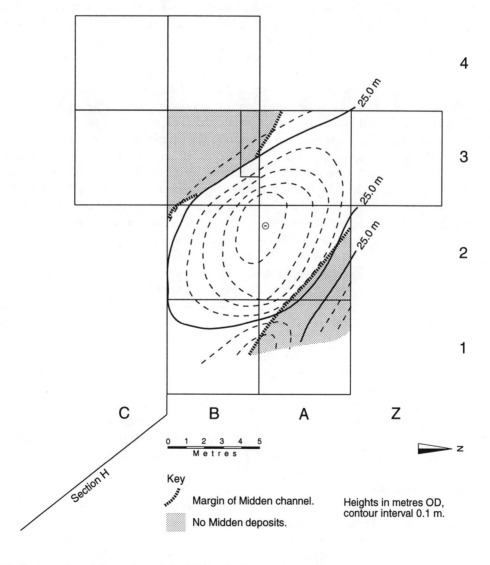

Fig. 7.7. Contour plan of the surface of the Midden in Squares A1 to C4

channels, occur throughout these beds. Calcareous concretions occur in the silty loams as nodular or irregularly tabular bodies. Rapid vertical and sometimes horizontal changes in lithology suggest that deposition was not continuous and there is evidence of a number of dry, or relatively dry, land surfaces (ie. localised concentrations of dry habitat molluscs - see below, scattered animal footprints - see Chapter 13, hearth blow and flint-working debris in a primary context - see Chapter 16). There are also erosional channels within the thickness of the stage Id deposits.

The irregular, tabular, calcareous concretions are clearly of secondary origin, frequently cutting across the bedding of the parent loam, and consist of up to 70% acid-soluble carbonate cementing loam particles. Their occurrence in thin irregular bodies at one or two levels suggests an origin controlled by fluctuations in the position of the surface of the local water table. Some pea-size nodular concretions show an indistinct cellular structure under the microscope and may be of primary, possibly algal, origin. Concretionary material of sand grade is a significant constituent (up to 11%) of the shell sand lenses, some of this may be of primary origin but the bulk of it was most probably derived from the erosion of loam already containing concretions.

Lenses of white shell sand occur throughout the main body of the Lower Loam and vary in thickness from 2 to 25 cm and from 0.3 to 5.5 m in width. The thinner lenses consist of medium/fine sand with scattered pebbles showing indistinct horizontal bedding and contain shells, and shell debris and algal oogonia which make up to 60% of the volume of the lens fill material.

The thicker shell sand lenses frequently show more complex structure (Plate 7.3), particularly in their lower parts which often comprise small cross-bedded sand units with silt drapes in the bedding planes. The upper part of the lenses show horizontal bedding, though an example in section H showed bedding inclinations of 12 to 15 degrees. Irregularities seen in the upper surfaces of thicker lenses most likely result from the de-watering of the lens fill material under subsequent sediment load (Plate 7.4). The floor of most of the channels is a smooth surfaced hollow though a number display shallow linear grooves up to 2 mm wide and extending 50 or 60 cm in directions parallel to the steepest slopes. They show a simple dendritic pattern and have the appearance of rain-water runnels (Plate 7.5). The floor of the channel in square C3 showed bioturbation structures in the form of worm casts.

The thickest shell sand lens was found in square B3. The excavated part of the lens had an area of 20 m^2 and a maximum thickness of 20 cm. The lower half of the infill consisted of horizontally-bedded sand with shells overlain in the upper part by sandy fine gravel. The lower surface of the lens was irregular in cross section and when the infill material was removed, showed in plan a number of roughly circular, often intersecting, depressions ranging in diameter from 10 to 30 cm (Plate 7.6). These depressions were up to 15 cm deep with sectional profiles varying from simple concavities to vertical-sided or undercut pits. The depressions were filled with shell sand and individual cavities contained one or more specimens of *Potomida littoralis* usually with both valves in juxtaposition (Plate 7.7). These cavities probably originated as water-modified animal footprints, or are perhaps the result of cavitation. This horizon was 45-50 cm above the junction of the Lower Loam with the Lower Gravel. The shell sand infill contained 22 flakes and 1 core (BM Reg. nos P1989.1-3.1140-1162), and was described in the records of the main area excavation as 'shelly sand in B3'. The vertical location given above superceeds that given by Waechter in the 1971 interim (Waechter *et al.* 1971, 73). Waechter's assertion that this shelly lens was near the bottom of the Lower Loam is probably a result of confusing this horizon with a second shell bed which was at the base of the Lower Loam in the western corner of the trench. This horizon contained no bones or artefacts.

Major erosional features occur within the main body of the Lower Loam and beneath the Surface Layer (Ie) in the north face of squares A1 and A2 (Figures 7.2 and Plates 7.1 and 7.8). The earlier of the two features, in square A1, was largely destroyed by gravel working operations (Plate 7.1) but the north-west margin was preserved and showed the profile of an undercut cliff 0.8 m high. The material deposited against the cliff is a sandy loam containing shells and with two irregular bands of tabular calcareous concretions which are cut by small faults with displacements of 1 to 2 cm. The faulting appears to be earlier than the Surface Layer in which sympathetic tension cracks occur. It is possible that failure could be the result of the adjacent quarrying operations. The second channel feature is about 3.5 m wide and shows an asymmetrical cross section with a near-vertical undercut cliff 0.8 m high on the west side (Plate 7.8). The filling of this channel consists of sandy clay with scattered small flint pebbles and there was a concentration of coarse sand and small pebbles in the undercut notch together with a small scatter of clay desiccation pellets. The loam cliff showed a small fault with a down-throw of 2 to 3 cm to the east with the fault plane partially filled with fine sand. This feature represents incipient failure, or slumping, of the channel bank, caused by localised overloading. Sympathetic tension cracks developed in the overlying Surface Layer and were filled with small pebbles. A third channel (Stage IIa; Plate 7.8; Figure 7.2), about 3 m wide and 0.8 m deep, showed a symmetrical cross section, and was cut in the filling of the second channel. The Surface Layer (Ie) follows the profile of this channel with a thickness of 20 to 30 cm and was emplaced before the fill material was deposited in the channel. The filling consisted of medium sandy gravel and appears to be undisturbed Lower Middle Gravel.

A further erosional channel was exposed in the south face of square A3 and showed an asymmetrical cross section with a near-vertical cliff 1 metre high on the west side and a width of about 4 m (Figure 7.3). The bottom 0.4 m of the channel infill comprised well-sorted, horizontally-bedded sand with a thick shell sand lens overlain by silty sand. Quarrying operations have partially or wholly removed the Surface Layer in the upper part of this section, but a thickness of 0.5 m is present over the initial channel fill. A small spread of conjoined worked flakes (complex 20; see Chapter 16) associated with an oval area (0.8 by 0.4 m) of carbon crumbs (? hearth blow) was found on the south-east side of the channel just below the Surface Layer. These data indicate that the knapping floor horizon lay to the south of, and was contemporary with, this ephemeral stream channel. The upper part of the channel fill comprised 0.6 m of fine/medium gravel which appeared to be undisturbed Lower Middle Gravel.

Also associated with the flint-working areas was a fauna of dry, or relatively dry habitat shells:

Hygromia hispida, Linne	52
Lymnaea peregra, Muller	2
Clausilia pumila, Pfeiffer	5
Cochlicopa lubrica, Muller	3
Ena montana, Drapernaud	6
Cepaea nemoralis, Linne	27
Arianta arbustorum, Linne	5

A marked feature of the main body of the Lower Loam was the presence of colour banding. The colours ranged from pale yellowish brown to deep yellowish orange in bands 1 to 5 mm in width at intervals of 10 to 20 mm. The configuration of the bands is variable, occurring concentrically about a sand lens or as plane parallel or undulating structures cutting across bedding. The banding is clearly of secondary origin and probably due to the dispersion of iron oxides allied to fluctuations in ground water chemistry. The colour banding cuts the Surface Layer of the Lower Loam and is therefore younger; but the relationship to the old quarry working face may suggest a very recent date.

The loam bodies of stage Id are indistinctly horizontally-bedded for the most part. In squares A1 and A2 the bottom 20 cm, resting on the surface of the Lower Gravel, showed contortions which disturbed the bedding. These structures are probably due to de-watering resulting from loading by overlying sediments and accompanying hydro-static pressure variations in materials of variable permeability. This accounts for the mixed zone of Lower Loam and Lower Gravel noted at the junction between the two units in some of the excavated squares. This was described in the excavation notebooks as LL/LG junction.

Small pebbles are scattered sparsely throughout the Lower Loam, but there was a concentration of rounded flint pebbles of fine/medium gravel grade in the 10 to 20 cm range immediately above the surface of the Lower Gravel.

A single layer of closely packed and arranged flint pebbles covering an area of 1.0 by 0.4 m was found 0.5 m above the base of the Lower Loam in square B2 associated with bone fragments (marked on some finds as B2 Pebble Complex). The origin of this patch of regularly arranged pebbles is difficult to explain in natural terms. Other than one slide in the archive, no further information exists concerning this enigmatic feature. It should be noted that the emplacement is at the same height as the relict land surface with water damaged footprints (or cavitation hollows) in square B3 that was described above.

A number of flattened flint cobbles in the upper part of the main body of the Lower Loam were found when carefully excavated to be lying on an edge with the flat faces at angles of 32 to 40 degrees to the horizontal. Had they been naturally emplaced they would have come to rest on a flat face. Their present attitude can be accounted for by their having been thrown or tossed into wet sediment under sub-aerial conditions as a result of human activity (Plate 7.9).

Scattered pebbles of plastic, yellowish orange clay occurred in the lower part of the Lower Loam, some of which yielded London Clay fossils, including fish teeth and worm tubes, *Ditrupa* sp. Derived London Clay fossils have also been individually recovered from the Lower Loam, including foraminifera (*Cibicides* sp.) and gastropods (*Turritella* sp.).

The bulk of the Lower Loam contains scattered shell debris with comparatively few complete shells expect for those of a small species of *Pisidium*. Shells are also concentrated in the lenses of pale clean sand which represent the bottom of stream channels (as above). They occur both as complete individuals and as debris, *Chara* oogonia and worm tubes are also plentiful and ostracods also occur. The shell sand lenses have yielded the following species:

Bithynia tentaculata, Linne	52
Lymnaea peregra, Muller	20
Ancylus fluviatilis, Muller	2
Valvata piscinalis, Muller	1
Succinea pfeifferi, Rossmassler	1
Planorbis carinatus, Muller	1
Potomida littoralis, Cuvier	13
Sphaerium corneum, Linne	2
Pisidium sp. (small)	4
Cepaea nemoralis, Linne	1
Hygromia hispida, Linne	3

(Aquatic species 96%, terrestrial species 4%)

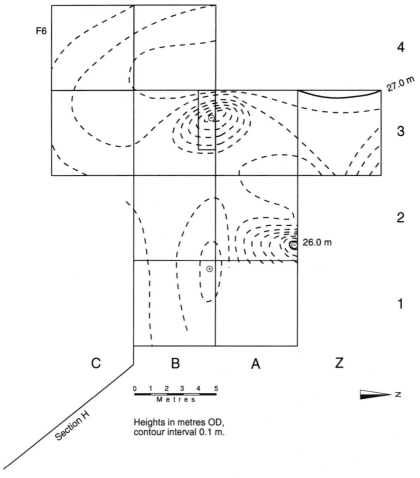

Fig. 7.8. Contour plan of the surface of the Lower Loam in Squares A1 to C4

Surface Layer of Lower Loam - Stage Ie (Unit 4 on Table 7.1; Figures 7.2-7.4; 7.6; and 7.9)

The Surface Layer of the Lower Loam consists of firm/hard brown silty clay with some sand, scattered pebbles, shells and broken and crushed bone. It is discontinuous and irregular in thickness with a maximum representation of 0.6 metres. The top of the stage Ie deposits is an erosional surface with irregularities of up to 0.8 m (Figure 7.8); its elevation ranges from 25.8 to 27.0 m OD. Where the Surface Layer is overlain by undisturbed Lower Middle Gravel (Stage Iia) the erosion surface was found to show large numbers of animal footprints (square C4; see Chapter 13) and to be decalcified. The decalcification was demonstrated chemically by PH measurements made on a vertical profile at the eastern end of the south face of square C3, passing through the Lower Middle Gravel through the Surface Layer and into the main body of the Lower Loam (this is shown on Plate 7.10). The measurements showed a marked decrease in alkalinity in the Surface Layer, followed by a steady increase with depth in the main body of the Lower Loam to 1 m (see Table 7.2).

Lithology	cm	PH
Lower Middle Gravel (Stage Iia)	0.50	
		8.4
Pale greyish orange (10YR 7/2)	0.40	
		8.3
fine/medium sandy gravel with	0.30	
		8.7
manganese staining of clasts.	0.20	
		8.6
	0.10	
		8.4
	0.00	
		7.1
Surface Layer of Lower Loam (Stage Ie).	0.10	
		7.2
Moderate brown (5YR 4/4) sandy	0.20	
		7.1
clay with scattered pebbles.	0.30	
		7.8
Main body of Lower Loam (Stage Id).	0.40	
		8.3
Pale yellowish brown (10YR 6/2) clayey loam with nodular	0.50	
		8.1
calcareous concretions below 0.65 m	0.60	
		8.4
	0.70	
		8.4
	0.80	
		8.6
White shell sand	0.90	
		8.6
	1.00	

Table 7.2. PH values for upper part of sequence in the Main Area, south face of square C3.

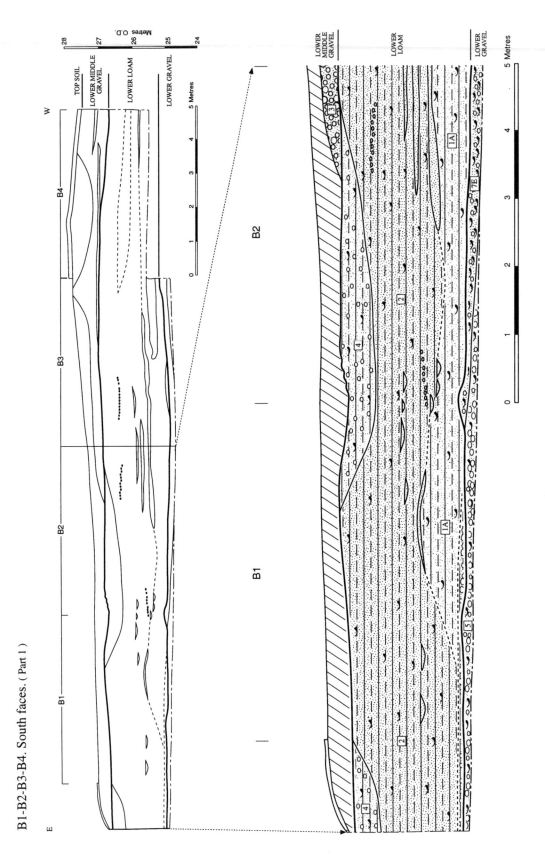

Fig. 7.9a. South sections of Squares B1 and B2 (continued in Figure 7.9b)

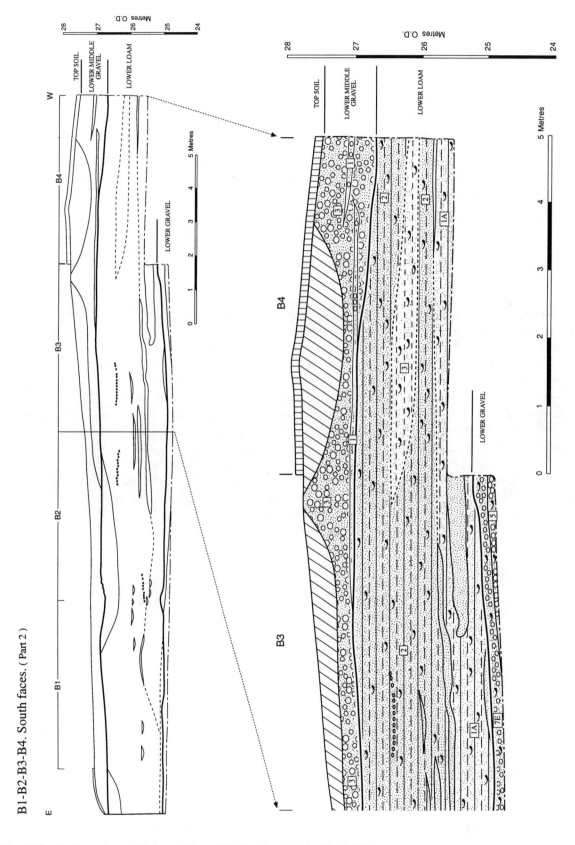

B1-B2-B3-B4. South faces. (Part 2)

Fig. 7.9b. South sections of Squares B3 and B4 (continued from Figure 7.9a)

Associated with the crushed bone material in this unit were large numbers of land shells as partially decalcified debris and as well-preserved shells, particularly *Cepaea* and *Hygromia*. The species represented included:

Cepaea nemoralis, Linne
Hygromia hispida, Linne
Ena montana, Draparnaud
Clausilia sp
Cochlicopa lubrica, Muller
Arianta arbustorum, Linne

Many of the *Cepaea* specimens were in an undamaged condition and were remarkable in that the shells retained their colour banding. Several examples were found in which the entire shell had fragmented *in situ* due to freeze/thaw conditions.

LOWER MIDDLE GRAVEL - Stage Iia (Units 1-3 on Table 7.1; Figures 7.2-7.4; and 7.9)

Commercial quarrying operations in Barnfield Pit ceased when gravel extraction reached the lower part of the Middle Gravels. In the area of excavation this has resulted in isolated patches of the Lower Middle Gravel being left in the irregularities on the surface of the Lower Loam.

The lower part of the Lower Middle Gravel was seen to a maximum thickness of 1 m and consisted of medium/coarse sandy flint gravel, well-sorted and horizontally bedded (Plate 7.10). Some irregularities in the surface of the Lower Loam were filled with shell sand, but where *in situ* material was present the Lower Loam surface was covered by 5 to 10 cm of coarse sand with flint boulders up to 25 x 15 x 10 cm resting on the erosion surface and occasional chalk and clay pebbles. The clay pebbles were of hard, dark yellowish brown clay, probably weathered London Clay. A number of derived fossils were recovered including a Jurassic *Ostraea* and a shark tooth (*Odontaspis*).

Shells and shell debris were scattered throughout the gravel and there were more sandy, shell-rich patches. The shells were partially decalcified, particularly the fresh-water mussel *Unio crassus* which occurred as conjoined valves. The following species were recovered:

Lymnaea peregra, Muller	5
Ancylus fluviatilis, Muller	23
Valvata piscinalis, Muller	24
Valvata macrostoma, Moch	2
Unio crassus, Philipsson	8
Corbicula fluminalis, Muller	1
Sphaerium corneum, Linne	1
Pisidium amnicum, Muller	2
Pisidium sp. (small) 25	
Hygromia hispida, Linne	3
Vallonia excentrica, Sterki	2
Vitrea crystallina, Muller	4

(Aquatic species 91%, terrestrial species 9%).

SECTION C

Section C (see Table 7.3 and Figure 7.10) was sited in the south-west corner of the NNR about 60 m south-west of the main excavation area. It was cut in the old pit face at the position where commercial

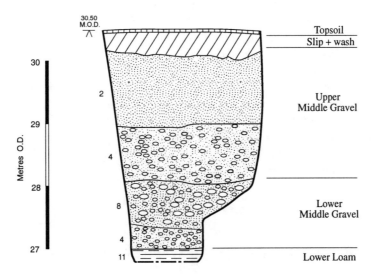

Fig. 7.10. Section C (description given below)

From	To	Thick		OD Ht.
0	0.05	0.05	SOIL	30.50
0.05	0.40	0.35	SLIP AND WASH	30.10
0.40	1.45	1.05	UPPER MIDDLE GRAVEL. Moderate yellowish brown (10YR 5/4) trough cross-bedded medium/fine sand with horizons of fine flint gravel. Light brown (5YR 5/6) soft/firm sandy clay with charcoal crumbs 1.00 to 1.05.	
				29.05
1.45	2.45	1.00	UPPER MIDDLE GRAVEL. Multi-coloured (white, yellows and oranges) planar cross-bedded medium/fine sand with some medium/fine gravel. Light brown (5YR 5/6) soft/firm sandy clay with silt laminations 1.45 to 1.50. Clay clasts up to cobble grade 1.90 to 1.95 and 2.35 to 2.45.	
				28.05
2.45	3.20	0.75	LOWER MIDDLE GRAVEL. Greyish orange (10YR 7/4) horizontally-bedded sandy medium gravel with large flint cobbles 3.05 to 3.20. Scattered, worn, biface thinning flakes throughout; 2 bifaces at 2.60.	
				27.30
3.20	3.52	0.32	LOWER MIDDLE GRAVEL. Very pale orange (10YR 8/2) horizontally-bedded medium sand with some fine/medium gravel. Iron oxide cementation 3.45 to 3.52. Scattered, worn, biface thinning flakes throughout; biface at 3.40.	
				26.98
3.52	3.70	0.18	LOWER LOAM. Moderate brown (5YR 4/4) firm silty clay with some light grey (N7) mottles. Several indeterminate bones fragments and two rolled flakes at 3.60.	
				26.80

Table 7.3 Section C. Nat. Grid Ref. TQ 59812 74234. The south face of the old workings in the NNR is about 8 m high, but the upper part is slipped, has had rubbish dumped over it, and is much overgrown. Section C was cut only in the lower part of the face, the upper part being unstable.

workings ceased in 1939. The old face, about 8 m high, was unstable and much overgrown in the upper part and consequently only the lower part was cut and cleaned. The purpose of cutting this section was to examine the relationship of the upper parts of the Barnfield sequence to the deposits in the detailed archaeological excavations. The face cleared was 2.5 m wide and 4 m high and showed 3.2 m of Middle Gravel (Stages Iia and b) resting on 0.18 m of the Surface Layer (Stage Ie) of the Lower Loam.

It was unfortunate that the instability of the upper part of the old pit face prevented a full section of the higher deposits being cleared, particularly as it was adjacent to the skull-find positions. However, sufficient of the Middle Gravels was seen to confirm their two-fold division into horizontally-bedded medium/coarse sandy flint gravel (Stage Iia) overlain by predominantly cross-bedded sands (Stage Iib). The horizontally-bedded Lower Middle Gravel yielded two small bifaces, a number of thinning flakes and several other struck flakes.

ASSESSMENT OF STAGE I DEPOSITS WITHIN THE NNR

Stage I deposits were laid down in a single, interrupted, temperate fluviatile episode commencing, in Barnfield Pit, with the cutting of an erosion surface in the Thanet Sand on which the aggradation rests.

The Basal Gravel (Stage Ia) had the unsorted and tumbled appearance of a slope-failure deposit. Localised concentrations of thermally fractured Tertiary and other flint pebbles together with scratched and striated pebbles and some struck flakes suggest an origin by down-slope sludging of material under cold climate conditions. The same gravitational process introduced the flint boulders which came to rest on the Thanet Sand surface and which were subsequently impressed into that surface by overburden loading. After emplacement most of the material underwent intermittent water re-sorting, resulting in the flushing out of much of the silt and clay fraction and its re-deposition on the surface of the Thanet Sand as a thin horizon of sticky clay.

The faunal remains found in the Basal Gravel during the present excavations were probably derived from the sludged land-surface material. A similar source may be ascribed to the worked flint flakes. The initiation of open fluviatile conditions is indicated by the presence of fresh-water mussel shells and the deposition of concretionary calcium carbonate on flakes and boulders.

The main body of the Lower Gravel (Stage Ib) was deposited under fully-developed fluviatile conditions with swiftly-flowing, carbonate-rich water occasionally flushing out ponds and quieter areas of water on the river floodplain. The horizon of chalk and clay clasts marked a temporary change in river conditions and is evidence of lateral erosion of the river channel at a point upstream where it cut through both Chalk and London Clay. Sand 'armouring' of both clay and chalk clasts took place during emplacement under conditions of fluctuating drying and wetting. Lateral erosion was also the source of introduction of shark teeth and gastropods from the London Clay and fragmentary belemnites from the Chalk. Deposits above the chalk clast horizon fine rapidly upwards and signify a steady reduction in water flow to the top of the Lower Gravel which is marked by an erosion surface.

The Midden Complex (Stage Ic) rests in a channel cut in the surface of the main body of the Lower Gravel, erosion having removed 0.8 to 1.0 m of the latter. An intermittent and variable water flow emplaced the channel fill, supporting a molluscan fauna of clear running-water, quiet water and pond forms. The midden lay in a shallow depression on the floodplain, occasionally washed over by flood-water and which periodically dried out. This muddy hollow was eventually covered by a moderate flow of clean, carbonate-rich water depositing a capping layer of sand over the midden level. Large numbers of fresh-water mussels flourished in the renewed flow which brought the open fluviatile conditions of Stage Ic to an end.

The fine-grained nature of the sediments of the main body of the Lower Loam (Stage Id) suggests deposition in a quiet back-water environment on the floodplain. Structures within the Lower

Loam show that deposition was neither continuous nor uninterrupted. Erosion and channelling took place at several levels and there were periods of temporary drying out as evidenced by horizons of desiccation pellets and pseudo-overconsolidation, flint-working areas and the development of rain-runnels. The molluscan fauna associated with the knapping floor suggests dry conditions and the adjacency of damp grassland with ponds and woodland. Narrow streams of clean, moderately flowing, carbonate-rich water crossed the dry or relatively dry sediments at a number of levels and supported a rich molluscan fauna. Land shells in the stream deposits indicate a damp grassland environment.

The Surface Layer (Stage Ie) of the Lower Loam represents a muddy land surface with a fauna of land shells indicating nearby woodland and damp grassland. The length of time taken for this land surface to develop is difficult to evaluate since it was partially or completely removed by a phase of renewed erosion, but its cessation was sudden and marked the end of Stage I. The length of time taken for the chemical weathering of the land surface, confirmed by PH measurements, is difficult to determine. The de-calcification process mobilised calcium carbonate and relocated it as nodular and tabular bodies in the lower parts of the profile. The irregular thickness of the Surface Layer represents a soil profile truncated by erosion. This soil marks the end of Stage I. Incoming water laid down sand which preserved the large numbers of animal footprints and land shells on the land surface in a virtually undamaged condition and initiated deposition of Stage II material.

The Lower Middle Gravel (Stage IIa) was deposited in clear, swiftly flowing, carbonate-rich water. The molluscan fauna includes pond and marsh species and land shells indicating adjacent grassland with subordinate woodland.

Plate 7.1. North face of Square A1. Full thickness of Lower Loam and Lower Gravel. Scales 1.80 m with lower scale resting on the surface of the Thanet Sand (35/4) (see Plate 7.8)

Plate 7.2. West face of Square A3. Full thickness of Lower Loam and Lower Gravel. Scale 60 cm resting on the surface of the Thanet Sand (122/12)

Plate 7.3. West face of Square B3. Lower Loam. Section through the shell-sand lens showing bedding of infill (117/4)

Plate 7.4. South face of square C3. Lower Loam. Section through the shell sand lens showing irregular upper and lower surfaces and bedding of infill (137/6 and 7)

Plate 7.5. Square B3. Lower Loam. Lower surface of the shell sand channel showing rain runnels. Scale 50 cm (116/5)

Plate 7.6. Square B3. Lower Loam. Lower surface of the shell sand channel showing development of potholes. Scale 50 cm (116/8)

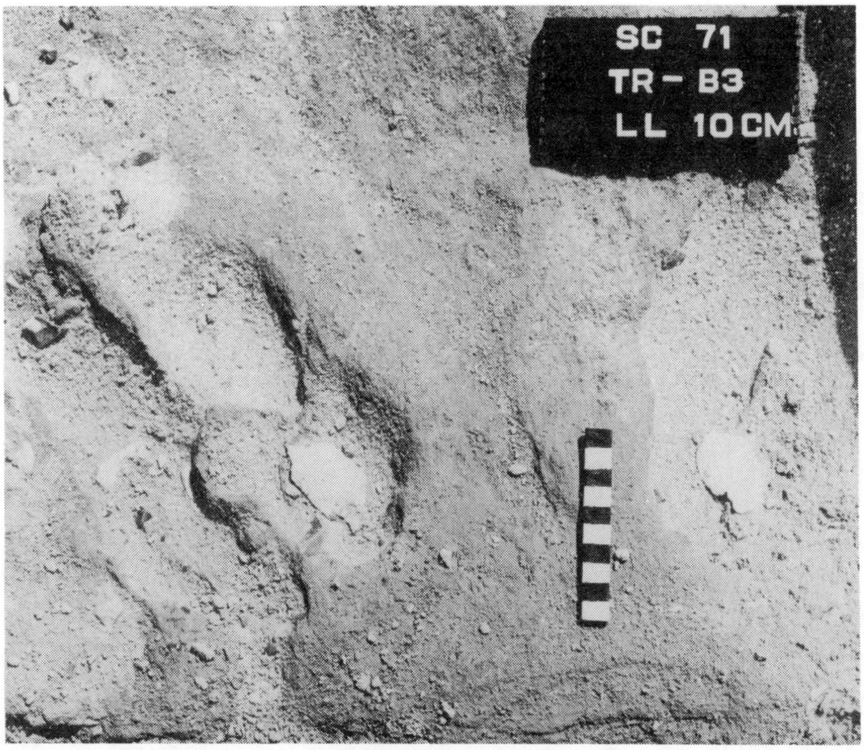

Plate 7.7. Square B3. Lower Loam. Lower surface of the shell sand lens with shells of *Potomida littoralis* in potholes. Scale 10 cm (115/5)

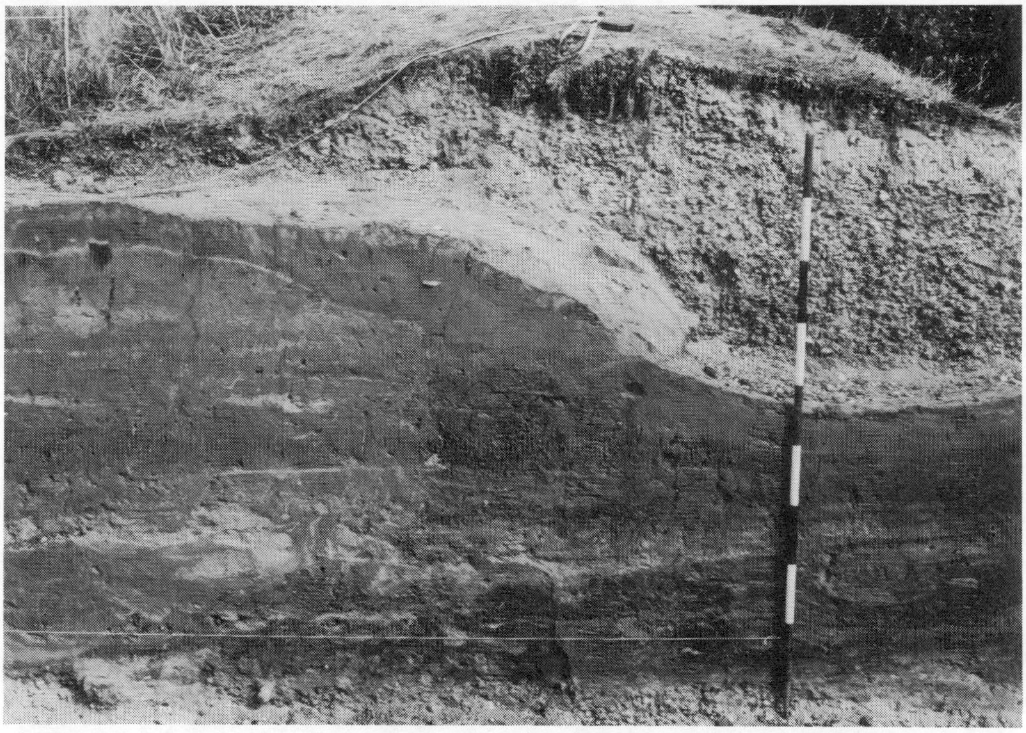

Plate 7.8. North face of Square A2. Full thickness of Lower Loam showing channel developed within it. Another channel, in the surface of the Lower Loam infilled with Lower Middle Gravel. Scale 1.80 m resting on the surface of the Lower Gravel (35/6)

Plate 7.9. Square O3. Lower Loam. Quartzite cobble lying with a flat face at ca. 40 degrees to horizontal. Scale 10 cm (136/7)

Plate 7.10. South face of Square C3. Lower part of Lower Middle Gravel, beneath backfill, overlying upper part of of Lower Loam with shell sand lens at foot of face. Scale 60 cm (122/5)

8. THE STRATIGRAPHY AND CHRONOLOGY OF THE PLEISTOCENE DEPOSITS OF BARNFIELD PIT, SWANSCOMBE

Bernard Conway

INTRODUCTION

This chapter discusses the stratigraphy of the Barnfield Pit as a whole drawing on the stratigraphic successions for the deposits inside and outside the NNR as outlined in Chapters 6 and 7 and relates them to the environmental evidence, where pertinent. Where possible, the bed descriptions of earlier workers, as outlined in Chapter 3, are equated with the sequence discussed below.

The geology and sequence of the Pleistocene deposits of Barnfield Pit have been known in general terms from the pioneering work of Smith and Dewey (1913 and 1914). As shown in Chapter 3 little serious geological work on the deposits was subsequently carried out until the Waechter excavations which commenced in 1968, and no overall account of the structural relationships of the beds had been given. The accounts which were written were largely re-digested versions of the work of Smith and Dewey or piecemeal and disparate descriptions of small and unrelated parts of the sequence. The present account attempts to critically assess early geological observations and relate them to the work done during the Waechter excavations. Some useful information has also come from retired quarrymen who took a professional, if somewhat paternalistic interest in the 1968-72 activities at Barnfield Pit.

Prior to the commencement of the Waechter excavations the sequence and relative chronology of the Thames terrace system most widely accepted was that of King and Oakley (1936). This required acceptance of certain eustatic gymnastics which were difficult to reconcile with geological reality in the Lower Thames. The motivating principal of their classification was the accommodation of stages in a perceived developmental sequence of artifact types (see Chapter 4). This often did violence to geological common sense and to the chronology. Much research since the end of the second World War in the fields of pollen analysis, isotope dating and the re-mapping of terrace deposits has enabled a more soundly based framework to be established (Bridgland 1994).

The deposits of Barnfield Pit have been mapped as Boyn Hill terrace by the Geological Survey and published on 1:50,000 Geological sheet 271 in 1977, based on surveys at 6 inches to 1 mile carried out between 1913 and 1921 with minor amendments made between 1951 and 1970. They comprise gravels, sands and loams resting on an eroded surface of Thanet Sand (Eocene) at about 22.5 m OD and reach a maximum height of 35.5 m OD. There are extensive areas of Boyn Hill terrace deposits on both the Kent and Essex sides of the river in the Dartford/Hornchurch areas, see 1:50,000 geological sheets 271 (Dartford) and 257 (Romford). At Upminster (NGR TQ 547874) Boyn Hill gravels were mapped resting on and banked against a glacial till - Chalky Boulder Clay (Holmes 1894, Dines and Edwards 1925). About 5 m of gravel with its surface at 32.5 m OD rests on a till surface at about 27.5 m OD which in turn rests on an eroded surface of London Clay (Eocene) at about 24.5 m OD (Bridgland 1994). The Chalky Boulder Clay of Essex is widely accepted as of Anglian age (Bridgland 1994) and therefore the Boyn Hill terrace must be considered as of post-Anglian age and the bench on which it rests of late-Anglian age. This provides a terminus *ante quem* for the chronology of the terrace sequence of the Lower Thames Valley.

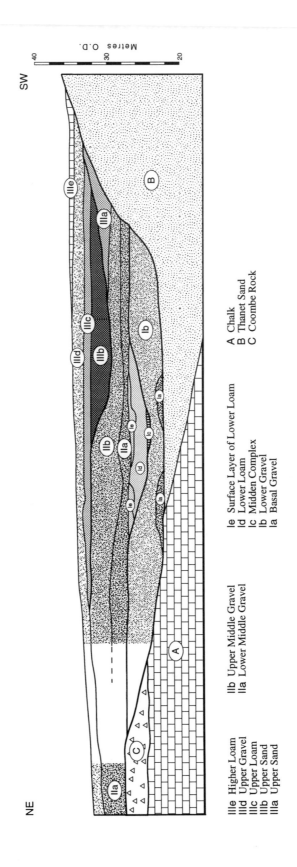

Metres O.D.

SW

NE

IIIe Higher Loam
IIId Upper Gravel
IIIc Upper Loam
IIIb Upper Sand
IIIa Upper Sand

IIb Upper Middle Gravel
IIa Lower Middle Gravel

Ie Surface Layer of Lower Loam
Id Lower Loam
Ic Midden Complex
Ib Lower Gravel
Ia Basal Gravel

A Chalk
B Thanet Sand
C Coombe Rock

Fig. 8.1. Schematic geological cross-section through the Swanscombe deposits

118

THE BASIS OF THE SUCCESSION

The Barnfield Pit sequence is based on Smith and Dewey's original work (1913 and 1914) subsequently confirmed and modified as a result of the 1968-72 excavations (Figure 8.1). Individual beds were delineated by changes of lithology, often associated with erosion surfaces. Few, if any, sequences of Pleistocene sediments give an uninterrupted representation of the total period of time during which material was deposited. Consequently the floral and faunal sequences contained within the deposits are also incomplete - an important factor when correlations and chronology are considered. Interruptions in sequences of sediments may be due to one or more of several causes with local or regional significance. In the interpretation of local successions the recognition of erosion surfaces is of major importance and their local or regional significance can only be determined by close and careful comparison with other sites.

Field evidence for erosion surfaces may take one or more of several forms: truncation of bedding (with or without angular unconformity), chemical and physical weathering (with or without soil formation), the presence of lag deposits signifying the base of a fluvial channel and disturbance of deposits by freeze/thaw processes - cryoturbation (with or without overlying solifluction material).

The Barnfield Pit deposits are no different from most other Pleistocene sites in that the sequence is interrupted by at least seven demonstrable erosion surfaces. One bed, the Lower Loam (Stage Id and Ie), less than two metres in thickness, shows a number of erosional phases of purely local significance. The principal factors governing erosional phases are changes in energy regimes in a fluvial environment and water level fluctuation either or both of which may be related to climatic changes.

The succession of erosional surfaces recognised in the Barnfield Pit sequence are labelled E1 to E7, and are shown in Figures 8.2 and 8.3 (see also Figure 8.1).

Erosion surface E1. This is the base of the channel, in which Stage I deposits rest, cut in Thanet Sand in the area of the Waechter excavations, but also recorded cut in Chalk in the northern part of the pit by early authors. The surface is marked by some cryoturbation disturbance of the top of the Thanet Sand on which rests a lag deposit and solifluction material.

Erosion surface E2. The top of the Basal Gravel (Ia) is irregular where the bed is present and is marked by a lag deposit resting on it. The lithological change is from an unsorted gravel in a clay/silt matrix (Ia) to a well-sorted, horizontally-bedded sandy gravel (Ib).

Erosion surface E3. The surface of the Lower Gravel (Ib) is irregular, bedding is truncated and the surface shows some decalcification. The lithology of the overlying beds, Midden Level (Ic) or the Lower Loam (Id), indicates a change to a much lower energy regime of deposition.

Erosion surface E4. The surface layer of the Lower Loam (Ie) has been weathered to a depth of about 50 cm and shows decalcification and the development of a soil. The surface is irregular, bedding is truncated and animal footprints are present in some number, a lag deposit of the Lower Middle Gravel (Iia) resting on it.

Erosion surface E5. The surface of the Lower Middle Gravel (Iia) shows considerable topography and marks a lithological change from a high energy environment of horizontally-bedded sandy gravels (Iia) to a lower energy environment of cross-bedded sands (Iib). Bedding of the Lower Middle Gravel is truncated.

Erosion surface E6. The upper part of the Upper Middle Gravel (Iib) shows cryoturbation disturbance and in places a solifluction deposit (IIIa) rests on the surface. The environmental change is from cool fluvial conditions to cold and at least partially terrestrial conditions.

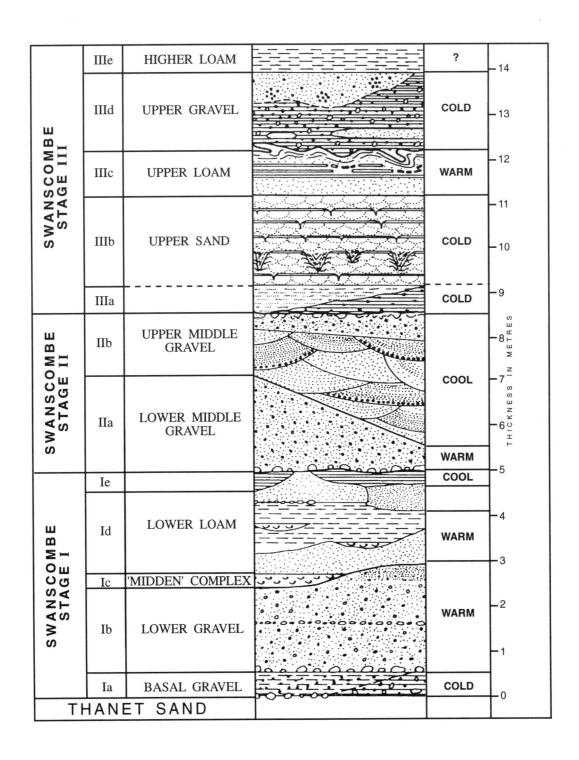

Fig. 8.2. Schematic geological section showing Stages I to III

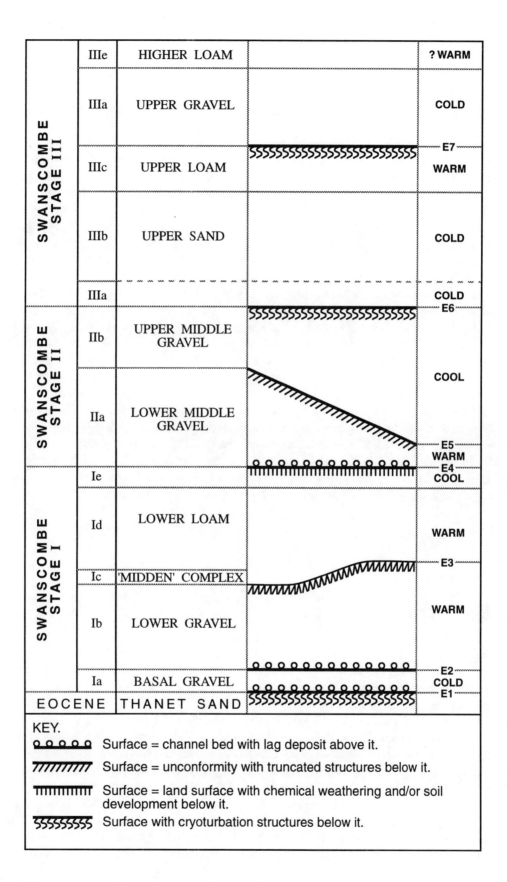

Fig. 8.3. Schematic section showing erosion surfaces 1 to 7

Erosion surface E7. The upper part of the Upper Loam (IIIc) shows marked cryoturbation disturbance together with ice-wedge casts with a solifluction deposit (IIId) resting on the surface.

Within the main body of the Lower Loam (Id) a number of phases of erosion have been recognised which are judged to be of very local significance and are not shown in Figure 8.3. They are demonstrated by channelling of fine-grained deposits, truncating bedding and by the presence of temporary dry-land surfaces.

At Barnfield Pit the Boyn Hill deposits were seen to rest on a bench cut in Thanet Sand at about 22.4 m OD in the Waechter excavations. Smith and Dewey (1913; 1914) recorded the gravels over-stepping the Thanet Sand and resting on a Chalk bench in the northern part of the pit at c. 22 m OD. This bench is considered to be of late Anglian age. The morphology of the late Anglian erosion surface is not known over most of its original extent since it has itself been eroded during subsequent periods of down-cutting and valley development. At Upminster the Chalky Boulder Clay, of late Anglian age, rests on an erosion surface cut in London Clay at about 24.5 m OD, ie. of somewhat earlier late Anglian age, see Figure 8.4. The Boyn Hill deposits there rest on a bench cut in the till at about 27.5 m OD. When these bench elevations are compared with the erosion surfaces in the Barnfield Pit sequence a correlation between the Boyn Hill Gravel bench at 27.5 m OD and erosion surface E4, the surface of the Lower Loam, is apparent as a surface of regional importance. The generalised descriptions of the dispositions of the several beds in the Barnfield Pit sequence by King and Oakley (1936) and Marston (1937A) show that the Stage I deposits (Lower Gravel and Lower Loam) lie in a channel about 500 m wide. The upper limit of this channel fill is the erosional surface (E4) at the top of the Lower Loam on which a soil developed at about 27.0 m OD. In other words, Stage I deposits are channel fill sediments and *not* part of a river terrace. The implication of this is that following emplacement of the Chalky Boulder Clay a river channel was eroded to a depth of 22.5 m OD in the Swanscombe area in late Anglian times (E1). Stage Ib deposits (Lower Gravel) aggraded in this channel to a height in excess of 27 m OD. Following the initial aggradation a narrower channel was eroded (E3) in the surface of the Lower Gravel down to about 25.0 m OD in which Stage Id and Ie deposits (Lower Loam) accumulated to a height in excess of 27 m OD. Stage I deposition terminated with and the deposits were truncated by a further erosion phase (E4) at about 27.0 m OD.

STAGE I

The Basal Gravel Ia

The three sub-divisions of the Lower Gravel, established in detail in the Waechter excavations, support early observations though some details were not confirmed. Where present the Basal Gravel examined in the Waechter excavations occurred as low mounds or hummocks and had been subjected to some sorting and re-deposition. Smith and Dewey's "basal red layer" appears to equate with Stage Ia of the present classification and was described by them as very coarse with large nodules of flint, "plentiful" mammalian remains and thick flakes. In his cumulative observations Dewey (1932) further records that the three-fold colour division of the Lower Gravel is not persistent and is not present in the eastern part of the pit, ie. in the central part of the channel in which it was deposited. Dewey also noted the large size of the material from Ia (1932; see Chapter 3).

Chandler's (1934B; see Chapter 3) brief description of the Lower Gravels as being clayey and unbedded with large flints appears to apply to the whole of the deposit and cannot be confirmed, though since the sections he examined were towards the western margin of the channel it may be that an area of thicker Basal Gravel was preserved there. Marston (1937A) repeats the earlier description of Smith and Dewey, but adds that the bottom 0.6 m of the Lower Gravel was covered by a layer of sticky brown clay; he later (1937B) described the pebbles in the bottom part of the Lower Gravel as

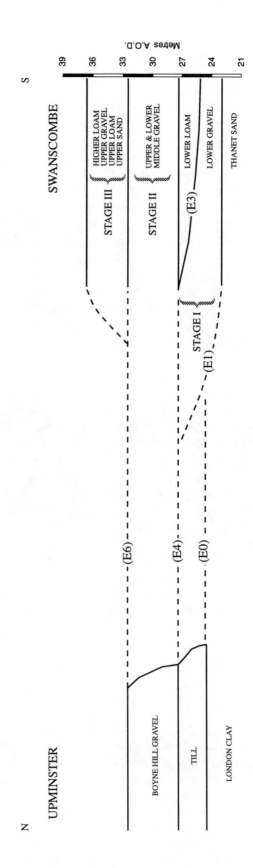

Fig. 8.4. Schematic geological section across the Thames between Upminster and Swanscombe

coated with tenacious brown clay. Paterson (1940) described the lower part of the Lower Gravel as compact, dark brown gravel with boulders and sub-angular sand. These observations are interpreted as being descriptions of the Basal Gravel Ia.

Many of the early authors describe both the large size and the quantity of mammalian remains associated with Ia. Dewey (1932) noted that the mammalian remains in the basal gravel were very friable and mentions a tusk of *Palaeoloxodon antiquus* about 2 m in length. In the 1930s a railway line was installed immediately to the east of squares A1 and B1 (in the Waechter excavations) to carry gravel to the washing plant. During the installation three wagon loads of bones were removed from the bottom of the (Lower) gravel (pers. comm. retired quarryman). Allowing for natural exaggeration I think the presence of a substantial amount of mammalian material in the Basal Gravel can be assumed.

The postulated solifluction origin for the Basal Gravel is supported by the extremes of texture and the size of the contained lithic and bone material. Marston (1937A) described the worked flakes as being "striated"; I examined his collection of worked flint from the Basal Gravel (1966-68) and was unable to confirm this statement in general, though there were quite convincing scratches on a small number of flakes. The poorly preserved mammalian remains give no indication of climate other than one purely temperate in nature. The texture, lack of bedding, and particularly the presence of some very large clasts are indicative of a solifluction origin - down-slope sliding of water-saturated material under gravity. That this took place in a cold climate, perhaps associated with the cutting of the channel in the Thanet Sand and Chalk, is more difficult to establish, though the presence of concentrations of thermally fractured pebbles, sharp splinters of flint, sub-angular coarse sand and some striated worked flakes is very suggestive. The mammalian remains from this unit are described in Chapter 11.

The main body of the Lower Gravels Ib

The earlier description of the Lower Gravel by Smith and Dewey as horizontally-bedded gravels subdivided on colour was repeated by Marston (1937B) who added that the gravels of the middle white layer were almost cemented by chalk wash-out. The Waechter excavations confirmed and refined this observation as resulting from a chalk clast horizon within the Lower Gravel (Chapter 7, unit 4 in Table 7.1). Light cementation of the gravels below this horizon was seen on the dressed sides of the excavation following a period of heavy rain. Smith and Dewey (1913) ascribe the colours of the three sub-divisions of the Lower Gravel to different states of oxidation of iron compounds. It would appear that the colour (red) of the lowest division is the result of clay coatings of the clasts and the clay content of the matrix. That of the middle division (white) is due to the presence of chalk and is a secondary feature appearing on weathered excavated faces. Both Smith and Dewey, and Marston describe the upper part of the Lower Gravel as finer than the lower part and well-bedded. This was confirmed by the Waechter excavations where the upward fining of the Lower Gravel as a whole was seen as a marked feature.

Kerney (1971) described the molluscan fauna of the upper part of the main body of the Lower Gravel (Ib) as dominated by aquatic species (90%), notably *Pisidium nitidum*, *P. henslowanum*, *P. subtruncatum*, *Bithynia tentaculata*, *Ancylus fluviatilis*, and *Lymnaea peregra*. Of the terrestrial species the Clausilids and *Retinella nitidula* are moderately common indicating the presence of woodland and scrub. *Vallonia costata* comprises 10-20% of the terrestrial element suggesting rather open conditions. Catholic species such as *Hygromia hispida* and marsh loving forms *Vallonia pulchella*, *Lymnaea truncatula*, *Zonitoides nitidus*, and *Carychium minimum*, predominate. Kerney also noted the presence of *Lauria* indicating fully temperate conditions with frost-free winters.

Early workers at Barnfield Pit recovered much mammalian material from the Lower Gravel which was studied by Sutcliffe (1964). This together with mammalian fauna recovered in the Waechter excavations suggests a mixture of open and closed environments (see Chapter 11)

The problems of pollen analysis in sand and gravel contexts are fully discussed by Hubbard (Chapter 15), but the pollen from the Lower Gravel generally support the molluscan evidence. The pollen profile extends through the Lower Gravel where it shows non-arboreal pollen dominating a mixed oak assemblage with some pine and a little alder, suggestive of the Early Temperate Zone II of an interglacial. The probable discovery of a pollen grain of the unidentified plant named "Type X" (Turner 1970) suggests that the main body of the Lower Gravel belongs to the Hoxnian interglacial.

The Midden Horizon Ic

Chandler (1928A) described shells and bones in the upper part of the Lower Gravel and his section shows a shell and bone bed at the top of the Lower Gravel. Marston (1937A) described the Lower Gravel as covered by a shell bed. Both these descriptions were confirmed by the Waechter excavations which recorded a great deal of detail in the Midden Level (Ic). The description by Paterson (1940) is difficult to reconcile with the 1968-72 excavations: he characterised the upper part of the Lower Gravel as containing large rafts of sand and many boulders, the upper part re-sorted. His section shows a thinned representation of the Lower Gravel rising up the Thanet Sand cliff feature at the western end (see Chapter 3, Figure 3.8). Depositionally this would represent an abnormal disposition of material under fluvial conditions, but it does suggest an erosional surface. If what Chandler saw was the eroded remnant of the Basal Gravel in a marginal part of the channel (as above), the description would be appropriate. Dewey (1932) seems to support this view when he recorded that the cliff of Thanet Sand against which the deposits were banked showed the Lower Gravel following the slope of the cliff, whereas higher deposits were horizontally bedded.

The Waechter excavations identified a Midden level for the first time (although the initial interpretation of it as being emplaced by human activity has not subsequently been confirmed - see Chapter 16), and also an erosional surface (E3) at the top of the Lower Gravel. Observations by earlier workers confirm the presence of this feature over an area extending beyond the detailed excavations within the NNR and also as a major stratigraphic break. Where this level is not marked by a shell bed, bone material is found on the erosion surface beyond the limit of the channel.

Except for the abundance of *Potomida littoralis*, which is otherwise rare in Stage Ib, the molluscan fauna of the Midden Level is comparable with that from the upper part of the Lower Gravel. The mammalian material (see Chapter 11) is qualitatively similar to that from the Lower Gravel, containing large bovids, proboscids, rhinoceros, bear, fallow and red deer.

The Lower Loam Id

For all its easy accessibility in sections over many years the Lower Loam has received far less attention than other beds in the lower part of the Barnfield Pit sequence. This may have been the result of Smith and Dewey (1913) characterising the bed as sterile with no archaeological or mammalian remains, a view repeated by most later authors. During extensive mechanised excavations in 1948 Ashley Montagu (1949) removed many tons of the bed and pronounced the Lower Loam sterile except for freshwater shells. The Waechter excavations showed convincingly that this is not so. As well as individual artefacts and bones scattered throughout the Lower Loam, primary context knapping scatters were present on fossil land surfaces.

Chandler's (1934B; Chapter 3), observations on the lenticular nature of the Lower Loam which he showed to rest in a channel cut in the upper part of the Lower Gravel were confirmed by the Waechter excavations. The fine-grained nature of the Lower Loam sediments indicates a low energy regime, a virtually still if not stagnant water environment. However, the Waechter excavations yielded evidence that within the Lower Loam deposition was interrupted at several levels by phases of channel cutting and infilling and by temporary relatively dry-land surfaces with desiccation features on which a network of small shallow streams flowed (see Chapter 7 and Figures 8.5 and 8.6).

This is supported by the molluscan evidence (Kerney 1971; Figure 8.5) which shows that there was an irregular cyclic fluctuation in the ratio of aquatic to terrestrial species in the main body of the Lower Loam (Id). The aquatic component of the fauna is similar to that from the upper part of the

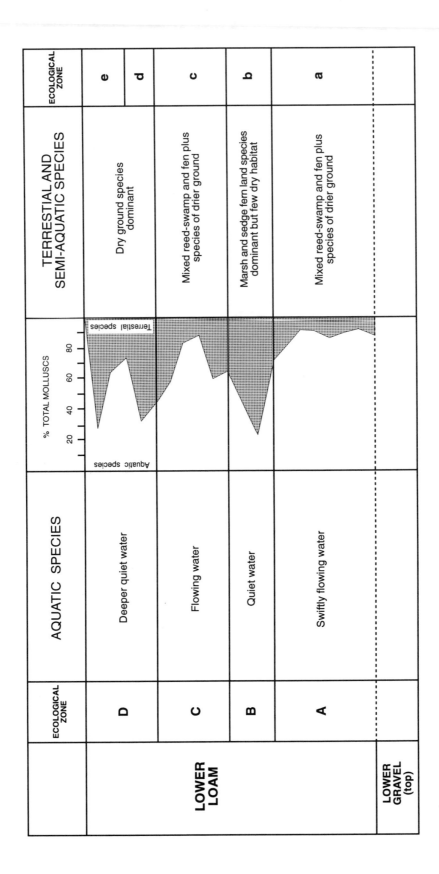

Fig. 8.5. Distribution of aquatic and terretsrial molluscs in the Lower Loam

Lower Gravel with the difference that *Pisidium nitidum*, *Planorbis crista* and *P. albus* are more abundant. The numbers of *Pisidium subtruncatum* decline in the upper half of the Lower Loam at the same time as *Valvata piscinalis* increases. Although the abundance of the latter species suggests lacustrine conditions *Ancylus fluviatilis*, which is present throughout the Lower Loam, is indicative of clear running water. The terrestrial component of the molluscan fauna of the lower part of the Lower Loam is comparable with that of the upper part of the Lower Gravel, but the marsh species *Lymnaea truncatula* and *Zonitoides nitidus* become scarcer in the upper part and c. 60 cms. from the top of the Lower Loam marshland species, with the exception of *Vallonia pulchella* disappear. Little change is apparent among the catholic and slum species, but species indicative of shaded habitats become more common while at the same time dry habitat species appear or increase in numbers. Kerney interpreted the semi-terrestrial component of the fauna as indicating reed-swamp and fen, while the terrestrial element recorded dry open grass-land in a wooded environment which, from the presence of *Azeca menkeana* and *Vallonia costata*, he concluded was dry, not heavily shaded, and probably contained hazel. The presence of *Lauria* and *Pomatias elegans* indicate mild winter conditions.

The ostracod fauna of the Lower Loam (Robinson 1971; Chapter 14) reflects a stagnant pond-like environment of an abandoned meander channel marginal to a sluggish river. Open water conditions are judged to have become more sedgy and overgrown with time. One species, *Scottia browniana*, is chronologically significant as it is not found in deposits later than the Hoxnian interglacial.

The pollen (see Chapter 15, Figure 8.6) suggests the presence of mixed oak forest with hazel throughout the main body of the Lower Loam, while a change to open conditions takes place about 60 cm from the top of the Lower Loam. The presence of pollen of Type X and of *Azolla filiculoides* permits correlation with the Hoxnian interglacial. The whole of the Lower Loam is placed by Hubbard within the Early Temperate Zone HoIIb of the Hoxnian interglacial.

The Weathered Surface of the Lower Loam Ie

In their first description of the Barnfield Pit deposits Smith and Dewey (1913) clearly accepted the top of the Lower Loam as an old land surface. Marston (1937A) recorded the presence of white-patinated flakes together with land shells on the surface of the Lower Loam. He also acknowledged in his unpublished report (Marston 1937B) that the top of the Lower Loam "became a land surface upon which plants grew, land snails lived, and Clactonian flakes remained sufficiently long to become patinated white by sub-aerial exposure". King and Oakley (1936) declared that the surface of the Lower Loam was "weathered". Zeuner (1959) noted that the weathered nature of the uppermost levels of the Lower Loam had been reported by many workers, but that it had never been confirmed chemically. He made Ph measurements which demonstrated decalcification of the upper part of the Lower Loam to a depth of 50 cm.

During the Waechter excavations measurement of a Ph profile was repeated and produced a more marked result than that shown by Zeuner, though with decalcification only to a depth of 30 cm (see Table 7.2). Kerney (1971) while accepting that there was a hiatus between the Lower Loam and the Lower Middle Gravel, suggested that decalcification of the top of the Lower Loam was due to leaching by water percolating from the overlying gravel. However, a detailed pedological examination carried out by Kemp (1985) substantiated the view that the surface layer (Ie) of the Lower Loam was a chemically weathered soil horizon which developed on a land surface before being truncated by erosion (E4) and buried.

The Waechter excavations yielded quite dramatic evidence to support the existence of a land surface at the top of the Lower Loam in the form of a large number of mammalian footprints associated with land shells (see Chapter 13).

The molluscan fauna occurring on the land surface at the top of the Lower loam is dominated by *Cepaea nemoralis*, *Hygromia hispida* is common and *Ena montana*, *Arianta arbustorum*, *Cochlicopa lubrica* and Clausilids are also present indicating the presence of dry grassland and scrub. It may be significant that the pattern of colour-banding most commonly exhibited by *C. nemoralis* is the one

The stratigraphy and chronology of the Barnfield Pit

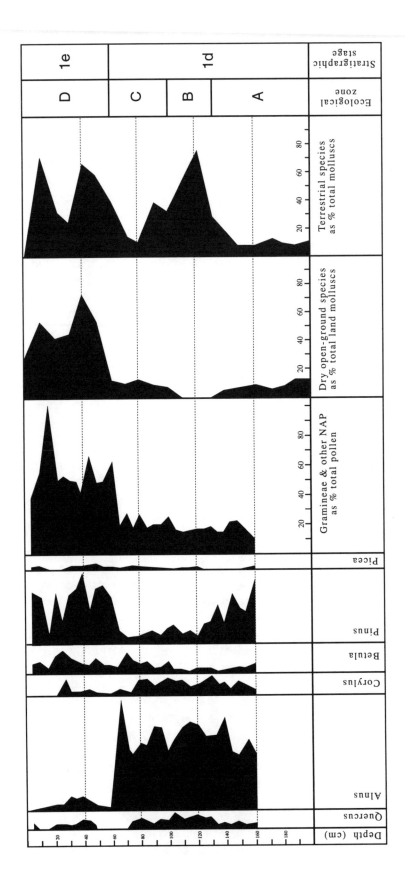

Fig. 8.6. Distribution of pollen and molluscs in the Lower Loam Stages Id and Ie

128

found most frequently in modern open environments. Pollen analysis also indicates an open environment in which the assemblage of open plants is very different to the main body of the Lower Loam (see Chapter 15).

STAGE II

The Lower Middle Gravel Iia

Stage II commenced with the flooding of the land surface at the top of the Lower Loam and aggradation of the Lower Middle Gravel. The initial stage of this aggradation was represented by a few centimetres of sand which were deposited very rapidly thus preserving the large number of animal footprints found on the land surface.

Dewey's cumulative description (1932) records the Lower Middle Gravel as 0.6 m thick throughout the pit which accords with the sections examined during the Waechter excavations where 1 m or less was seen. He also identified the Lower Middle Gravel as the source of the majority of the bifaces from the pit. When the Barnfield Pit deposits had their maximum exposure and availability to inspection Smith and Dewey (1912) recorded thickness variations for the Middle Gravels from 2.4 to 5.5 m in the southern part of the pit, thinning northwards to 1.8 m The implication of this description is that throughout the pit 0.6 m of Lower Middle Gravel occurred at the base of the Middle Gravels and that the balance in thickness of material was Upper Middle Gravel, described as gravel in the southern part of the pit passing laterally into current-bedded sands on the north side. The sections examined during the Waechter excavations confirm Dewey's description of the Lower Middle Gravel but present difficulties in accommodating his description of the Upper Middle Gravel. The 1968-72 excavations recorded the Upper Middle Gravel as markedly cross-bedded sands, not as gravels, even though the sections were in the southern part of the old pit. Chandler (1928A), on the other hand, described sections displayed in the southern face of the pit which appear to disagree with Dewey. Chandler recorded 0.5 to 1.5 m of gravel (Lower Middle Gravel) overlain by 3.1 to 3.7 m of cross-bedded sands (Upper Middle Gravel). Later Chandler (1934B) recorded a somewhat different section with 1.5 to 2.4 m of sand and gravel as undifferentiated Middle Gravel. It appears that he included a part of the Upper Middle Gravel (cross-bedded sands and fine gravel) in his "Middle Loam". These varying descriptions were made at a time when the southern face of Barnfield Pit was being commercially worked, sections observed one year had been cut back some tens of yards three or four years later. Dewey's record of 2.4 to 5.5 m of undifferentiated Middle Gravel is probably of a much fuller development of the Lower Middle Gravel which escaped the erosional phase (E5) which terminated the aggradation of Stage Iia.

The molluscan fauna of the Lower Middle Gravel is quite different from that on the surface of the Lower Loam (Kerney 1971). Terrestrial species make up less than 10% of the total and the aquatic element is similar to that of the Lower Gravel and Lower Loam with corresponding environmental implications. Several species make an appearance in the Barnfield sequence for the first time; *Unio crassus, Valvata naticina, Pisidium clessini, Sphaerium rivicola,* and the thermophilous species *Corbicula fluminalis* and *Belgrandia marginata; Theodoxus serratiliniformis* is widespread and marshland species seem to be absent. The terrestrial molluscs were considered by Kerney to indicate a more closed environment than in the Lower Loam. Species such as *Acicula, Theodoxus, Belgrandia,* and *Corbicula,* are "southern" species whose arrival late in the interglacial has arguably been ascribed to the establishment of a geographical connection between the Rhine and the Thames river systems (Castell 1964); their presence implies a warm climate.

The early collections of mammalian material from Swanscombe were labelled "Middle Gravel" with no differentiation made between Lower and Upper (Sutcliffe 1964). Sutcliffe has argued that they show a change from those of Stage I deposits, suggesting more open conditions. Those recovered from the Waechter excavations were not of sufficient quantity to draw firm conclusions (see Chapter 11).

Pollen concentrations in the Lower Middle Gravel was low but there was no evidence for differential destruction (see Chapter 15). The assemblage is similar to that of the Lower Gravel and reflects an open environment with grass and herbs making up 70% of the pollen; trees and shrubs clearly indicate temperate conditions.

The Upper Middle Gravel IIb

The account given by Marston (1937A) of the deposits from which he recovered the fragments of the now famous skull described a phase of erosion and channelling between the Lower and Upper Middle Gravels in which a channel cut through the Lower Middle Gravel, Lower Loam and the Lower Gravel to within 0.3m of the Thanet Sand surface was infilled with Upper Middle Gravel. The examinations by Smith and Dewey and Chandler (above) were made at a time when very extensive sections were exposed in a working pit. Neither account records seeing channelling cutting through the Lower Middle Gravel and lower deposits (see especially Chapters 3 and 4.) Careful examination of the Middle Gravels sections exposed during the Waechter excavations do not confirm the existence of a channel as described by Marston. However, this examination did confirm the erosional nature (E.5) of the junction between the Lower Middle and Upper Middle Gravels.

Wymer's excavations at Barnfield Pit from 1955-60 (in Ovey 1964) recorded an area of subsidence in the lower part of the Upper Middle Gravel adjacent to his find position of the third part of the human skull. Small-scale faulting of the current-bedded sands was associated with this subsidence. The 1968-72 excavations outside the NNR and about 160 m NNW of Wymer's excavation also recorded faulting and slumping in the lower part of the Upper Middle Gravel on a larger scale (Chapter 6). The faulting and slumping in the Upper Middle Gravel was clearly gentle in nature, involving progressive down-throws of only a few centimetres at a time, and was caused by cambering in an area marginal to a major solution structure. The subsidence collapse of the sediment fill of the solution feature ceased by the time that the Upper Middle Gravel was deposited and only minor volume accommodations were taking place. Cessation of solution subsidence takes place when the water table drops to a position where fissure systems are developed by solution only in competent Chalk (Walsh *et al.* 1973).

Dewey's Stopes Memorial Lecture photograph described and figured in Chapter 3 shows a sag-syncline in Pleistocene deposits in-filling a solution structure in the Chalk surface on the north face of the Barnfield Pit. Solution subsidence affected the Lower Gravel, Lower Loam and Lower Middle Gravel and higher beds appear to be unaffected and pass over the area of disturbance horizontally. The structure resulted from the formation of a sub-surface solution cavity which was roofed over during the deposition of the Stage I and IIa sediments and which collapsed when that sedimentation ceased with the erosion of the surface of the Lower Middle Gravel, E5. The gravitational collapse was quite a gentle process and the primary sedimentary features of the deposits were faithfully preserved. Edmunds (1983) has recorded cambering associated with solution subsidence, though evidence of this is not visible on Dewey's photograph. Marston's claim (1937B, and unpub. notes) of having found a hand axe within 0.3 m of the surface of the Thanet Sand seems likely to have been a misunderstanding of features associated with a solution hollow of the kind illustrated by Dewey. The presence of slumping seen in both the Wymer and Waechter excavations and Dewey's observations may suggest a preferred and linear disposition of solution features.

The molluscan fauna of the Upper Middle Gravel (IIb) is only known from a number of early collections (Kerney 1971). It is dominated by aquatic species. The "southern" species *Theodoxus serratiliniformis* and *Corbicula fluminalis* are present though not common, but *Belgrandia* is not recorded. The terrestrial element of the fauna is virtually restricted to one species *Hygromia hispida*. An open grassland is indicated and a distinct cooling of the climate, though specifically cold climate molluscs are absent.

The large mammal fauna of the Upper Middle Gravel is similar to that of the Lower Middle Gravel (Sutcliffe pers. comm.), but against this indication of temperate conditions must be set the finding of *Lemmus* (Schreuder 1950; see Chapter 11). Other rodents are of species not particularly associated with arctic conditions, while pollen from only one sample also suggests interglacial conditions (see Chapter 15).

STAGE III

The Upper Sand, Stages IIIa and IIIb

As a result of the Waechter excavations in the south-western part of Barnfield Pit, outside the NNR, a new stratigraphic unit was recognised and added to the sequence - "Upper Sand", (see Chapter 6), classed as Stage III a and b. This was seen to rest in a channel about 75 m wide with a depth of about 2.9 m. The surface of the Upper Middle Gravel on which the Upper Sand rests (E.6) showed cryoturbation disturbance to a depth of 15-20 cm. At the western end of the section this zone of disturbance was overlain by a solifluction deposit (IIIa) at the base of the Upper Sand, confirming Paterson's observation (1940). The main body of the Upper Sand (IIIb) comprises banded sands and clays with well-developed ice-wedge casts at several levels; the deposits clearly having accumulated under periglacial conditions.

The Upper Loam IIIc

The Upper Sands pass up conformably into the Upper Loam, first described by Smith and Dewey (1913). Chandler (1928A) described them as consisting of more than 3 m of current-bedded sands with a clayey loam above. It is clear that he included the cold-climate Upper Sand in this account. In a later paper (Chandler 1934) he described the bed as a fine-bedded sandy loam which he named "Middle Loam". Marston (1937A) described the Upper Loam as a horizontally laminated loam.

The Waechter excavations showed the Upper Loam to comprise horizontally bedded clayey sands with thin clay horizons and with patches of carbon crumbs on bedding planes. The upper part was penetrated by ice-wedge casts to a depth of 0.4 m.

The Upper Loam yielded no faunal material, but sparse pollen suggests that the lower part of the bed belongs to the early temperate mixed oak forest Zone Iib of an interglacial. The upper part of the bed shows a marked increase in hornbeam, no increase in spruce, and fir is absent, suggesting deposition during the post-temperate Zone III of an interglacial (see Chapter 15).

The Upper Gravel IIId

Smith and Dewey (1913) first described the Upper Gravel as a stiff clay, variable in thickness, with pockets of gravel resting on the irregular surface of the Upper Loam and claimed that it originated as a "hill wash" and not as a river deposit. The Waechter excavations revealed a raft of apparent Upper Loam material about 3 m in length within the Upper Gravel with listric surfaces developed at the base. Ice-wedge casts descend from the surface on which the Upper Gravel rests (E7) into the Upper Loam (section LA1, Figure 6.6). They were seen to be inclined at about 60° from the vertical in an easterly direction - the result of drag distortion by downslope movement of the Upper Gravel from west to east over the Upper Loam surface.

Chandler (1934B) recognised a further bed of loam above the Upper Gravel, and this was confirmed by Paterson (1940). In the Waechter excavations all the sections cut outside the NNR area showed Upper Gravel to pass upwards, with a reduction in the number of pebbles, into a loose clayey silt with scattered pebbles which appears to be the "Brickearth" of earlier authors. The "Brickearth" has yielded faunal material in the form of indeterminate crushed bone fragments together with some well-preserved shells - *Pomatias elegans*, *Ostraea* and *Patella*. Several small scatters of probably later prehistoric flakes were also found which, together with the molluscs, are clearly intrusive. The "Brickearth" appears to represent the deeply weathered and disturbed upper part of the Upper Gravel.

Higher Loam IIIe

During the 1968-72 excavations a number of shallow inspection trenches were cut up to 85 m south west of the south west corner of Barnfield Pit, ie. beyond the original extent of the pit and in the undisturbed land surface. Two of these revealed a horizontally-bedded clayey loam with a scatter of worked flakes in a very sharp condition, but no faunal material. This bed does not appear to have been described by earlier workers and is tentatively labelled "Higher Loam" until such time as more extensive sections are available.

CHRONOLOGY

On the basis of his studies of loess in Central Europe Kukla (1977) concluded that the Holstein interglacial, which has been confidently correlated with the Hoxnian of England, corresponded with Oxygen Isotope Stage 11 of Shackleton and Opdyke (1973). Bridgland (1994) equates the Anglian glaciation with Isotope Stage 12 and uses the term "Hoxnian *sensu* Swanscombe" to identify the first interglacial period following the Anglian. This has been used to distinguish the deposits from those at Hoxne, which on the basis of Amino Acid Racemisation suggests a Isotope Stage 11 date for Swanscombe, and a Isotope Stage 9 date for Hoxne (Bowen *et al.* 1989). In the discussion below the term Hoxnian is used *sensu* Swanscombe.

The Anglian age of the Chalky Boulder Clay of Upminster is the fixed point on which the chronology of the Swanscombe local sequence is based, and also on which the Lower Thames regional sequence is anchored. The Boyn Hill Gravels (= Orsett Heath Gravels of Bridgland) were shown earlier to be post-Anglian in age. The gravels resting on Chalky Boulder Clay at Upminster at a height of 27.5 m OD have been correlated with Stage II deposits at Barnfield Pit which rest on erosion surface E4 at 27.0 m OD (see Figure 8.4). Evidence from the molluscan and mammalian faunas of Stage II, might suggest that the Lower and Upper Middle Gravels are from the latter half of the Hoxnian interglacial. The palynological evidence, however, suggests a Hoxnian Zone Iib age.

A similar strength of floral and faunal evidence places most or all of the Stage I deposits in the early part of the Hoxnian, the Lower Gravel (Stage Ib) in pollen Zone HoII; the Lower Loam (Stage Ic-e) in HoIIb. Stage I deposits were laid down in a channel eroded in Thanet Sand and Upper Chalk, resting on erosion surface E1 which shows some cryoturbation disturbance beneath it. These deposits are not part of the Boyn Hill terrace. Stage I deposits are unequivocally the oldest part of the gravels mapped as Boyn Hill Gravels, but they are not part of the terrace (= the eroded remnant of a flood pain) but a complete channel fill, the deposits in which were truncated by erosion surface E4 at 27.0 m OD.

Are both Stages I and II to be considered as part of the same Hoxnian interglacial? There is floral and faunal evidence for continuity between the two stages, although there are significant differences. Lithologically both Stages consist of an upwards - fining fluviatile sequence, separated by an erosion (E4) and land surface. In the molluscan faunas "southern" forms appear for the first time at Swanscombe in Stage Iia and there are quantitative differences in the mammalian faunas which might reflect environmental changes. Geologically the two Stages are separated by a period of unknown duration of non-deposition and soil formation, followed by erosion (E4). It is in this hiatus that some authors (King and Oakley 1936; Gibbard 1988) believe that a direct link developed between the Rhine and Thames river systems permitting the migration of "Rhenish" or "southern" molluscan species into the Lower Thames. Kemp (1995), however, has argued that the hiatus is only of local significance. This is supported by amino acid ratios from the Lower Gravel to Upper Middle Gravel which all correlate with Isotope Stage 11 (Bowen *et al.* 1989).

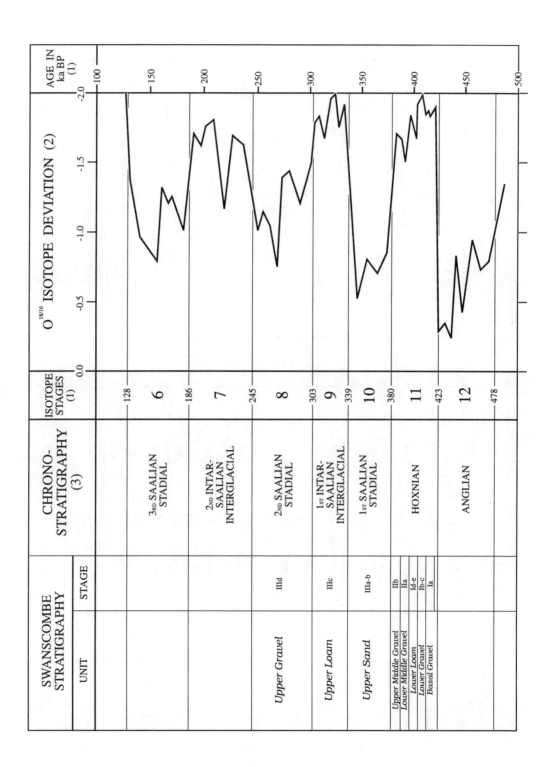

Fig. 8.7. Possible correlation between the Oxygen Isotope curve and the Swanscombe sequence

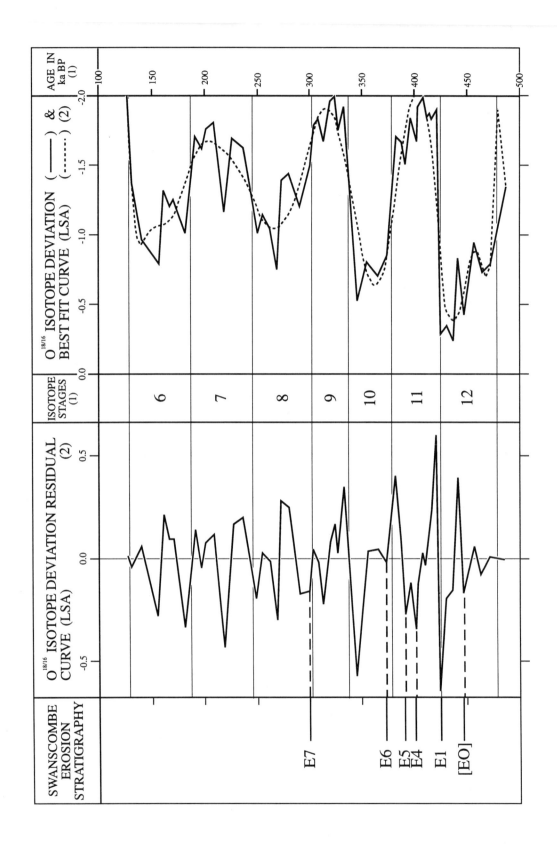

Fig. 8.8. Possible correlation between erosion surfaces and Oxygen Isotope deviation residual curve

One of the difficulties of accepting the botanical definition of an interglacial period is that the model presented by West and Turner (1968) provides only for uni-directional development of the floral sequence. There is no possibility in this simple model in which short-term, sharp fluctuations of climate can be accommodated. The implication is that floral, and to some extent faunal responses to sudden changes of climate are very slow, and not identifiable in the fossil record. The response in sedimentary regimes may be much more immediate and identifiable as periods of erosion.

The Oxygen Isotope deviation curves produced by Shackleton and Opdyke (1973) are an index of the global budget of land ice, with variations interpreted in terms of climate. Stage boundaries are drawn where steep gradients indicate major changes and ages for the boundaries by Campbell and Bowen (1989) on the basis of magnetic stratigraphy, accepting the Matuyama/Brunhes magnetic reversal to have taken place 750,000 years BP.

Figure 8.7 is based on Shackleton and Opdyke (1973) and is a composite curve based on the results from cores Vema 28-238 and 239, in which Oxygen 16/18 deviation from the standard is plotted against age in thousands of years as determined by Campbell and Bowen (1989). From this curve it can be seen that no Stages are uniformly "cold" or "warm", but all show short-duration, sharp contra events: two in Stage 12 (Anglian) and at least three in Stage 11 (Hoxnian). The fluctuations in Stage 11 for example represent short-lived cold periods and these could be expected to have an effect on climate, albeit a minor one. A temperature curve for the interglacial would not be a simple rise to a peak followed by a fall (as implied by West and Turner's model) but rather rises to three peaks of warmth separated by cooler troughs. There would then be difficulty in reconciling West and Turner's vegetation model for the interglacial period with the temperature model for the same period. The difficulties of interpretation are compounded by the incomplete nature of the sedimentary record and hence of the floral and faunal material, the incompleteness itself being a function of non-deposition and erosion resulting from the short, sharp cold events.

In an attempt to assess and focus the fluctuations in the isotope deviation curve as shown in Figure 8.7, the data was subjected to a least squares analysis (LSA) and a best-fit curve calculated, see right hand side of Figure 8.8. The difference between the deviation curve and the calculated best-fit curve is shown on the left hand side of Figure 8.8 as the isotope deviation residual curve. It is apparent that a series of marked, short-duration maximum and minimum events are partially masked by the generalised isotope deviation curve. Cold micro-events within an overall warm period might not have a positive detectable presence in the floral or faunal record because of slow response times but the climatic effect, particularly on sea levels, would be more immediate and obvious. In the lower reaches of fluvial regimes this might be expected to manifest itself in terms of non-deposition (still stands) and in erosion.

The stratigraphic sequence at Barnfield Pit has been shown to be interrupted by a number of phases of erosion and some of these are correlated with the micro-events shown in Figure 8.8 in Isotope Stages 12 to 9. The following chronology is proposed for the Pleistocene deposits of Barnfield Pit, Swanscombe:

1. The erosion of the channel (E1) in which Stage I deposits accumulated took place towards the end of the Anglian cold event (Isotope Stage 12) about 420 ka BP and was accompanied by solifluction represented by the Basal Gravel (Stage Ia). The Basal Gravel was originally a late Anglian deposit but much of it was re-sorted or incorporated in the aggradation of the Lower Gravel Stage Ib which followed.

2. Where Basal Gravel is present the upper surface is truncated by erosion surface E2 which is believed to be of terminal Anglian age. Where the Basal Gravel has been incorporated in the Lower Gravel the two erosion planes (E1 and E2) coalesce. E1 sometimes shows cryoturbation disturbance beneath it. Faunal material recovered indicative of a fully temperate climate has been identified with pollen Zone II of the Hoxnian warm event. Evidence of lateral erosion of the channel banks is believed to be only of local significance.

3. The main body of the Lower Gravel (Stage Ib) has yielded faunal material indicative of a fully temperate climate and has been identified with pollen Zone II of the Hoxnian warm event.

Evidence of lateral erosion of the channel banks is believed to be only of local significance.

4. The top of the Lower Gravel is an erosional surface, E3, which shows slight chemical alteration beneath it and marks a break between the high energy regime below and the low energy regime above. The Middle Level (Stage Ic) and the main body of the Lower Loam (Stage Id) have yielded faunal and floral evidence of a fully temperate climate of pollen Zone IIb of the Hoxnian warm event. There is evidence of several phases of erosion and of dry land surfaces developing within the main body of the Lower Loam, these are believed to be of local significance only.

5. The Surface Layer (Stage Ie) of the Lower Loam has yielded floral and faunal evidence of a marked environmental change to dry, open-ground conditions. The top of the Surface Layer had a soil profile developed on it which was truncated by erosion surface E4 and there is evidence for it having been a land surface at perhaps 410 ka BP.

6. The Lower Middle Gravel (Stage IIa) shows a return to high energy fluvial conditions and the faunal evidence might indicate the latter part of the Hoxnian warm event. The top of the Lower Middle Gravel is erosion surface E5 which accompanies some channelling and took place perhaps about 400 ka BP.

7. The Upper Middle Gravel (Stage IIb) though still fluvial shows a distinctly lower energy regime than that of the Lower Middle Gravel. Faunal evidence suggests that it can be assigned to the later stages of the Hoxnian warm event, with indications that a somewhat cooler climate prevailed. The top of the Upper Middle Gravel is marked by erosion plane E6 assigned to about 380 ka BP.

8. Erosion surface E6 shows cryoturbation structures beneath it and is overlaid by cold-climate solifluction material of the lower part of the Upper Sands (Stage IIIa). The upper part of the Upper Sands is also of cold climate origin, both Stages IIIa and b are assigned to the first Saalian cold event, Isotope Stage 10.

9. The Upper Loam (Stage IIIc) has yielded floral evidence of a fully temperate climate and can perhaps be assigned to the first intra-Saalian warm event, between about 339 and 303 ka BP, Isotope Stage 9.

10. The surface of the Upper Loam is erosion plane E7 and shows cryoturbation disturbance beneath it. The Upper Gravel (Stage IIId) is a cold climate solifluction deposit and as such can possibly be assigned to the second Saalian cold event, Isotope Stage 8, 303 to 245 ka BP.

11. Higher deposits in the sequence are not known sufficiently well for them to be characterised in chronological terms.

9. THE AVIFAUNAL REMAINS

Steven Parry

INTRODUCTION

A small collection of avifaunal remains from Swanscombe, recovered prior to the Waechter excavations, has been described by Harrison (1979; 1985). He also assigned a coracoideum fragment recovered by Waechter to Common Scoter *Melanitta nigra* (Linnaeus) 1758. This report describes 13 previously undescribed specimens recovered during the Waechter excavations, held in the collections of the Department of Palaeontology, Natural History Museum, London. The specimens are all poorly preserved and highly fragmentary, while some lack provenances but are very probably referable to the Lower Loam (Currant, pers. comm.). These unprovenanced specimens have been designated individual museum accession numbers. The provenanced specimens had not been designated individual accession numbers at the time this report was submitted.

Given the limitations of the recovery techniques employed during the excavations (see Chapter 12) the avifaunal remains here described cannot be regarded as representative and are very probably biased towards larger taxa. Furthermore, there is no evidence to suggest that their deposition was in any way related to anthropogenic behaviour. Given the obvious limitations of the material no attempt has been made to undertake quantitative analysis. All specimens were identified by comparison with the osteological reference collections of the Natural History Museum, Sub-Department of Ornithology, Tring, Buckinghamshire. Wherever possible identifications have been supported by morphometric data. All measurements were taken with a pair of electronic callipers with a resolution of 0.01mm and an instrumental error of ± 0.02 mm. The taxonomy and sequence utilised in this report follows Clements (1991). English language names follow British Birds (1993) for western Palaearctic neospecies and anatomical nomenclature follows Baumel *et al.* (1979). As all specimens were fused there is no evidence for the presence of nestlings or juvenile birds.

PALAEONTOLOGY

Phalacrocorax carbo (Linnaeus) 1758, Great Cormorant

Lower Loam, SC 70 A3

Coracoideum, sinister, incomplete. A fragment of the Extremitas omalis and Corpus, lacking the Processus acrocoracoideus and exhibiting abrasion of the Facies articularis humeralis.

The degree of fragmentation exhibited by this specimen precluded biometric analysis, however, comparison with recent reference material indicates that this specimen is indistinguishable in both size and morphology from the coracoideum of the neospecies *P. carbo*. This taxon is the largest extant cormorant in western Eurasia (Cramp and Simmons 1977). Harrison (1979), working with less fragmentary material recovered by Kennard, was able to demonstrate that *P. carbo* was represented at Swanscombe but the Lower Loam provenance assigned to these specimens by Kennard may now be regarded as questionable (see Chapter 12).

Bucephala clangula (Linnaeus) 1758, Common Goldeneye.

Lower Loam, SC 69 B1, 33.

Humerus, dexter, incomplete. Comprised of eight conjoining fragments constituting the Extrematis proximalis, the Corpus and the Condylus dorsalis. These fragments were united with an adhesive following excavation. An isolated fragment of the Caput is also represented. Despite the degree of fragmentation there has been little surficial erosion.

Ulna, dexter, complete. Comprised of two exactly conjoining fragments which were united with adhesive as above. The Extrematis proximalis has been subject to limited surficial erosion, the Extrematis distalis has been more severely eroded.

Radius, dexter, complete. Comprised of three exactly conjoining fragments which were united with adhesive as above. The Extrematis proximalis and particularly the Extrematis distalis have been subject to surficial erosion.

Carpometacarpus, dexter, incomplete. A fragment of the Extrematis proximalis and the Os metacarpale majus which has been fractured close to the midpoint. The Os metacarpale minus has been largely lost due to a fracture close to its proximal limit. This specimen exhibits evidence of more severe erosion than those described above.

These four specimens are complementary in proportions, share identical laterality and were recorded as 'articulated' when exposed *in situ*. This is taken as compelling evidence that they represent the remains of an articulated wing. In an assessment of 34 extant Holarctic anatid ducks these specimens were found to be closest in size to the complementary elements in four Palaearctic neospecies; Northern Shoveler *Anas clypeata* Linnaeus 1758, Ferruginous Duck *Aythya nyroca* (Güldenstädt) 1770, Tufted Duck *Aythya fuligula* (Linnaeus) 1758 and *B. clangula*. The humerus and antebrachial elements of these taxa all overlap in greatest length (Table 9.1).

The identification of the post-cranial osteology of the Holarctic Anatidae has been regarded as notoriously difficult by zooarchaeologists who have tended to use standardised mensural criteria in identification. In fact, from an ornithological perspective, character differences and proportional differences exhibited by key skeletal elements are clearly apparent in the members of this family (Parry in prep.). These differences reflect the phylogeny and ecomorphology of the taxa in question and, in many instances, they may be readily demonstrated by biometry if measurements are designed to highlight them. In this instance the humerus was found to be the most useful specimen for the purpose of identification and proved to be referable to *B. clangula* on the basis of the distal structure of the Crista pectoralis, the form of the circumscription of the Crista bicipitalis on the Facies cranialis, and the cross-sectional form of the most proximal Corpus which is more rounded in *A. clypeata* and the smaller *Aythya* ducks. Furthermore, the relative dorsal length (from the most distal point of the Crista pectoralis to the most distal point of the Condylus dorsalis) of the humerus is relatively shorter in *B. clangula* than in the other taxa considered. This proportional difference in the humerus enables clear separation even from *A. nyroca* (Table 9.1, Figure 9.1). *B. clangula* exhibits marked sexual dimorphism and the Swanscombe wing bones are within the size range of recent females (Table 9.1 and Figure 9.1)

The congeneric Barrow's Goldeneye *B. islandica* (Gmelin) 1789 is morphologically similar to *B. clangula*. However, this essentially Nearctic neospecies is markedly larger and more robust in its post-cranial osteology than *B. clangula* (Parry in prep.). Thus, both morphological and biometrical evidence indicates that these specimens are best referred to *B. clangula* and, allowing for surficial erosion and mensural error, not significantly different in size and proportion from the complementary elements in recent females (for dorsal length of humerus; $t_s = 0.1954$, $t_{0.9[3]} = 0.137$).

Anatidae sp. indet.

Midden, second floor, SC 70 A3

Scapula, sinister, incomplete. A fragment comprised of the Extrematis cranialis and the most cranial component of the Corpus.

The conformation of the Extrematis cranialis provides sufficient evidence to refer this specimen to a small anatid duck, however, the degree of fragmentation precluded generic diagnosis.

Lower Loam/Lower Gravel, SC 68 A Level 2B

Ulna, sinister, incomplete. A proximal fragment comprised of the Extrematis proximalis and the Corpus fractured close to the Foramen nutricium. The Olecranon and Processus cotylaris dorsalis have been subject to erosion.

Humerus	GL	1	2	3
A.clypeata				
Both sexes (n=8)				
Range	73.1 - 77.5	20.9 - 25.6	6.51 - 7.18	53.9 - 57.5
x ± sd	76.0 ± 1.5	23.1 ± 1.8	6.75 ± 0.2	55.8 ± 1.1
A.nyroca				
Female (n=1)	76.4	23.2	6.79	56.3
A.fuligula				
Both sexes (n=7)				
Range	77.4 - 83.0	23.5 - 26.0	6.56 - 7.22	57.5 - 62.0
x ± sd	80.3 ± 1.8	24.7 ± 1.0	6.77 ± 0.4	58.6 ± 1.6
B.clangula				
Males (n=4)				
Range	80.5 - 81.2	26.3 - 27.6	7.24 - 7.71	57.7 - 59.3
x ± sd	80.9 ± 0.3	27.1 ± 0.6	7.56 ± 0.2	58.9 ± 0.8
Females (n=4)				
Range	70.0 - 72.7	22.4 - 24.5	6.27 - 7.67	50.7 - 52.3
x ± sd	71.4 ± 1.2	23.3 ± 1.1	7.1 ± 0.4	51.3 ± 0.7
Swanscombe (n=1)				
Sc69 Sq B1 33	NA	22.2	6.63	51.5

Ulna and Radius	Ulna GL	Radius GL
A.clypeata		
Both sexes (n=7)		
Range	65.1 - 66.7	58.9 - 61.4
x ± sd	65.7 ± 0.6	60.6 ± 0.9
A.nyroca		
Female (n=1)	64.8	60.3
A.fuligula		
Both sexes (n=7)		
Range	68.1 - 72.6	64.3 - 68.2
x ± sd	70.3 ± 1.6	66.0 ± 1.6
B.clangula		
Males (n=4)		
Range	68.9 - 70.2	64.1 - 66.2
x ± sd	69.3 ± 0.6	64.7 ± 1.0
Females (n=4)		
Range	60.8 - 63.7	57.0 - 59.5
x ± sd	62.1 ± 1.2	58.0 ± 1.1
Swanscombe (n=1)		
Sc69 Sq B1 33	63.7	60.3

Table 9.1. Measurements (mm) of the humerus, ulna and radius of *Anas clypeata, Aythya nyroca, Aythya fuligula* and *Bucelpha clangula* compared with the articulated sub-fossil specimens from the Lower Loam (SC 69 Sq B1 33). Abbreviations: GL - greatest length; 1 - minimum length from the most distal point of the Crista pectoralis to the most proximal limit of the Foramen nutricium; 2 - maximum breadth of the Corpus at the most distal limit of the Crista pectoralis; 3 - maximum dorsal length from the most distal point of the Crista pectoralis to the most distal point of the Condylus dorsalis. * In the case of *A. nyroca* data has been supplemented with the measurements of Woelfle (1976).

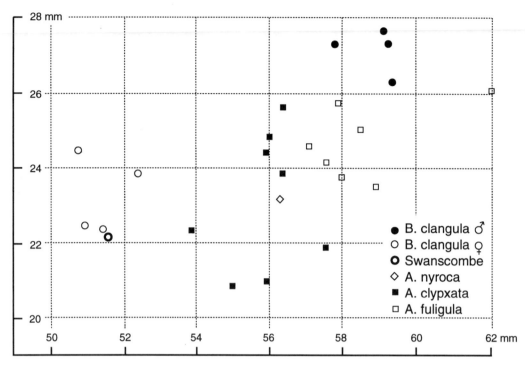

Fig. 9.1. Measurements of the humerus of Holartic anatid ducks. The maximum dorsal length from the most distal point of the Crista pectoralis to the most distal point of the Condylus dorsal is plotted against the minimum length from the most distal point of the Crista pectoralis to the most proximal limit of the Foramen nutricium

Although surficial erosion precluded morphometric analysis this specimen is of the same order of size as the ulna in such neospecies as *Anas clypeata, Aythya fuligula* and *B. clangula*.

Lower Loam? Unprovenanced, NHM Acc. No. A4277

Carpometarcarpus, dexter, incomplete. A fragment comprised of the Os metacaple majus lacking the Extremitas proximalis and the Extremitis distalis. The Os metarpale minus is largely absent due to a fracture close to the proximal termination.

      The overall morphology and cross-sectional form of the Os metacarpale majus together with the conformation of the proximal termination of the Os metacaple minus provided sufficient evidence to assign this fragment to the Anatidae. However, the specimen was deemed too fragmentary for generic diagnosis. This specimen is of the same order of size as the carpometacarpus in such neospecies as *Melanitta nigra* and Goosander *Mergus merganser* Linnaeus 1758.

Pandion haliaetus (Linnaeus) 1758, Osprey

Lower Loam/Lower Gravel, SC68 A, level 2B

Tibiotarsus, sinister, incomplete. A distal fragment, fractured proximally at the proximal limit of the Sulcus extensorius and distally at the Pons supratendineus. The Condylus medialis and Condylus lateralis have been lost through fragmentation but the most lateral limit of the Pons supratendineus is preserved.

      The morphology of the tibiotarsus in the neospecies *P. haliaetus* is unique amongst the Falconiformes (Jollie, 1977; Parry, in preparation) thus, despite the degree of fragmentation, the Swanscombe specimen is readily referable to this taxon. A comparison of the breadth and depth of the Corpus at the proximal limit of the Sulcus extensorius indicates that this specimen is similar in size and proportions to the tibiotarsus of the largest recent form, the Palaearctic subspecies *P. haliaetus* (see Table 9.2).

Columba palumbus Linnaeus 1758, Common Wood Pigeon

Lower Loam/Lower Gravel, Sc70 A3

Femur, dexter, incomplete. This specimen is comprised of two fragments representing the Corpus and the Extremitas distalis, the Extremitas proximalis having been lost. The Condylus medialis, Condylus lateralis, the Epicondylus medialis and the Epicondylus lateralis have all been subject to limited surficial erosion. Following excavation the two fragments were united with an adhesive and a splint of wood was inserted into the Cavitas medullaris to reinforce the repair thus obliterating any potential evidence of Os medullare.

The femur of *C. palumbus* is morphometrically distinguishable from those of the smaller European neospecies Rock Pigeon *C. livia* Gmelin 1789 and Stock Pigeon *C. oenas* Linnaeus 1758. This specimen is indistinguishable from the femur of the neospecies *C. palumbus* and is not significantly different in size (Table 9.3) from the femur in the recent European subspecies, the nominate *C. palumbus* (for minimum breadth of the corpus $t_s = -0.676$, $t_{0.5[10]} = 0.700$). Whereas European populations of *C. livia* appear to have experienced repeated size variation during the Middle and Upper Pleistocene the size of *C. palumbus* is regarded as having remained relatively constant (Mourer-Chauviré 1975, 145-158).

In addition to the specimens described in the systematic section three specimens are regarded as *incertae sedis* and are listed as follows.

Lower part of Lower Loam, SC 71 B2. Radius, dexter, incomplete. A fragment of the Extrematis proximalis and proximal Corpus which has been subject to surficial erosion.

Lower Loam ? NHM Access. No. NHM A4275. Limb bone Corpus fragment.

Lower Loam/Lower Gravel, SC 68 A 2B. Pedal Phalanx, complete.

Tibiotarsus	BC	DC
P.haliaetus Both sexes (n=5)		
Range	7.63 - 8.02	5.62 - 6.54
x ± sd	7.86 ± 0.2	6.05 ± 0.4
Swanscombe (n=1) Sc68 2B LL/LG	7.81	5.87

Table 9.2. Measurements (mm) of the tibiotarsus of *Pandion haliaetus* compared with the fossil specimen from the Lower Loam (SC 68 A 2B LL/LG). Abbreviations: BC, breadth of the Corpus at the proximal limit of the Sulcus extensorius; DC, depth of the Corpus at the proximal limit of the Sulcus extensorius.

Femur	BC	DC	DD
C.palumbus Both sexes (n=11)			
Range	3.49 - 4.07	3.47 - 3.96	6.82 - 7.80
x ± sd	3.82 ± 0.2	3.72 ± 0.2	7.21 ± 0.3
Swanscombe (n=1) Sc68 2B LL/LG	3.69	3.66	6.4*

* Minimum measurement due to surficial damage

Table 9.3. Measurements (mm) of the femur of *Columba palumbus* compared with the fossil specimen from the Lower Loam (SC 70 A3 LL/LG). Abbreviations: BC, breadth of the Corpus at the Foramen nutricium; DC, depth of the Corpus at the Foramen nutricium; DD, depth of the Condylus lateralis.

DISCUSSION

Given the extreme limitations of the material, the apparent lack of biostratigraphic evidence of seasonal turnover in the faunal assemblages and the absence of clear evidence of breeding such as the presence of Os medullare and the remains of eggs or nestlings, it is uncertain whether the four avian taxa occurred as residents, non-breeding visitors or migrants. Nor should it be assumed that the recent distributions and status of neospecies provide direct analogues for palaeoecological reconstruction (Sher 1990). There is an increasing body of evidence which suggests that many Pleistocene mammalian assemblages have no recent analogues (Lundelius 1989; Sher 1990; 1991) and current research suggests that similar patterns are evident in Pleistocene avifaunal assemblages (Parry in prep.). Furthermore, traditional models for the evolution of Eurasian avian migration systems during the Pleistocene (eg Moreau 1972) are increasingly difficult to reconcile with the evidence of the rapidity and complexity of climatic change furnished by the oxygen isotopic record (Dansgaard *et al.* 1993; Greenland Ice-core Project Members 1993; Grootes *et al.* 1993). For example, the present Holarctic populations of *Pandion haliaetus* undertake long distance tropical migration and occur as summer visitors in northern high latitudes (Poole 1989). It is generally accepted that this behaviour is related to mean winter water temperatures in northern high latitudes which cause prey species to retreat to deep water (Newton 1979). However, small numbers of *P. haliaetus* are able to overwinter in the Mediterranean and other populations in the Caribbean and Australia are sedentary (Poole 1989). Thus, it cannot be assumed that the current Holarctic distribution and seasonal status of *P. haliaetus* are directly applicable to the ospreys of the Middle Pleistocene.

Despite these reservations, the avifaunal material recovered by Waechter is not without interest or significance. The record of *P. haliaetus* appears to be by far the earliest known from north-western Europe (cf. Brodkorb 1964; Harrison 1988) and the implications of this for Middle Pleistocene taphonomy are discussed below. Both *P. carbo* and *Bucephala clangula*, a diving duck, are mid-water and bottom feeders which may indicate the presence of deep water as well as eutrophic shallows. The recovery of an articulated wing of *B. clangula* provides clear evidence of the presence of underived faunal material in the Lower Loam. However, this latter record should not be taken as evidence of rapid depositional rates in a low energy environment as bird carcasses may float for up to 38 days (Schafer 1972) and the wings of strandline carcasses may remain articulated for months (Parry in prep.).

The presence of the piscivorous *P. carbo* and *P. haliaetus* has significant implications for the interpretation of fish remains from Middle Pleistocene fluvial and lacustrine deposits. The potential role of avian predators in the formation of piscifaunal assemblages has rarely been considered in the literature although perceptively anticipated by Weigelt (1927). In fact, a considerable body of evidence indicates that these predators may be primary agents in the formation of piscifaunal assemblages and that their variable feeding ecology may result in a plethora of taphonomic biases which may not be readily resolved (Parry and Irving in prep.). Such processes may have influenced the taxonomic, sex and age representation of fish in recovered assemblages. Both of these predators are opportunistic, taking a wide diversity of fish in the range 0.1-0.5 m in length and, as their prey selection is linked to relative availability and density, dramatic short-term shifts in the taxa exploited are commonplace (Cramp and Simmons 1977; 1979; Poole 1989). Furthermore, both *P. carbo* and *P. haliaetus* may travel over 25 km between their feeding grounds and the nest and roost sites where prey remains are deposited (Cramp and Simmons 1977; 1979; Poole 1989). Such feeding strategies often result in the deposition of the remains of allocthonous fish caught in different catchments and environments to those in which nests and roosts are located (Jamieson *et al.* 1982; Parry and Irving in prep.). In the case of Swanscombe the fish remains recovered from the Lower Loam and Lower Gravel are dominated by those of large salmonids (see Chapter 10). Whilst this taxonomic and size representation may be attributable to recovery bias (see Chapter 10) the presence of salmonids is of interest given that, in Britain today, both *Phalacrocorax carbo* and *Pandion haliaetus* frequently specialise in salmonid predation (Carss and Brockie 1994; Cramp and Simmons 1977; 1979). Although the reconstructed size of the fish represented at Swanscombe is greater than those normally taken by these birds (see Chapter 10), the possibility that some of these remains may have been deposited by ospreys scavenging

S.Parry

carcasses of fish beyond their prey-weight threshold (Parry in prep) of 2.5-3.0 kg in live-weight requires consideration (Parry and Irving in prep.).

10. THE ICHTHYOFAUNA FROM THE WAECHTER EXCAVATIONS, BARNFIELD PIT, SWANSCOMBE

Brian Irving

INTRODUCTION

A small assemblage of fish material (26 fragments) from the Waechter excavations at Barnfield Pit have produced one identification to species, three to genus, one to family and one to order. Twenty fragments were not referable higher than class. All of the material is in poor preservation condition, limiting the amount of information which could be retrieved. The bones are probably all surface finds as no sediment from the excavations was systematically screened (see Chapter 12). This of course will have placed an unknown level of bias towards larger bone fragments.

The material was identified using the osteological reference collection at the Environmental Archaeology Unit, Department of Biology, University of York. Few measurements were taken as the bones were too eroded for accurate comparison; however, two vertebrae were measured which were much better preserved (measurements are those of Morales and Rosenlund (1979)). The anatomical nomenclature combines the schemes of both Wheeler and Jones (1989) and of Lepiksaar (1983). The systematic taxonomy is that described by Wheeler (1969).

PALAEONTOLOGY

Salmo salar (Linnaeus 1758), Atlantic Salmon.

Lower Loam, SC 68 A(2B) 145-165.

Abdominal vertebral corpus, complete. A fully intact corpus with processus transversus intact. Both the processus spinosus superior and processus spinosus inferior are missing; this is typical in the Salmonidae as they are not fused to the corpus of the abdominal vertebrae.

The vertebra has been referred to species as both overall morphology and the identification of migratory history has been established. Migratory fishes show 'annuli' within the systemic osseus growth of the vertebral centrum. These growth bands are very clear on this specimen showing that, after two years, growth increased three-fold, something which is normally associated with accelerated growth in the marine environment (Irving in prep). The migratory phase of the brown trout *Salmo trutta fario* L., the sea trout *Salmo trutta* L. can be confused with *S salar* L. on the identification of annuli; however the abdominal vertebrae are very species distinct (Irving in prep).

Salmo (Linnaeus 1758), species indeterminate.

Lower Loam, SC 68 A(2B) 145-165.

Dentary tooth, complete. The tooth is typical of *Salmo* species but cannot be identified to species as *S. trutta* and *S. salar* share an identical dentary tooth morphology.

Lower Loam, SC 71 B3 #51.

Caudal vertebra, corpus complete. Processus transversus are both intact. Both processus spinosus superior and processus spinosus inferior have broken off, leaving part of the canalis haemalis and canalis neuralis attached to the corpus.

The vertebra is the best preserved fish bone within the assemblage. The points of breakage are fresh and uneroded so may have been lost either during excavation or later. The vertebra could not be assigned to species as the caudal vertebrae of *S. salar* and *S. trutta* are indistinguishable. The vertebra shows distinct annuli on the centrum which indicates a migratory history.

Weathered surface of Lower Loam, SC71 C3.

Abdominal vertebra, corpus intact. Very eroded condition but shows characteristic salmonid morphology.

Gadidae, species indeterminate.

Lower Loam, SC71 B3 41.

Rib fragment, distal portion, representing approximately one third of the total length. A single distal rib fragment has the 'wavy' morphology seen in the Gadidae, especially the cod *Gadus morhua* and the haddock *Melanogramus aeglefinus*.

Isospondyli, family indeterminate.

Base of Lower Loam, SC71 B3.

First vertebra, lateral fragment of facies articularis posterior. A small fragment which is probably Salmonid but is indistinguishable from the charr's *Salvelinus* sp in overall morphology.

A number of fragments could only be assigned to class and are listed here for completeness.

Lower Loam, SC 71 B3. Rib fragments, 19.

Base of Lower Loam, SC 70 B2. Rib fragment, 1

	SC71 B3 LL 51	SC68 A(2B) 145165
greatest dorso ventral height of centrum	8.9	11.9
greatest medio lateral breadth of centrum	9.7	12.3
greatest cranio-caudal length of centrum	8.9	6.7

Table 10.1. Measurements (in mm) of *Salmo* centrums

DISCUSSION

The fragments come from the lower part of the sequence and contain both marine stenohaline and diadromous (migratory) euryhaline species. This would suggest that the site of deposition is probably estuarine or the marine littoral.

Parry (see Chapter 9) suggests that the material may have been deposited by piscivorous birds. The evidence from the ichthyofauna suggests otherwise, as the fossil material is large in size and represents individuals larger than those taken by the avian predators identified. However, as suggested above, bone recovery was from surface finds and small fragments of fish material may have been missed through a lack of sieving. Irving (1994) discusses the role of avian predators as accumulators of fish remains, concluding that none of the western palaearctic bird species are capable of taking medium- to large-sized migratory salmonids or large gadids.

If an accumulator is responsible for the ichthyofaunal assemblage at Barnfield Pit then it is more likely to be a large mammal such as one of the seals (Phocoidea) or the dolphins (Delphinidae) and porpoises (Phocoenidae). The bottle-nosed dolphin *Tursiops* cf *truncatus* has been identified from an unprovenanced find in the adjacent Ingress Vale Pit (Sutcliffe 1964). It is thought that this specimen is also from the lower part of the sequence.

Evidence for predators cannot be deduced from the ichthyofaunal material; it is likely that the material reflects a natural 'tidal strand line' death assemblage. It is difficult to establish accumulating agencies when dealing with such a small and poorly preserved assemblage.

As most of the material has suffered mechanical abrasion, probably due to hydraulic transport, the material is not thought to be *in situ* and therefore cannot accurately reflect local environmental conditions. However, the presence of marine and migratory species in association suggests a brackish estuarine intertidal zone or a coastal littoral intertidal zone. The above-mentioned find of dolphin attests to the view of a tidal strand death assemblage.

11. THE MAMMALIAN FAUNA FROM THE WAECHTER EXCAVATIONS, BARNFIELD PIT, SWANSCOMBE.

Danielle Schreve

INTRODUCTION

The mammalian fossils described below were collected from Barnfield Pit, Swanscombe between 1968 and 1972. They come primarily from two horizons at the site, namely the Lower Loam and Lower Gravel, although occasional specimens from the Middle Gravels were also obtained. Only a small amount of the material is in a fresh state, much of it being either rolled or weathered and most of it highly fragmentary. Although this may provide some indication of both the depositional environment and the taphonomic processes that were in operation at the time of deposition, the poor condition of the fossil material also reflects the methods of recovery that were employed at the site. This is particulary true in the case of the small mammal remains, many of which were trowelled through during excavation.

A list of the mammalian species recorded is provided below, showing their presence/absence in various horizons (see Table 11.1). This is followed by descriptions of the identified bones, teeth and bone fragments. The material is listed according to stratigraphic order which is as follows (from the base of the deposits to the top):

Lower Gravel units 1-4
Lower Gravel midden
Lower Loam/Lower Gravel junction
Base of Lower Loam
Lower Loam sandy horizon in B3
Lower Loam main body
Top of Lower Loam
Weathered Lower Loam
Lower Loam (LL) weathered surface
Base of the Lower Middle Gravels (LMG)

Every effort has been made to provide as many details as possible concerning each specimen (Natural History Museum London accession number, year of excavation, location ie. trench/square and finds number where available, followed by a brief description of the specimen). A certain amount of the fossil material was never assigned a finds number at the time of its excavation and as a result, it has been impossible to relate all the specimens to their correct horizon at the site. In other cases, the same finds number has been allocated to several different specimens which has further served to confuse the picture. Furthermore, according to the excavation notebooks, certain specimens were apparently discarded (seemingly at random) by Waechter although some of these have since been rediscovered in the collections. It is therefore advisable to be aware of the considerable problems and sample biases inherent in the material: certain horizons (in particular the Lower Gravel midden, formerly believed to be a humanly-derived accumulation) are over-represented in terms of the number of fragments collected whilst some major faunal groups of potential biostratigraphic significance (such as the small mammals) are markedly under-represented, again due to bias in recovery techniques.

Species	LG Midden	LG junct	LL/LG undif	LL m.b.	LL weath.	LL	LMG
Primates							
Macaca sylvana, macaque				+			
Insectivora							
Talpa minor, extinct mole			+				
Talpa cf. *europaea*, mole					+		
Lagomorpha							
Oryctolagus cuniculus, rabbit		+	+	+	+	+	
Rodentia							
Castor fiber, beaver				+			
Arvicola cantiana, water vole	+		+	+	+		
Microtus oeconomus, northern vole			+				
Microtus cf. *agrestis*, field vole			+				
Microtus (Terricola) subterraneus, pine vole				+	+		
Murid indet., mouse					+		
Carnivora							
Ursus sp., bear	+	+	+		+		
Martes cf. *martes*, pine marten						+	
Canis sp., wolf		+			+		
Panthera leo, lion					+	+	
Felis sylvestris, wild cat		+					
Proboscidea							
Palaeoloxodon antiquus, st. tusked elephant		+					+
Elephant sp. indet.	+	+			+		
Perissodactyla							
Equus caballus, horse	+						
Stephanorhinus hemitoechus, narrow-nosed rhinoceros		+					
Stephanorhinus kirchbergensis, Merck's rhinoceros	+	+					
Stephanorhinus sp. indet., rhinoceros		+	+	+	+	+	
Artiodactyla							
Sus scrofa, wild boar			+	+	+	+	
Cervus elaphus, red deer	+	+	+	+	+	+	
Dama dama clactoniana, fallow deer	+	+	+	+	+	+	+
Megaloceros giganteus, giant deer						+	+
Bos primigenius, aurochs	+		+		+		
Bison cf. *priscus*, bison	+						
Bovini sp. indet.	+	+	+	+	+	+	+

Table 11.1. Presence/absence of species in selected horizons.

PRIMATES

Cercopithecidae (macaques, mandrills and baboons)

Macaca sylvana (L.), Barbary macaque

Lower Loam main body
SC70 B2 #44 R ulna prox. end

INSECTIVORA

Talpidae (moles and desmans)

Talpa minor (Freudenberg), extinct small mole

Lower Loam undifferentiated
SC70 B2 radius

Talpa cf *europaea* L., mole

Lower Loam main body
SC72 C3 #97 frag. R lower M1

LAGOMORPHA

Leporidae (rabbits and hares)

Oryctolagus cuniculus L., rabbit

Lower Gravel midden
R tibia dist. end (weathered),

Lower Loam/Lower Gravel junction
SC69 A2 #105 incomplete R calcaneum, SC70 B1 #82 (part) 2 lower cheek teeth, SC68 TrA 2B R tibia (lacks both articular ends), L humerus dist. end and L scapula (glenoid, neck and part of blade), possibly one individual, SC70 B2 L ulna (lacks part of prox. articulation and dist. end) and L radius shaft

Lower Loam sandy horizon
SC71 B3 #49 R tibia (lacks prox. end)

Lower Loam undifferentiated
SC70 B3 'near Complex 4' incomplete L calcaneum (weathered), SC71 C3 L upper I1, 2 upper cheek teeth, SC70 TrE #8 (30 cm) L calcaneum, R 4th metacarpal, phalanx and metapodial frags., SC70 B2 incomplete L calcaneum, SC71 B4 L calcaneum, SC71 C3 R calcaneum, SC70 B2 L calcaneum, SC71 C3 lower P3, cheek tooth and mand. frag., SC70 B1 #65 upper cheek tooth (very fragmentary), SC70 B2 #47 R femur (lacks dist. end), SC70 A3 juvenile cervical vertebra (cf. *O. cuniculus*), SC70 B2 L innominate frag., SC70 TrE #12 L tibia dist. end (possibly associated with SC70 TrE #8), SC70 TrE #20 L upper I1

Lower Loam main body
M29618 SC72 C3 #99 upper I frag., SC70 B1 #70 lower P3 (very fragmentary), SC70 B3 #5 damaged phalanx, SC72 C3 #95 L and R innominate bones (damaged and weathered), SC72 C3 #93 incomplete L mand. ramus with L P3-M3, SC70 B3 #8 R tibia dist. end (weathered), SC68 TrA 2B 145-165 cm L calcaneum, SC70 B2 #37 R calcaneum (damaged), R astragalus, L humerus dist. end, SC71 B2 #112 upper I, SC70 B2 #25 frag. lower P3 (juvenile)

Top of Lower Loam
SC70 B2 lower I, upper I1, R premaxilla with upper R I2, upper cheek tooth and R scapula prox. end, SC70 B3 R mand. ramus frag. with lower I, lower P3, lower I, 2 cheek teeth and mand. frags.

Weathered Lower Loam
SC70 B3 upper I1, L premaxilla, L 1st metatarsal, 2 isolated cheek teeth and metatarsal frags.

Unprovenanced
SC70 B2 L tibia shaft, R tibia shaft (weathered), SC68 'TrB 2D' L femur prox. end, SC71 'LL/WL June' R 4th metacarpal

RODENTIA

Castoridae (beavers)

Castor fiber L., beaver

Lower Loam undifferentiated
M49695 SC72 associated L and R crushed mand. rami with L and R lower I, lower P4-M3, SC71 B3 R lower M1

Cricetidae (voles and lemmings)

Arvicola cantiana (Hinton), extinct water vole

Lower Gravel surface
M29494 SC71 B3 lower M1

Lower Loam/Lower Gravel junction
M29490 SC70 A3 upper I (cf. *A. cantiana*)

Lower Loam undifferentiated
M29496 SC70 A3 associated teeth and bones, M29620 SC72 C3 L dentary with upper M1, upper M2, M29621 SC72 C3 associated teeth and bones, M29622 SC72 C3 associated teeth and bones, M29491 SC70 B3 'near flint complex 4' lower M2 (cf. *A. cantiana*)

Lower Loam main body
M29492 SC70 B2 #38 associated teeth and bones, M29607 SC69 A2 #43 frags. of dentary with teeth (cf. *A. cantiana*), M29608 SC69 A2 #44 associated frags. of cranium and dentary with teeth, M29610 SC69 A2 #35 frags. of dentary with teeth, M29611 SC69 A2 #30 frags. of dentary and I (cf. *A. cantiana*), M29612 SC69 A2 #33 frags. of dentary and teeth (cf. *A. cantiana*), M29613 SC69 B1 #49 tooth frags. (cf. *A. cantiana*), M29614 SC69 B1 #50 associated teeth and bones, M29615 SC69 B1 #53 upper I frag.

Arvicolid indet.

Lower Loam main body

M29606 SC69 A2 #34 lower I frag., M29609 SC69 A2 #73 tooth frags., M29616 SC72 B4 #100 tooth frags., M29617 SC72 B4 #102 dentary frag.

Microtus oeconomus (Pallas), northern vole

Lower Loam/Lower Gravel junction
M29493 SC70 B1 #82 (part) 2 teeth incl. lower M1 of *M. oeconomus*, M29495 SC70 B1 associated teeth and bones (part of probable pellet accumulation)

Microtus cf. *agrestis* (L.), field vole

Lower Loam/Lower Gravel junction
M29495 SC70 B1 associated teeth and bones (part of probable pellet accumulation)

Microtus sp. indet.

Lower Loam/Lower Gravel junction
M29495 SC70 B1 associated teeth and bones (part of probable pellet accumulation)

Microtus (Terricola) subterraneus (= *Pitymys arvaloides* Hinton), European pine vole

Lower Loam/Lower Gravel junction
M29495 SC70 B1 associated teeth and bones (part of probable pellet accumulation)

Lower Loam undifferentiated
SC70 B1 LL (incorrectly numbered as #69) associated teeth

Muridae (mice)

Murid indet.

Lower Loam main body
M29619 SC72 C3 #105 upper and lower I frags.

Indeterminate small mammals

Lower Loam weathered surface
SC71 C3 incisor frag.

Lower Loam/Lower Gravel junction
SC68 TrA 2B long bone shaft frag.

CARNIVORA

Ursidae (bears)

Ursus spelaeus Rosenmuller and Heinroth, cave bear

Lower Gravel undifferentiated
damaged skull with R upper M2 and L upper M1-M2 (rolled and abraded)

Ursus sp., bear

Lower Gravel unit 2?

SC71 A3 60-80 cm R radius shaft frag.

Lower Gravel unit 1
L lower M1 (very worn)

Lower Gravel midden
M43923 SC71 B3 #56 L humerus shaft, SC69 A2 #109/B R zygomatic arch frag.

Lower Loam/Lower Gravel junction
M43922 SC68 TrA 2B L lower M2 mesial frag. (slightly rolled)

Lower Loam main body
M43927 SC68 TrA 2B 145-165 cm 2nd phalanx of juvenile (rolled), SC71 B4 #45 'antler and bone complex' frag. of horiz. mand. ramus, SC68 TrA 2B 145-165 cm skull frag. (sagittal crest)

Mustelidae (mustelids)

Martes cf. *martes* L., pine marten

Weathered Lower Loam
M43920 SC71 C3 associated upper C, isolated R P, incomplete L mand. ramus with L lower P2-M1 (damaged) and frag. R mand. ramus with broken R lower M2

Canidae (dogs)

Canis sp., wolf

Lower Gravel midden
SC70 A3 #69 L humerus shaft nr. dist. end

Lower Loam main body
M43926 SC71 B2 #118 R 3rd metacarpal prox. end (abraded), M43924a and M43924b SC71 C3 #79 associated R radius shaft frag. and complete R ulna

Unprovenanced
M43928 1st phalanx

Felidae (cats)

Panthera leo (L.), lion

Lower Loam main body
SC71 B2 #113 L 5th metacarpal

Weathered Lower Loam
SC70 B3 R mand. ramus frag.

Felis sylvestris Schreber, wild cat

Lower Gravel midden
M43921 SC71 B3 #76 L humerus shaft and distal condyles

Small carnivore, probably felid

Lower Loam undifferentiated
M43925 SC70 B3 scapula (glenoid)

PROBOSCIDEA

Elephantidae (elephants)

Palaeoloxodon antiquus Falconer and Cautley, straight-tusked elephant

Lower Gravel midden
SC70 B3 #71 R calcaneum, M43929 SC70 B2 #94 molar fragment (slightly rolled), SC68 TrA occipital part of skull, SC68 TrA 2B 165 cm thoracic vertebra and M49697 SC68 TrA 2B 165 cm thoracic vertebra (probably associated), SC68 TrA occipital

Base of Lower Middle Gravel
SC 70 A3 #1 mandibular symphysis (heavily rolled)

Unprovenanced
M43930 SC72 incomplete lower R M3 (very worn)

Elephant sp. indet.

Lower Gravel unit 1
SC69 A2 'top of LG' large bone frag, cf. elephant, SC71 A3 0-20 cm rib (lacks prox. end), rolled

Lower Gravel midden
SC70 B2 #91 innominate frag. of juvenile very large mammal, cf. elephant, SC69 A2 #114/DD neural spine of thoracic vertbra of juvenile

Lower Loam main body
SC68 TrA 2B 145-165 cm rib, SC68 TrA 2B rib frag. (heavily rolled), SC68 TrA 2B frag. vertebra

Unprovenanced
A3 or B1 Floor? R innominate frag., SC68 TrA Floor? damaged cervical vertebra

PERISSODACTYLA

Equidae (horses)

Equus caballus L. (= *E. ferus* Boddaert), horse

Lower Gravel unit 1
SC71 A3 L lower M3, M43938 SC71 A3 frag. of distal metapodial

Lower Loam weathered surface
SC71 C3 upper M frag., SC71 C3 #48 horizontal mand. ramus frag. (cf. *Equus*)

Rhinocerotidae (rhinoceroses)

Stephanorhinus (*Dicerorhinus*) *hemitoechus* (Falconer), narrow-nosed rhinoceros

Lower Gravel midden
M43933 #139/K L upper M3, M43937 SC70 A3 #74 skull lacking palate and teeth.

Stephanorhinus (*Dicerorhinus*) *kirchbergensis* (Jaeger), Merck's rhinoceros

Lower Gravel midden
M43934 SC71 B2 #106 R 3rd metacarpal

Lower Gravel undifferentiated
M43932 SC70 A2 R upper M2 (damaged)

Lower Loam sandy horizon
M43935 SC71 B3 #47 L lunar (*S.* cf. *kirchbergensis*)

Stephanorhinus (*Dicerorhinus*) sp. indet.

Lower Gravel midden
M43939 SC70 A3 3rd phalanx of 4th podial (slightly rolled), SC70 A3 #105 skull frag. (L orbital region), SC69 A2 #222 lower M frag. (very worn)

Lower Loam/Lower Gravel junction
SC70 B2 'near large flint complex' 3rd phalanx of 2nd podial (weathered)

Lower Loam main body
SC72 B4 #92 R innominate frag.

Weathered Lower Loam
M43936 SC71 B3 #38 L humerus prox. articulation (crushed), SC71 B4 3rd phalanx of 3rd podial

Lower Loam undifferentiated
M43931 SC71/2 B3 incomplete R mand. ramus (crushed) with lower R DP 2-4

ARTIODACTYLA

Suidae (pigs)

Sus scrofa L., wild boar

Lower Loam/Lower Gravel junction
M43945 SC68 TrA 2B L upper DI2, SC70 A3 R tibia midshaft frag., SC71 B2 C frag.

Lower Loam main body
SC71 B2 #105 incomplete R upper C

Weathered Lower Loam
M43944 SC71 C3 #15 L lower I1, M43942 SC71 C3 #5 L upper P2, M43943 SC71 B4 R upper P2, M43941 SC71 B3 #36 L upper P3-M2 and palatal frags.

Lower Loam undifferentiated
M43940 SC71 B3 associated R upper M2-M3

Cervidae (deer)

Cervus elaphus L. and cf. *Cervus elaphus* L., red deer

Lower Gravel unit 4
SC71 A3 'base of solifluction' L humerus dist. end (rolled)

Lower Gravel unit 1
SC71 A3 0-20 cm R humerus dist. end (cf. *C. elaphus*)

Lower Gravel midden

SC71 B2 #115 L frontlet and pricket (slightly weathered), SC70 B2 #72 L metatarsal prox. end (weathered), SC68 TrA 2B 165 cm R humerus dist. end (heavily rolled)

Lower Gravel undifferentiated

SC68 TrA R tibia

Lower Loam/Lower Gravel junction

SC68 TrA 2B R lower P4, SC68 TrA 2B R metacarpal (juvenile)

Lower Loam main body

SC71 B3 #40 R lower M1, SC71 B3 #33 L humerus shaft and distal condyles (slightly rolled), SC71 B4 #11 R astragalus (weathered), SC71 B4 #53a R tibia dist. end, SC69 A2 #9 R lower M3 frag., SC71 C3 #73 L antler (complete and shed)

Weathered Lower Loam

SC71 C3 #9 R maxilla with R upper P2-M2 crushed onto cervid innominate in sediment block

Lower Loam weathered surface

SC71 B3 #80 R lower DP4

Lower Loam undifferentiated

SC69 B1 associated incomplete cranium (crushed) with L and R frontlets and complete, unshed antlers, SC70 B3 pricket

Dama dama clactoniana (Falconer) and cf. *Dama dama clactoniana* (Falconer), fallow deer

Lower Gravel unit 4

SC71 A3 'base of solifluction' L antler base, shed (coronet, broken brow tine and part of beam)

Lower Gravel unit 3

SC71 A3 60-80 cm R scapula (glenoid, neck and part of blade)

Lower Gravel unit 1

SC70 A2 0-20 cm L antler base, shed and rolled, SC70 B1 #132 R radius prox. end, SC69 A2 'top of LG' L antler base, shed (coronet, broken brow tine and part of beam), SC71 B3 'LG surface' R lower M1 or M2 (cf. M2), SC71 A3 20-40 cm R metatarsal (rolled), SC71 A3 0-20 cm antler frag., M50606 SC71 A3 0-20 cm R tibia dist. end

Lower Gravel midden

A2 '0' L frontlet and antler (brow and middle tines and 3 point palmation), SC71 B3 #69 antler frag., SC71 B3 #57 L frontlet and antler (pedicle, coronet, brow tine and part of beam), SC71 A3 #113 palmate part of antler, SC69 A2 #123/D L metacarpal prox. end, SC70 A3 #59b R femur dist. end, SC70 B2 #61 L tibia, lacks prox. end (weathered), SC70 A3 #107 R humerus dist. end (rolled), SC70 B2 #78 L tibia dist. end, SC69 A2 #138/T R tibia prox. end (slightly rolled), SC70 A3 #42 L antler base, shed and weathered (coronet, brow tine and part of beam), SC70 A3 #29 L antler, shed and weathered (coronet, brow tine and part of beam), SC70 A3 #106 R antler (coronet, brow and middle tines), SC70 A3 #30 L antler base, shed (rolled), SC70 A3

#34 L antler base (coronet, part of brow tine, beam frag.), SC70 A3 #73 L lower M1, SC69 A2 #101/R R femur prox. end and shaft frag., SC71 B2 #102 R antler, shed (coronet, brow and middle tines), SC70 A3 #109 R antler, unshed (frontlet, coronet, brow and middle tines), SC69 A2 #130/Z antler frag., SC69 A2 #223/MN R antler base, shed (coronet, brow tine and beam), SC69 A2 #209/DE R antler, shed (coronet and beam), SC71 B1 #146 axis vertebra (complete, slightly rolled), SC71 A3 #118 tine (cf. *Dama*), SC69 A2 #137 L scapula prox. end (glenoid, neck and part of blade), SC70 B2 #56 L antler base (rolled and weathered), SC68 TrA 2B 165 cm 2 palmate portions of antler, detached tine and 6 antler frags., SC69 A2 #112/F associated L upper M2-M3, SC70 B2 #65 L frontlet and antler, unshed (pedicle, coronet, brow tine and part of beam), SC70 A3 #71 R antler, unshed (frontlet, pedicle, coronet, brow tine) and slightly abraded, SC71 B3 #60 antler frag.

Lower Gravel undifferentiated

R frontlet and antler, unshed and rolled (pedicle, coronet and broken brow tine cf. *Dama*)

Lower Loam/Lower Gravel junction

SC70 A3 L metacarpal prox. end (rolled), SC70 A3 L antler base, shed (heavily rolled), SC71 B2 antler frag.

Base of Lower Loam

SC70 A3 #16 complete L antler of juvenile (shed), SC71 B2 #102 R antler base (coronet, brow tine and part of beam)

Lower Loam sandy horizon

SC71 B3 #39 1st phalanx, SC71 B3 #48 antler frag., SC71 B3 antler frag., SC71 B3 R lower P4 (very worn)

Lower Loam main body

M49718 SC71 B4 #21 L lower P4, SC71 C3 #60 L upper P2, SC70 B3 #12 R lower M1 or M2 (cf. M2), SC71 C3 #58 L upper M1, SC71 C3 #59,#60 associated L upper M2-3, SC71 C3 #72 associated R upper M1-3, SC71 C3 #61 R lower M1, SC71 B2 #101 axis vertebra, SC71 B4 #26 2nd phalanx (weathered), SC71 B4 #53a associated antler frags. (crushed) in 7 separate sediment blocks, shed antler base and brow tine (crushed in sediment block), L upper P3, associated R upper P2-M3, R antler base (part of coronet and brow tine), shed (cf. *Dama*) and detached tine, SC70 B2 #6 L femur dist. end, SC70 B2 #30 R metacarpal dist. end (fractured when green), SC71 C3 'knapping floor' #63 and #64 skull with complete L and R antlers (crushed in sediment block), SC71 B4 #53b R lower M1 or M2 (cf. M2) and L antler base (part of coronet and brow tine), shed and weathered, SC70 B1 #62 tine, SC70 A3 #11 tine, SC70 B3 #4 1st phalanx, SC70 B3 #13 R lower M2, SC70 B3 #30 R upper M3, SC71 B4 #25 L astragalus (weathered), SC70 B3 #29 L antler base, shed (coronet and part of brow tine), SC70 B3 #19.S 'from flint complex' L radius prox. end, SC68 TrA 2B 145-165 cm R tibia dist. end, SC68 TrA 2B 145-165 cm R tibia dist. end and part of shaft (cf. *Dama*), SC70 B3 'near complex 4' enamel frag. of molar (cf. *Dama*), SC68 TrA 2B R antler base (coronet and brow tine), SC70 TrE #25 fragmentary L upper M3, SC71 C3 #57 antler frag.

Weathered Lower Loam

SC72 Z3 #1 L. antler, shed and crushed (coronet, brow and middle tines and palmation), SC71 B4 R upper M1 or M2, M49711 SC71 C3 #7 R mand. ramus with R P2-M3 (crushed in sediment block), SC71 B4 R metatarsal prox. end (laterally crushed and weathered), M49712 C3 incomplete L mand. ramus with L lower I2 and lower P3-M3 (crushed in sediment block)

Lower Loam weathered surface

SC71 C3 #39 L mand. ramus with L lower P2-M3 (crushed in sediment block), SC71 B3 #77 R metatarsal, lacks dist. end (weathered), M49720 SC71 B3 #50 associated R lower P3-M3, SC71 C3 R upper M1 or M2 (cf. M2), SC71 C3 #1 L frontlet and antler, unshed (pedicle, broken brow tine, part of beam and detached tine), slightly rolled

Lower Loam undifferentiated

M49722 SC71 B4 L lower M3, M49723 SC71 B4 associated R lower P4-M2, SC71 B4 R lower M3, SC71 B4 R lower M3, SC71 B4 L upper M1 or M2 (cf. M1), M49724 SC69 B1 incomplete R mand. ramus with R P2-P4 (possibly associated with *C. elaphus* cranium and antlers in B1), SC70 A3 L lower P3 frag., SC71 B4 L antler base, shed (weathered), SC70 TrE #31a antler frags. (cf *Dama*), antler, shed (shattered and crushed in sediment block), SC70 TrE #23 L scapula (cf. *Dama*), crushed in sediment block

Lower Middle Gravel

SC72 C4 tine

Middle Gravels

SC68 L scapula prox. end (glenoid, neck and part of blade)

Unprovenanced

M49713 incomplete R mand. ramus with R lower P2-M1 (crushed in sediment block), SC70 E3 L upper M2, possibly associated lower I, R lower P4, R lower M1 and R lower M2, SC70 TrH incomplete L mand. ramus with L lower M2-M3, complete R antler (shed), SC70 LG 0-20 cm (no square given) #119 L tibia dist. end, SC68 TrA R antler (complete), SC69 #125/R antler frag., SC71 ?B4 #4 (incorrectly numbered) incomplete R mand. ramus with R lower P2 and M3 (crushed in sediment block), SC71 A3 140-160 cm L metatarsal shaft frag. (anterior side)

Megaloceros giganteus (Blumenbach), giant deer

Weathered Lower Loam

M49727 SC71 B4 L humerus dist. shaft lacking articular end (weathered)

Lower Middle Gravel

SC72 C4 frag. L metacarpal shaft

Cervidae, sp. indet.

Lower Gravel unit 4

SC71 A3 tine tip (rolled), SC71 A3 R calcaneum (rolled and abraded), SC71 A3 'base of solifluction'

metacarpal shaft frag., M50608 SC71 A3 'base of LG' L tibia shaft frag. (posterior side)

Lower Gravel unit 3

SC68 TrB 3 R humerus dist. frag. and 2 dist. articulations of metapodia, SC68 TrA 3 310 cm tine (heavily rolled)

Lower Gravel unit 2

SC68 TrB 2 L astragalus (abraded), SC68 TrA 3 280-300 cm tibia shaft frag., SC71 A3 60-80 cm (unit 2?) metapodial shaft frag.SC70 A2 3m 70-60 cm metatarsal shaft frag.

Lower Gravel unit 1

SC70 B1 'top of LG' #93 tine, SC70 A2 0-20 cm centrum of thoracic vertebra (highly fragmentary), SC70 A2 'top of LG' tine, SC70 A2 'top of LG' tine, SC70 A2 'top of LG' femur shaft frag. (cf. Cervidae), SC70 A2 'top of LG' R humerus dist. frag., SC70 A2 20-40 cm L tibia shaft frag., SC71 B1 #88 'top of LG' L femur shaft nr. dist. end, juvenile, SC70 B1 #138 tine, SC71 B3 'below floor' 3 tines, SC71 B3 'below floor' rib prox. end (cf. Cervidae), SC71 A3 20-40 cm R humerus shaft frag. (posterior side near dist. end), SC71 A2 #113 tine tip, SC71 B2 #109 antler base (heavily rolled), SC71 A3 R metatarsal shaft frag. (anterior side), SC71 A3 20-40 cm antler frag., M50609a SC71 B3 'LG surface' L humerus shaft frag. near dist. end (posterior side), M50609b SC71 B3 'LG surface' humerus shaft frag. (rolled), M50609c SC71 B3 'LG surface' humerus shaft frag. (cf. Cervidae)

Lower Gravel midden

SC71 A3 #49 L femur shaft (weathered), SC70 B2 #90 R humerus shaft, SC68 A2 #110/B L humerus dist. end, SC70 B2 #72 R humerus dist. end (very rolled), SC69 A2 #221/LK L metacarpal shaft frag. (rolled), SC69 A2 #171 L tibia dist. end (rolled), SC69 A2 #93/X thoracic vertebra (damaged and rolled), SC69 A2 #217/HJ L ulna prox. end, SC69 A2 #192/CD tine (rolled), SC70 B2 #69 basioccipital frag., SC70 B2 #57 tine (rolled), SC70 B2 #77 R metatarsal prox. frag., SC71 B2 #116 R magnum (rolled), SC70 A3 #89 tine (abraded), SC70 A3 #100 tine (rolled), SC70 A3 #46 tine (rolled and abraded), SC70 A3 #23 L femur dist. medial condyle, SC70 A3 #47 antler frag., SC70 A3 #40 shed antler base, part of brow tine, SC70 A3 #43 occipital frag. (nuchal crest), SC70 A3 #26 antler frag., SC70 A3 #36 tine frag., SC70 A3 humerus shaft frag., SC70 A3 #33 metacarpal shaft frag. (anterior side), SC70 A3 #58 skull frag., SC70 A3 #44 L metacarpal dist. end and shaft frag. (anterior side), SC70 A3 #70 3rd phalanx, SC69 A2 #95/HH L femur midshaft frag., SC69 A2 #98/S L scapula (glenoid, neck and part of blade), SC69 A2 #190/BC L femur midshaft (rolled), SC70 B2 #91 tine (weathered), SC70 B2 #95 radius shaft frag. (posterior side), SC70 A3 L metatarsal shaft frag. (posterior side), SC70 A3 R femur shaft frag. (posterior side), SC70 A3 2 tine tips (abraded), SC70 A3 cf. tibia midshaft frag., SC70 A3 metatarsal shaft frag., SC70 B2 tibia midshaft frag., SC70 A3 metatarsal shaft frag. (anterior side), SC70 A3 metacarpal shaft frag. (anterior side), SC70 A3 L tibia dist. end (heavily rolled), SC69 A2 tine (rolled), SC70 A2 #121/A tine (rolled), SC68 TrA 2B 165 cm R ascending mand. ramus (slightly rolled), SC68 TrA 2B 165 cm antler base (very eroded), SC70 A3 #?79 metatarsal shaft frag. (anterior side), SC71 A3 #119 metatarsal dist. condyle and part of shaft, SC70 B2 #100 R femur prox. end, M50604 SC71 B3 #70 R humerus shaft frag. near dist. end, M50607 SC71 B2 #124 L femur shaft frag. (posterior side), slightly rolled, SC69 A2 metacarpal shaft frag., SC71 A3 'shell sand above midden' L humerus dist. end frag. (cf. Cervidae), SC70 A3 thoracic vertebra

Lower Gravel undifferentiated
SC71 B2 humerus shaft frag., SC71 B2 metatarsal shaft frag. (anterior side)

Lower Loam/Lower Gravel junction
SC70 A3 R metatarsal prox. frag., SC70 A3 metacarpal shaft frag., SC68 TrA 2B tine, SC70 A3 metatarsal shaft frag., SC70 A3 cf. tibia shaft, SC68 TrA 2B R innominate frag., SC70 B2 'near large stone complex' metapodial shaft frag. (weathered), SC70 B2 'near stone complex' innominate frag. (slightly rolled), SC70 B2 'near stone complex' skull frag., SC70 A3 frag. of L? metatarsal shaft, SC70 A3 L femur shaft frag., SC70 A3 tibia shaft frag., SC70 A3 tine tip (weathered and rolled), SC70 A3 antler beam frag. (rolled), SC71 B1 R radius midshaft frag. (weathered and rolled), SC68 TrA 2B 12 skull frags. (probably one individual), SC68 TrA 2B femur shaft frag., SC68 TrA 2B 1st phalanx dist. frag., SC70 A3 R antler base (shed), SC68 TrA 2B R magno-trapezoid, SC71 B2 1st phalanx (weathered), M50603 SC69 A2 #138/T R tibia prox. end frag., M50605 SC68 TrA 2B R ascending mand. ramus

Lower Loam sandy horizon
SC71 B2 L tibia shaft frag., SC71 B3 #47 occipital frag. (nuchal crest), SC71 B3 2 L femur shaft frags. (posterior side near dist. end), SC71 B3 #46 incomplete R astragalus (heavily rolled)

Lower Loam main body
SC72 B4 #70 R radius shaft, SC69 A2 #62 tine (slightly rolled), SC69 B1 #55 cervical vertebra frag., SC69 A2 #74 L scapula (glenoid) frag., SC70 B2 #22 cervical vertebra frag., SC71 B1 #83 vertebra frag., SC71 B4 #66 L femur shaft (weathered), SC71 B4 #27 R humerus shaft (weathered), SC71 B4 #25 1st phalanx prox. end (weathered), SC71 B4 #26 L tibia (lacks prox. end) weathered, SC71 B4 #31 R ulna prox. end, SC71 B4 #7 humerus dist. frag (weathered), SC71 B4 #7 R radius dist. frag. (crushed), SC71 B4 #45 'antler and bone complex' tine (weathered), 2 innominate frags. (weathered), vertebra frag., SC71 B4 #47 tine (rolled and weathered), SC71 B4 #48 L tibia shaft frag. (weathered), SC71 B4 #30 radius midshaft frag (weathered), SC71 B4 #64 rib, lacking prox. articulation (weathered), SC71 B4 #23 incisor and M frags. in sediment block, SC71 B4 #11 R calcaneum frag. (weathered), SC70 B1 #76 R metacarpal prox. and shaft frag., SC71 B4 #17 humerus shaft frag., SC70 B3 #17 cf. L tibia shaft frag., SC70 B2 #23 atlas vertebra, SC70 B4 #57 tine (rolled and weathered), SC70 B3 #26 tine, SC70 B2 #23 fragmentary cervical vertebra (crushed in sediment block), SC71 B3 #34 atlas vertebra (complete), SC70 B3 #13 R radius shaft frag., SC71 B4 #38 L calcaneum (weathered), SC71 B4 #53a damaged centra of 2 lumbar vertebra of juvenile, rib

frag., tibia shaft and R dist. malleolus (probably associated with *Dama* remains SC71 B4 #53a), 4 skull frags. (cf. Cervidae), SC71 B4 #32 R lower I1, SC72 C3 #94 L lower I1 and L lower I2 (probably associated), SC72 C3 #100 R lower I2, SC72 C3 #102 R lower I2, SC71 B4 #61 rib frag., SC71 B4 #9 L magno-trapezoid, SC70 B2 humerus shaft frag., SC68 TrA 2B 145-165 cm antler base (heavily rolled), SC68 TrA 2B 145-165 cm L metacarpal shaft frag., SC68 TrA 2B tine and antler frag., SC71 B2 #111 antler frag., SC71 C3 #77 incomplete L calcaneum (weathered), SC71 B3 #45 L radius dist. end (lacks epiphysis) of juvenile, M50601 SC71 C3 #70 rib prox. end, M50602 SC70 A3 #6 incomplete atlas vertebra, SC71 B4 #25 R metatarsal midshaft frag., SC70 B2 #20 rib prox. end, SC72 B4 #77 R metacarpal prox. frag. (anterior side), SC70 TrE #21 cervical vertebra frags., SC72 B4 'below knapping floor' sacrum frag., SC70 TrE #13 '62 cm below datum' vertebra frags., SC72 C3 #87 R scapula prox. end (glenoid, neck)

Weathered Lower Loam
SC71 B4 L femur shaft (weathered), SC71 B4 R humerus dist. (weathered), SC71 R metatarsal shaft (weathered), SC71 C3 #14 frag. of dist. articulation of metapodial (weathered), SC71 C3 #12 frag. of dist. articulation of metapodial (weathered), SC71 B3 #37 R scapula prox. end (glenoid, neck), crushed in sediment block, SC71 C3 #23 L scapula prox. end (glenoid, neck), crushed in sediment block, SC72 Z3 #1 antler tine, SC71 C3 centrum of thoracic vertebra (weathered), SC71 C3 #17 tine (weathered)

Lower Loam weathered surface
SC71 C3 #43 cervical vertebra, (crushed in sediment block), SC71 B2 cervical vertebra (weathered), SC71 B2 L scapula (glenoid, neck), SC71 B3 #77 cf. innominate frag., SC71 B2 metatarsal shaft frag. (posterior side), SC71 C3 R radius (prox. medial articulation), SC71 C3 2 centra of thoracic vertebra (weathered), SC71 C3 #48 tine tip (weathered), SC71 C3 #29 R metacarpal shaft, SC71 C3 #31 R scapula (glenoid), SC71 C3 #26 tine (weathered), SC70 TrE #6 L calcaneum (damaged and weathered), SC70 TrE #6 incomplete R astragalus, SC71 C3 #51 L scapula (blade frag.), weathered, SC71 C3 #41 L humerus shaft frag. (weathered)

Lower Loam surface
SC69 cervical vertebra frag.

Lower Loam undifferentiated
SC71 B4 tine, SC70 B3 L upper M1 frag., SC71 C3 innominate frag., SC71 B2 rib (lacks dist. end), SC71 B2 metatarsal shaft frag. (posterior side), SC71 B2 L metatarsal shaft frag. (posterior side), SC71 B3 metatarsal shaft frag. (anterior side), SC70 TrE #22 tine tip (weathered)

Unprovenanced
innominate frag., SC69 A2 metacarpal shaft frag., frag. of dist. articulation of metapodial (weathered), tine (weathered), R lower I2, SC70 #91 'top of LG' no square given R antler base (shed and rolled)

Bovidae (cattle)

Bos primigenius Bojanus and cf. *Bos primigenius* Bojanus, aurochs

Lower Gravel unit 2
SC68 TrA 3 240-260 cm L upper M1 or M2

Lower Gravel unit 1
A2 #99 and #103/W associated L acetabulum frag. and femoral head, SC70 B1 #139 L lower M1 or 2, SC70 B1 #127 lower molar frag., B2 'S. baulk' 0-20 cm R metatarsal dist. end (rolled)

Lower Loam/Lower Gravel junction
SC70 A3 L upper P3

Lower Loam main body
SC70 B3 #15 upper P frag., TrE lower molar frag.

Bison cf. *priscus* Bojanus, bison

Lower Gravel unit 1
SC70 A2 20 cm L tibia dist. end

Bovini indet. sp.

Lower Gravel unit 4
SC68 A3 360 cm R lower M3, SC71 A3 'base of solifluction' L metacarpal prox. end (damaged during excavation)

Lower Gravel unit 1
SC70 A2 20-40 cm L innominate frag., SC70 A2 20-40 cm L lower P4 frag. (worn)

Lower Gravel midden
SC70 A3 #45 6 horn core frags., SC70 A3 R dist. malleolus (rolled), SC70 A3 #23 L ulna prox. frag. (part of semilunar notch), SC70 A3 #103 metatarsal shaft frag. (anterior side), SC70 A3 #62 metatarsal shaft frag. (cf. Bovini), SC69 A2 #HI? thoracic vertebra of juvenile (damaged), SC70 B2 thoracic vertebra, damaged (rolled), SC70 A3 Frag. of dist. condyle of metapodial (cf. Bovini), SC69 A2 #136/U rib frag. of juvenile cf. Bovini (weathered)

Lower Loam/Lower Gravel junction
SC68 TrA 2B fused L ulna and radius shafts, SC68 TrA 2B R radius shaft, SC68 TrA 2B 2nd phalanx prox. surface (rolled), SC70 A3 L tibia shaft frag.
Lower Loam sandy horizon
SC71 B3 tibia shaft frag. (posterior side)

Lower Loam main body
SC71 B4 #37 7 small horn core frags. and 9 skull frags. including basi-occipital, SC70 B3 #14 L lower M3, SC71 B3 #33 L metatarsal midshaft of juvenile cf. Bovini (weathered)

Weathered Lower Loam
SC72 C4 'footprint complex' metacarpal shaft dist. end frag. (crushed)

Lower Loam weathered surface
SC71 C3 #56 very badly fractured frag. of cf. humerus of Bovini

Lower Loam surface
SC69 B2 base of horn core frag., SC68 C4 horn core frag.

Lower Loam undifferentiated
SC70 B2 incomplete thoracic vertebra, SC69 B2 2nd phalanx (cf. *B. primigenius*)

Base of Lower Middle Gravel
SC69 B1 #2 skull frag.

Unprovenanced
SC68 TrB 2C frontlet and horn core base frag. of juvenile (very weathered), A2 #100/Q thoracic vertebra (incomplete), juvenile

INDETERMINATE BONE FRAGMENTS

Lower Gravel unit 4
SC68 TrA 3 360 cm 2 indet. bone frags., SC68 TrA 3 260-280 cm 4 skull frags.

Lower Gravel unit 2
SC71 A3 40-60 cm 4 long bone frags., SC68 TrA 3 280-300 cm rib frag., SC68 TrA 3 280-300 cm indet. bone frag., A3 40-60 cm large indet. frag., SC71 A3 60-80 cm (unit 2?) 7 indet. bone frags., SC70 A2 3m 60-70 cm (unit 2?) 6 indet. bone frags.

Lower Gravel unit 1
SC68 A3 indet. bone frag., SC69 A2 indet. bone frag., SC70 B1 'top of LG' 16 indet. bone frags., SC71 A3 0-20 cm 9 indet. bone frags. (1 heavily rolled), SC70 A2 'top of LG' 14 indet. bone frags. (rolled), SC70 B1 'top of LG' #94, SC70 B1 #89, SC69 A2 'top of LG' skull frag., SC70 A2 20-40 cm long bone shaft frag., SC71 A3 0-20 cm long bone frag., SC71 A3 20-40 cm 2 indet. bone frags., SC71 A3 20-40 cm horizontal mand. ramus frag., SC71 A2 #113 4 indet. bone frags., rib frag. and cf. tibia shaft frag., SC71 B2 #107 2 indet. bone frags. (1 rolled), SC71 B2 #108 skull frag., SC71 B3 indet. bone frag., SC71 B3 cf. neural spine frag.

Lower Gravel midden
SC69 A2 #204/GH indet. bone frag. (corroded through being digested), SC69 A2 #219/HI, SC69 A2 #197/EF, SC69 A2 #208/19, SC69 A2 #173, SC69 A2 #218, SC69 A2 #131/Z, SC69 A2 200/17, SC69 A2 #169/GG, SC69 A2 #199/C, SC69 A2 #193/CD, SC69 A2 #163/Y, SC69 A2 #187/AB, SC69 A2 #164, SC69 A2 #168/GG, SC69 A2 #167/GG, SC69 A2 #194/EF, SC69 A2 #162/N, SC69 A2 #216/19, SC69 A2 #172 indet. bone frag. (corroded through being digested), SC69 A2 indet. bone frag., SC70 B2 3 indet. bone frags., SC70 B2 #98 skull frag., SC70 A3 #72, SC70 A3 #102, SC70 A3 #99 cf. innominate frag., SC70 A3 #83, SC70 A3 #53, SC70 A3 #35, SC70 A3 #39, SC70 A3 #48, SC70 A3 #52 rib frag., SC70 A3 #59a, SC70 A3 #41a, SC70 A3 #31, SC70 A3 #54, SC70 A3 #25, SC70 A3 #51 long bone frag. cf. humerus shaft, SC70 A3 #60 skull frag., SC70 A3 #57a, SC69 A2 #201/FG rib frag. of large mammal, SC70 B2 #84, SC70 B2 #96, SC70 B2 #88 skull frag., SC70 A3 18 indet. bone frags., SC70 A2 indet. bone frag., SC70 B2 cf. tibia midshaft frag., SC70 A3 vertebra frag., SC71 B2 #122 and #119 2 very large bone frags. (weathered and rolled), SC69 A2 frag. cf. zygomatic

arch, SC70 B2 #95, SC70 B2 #89, SC70 B2 #98 skull frag., SC70 A3 #80 (incorrectly numbered), SC70 A3 #32 ?skull frag., SC70 A3 #58 skull frag., SC71 B2 #123, SC71 B3 #64, SC71 B3 #75 3 indet. bone frags., SC71 A3 'shell sand above midden' 5 indet. bone frags.

Lower Gravel undifferentiated

SC68 A3 indet. bone frag., SC70 A2 long bone shaft frags., SC71 B2 2 indet. bone frags., SC71 A3 indet. bone frag of very large mammal, SC71 A3 280-300 cm indet. bone frag. (very rolled), TrB eastern extension 1 90-100 'red gravel' indet. burnt? frags.

Lower Loam/Lower Gravel junction

SC70 A3 36 indet. bone frags., SC70 TrA 2B 7 indet bone frags., SC70 B2 'near stone complex' indet. bone frag. (rolled), SC70 B2 'near large flint complex' indet. bone frag., SC70 B1 base of Lower Loam/Lower Gravel junction 5 indet. bone frags., SC71 B1 5 indet. bone frags., SC70 A3 skull frag., SC70 A3 bone shaft lacking both articular ends (possibly carnivore metapodial), heavily rolled and abraded, SC71 B2 4 indet. bone frags.

Lower Loam sandy horizon

SC71 B4 #48, SC71 B3 indet. bone frag.

Base of Lower Loam

SC70 B2 #66 (incorrectly marked as 'Floor'), SC71 B3 3 indet. bone frags., SC70 B2 #83 vertebra frag. (heavily rolled)

Lower Loam main body

SC71 B4 #26 long bone (cf. tibia) frags. (weathered), SC71 B4 #66, SC71 B4 #26, SC70 B2 #8 and #9 femur shaft frags. (rolled), SC71 B4 #54, SC70 B2 #16, SC70 B3 #23 5 skull frags., SC71 B4 #15, SC71 B4 #53a, SC68 TrA 2B 146-165 cm 4 skull frags., SC68 TrA 2B 145-165 cm 2 indet.

bone frags., SC70 B2 #22 (incorrectly marked as 'Floor'), SC70 B3 #20 'below flint complex', SC70 B3 'flint and bone horizon' indet bone frag., SC70 B1 #63 crushed humerus lacking both articular ends of very juvenile animal (probably neonatal), SC71 C3 #77, SC71 B3 #40, SC71 B3 #45, SC71 C3 #68, SC71 C3 #78, SC72 C3 #110 part of scapula blade, SC72 C3 #109, SC71 B4 #25 multiple small indet. frags., SC71 B4 #6, SC68 TrA 2B 145-165 cm 2 skull frags., SC70 B2 #36 2 indet. bone frags., SC72 C3 #115, SC72 C3 #116, SC70 B2 #25, SC72 Z3 #12, SC69 B1 #24 indet. bone frags., SC72 C3 #112 multiple indet. bone frags., SC72 B4 #68 multiple indet. bone frags., SC72 B4 #81 'below knapping floor' 2 indet. bone frags.

Weathered Lower Loam

SC70 B3 indet. bone frag. (weathered), SC71 C3 2 indet. bone frags., SC71 B4 multiple indet. bone frags., SC71 B4 #10 (probably incorrectly numbered), SC71 C3 #8 skull frags.

Lower Loam weathered surface

SC71 C3 5 indet. bone frags.

Lower Loam undifferentiated

SC70 A3 indet. bone splinter, indet. bone frag., SC71 B4 indet. bone frag., SC70 B3 indet. bone splinter, SC71 B2 rib frag. (juvenile), SC71 B2 2 indet. bone frags., SC70 B2 'stone complex' indet bone frag., B2 'stone complex' indet bone frag. (rolled and weathered), SC70 B2 #21 (incorrectly marked 'Floor'), SC71 B2 vertebra frag., SC71 B3 6 indet. bone frags., SC71 C3 indet. bone frag.

Lower Middle Gravel

SC71 C3 3 indet. bone frags., SC72 C4 15 indet. bone frags.

Unprovenanced

A2 #213/HJ rib frag. of large mammal

PALAEOECOLOGICAL SIGNIFICANCE OF THE MAMMALIAN FAUNA

The validity of using Pleistocene fossils to reconstruct past environments has frequently been discussed, for example by Stuart (1982) and Currant (1986). Traditionally, it was widely assumed that the ecology and biogeography of individual taxa has not changed significantly over the relatively short geological timespan of the Pleistocene and that fossil species still extant at the present day or their near relatives could provide direct information about past ecologies, a clear case of the present being the key to the past. In reality, the picture is not quite so simple. Some Pleistocene biotopes have no modern analogue and most Pleistocene assemblages contain a significant percentage of extinct species, particularly large herbivores, for which we clearly have no concrete ecological information. Even when the species concerned (or a close relative) is still alive at the present day, it is a very big assumption to state that its ecology has remained unchanged over hundreds of thousands of years.

Furthermore, since many palaeoenvironmental reconstructions are made on the basis of a very small number of fossil examples, the possibility for error is even greater. How valid are these reconstructions when they are based on the presence of so few individuals? Indeed, mammals in general provide us with a much poorer environmental and climatic picture than either herpetofauna or ichthyfauna as they are much less influenced by direct climatic factors such as temperature and precipitation. Present day distribution approximates at best to a biotope characterised by a particular regional vegetation type (Stuart 1982, 73) although the information that may be derived from this is in itself limited by our lack of knowledge of past environments, mammalian distribution patterns and community ecology. The considerable biases encountered in many samples (usually due to collecting methods) must also be taken into account, since they will undoubtedly colour any palaeoenvironmental reconstruction.

These problems certainly present themselves at Swanscombe. The mammal fauna recovered during the Waechter excavations of the Lower Loam and Lower Gravel is heavily biased towards large mammal remains, a substantial proportion of which are extinct species, including the straight-tusked elephant *Palaeoloxodon antiquus*, two species of rhinoceros *Stephanorhinus hemitoechus* and *Stephanorhinus kirchbergensis*, aurochs *Bos primigenius* and giant deer *Megaloceros giganteus*. As a rule, little can be gained from comparisons with, for example, extant species of elephant and rhinoceros since the phylogenetic relationships of the extinct taxa with their modern counterparts remain for the most part very unclear. Furthermore, the potential for resolution of past environments through comparison with present-day species has been entirely lost as virtually all species of modern megafauna have had their natural habitats dramatically altered, reduced or indeed obliterated by human activity.

The only palaeoecological observations concerning these extinct large mammals which retain some validity are of a general nature and relate to anatomical features or adaptations. For example, the outsize antlers of *M. giganteus* make it extremely unlikely that this species inhabited closed woodland. Similar deductions using morphological characters have also been made regarding the Middle Pleistocene rhinoceroses, which appear to fall into distinct ecological classes. For instance, the long-limbed proportions of *Stephanorhinus etruscus* and *Stephanorhinus hundsheimensis* indicate that they were cursorial, open-environment animals, whilst the dentition of *Stephanorhinus kirchbergensis* combined with a high head posture and strongly concave limb joints suggest a predominantly browsing animal operating in a closed forest environment. Finally, the more compact body, dentition and other anatomical features of *Stephanorhinus hemitoechus* appear to indicate that this animal inhabited a more open habitat with low growing vegetation (Fortelius *et al.* 1993, 119). Even then, these are only general indications of habitat preference and the coexistence of three separate species of rhinoceros in the Lower Gravel at Swanscombe (see Chapter 12) has posed some interesting questions.

The Carnivora also reveal little about the contemporary environment since their distribution is influenced by factors other than regional vegetation type. They occur in both the Lower Gravel and the Lower Loam, although in small numbers. As at other British Pleistocene sites, bears and wolves are the most commonly-occurring carnivore fossils at Swanscombe. Both are now largely extinct from western Europe and survive only in small and fragmented populations, having suffered like the lion *Panthera leo* and the pine marten *Martes martes* from human hunting pressure. In the same way, the wild cat *Felis sylvestris*, present in the Lower Gravel at Swanscombe, has been prevented, in the present day, from following a natural migration southward into England by the central Scottish industrial belt (Corbet and Harris 1991, 434). None of these species can therefore be realistically used to interpret past environments whilst their present ranges are so artificially controlled.

However, certain other mammalian species that appear to have been particularly constant in their habitat preferences over time may yet shed some light on the nature of the palaeoenvironment at Swanscombe.

1. Fallow deer

By far the most common species in both the Lower Gravel and Lower Loam is the fallow deer, attributable to the subspecies *Dama dama clactoniana* (Lister 1986). The modern fallow deer *Dama dama* is today characteristic of temperate deciduous or mixed woodland (Corbet and Harris 1991, 512) and Pleistocene occurrences have similarly been entirely restricted to wooded interglacial episodes. Although caution must be exercised since the Clacton subspecies is now extinct, it would not be unreasonable to assume a similar habitat preference for this subspecies and concomitantly to propose the existence of temperate woodland at the site. A co-abundance of wood mouse *Apodemus sylvaticus* and bank vole *Clethrionomys glareolus* in Pleistocene faunas has been cited by Currant (1986, 50) as a reliable indicator of a wooded environment and would normally be verified by associated biota such as the fallow deer. The absence of these two common small mammal species in the Lower Loam more probably reflects the highly selective collecting methods of the excavators rather than a genuine absence of woodland.

2. Beaver

The beaver *Castor fiber* was formerly widespread throughout the Palearctic and its postglacial survival into historic times in Britain is documented up until the 12th century. At the present day, beavers are associated with deciduous forest (in particular aspen and birch woods) on the shores of lakes and rivers. Remains of beaver are uncommon at Swanscombe and occur only in the Lower Loam but their presence is confirmation of the existence of a slow-flowing body of water at the site and of temperate deciduous woodland in the vicinity.

3. Water Vole

The living British water vole *Arvicola terrestris* occurs most commonly on the densely-vegetated banks of rivers and streams, generally where the current is slow and water is present throughout the year (Corbet and Harris 1991, 214). Like the beaver, *Arvicola cantiana*, the fossil relative of the living species almost certainly confirms the presence of water at Swanscombe in the Lower Gravel and Lower Loam horizons. However, modern continental European water voles appear to be less aquatic than their British relatives and are frequently found in grasslands and other habitats at considerable distance from water. Whilst this probably reflects a recent alteration in habitat preference, it should be borne in mind that Pleistocene populations may have occupied a considerably wider range of habitats than at the present day.

Palaeoecological significance of mammals from the Lower Gravel

The Lower Gravel appears to be divisible into two parts. The lowest (units 3 and 4) have yielded only a handful of bones of a restricted number of species, namely fallow deer *Dama dama clactoniana*, red deer *Cervus elaphus* and large bovids. These bones are marked 'base of solifluction' and originate from the basal part of the Lower Gravel, which Marston (1937A, 31) and later Conway (1969, 1970) considered to be of periglacial origin. Kerney (1971) refuted this on the basis of molluscan evidence collected from near the base of the Lower Gravel, which indicated a climate as temperate as that of the Lower Loam. It is quite possible however, that these conflicting results have arisen from observations of sections in different parts of the site. Bridgland (Bridgland *et al.* 1985) also concluded that this basal layer might date from the final part of the cold stage that preceded the deposition of the overlying interglacial deposits but considered the basal gravel to be fluvial in origin. They were unable to find any fossil material in this layer (again, probably as a result of local lithological differences and lateral variation in the sediments). The recovery of mammalian remains by Waechter from this basal layer cannot however confirm either interpretation as the species recovered are so few in number.

The upper part of the Lower Gravel (units 1 and 2) has yielded a mammalian fauna very similar to that documented by Sutcliffe (1964) and which indicates fully temperate conditions. The abundance of fallow deer suggests the presence of local deciduous woodland but other supporting taxa such as beaver *Castor fiber*, macaque *Macaca sylvana* and wild boar *Sus scrofa* (which are present in the overlying Lower Loam) are apparently absent. No small mammal remains were recovered by Waechter, with the exception of an isolated water vole molar from the surface of the Lower Gravel. Various large herbivores, including bovids, straight-tusked elephant *Palaeoloxodon antiquus*, horse *Equus ferus* and Merck's rhinoceros *Stephanorhinus kirchbergensis* were recovered in small numbers from the Lower Gravel by the Waechter excavations. As previously stated, little is known about the habitat preferences of the Pleistocene megafauna during this period but these animals are all likely to have grazed the open grasslands of the river floodplain. The Lower Gravel 'midden' contains a virtually identical assemblage reflecting similar environmental conditions, with the addition of a single specimen each of the following species: wolf *Canis* sp., wildcat *Felis sylvestris*, narrow-nosed rhinoceros *Stephanorhinus hemitoechus* and rabbit *Oryctolagus cuniculus*. Horse *Equus ferus* is apparently absent.

Palaeoecological significance of mammals from the Lower Loam

In the Lower Loam, the mammalian fauna is again wholly consistent with a temperate climate and a regional vegetation of mixed deciduous woodland with areas of dry grassland in the river floodplain. No direct climatic information is provided by the mammalian remains, with the possible exception of the mole *Talpa* cf. *europaea* and the extinct small mole *Talpa minor* (both new records for the site) which are clearly adapted to a fossorial existence and thus presumably required a habitat where the soil was not subject to permanent or seasonal freezing. The proximity of the river is suggested by the water vole *Arvicola cantiana*, whilst the presence of nearby relatively open woodland is supported by the abundance of fallow deer and echoed by much smaller numbers of beaver, wild boar and macaque.

The rabbit *Oryctolagus cuniculus* also prefers open woodland and grassland (Stuart 1982, 76) and has been found in moderate numbers throughout the Lower Loam. Other rodents, such as the field vole *Microtus agrestis*, European pine vole *Microtus (Terricola) subterraneus* (= *Pitymys arvaloides*) and northern vole *Microtus oeconomus* have only been recovered in extremely small numbers as part of a probable pellet accumulation and are therefore unsuitable for use as environmental indicators. The existence of substantial areas of grassland beside the river is again attested to by the presence of large herbivores, such as horse *Equus ferus*, rhinoceroses and large bovids.

Palaeoecological significance of mammals from the Lower Middle Gravel

The fauna recovered during the Waechter excavations from the Lower Middle Gravel is extremely sparse and in rather poor condition. Four species are recorded from the base of the Lower Middle Gravel by a single specimen in each case: straight tusked elephant *Palaeoloxodon antiquus*, fallow deer *Dama dama*, giant deer *Megaloceros giganteus* and a large bovid. A further fragment of scapula of *Dama dama* is marked simply 'Middle Gravels'. Given the paucity of evidence and the fragmentary and heavily rolled nature of the bones, further attempts to use the mammalian remains to portray the palaeoenvironment at the time of deposition of the Lower Middle Gravels would be unwise.

12. NOTES ON THE MAMMALIAN REMAINS FROM BARNFIELD PIT, SWANSCOMBE.

Andrew Currant

INTRODUCTION

The mammalian remains recovered from Pleistocene terrace deposits at Barnfield Pit, Swanscombe are important because they constitute the oldest known faunal assemblage from the Lower Thames Valley. Little attention has been given to the context of most of these finds other than attribution to a particular horizon within the Swanscombe sequence. In these notes, particular attention is given to factors which may limit the interpretation of the mammalian fossils, and to important material which has been overlooked or misinterpreted in the past and which has a direct bearing on the possible age of the site.

The extensive collections of mammal remains from the 'High Terrace' deposits at Swanscombe, arising mainly from the work of A.T. Marston, A.S. Kennard, L.S.B. Leakey, and B.O. and J. Wymer between 1934 and 1960, were described and summarised by Sutcliffe (*in* Ovey (ed), 1964). Sutcliffe's account underlined the paucity of information then available about the fauna of the Lower Loam, a major stratigraphic unit representing a phase of relatively low energy deposition within the 'High Terrace' sequence. Given the well known difficulties associated with the interpretation of faunal remains from river gravels, the Lower Loam represented one of the few parts of the Swanscombe succession which was likely to contain reliably autochthonous material.

John Waechter's excavations concentrated on recovering faunal and archaeological collections from the lower units represented at Swanscombe, principally the Lower Loam and the upper part of the Lower Gravel. With the exception of some of the microtine rodents, which are commented on in Sutcliffe and Kowalski (1976), none of Waechter's material has been published prior to this volume. Details of the identity and provenance of the preserved faunal remains from Waechter's excavations, now in the Natural History Museum, London, are given in Chapter 11.

It is not intended here to repeat the excellent work already done on the Swanscombe fauna by Sutcliffe, but attention is drawn to particular features of the mammalian collections recovered from the site which have not been discussed previously and which have a bearing on their overall interpretation.

COLLECTION BIASES AND THE RELIABILITY OF COLLECTION DATA

Letters from A.S. Kennard to M.A.C. Hinton (N.H.M. Pal. Dept. archive) indicate that Kennard was excavating a limited number of specimens himself, but the majority were being 'put on one side' for him by the pit workmen. He also suggests that he was learning to recognise the provenance of particular fossils according to their state of preservation.

It is interesting to note that nearly all of the material in both the Kennard and the Marston collections is labelled according to the bed in which it was said to have been found. There are two ways in which this information might have been obtained. The first presupposes that the workmen were noting precisely where finds were coming from and keeping them in such a way that there could be no confusion about their provenance. The second is that Marston and Kennard were assigning unprovenanced specimens to particular beds on the basis of their preservation. Whichever is closer to the truth, it is now impossible to assess how reliable or consistent this information may have been. There are certainly mistakes in attribution, a particularly obvious example being two virtually identical *Stephanorhinus kirchbergensis* upper premolars (NHM P.D. M20604 and unregistered), very possibly from the same individual, one of which is marked 'Basal' (=Lower Gravel) and the other 'Middle Gravel'.

Looking at the surviving collections, there is an impression that Kennard may have been more selective in what he kept than Marston. There seems to be a greater proportion of complete or specifically diagnostic specimens among Kennard's material and far more fragmentary or undiagnostic material among Marston's.

The Wymer Collection was the first assemblage of material from Swanscombe to be systematically excavated. The Wymers attention was concentrated on the Middle Gravels, source of the human skull fragments found earlier by Marston. The condition of the specimens in the Middle Gravels had deteriorated significantly in those areas stripped of the overlying parts of the terrace deposits and many of the finds from their excavations are in very poor condition when compared with those found by earlier collectors. There is, nonetheless, considerably less collector bias than in the Marston and Kennard collections.

The author was present during the closing phases of the final season of John Waechter's excavations. In the course of Waechter's work at Swanscombe, virtually everything discovered was kept, at least initially, but a good deal of fragmentary and indeterminate material was disposed of soon after the excavation. Most of the material from the Lower Loam was three-dimensionally recorded. The Lower Loam was quite tough material to excavate by hand, and because it contained many tiny calcareous nodules it had a notably 'crunchy' texture. The method of excavation - trowelling down in shallow spits - and the absence of any form of sieving lead to the damage, destruction or loss of most of the contained vertebrate microfauna. All of that which survives is very fragmentary and consists mainly of the largest species represented, *Arvicola cantiana*, the smaller species being generally overlooked or destroyed other than in the one instance where several species were found together in what may have been a preserved raptor pellet.

Many of the larger specimens found in the Lower Loam were removed on plinths of sediment which were taken into the finds hut for further cleaning and a limited amount of on-site conservation. Regrettably, much of this work was carried out less than skilfully by untrained volunteers and considerable damage was done to some otherwise good specimens. Future users of the collections should be aware that surface damage to Lower Loam specimens in the Waechter Collection is common, and may have been caused by a wide variety of wooden and metal instruments. It was largely for this reason that a search for original butchery marks on the Waechter specimens was abandoned as inconclusive.

THE PROBLEM OF DERIVED MATERIAL

Much of the Swanscombe High Terrace material is composed of sands and gravels, Marston and Kennard both made extensive collections from the Middle and Lower Gravel units, and both commented at various times about the 'derived' state of some of the material that they encountered.

Care should be taken here about making a distinction between contemporaneous fossils which may have been rolled, more or less extensively in the process of initial deposition, and genuinely derived material which represents reworking from earlier deposits. Waechter's midden feature at the top of the Lower Gravel is without doubt a winnowing horizon - minor events of non-deposition or active erosion which served to concentrate vertebrate and lithic material at particular horizons. Almost all specimens from this feature are heavily broken and rolled, the rounded surfaces showing the same dullness one might find in modern fluviatile accumulations, for instance the material which is still so common on the modern Thames foreshore in the area of the City of London. Some of the rolled material in the Lower Gravel may represent similar contemporaneous processes, but other specimens have features which suggest complex depositional histories.

Distinguishing between these two possible categories is not necessarily easy, but there are critical fossils in the Swanscombe collections which do appear to demonstrate that at least some of the fauna from the gravel units may significantly pre-date the age of the deposits in which they were finally preserved.

A characteristic example of these derived fossils is a third upper molar (NHM P.D. M16532) of an arvicolid rodent from a silt layer in the Upper Middle Gravel previously identified by Schreuder (1950) as *Clethrionomys* sp. This large, slightly rolled and heavily mineralized tooth appears to belong to a water vole. It is of particular interest because the pulp cavities of the tooth show the first stages of closure, a precursor to root formation, indicating that the tooth is either from a young individual of *Mimomys savini*, a form possessing rooted cheek teeth, or represents a member of a transitional population between this form and its lineal descendant *Arvicola cantiana*, which is characterised by unrooted cheek teeth. Whichever of these two possibilities is the case, this fossil clearly pre-dates water voles represented by material from the underlying Lower Loam which are consistently unrooted forms of *Arvicola cantiana*.

Other fossils appear to show evidence of rolling which post-dates an initial phase of mineralisation, and hence are also plausibly derived. Here one has to make a subjective judgement about the significance of rolling or abrasion to any one specimen.

A good example is the fragment of rhinoceros upper molar from Kennard's collection, figured (reversed) by Sutcliffe (1960, fig. 30d as *Stephanorhinus hemitoechus*. NHM P.D. M20579). Unusually this specimen is marked 'horizon uncertain', though the heavy iron staining and remaining matrix fragments suggest it is from one of the gravels. It is heavily rolled and abraded, but the surfaces show a distinctive polish. Another rhinoceros tooth (NHM P.D. M20603, a worn upper premolar of *Stephanorhinus* sp.) is also heavily mineralized and rolled. It is almost certainly a derived specimen. A large number of the Swanscombe specimens from the gravel units show a greater or lesser degree of damage that may be attributable to a derived origin.

It should be borne in mind that numerous fossils from the gravel units, particularly the Lower Gravel, are absolutely fresh and show no sign whatever of abrasion or rolling. In this category one can include two associated dorsal vertebrae and a complete rib of *Palaeoloxodon antiquus* from Waechter's excavation (Sc68 A 2B 145-165) which are relatively lightly stained and show very fine, crisp surface detail. The very fact that such large yet delicate material could survive intact in the depositional environment of the Lower Gravel makes it all the more likely that specimens with significant edge rounding may represent derived material.

BIOSTRATIGRAPHY OF THE SWANSCOMBE FAUNAS

Other than in palynological circles, Swanscombe has become synonymous with the concept of the Hoxnian interglacial. The vertebrate fauna at the type locality, Hoxne, Suffolk, is mainly confined to deposits overlying the interglacial lake beds, with only limited finds from the lake beds themselves (Stuart 1982). Swanscombe has long been taken to represent the true Hoxnian temperate vertebrate fauna. The Hoxnian is usually interpreted as being the first major interglacial stage to follow the Anglian/Elsterian Glaciation, the major cold stage of the Middle Pleistocene.

Even the old collections from Swanscombe still hold a few surprises. Three associated upper teeth (P^3 to M^1) from the Lower Gravel in A.S. Kennard's collection (NHM P.D. M20586; M18968; M20580), none of which show significant evidence of abrasion or derivation, belong to *Stephanorhinus etruscus*. The later forms of *S. etruscus* have recently been assigned to a seperate species *S. hundseimensis* by Fortelius, Mazza and Sala (1993). These teeth have been examined by the author, Dr. Mickael Fortelius of Helsinki and most recently by Prof. C. Petronio of Rome: we all agree on the determination. It should be noted that Simon Parfitt disagrees with this classification (pers. comm.).

Etruscan rhinoceros is most definitely not one of the animals that one would have expected to find at Swanscombe. There is no other record of this animal in a Hoxnian/Holsteinian context in Europe. The picture is made all the more complex because the same deposit, the Lower Gravel, also contains clearly identifiable specimens of *Stephanorhinus kirchbergensis* and *Stephanorhinus hemitoechus*, creating a palaeoecological as well as biostratigraphic nightmare. Three species of rhinoceros in the same place at the same time is not easy to explain, but the fact remains that this appears to have been the case.

So, what else is there in the Swanscombe fauna which helps to clarify where it might belong in the British Quaternary succession? The water voles, as mentioned, are all of the *Arvicola cantiana* morphology, so they must post-date the type Cromerian. Other than this, the small mammal fauna doesn't really help very much because so little has been collected.

In an attempt to examine the evolution of British temperate woodland faunas throughout the Middle and Late Pleistocene, the author has previously proposed an informal five-fold grouping of such interglacial mammalian assemblages, Group 5 representing the Cromerian of West Runton, Norfolk and Group 1 representing the Last Interglacial as characterised by faunas with abundant *Hippopotamus* (Currant 1989). In this scheme Swanscombe was used as one of the sites typical of Group 3 assemblages. The addition of *Stephanorhinus etruscus* to the Group 3 faunal list doesn't actually make much difference to the picture. The Swanscombe bears are still 'spelaeoid', differentiating them from later Middle Pleistocene sites with *Ursus arctos* (Group 2 assemblages). The model is still intact, but the presence of *S. etruscus* tends to suggest the Swanscombe fauna (and other Group 3 assemblages) may be older than had previously been anticipated.

Here we have a real dilemma. The fossils are may indicate that Swanscombe could predate the Anglian/Elsterian glaciation, or perhaps represent an inter-Anglian temperate phase of some kind. At present there is nothing in the fauna that would preclude such a suggestion. This would not be a popular suggestion, but it should not be dismissed without a fair hearing. The alternative is that one would have to accept the presence of post-Anglian/Elsterian *S. etruscus* in Europe, which would not find ready acceptance either.

Martin Hinton firmly believed that the High Terrace deposits around Swanscombe and their contained fauna represented a very early phase in the Pleistocene, closer in time to the Forest Bed sequences of East Anglia than to the rest of the fossiliferous deposits of the Lower Thames Valley. Bridgland (1994) in the most recent overview of the Lower Thames Pleistocene deposits notes the traditional correlation of Swanscombe with the Hoxnian, but draws attention to the problems of dating the Hoxne interglacial deposits in their own right. He proposes that the Swanscombe deposits should be adopted as the type locality for the first post-Anglian interglacial, which he correlates with stage 11 of the deep-sea oxygen isotope record.

It is here that attention turns again on the presence of derived fossils at Swanscombe. It is usually the case that such fossils come from earlier fluviatile deposits along the course of the same river valley. If it is proposed that Swanscombe represents the first post-Anglian interglacial, it also presumably represents the first post-diversion terrace, in which case from where are the earlier derived fossils derived? In the earliest phase of post-diversion valley modification one might expect considerable landscape modification and the deposition of massive outwash deposits from the Anglian glacial front. Under such circumstances it is unlikely that earlier terrace deposits representing entirely different river systems and containing interglacial mammalian fossils would be available for reworking during the succeeding interglacial phase.

The present author believes that it would be premature to try to assign Swanscombe to any particular phase of the global Quaternary succession. As Bridgland emphasised, there is still a great deal to be learned about this site, and there is in any event little general or specific agreement about the correlation of any Middle Pleistocene terrestrial sequence with the oxygen isotope record.

A detailed re-evaluation of the entire Swanscombe mammalian fauna is currently being undertaken by Schreve, and further samples of Swanscombe matrices collected in 1986 are also being processed for small vertebrates.

CONCLUSIONS

Waechter's excavations have filled a major gap in the faunal collections from the Swanscombe terrace deposits and provided several interesting new records (see Chapters 9 to 11). The methods of recovery employed have done little to redress the bias against the smaller elements of the fauna, and it is these which might give us a much clearer fix on the true relative age of the site. It is also clear that there is much to be gained from closer study of existing collections and data, once freed from the constraints of assumed correlations.

13. THE FOOTPRINT SURFACES AT BARNFIELD PIT, SWANSCOMBE

Peter Davis

THE RESULTS OF ANALYSIS OF A POTENTIAL HUMAN FOOTPRINT

Alan Walker

During the 1968-1972 excavations at Barnfield Pit several horizons within the Lower Loam were identified as being fossil land surfaces. Footprints were associated with some of these surfaces, although only three of the surfaces were recorded in any detail (E, C4, B3 sandy horizon). On one of these surfaces (B3 sandy horizon) the footprints (? cavitation hollows - see Chapter 7) were indistinct and other than a photographic record no detailed work on the depressions was possible. The geological context of this horizon is discussed by Conway in Chapter 7. The footprints from the other two surfaces were examined in greater detail, and the results of these investigations are presented below.

TRENCH C4

Description

The excavation and contemporary recording. The top surface of the Lower Loam was variably covered with a thin layer of pale gritty sand with pebbles and occasional mollusc shells. This was cleared by manual removal of loose pebbles, followed by careful brushing away of the gritty sand; where this sand appeared to be filling surface depressions it was removed by sucking or blowing it out by air from a domestic vacuum cleaner nozzle. Any stones embedded into the Loam surface were retained. The Loam surface of many of the depressions thus exposed was discoloured to a depth of a few millimetres, being of various shades of brown or grey, which allowed accurate cleaning of the hollows. Footboards were used as required to protect the exposed surface.

During excavation it became clear that the depressions were mostly animal footprints. A few photographs were taken as work progressed, the depressions being indicated by pointers. Once the surface was completely exposed, numbered white card labels were placed alongside most of the depressions and a list was made of their possible or probable origins as determined by John Waechter and assisted by the author. A street light inspection vehicle was then used to place its platform centrally over the excavation from which a series of overhead colour slides of the whole and parts of the surface were taken. Further oblique photographs were also obtained from positions around the surface. A further series of overhead photographs was taken when the surface had been covered with a 10 cm grid to allow accurate location of the hollows.

It proved impossible to acquire a satisfactory permanent cover for the excavation. As bad weather was becoming imminent, the exposure was dressed with a stabilising solution and cloth reinforced latex moulds were made of the surface for later study. There is no record of any subsequent study being completed and published. The surface was backfilled for protection.

Preliminary examination of the latex moulds in 1973 proved them to be of little value, and they were transferred to the Institute of Archaeology. One section of the mould is currently in Dartford Museum, the remaining sections are being curated by the Natural History Museum at Tring.

Trench C4

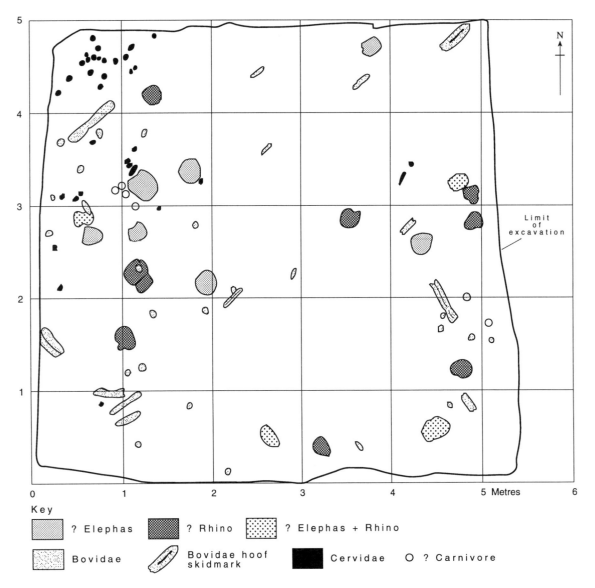

Fig. 13.1. Complete footprint plan in Square C4

There is no trace of the overhead photographs taken with the 10 cm grid in place. What survives are twelve colour slides taken by Waechter from the overhead platform (OH1-3, 21-29), of which OH21 is of the whole surface with labels in place; nine colour slides taken by the author (OH4-12); eleven colour slides taken by Waechter of close up photographs of individual features (BM6, 33, 34a, 34b, 35, 43, 56, 68, 72, 81, 82).

A preliminary species identification list was compiled by Waechter and the author which has survived. This list, amended in the light of more recent work by the author, forms the basis of the species list presented below.

170

Recent work, 1994, by P.R. Davis

A 1/10th scale diagram of trench C4 was obtained by projecting OH21 onto graph paper at an appropriate enlargement. The number slips in OH21 are illegible, so the numbers were inserted by reference to OH1, OH5, OH22, OH23, OH28 and OH30, in which they are clearly visible. It should be noted that a few numbers in OH1 and OH5 appear to have been displaced before the photographs were taken, but the other sources and the field notes allowed correction of this fault. Unfortunately there are no legible number cards for numbers 53, 54, 55, 58, 60, 61, 72A, 88A; but the outlines visible in OH21 allowed a tentative allocation using the descriptions in the field notes.

The master diagram, Figure 13.1, was compiled from OH21 and was given co-ordinates from an arbitrary zero point near the north-west corner of the trench, the X axis running north-south and the Y axis running west-east. This enabled a record to be made of the position of each feature, and greatly eased the task of inter-picture recognition and analysis. The X and Y co-ordinates of each feature are given in the list below.

Each numbered feature was then examined in every slide in which it could be seen, enlarging the relevant part of the picture where necessary. This allowed confirmation of the tentative diagnosis in some prints, and a better description in others. Some additional footprints were revealed, and these have been numbered 27A, 28A, 41A, 81A, 90A.

The detailed inspection also allowed measurement of the print sizes in many cases. Some slides include a scale so that measurement was straight forward, while in others indirect methods were employed, such as using the size of a feature measured in another slide as a scale for the picture in question.

The footprint list

In Table 13.1 below, the original field note description appears in italics. The numbers of pictures in which the print can be seen well follows, together with any further information gleaned from the photographs, including an opinion on the species in some cases. The lengths and widths of as many prints as possible have been measured. The measurements for well circumscribed prints are given as cm and mm, eg. length 6.0. Prints lacking such clarity are given as cm only, eg. length 6. The photographs used to take the measurements are indicated by an asterisk.

Thus each print in Table 13.1 is listed as:-

Number; *Original note*, Photo. nos. (*) and other notes; Length; Width; Coordinates (X and Y).

Table 13.1. Identification of Footprints from Square C4.

No.	Description and notes	Size		Coordinates	
		L.	W.	X	Y
1.	*Cervid skid mark in Loam*, OH3, OH5, OH22*. Not clear in photo., diagnosis from field notes.	5	4	13.4	48.5
2.	*Shallow slot, ?Cervid in Loam surface*, OH5, OH22*. Not clear in photo, diagnosis from field notes.	4	3	10.8	47.2
3.	*Shallow Cervid print in Loam surf.*, OH5, OH22*. Not clear in photo., diagnosis from field notes. Stained deep brown.	5	4	6.7	48.2

4.	Shallow Cervid print in Loam surf., OH5, OH6*, OH22*. Short skid, stained deep brown.	5	4	6.7	46.0
5.	Cervid print in Loam, OH5, OH22*. Deep print, stained brown.	5	4	7.2	47.0
6.	Cervid slot in Loam, OH5, OH22*. Deep print, stained deep brown.	4	4	9.0	45.7
7.	Small Cervid print in Loam with splash surround, OH5, OH22*. A medium sized print imposed on another. Stained brown.	5	4	10.2	46.1
8.	Jumble of Cervid prints in Loam, OH5, OH22. Indistinct in photo.	-	-	11.2	44.8
9.	V. small Cervid print oblique in Loam with splash surround, OH22. Partly hidden by label, stained deep brown.	3	2	7.9	45.7
10.	Single slot in Loam, OH5, OH22*. Other unnumbered slots in line to right. All deeply coloured, with splash surrounds, Cervid, part of the trail of an adult with a fawn.	3	2	5.6	45.6
11.	Small print in loam, ?species, OH22* ?Cervid, clearly fissiped, some splash surround, stained brown.	5	4	4.0	43.8
12.	Cervid print in Loam, OH5, OH22*. Deep, no detail in picture, stained brown.	3	2	6.3	44.5
13.	Shallow Cervid print in Loam, OH5, OH22*. Shows well, brown stain.	4	3	7.9	44.0
14.	Shallow Cervid print in Loam. Slight skid. OH5, OH6, OH22*, OH27. Shows well, stained dark brown.	7.0	5.3	7.7	42.9
15.	Shallow print in loam, ?species OH5, OH22. Clearly Cervid in OH22, stained brown.	3	3	3.0	42.3
16.	Bovid skid mark in Loam with occasional embedded pebble, one indicating direction of skid OH5, OH6, OH22*, OH27*. Stained blue grey throughout.	50	10	4.3 to 8.7	37.5 41.3
17.	Deep large print, gravel embedded into Loam, with raised edge, ?rhino. OH5, OH22* Raised edge visible by west margin.	30	25	12.7	41.8
18.	Circular pit in Loam with splash surround, OH5, OH6, OH22*, OH27*. Obscured by label, deep brown stain, lining separating.	7.9	6.6	3.4	37.3
19.	Cervid footprint in Loam, OH5, OH6, OH22*. Deep brown stain.	5	4	6.7	37.0
20.	?Bovid footprint in Loam with occasional pebble, beside(s) small depression, ?cause, OH6, OH22*. Front of print shows well, is elongate and typically Cervid. Dark brown stain.	7	6	7.4	38.5
21.	Shallow pit in Loam, ?species, OH21, OH22*. Clearly bovid. Lightly stained brown, some embedded gravel visible.	7.7	5.5	12.3	38.1
22.	Bovid print in Loam, OH5, OH9, OH22, OH28*. Brown stain.	6.0	7.2	5.3	34.2

23.	*Cervid print in Loam*, OH5, OH22*. Indistinct in photo, diagnosis from field notes.	9	6	11.2	36.1
24.	*Small print in Loam*, ?species, OH4, OH9*, OH22, OH28*. ?Cervid Lightly stained.	6.6	6.0	5.4	31.1
25.	*Shallow print in Loam*, ?species, OH4, OH5, OH22, OH28*. ?Cervid, Lightly stained.	5.0	4.3	4.9	30.8
26.	*Bovid print in loam with occasional pebble. Also a skid mark.* OH4, OH5, OH9*, OH22 OH25, OH28*. Dark staining.	16.4	8.8	6.0	30.0
27.	*Small print with claw marks in Loam*, ?species, OH5, OH9, OH22, OH28*. Adjoins 27A, 28 and 28A, all in splash from 30. All light brown in colour, probably 1 animal, probably a carnivore.	2.5	2.4	9.2	31.8
27A.	By 27, no original no., see 27. Canine like print with 3 clear marks, OH5, OH9, OH22, OH28*.	2.5	2.2	10.0	32.2
28.	*Shallow pit in Loam*, ?cause, see 27, OH5, OH9, OH22, OH28* Canine form, deformed by slip on pebble?	3.6	3.8	10.4	31.3
28A.	By 28, no original number, see 27. Canine form, possibly claw marks, OH5, OH9, OH28*.	4.0	2.8	11.6	30.0
29.	*Small skid mark in Loam*, ? species, OH5, OH22, OH28* Probably Cervid, colour is indeterminate.	9	4	11.2 to 10.7	34.2 33.6
30.	*Large pit with splash surround, gravel embedded in Loam*, ?Elephas OH5, OH9, OH22, OH28*.	41.8	27.5	12.2	32.5
31.	*Circular hole in loam*, ?cause, OH5, OH22, OH28*. Edge indefinite ?bovid.	15	10	2.0	27.2
32.	*?bovid footprint superimposed on edge of 47*, OH5, OH28*. Pale colour, splash surround.	7.2	8.3	11.7	23.2
33.	*Clean bovid skid mark in loam surface. Divided by central ridge*, OH5, OH7, OH24, BM33*. Slight side slip visible at end, pale brown stain.	38.4	11.0	3.2	14.1
34.	*Clean Cervid print in Loam*, OH23, BM34A and B. Curved ridge ? turning. Brown stain visible in BM34B.	6.3	5.8	7.7	8.7
35.	*Skid mark in gravel on Loam*, ? species, OH23, OH24*. Clearly bovid. Colour indeterminate.	18	6	11.4 to 8.8	9.7 7.9
36.	*Shallow bovid print in Loam with a little gravel embedded*, OH22, OH28*. Pale brown stain.	13	15	2.4	31.1
37.	*Small Cervid print, some gravel in lining*, OH4, OH5, OH25*, OH28*.	3.3	3.7	2.5	25.5
38.	*Shallow Cervid print with some gravel in lining*, OH4, OH5, OH25, OH28*. Colour indeterminate.	4	3	3.1	21.2
39.	*Deep large concavity in gravel rhino?*, OH5, OH24*. Some brown stain.	27	25	10.2	15.7

No.	Description				
40.	*Bovid imprint on raised edge of 39, gravel lining*, OH5, OH23 OH24*. Colour indeterminate. OH25.	12	15	10.4	12.2
41.	*Long narrow skid mark in Loam*, OH23*. Closer examination shows two parallel grooves, from the two sides of a bovid hoof. Partly stained medium brown.	45	12	10.0 to 6.9	10.0 10.2
41A.	Skid, ?bovid, in gravel, OH23*. Edges indistinct. No original number, located by description, pale brown stain.	55	15	11.7 to 8.9	7.8 6.4
42.	*Bovid footprint, gravel lined, with splash surround*, OH23, OH24*. Could be one of two prints in OH24, clearest measured.	8	7	12.0	12.7
43.	*Clean equid print in Loam surface*, OH23, OH26*, BM43*. ?equid, but front end appears bifid, and frog is inverted. Has ends of bovid slot projecting from the front. Very probably two bovids superimposed. Brown stain in part.	13.6	10.8	11.4	4.7
44.	*Print, ??bovid in Loam surface*, OH21, OH30*. Measures very approximate, no better speciation or colour possible.	8	7	21.5	1.3
45.	*Oval depression, ?species print, splash surround*, OH21, OH30*, no detail or size visible.	-	-	16.5	8.7
46.	*Print and splash surround in Loam, ?species*, OH21, OH30*, ?rhino. No colour determination possible.	25	25	26.2	5.0
47.	*Ill defined large print, splash surround, ?rhino (with 32)*, OH28* 32 and 48 superimposed. Rough trifoliate appearance. Colour indeterminate.	35	30	12.0	21.7
48.	*Skid mark, ?bovid, in splash surround of 47*, OH28*. Dark brown.	15	6	13.2	18.5
49.	*Large print with gravel base and splash surround, ? Elephas*, OH28*. Ill defined. Colour indeterminate.	40	27	19.9	21.9
50.	*Round hole, gravel lined, ?cause*, OH28*. Species and colour indeterminate.	8	8	18.8	18.9
51	*Clean Cervid print in Loam in splash from 52*, OH22, OH28*. Brown stain.	3.2	2.8	18.5	32.7
52.	*Large print with gravelled base splash surround, ?Elephas*, OH5, OH22, OH28*. Colour indeterminate.	27	25	17.5	33.9
53.	*Bovid skid mark, gravel lined*. No label found, tentative position in OH21* master diagram from description only. Shows well in OH30, brown staining.	40	8	23.0 to 26.5	43.5 45.5
54.	*Bovid skid mark, clean in Loam*. No label found. Position in OH21* master diagram from description only. Colour indeterminate.	35	8	25.2 to 26.1	35.8 38.1
55.	*Bovid skid mark, lined with gravel splash at one corner*. No label found, tentative position in OH21 master diagram from description only. Shows well in OH30, dark brown.	30	9	30.0 to 28.6	21.0 23.9

No.	Description				
56.	2 skid marks (? 1 large bovid), gravel lined, splash surround, OH1, OH8, BM56*. Imposed on side of 79. Some brown staining.	18.5	16.7	48.5	8.8
57.	Footmark in gravelly Loam, ?species. Fissiped, probably bovid, OH1, OH8*. Imposed on end of 79. Brown stain.	10	10	46.1	8.7
58.	Footmark in gravelly Loam, ? species. No label, tentative position in OH21 master diagram from description. Poor view in OH30.	-	-	25.3	23.0
59.	Long skid mark, ?species, gravel lined, OH28*. Very ill defined no clear width possible. Possibly bovid.	27	-	23.3 to 21.2	21.2 19.4
60.	? bovid, side-slip mark from 59. Gravel lined. No label found, position in OH21 master diagram from description. Indeterminate.	-	-	22.9	21.5
61.	Deep skid mark, gravel lined, ?species. No label found, tentative position in OH21 diagram from description. Shows well in OH30. Dark brown staining. Bovid.	40	9	45.5 to 48.9	47.2 49.9
62.	Large print gravel lined, ?Elephas, (splash surround), OH21, OH30*. In OH30 looks like 2 prints superimposed.	30	25	38.0	47.0
63.	Bovid skid mark, shallow, gravel lined, OH21, OH30*. Light staining.	30	9	35.6 to 37.9	42.7 44.4
64.	Bovid print, gravel lined, splash surround, OH22, OH28*, Slight colour.	7.8	7.2	18.0	28.2
65.	No entry in rough notes, no label found.				
66.	Bovid print in Loam, gravel lined, OH1*, OH2*. Slight colour.	13.0	11.5	45.3	16.0
67.	Hoofprint, ?equus, gravel lined, OH1*, OH2*. Partial colouring. Again, difficult to believe from the outline; ?bovid.	10	8	48.5	16.1
68.	Bovid skid mark, gravel lined, splash surround, OH1*, OH2*, OH24 BM68*. Some brown staining.	40.2	8.5	46.6 to 44.5	17.9 22.0
69.	Print, gravel lined, ?species, OH1*, OH2*. Fissiped, probably Bos. Ill defined, slight colouration.	7	8	48.0	20.5
70.	Large print, gravel lined, splash surround. Trifoliate, ?rhino. OH1*. Good definition but poor colour.	38	29	49.2	28.3
71.	Bovid skid mark, gravel lined, OH1*, OH2. Poor definition, some weak brown staining.	28	13	41.6	28.0
72.	Deep, large impression, gravel lined, splash surround, ?Elephas, OH1*, OH2, BM72*. More like a rhino in the photograph. Colour poor.	27.4	22.0	49.0	31.4
72a.	Circular large impression ?Elephas, OH1*, Unnumbered in photo, Has a raised edge and some, More like rhino picture.	37	37	46.8	34.5

73.	*Ill defined large impression, gravel lined, splash surround, ?Elephas*, OH1*, Looks trifoliate, ?rhino, Colour poor.	-	-	35.7	28.8
74.	*Clean Cervid print in loam*, OH1* Dark brown.	12	6	41.8	34.6
75.	Skid and print, gravel line, ?equus, No label found, doubt equus, Tentative position in OH21 master diagram from description only.	-	-	36.3	4.2
76.	*Skid mark, gravel lined, with splash surround*, No label found, position in OH21 diagram from description, No measure possible.	-	-	39.7	6.5
77.	*Ill defined large impression, gravel line, splash surround, ?rhino, and 85* No label, position in OH21 diagram from description, and match with super-imposed flint tool (85), Colour poor.	30	30	45.0	6.0
78.	*Ill defined print, gravel lined, ?species ?rhino*, No label, tentative position in OH21* diagram from description only.	28	25	32.5	4.0
79.	*Large print in loam, gravel lined, splash surround ?rhino*, OH1*, OH8*, 56, 57 superimposed, Colour poor.	30	30	48.0	12.0
80.	No entry in rough notes, no label found .				
81.	*Small footprint, gravel present, ?canis*, Dark brown BM81, to right of board at end of straw indicator,	3.2	3.2	50.7	17.5
81A.	Unnumbered, In BM81* Clean bovid print below marker board.	7.8	9.3	50.8	16.9
82.	*Bovid imprint in splash of 68*, OH1*, BM82, Label in BM82 hides the imprint, and labelling confused, However, this description appears correct, it fits with other views.	7	6	45.4	18.4
83.	*Large impression, gravel lined, splash surround, in centre of area of jumbled impression ?species, ?2 superimposed*, OH1*.	40	30	43.6	25.9
84.	*Skid mark, ?species, gravel lined*, OH1* Possibly Cervid skid.	42	5	40.8	33.0
85.	*Flint, worked flake, in loam surface, and 77*, Position in OH21 master diagram from description, and from 77, q.v.			43.9	4.2
86.	*Clean Cervid print*, OH5*, OH9, OH22, OH28 Brown.	4	4	11.6	32.8
87.	*Bone fragment, ?Cervid, Not in contact with loam*, OH4*, OH5*, ?lower end of cannon bone, Where is it now?	-	9	5.4	20.5
88.	*Large impression, gravel line, splash surround ?Elephas*, OH4, OH5, OH9, OH22, OH25*, OH28*, Splash round ½ circumference.	30.4	32.8	6.6	26.5
88A.	*Large circular impression ?Elephas*, Splash surround, OH4, OH5, OH28* No number in slides, but location given fits description.	30	30	11.0	26.6
89.	*Shallow fissiped print in loam*, OH5, OH9, OH22, OH28* ?Cervid.	5	4	10.4	34.9
90.	*Shallow pit in loam, ?cause*, OH28* ?part of 27 Cervid step series.	4	3	13.9	29.8
90A.	Large print with splash surround, OH21* Not in numbers or notes.	35	30	14.0	29.6

	Cervid	Bovid	Carnivore	Large
Firmly indicated in rough notes	21	16	0	0
Possibles in rough notes	2	5	1	17
Firmly added by P.R.D.	0	5	3	0
Possibles added by P.R.D.	7	10	1	3
Totals	30	36	5	3

Table 13.2. The source of the identification of the footprints

Trench E	Square C3	Square B3
		Complex 19 26.24 m
		Complex 22C 26.10 m
	---	
	antler/skull 26.05 m	
	(Sc.71 C3 63/64)	
	76 25.83 m	

E5 25.03 m		
E33 24.90 m		
E6 24.81 m		

Table 13.3. Comparison between the heights of the footprints in Trench E, and the knapping floor in squares C3 and B3.

Results

Formation of the footprints. Some prints occurred in the top surface of the Loam, others in a shallow layer of water rolled gravel driven by the pressure of the feet into the Loam surface. The gravel mainly lay on the east side of trench C4; slide OH3 suggests that it lay in a shallow water channel running along that side of the excavation.

There were several large prints 20-30 cm across in both parts of the horizon, partially or completely surrounded by a raised ridge of fine material expressed from the print by the pressure of the foot. While some of these large prints were of reasonable quality, others had clearly been partially washed out. Several had medium sized and smaller prints superimposed; no example of the reverse has been seen.

The smaller prints were generally of good quality. They appeared in both the gravelly and clean Loam parts of the surface, many also having a surround of expressed material. Additionally some had marks around them consistent with mud splashes outwards from the print site, but these do not appear in the photographs. Many medium sized prints clearly show that the foot skidded on the surface before coming to rest, skids being up to over a half a metre in length. Some parts of the undisturbed Loam surface bore marks consistent with rain drops, but again this can not be seen in any of the photographs.

All prints were infilled with a pale gritty sand, and it was by brushing this out that they were first discovered. The resultant sand lenticles, the unprinted Loam surface and the gravel bed of the water channel were covered by further layers of coarse sand and gravel, including many rolled pebbles.

The general colour of the Loam was a light yellowish brown. The prints in the clean Loam surface were lined by a layer 1-5 mm thick of dark brown or grey brown material; those in the gravel area varied, some having a deep coloured lining, others with a lighter coloured lining. In a few of the darkest prints, as the surface dried after excavation, the lining material cracked away from the surrounding Loam.

One can speculate on the conditions resulting in the formation of the prints. The majority were formed by bovids, Cervids and one or more large mammals. From the relationships shown by the superimposition of prints the large animals crossed the surface first when it was possibly still under shallow water, as some of the well heaped surrounds expressed from under their feet are not as sharply defined as those of many of the smaller animals. The surface then drained to leave a firmer clayey

Trench C4

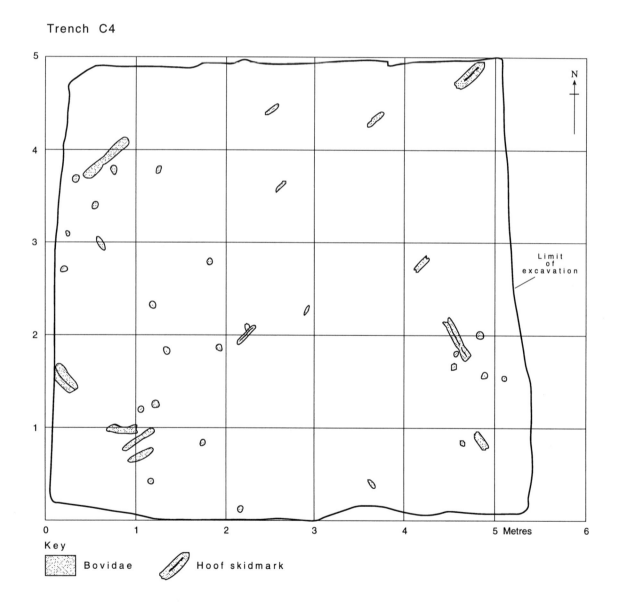

Fig. 13.2. Plan of Bovid footprints in Square C4

mud, and the smaller animals then crossed, generally leaving very sharply defined footprints. It may be that the surface had dried out, and then been dampened by rain to leave an excellent surface for imprinting. The bovid prints show frequent and substantial evidence of slipping, whereas only three Cervid prints showed any evidence of slipping. Thus it may be that the surface was wetter for the bovids than when the Cervids came. No evidence has been found as to which came first. It is possible that the imprinted surface was then baked hard by the sun, thus preserving the prints in fine condition. Subsequent aggradation on this surface was in the form of fine sand infilling the prints. This gentle encroachment was followed by a flood carrying the coarser sand and gravel to cover the whole surface. As time passed, water percolating through the gravel and loam layers carried dissolved salts, probably ferriferous, and these were trapped in the compressed materials lining the footprints to produce the coloured lining.

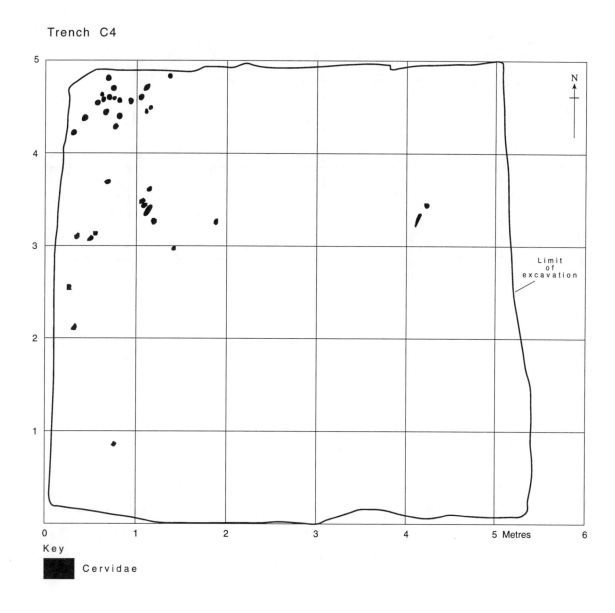

Fig. 13.3. Plan of Cervid footprints in Square C4

Species. During the excavation each print was inspected by John Waechter with some help from myself, and either firmly identified, provisionally identified, or left unidentified; the final list formed the rough notes. While looking at the pictures in detail, I was able to compare unlabelled or unknown prints with others in which the species were known, and this is the basis of the later identifications. The identification sources are summarised in Table 13.2.

Cervid and Bovid prints. Many of the prints in C4 were similar in shape to the first footprint found during the excavation, a Cervid print, found in 1969 (E5, Waechter, 1976, 52; see below). Although many of the C4 prints had the same characteristics as this diagnostic footprint, it was felt that they came from two differently sized series of animals. In the smaller series, a smaller set of prints suggested a foal accompanying an adult. Preliminary identifications suggest that the smaller prints are *Dama* and the larger ones *Cervus* (see Figure 13.3)

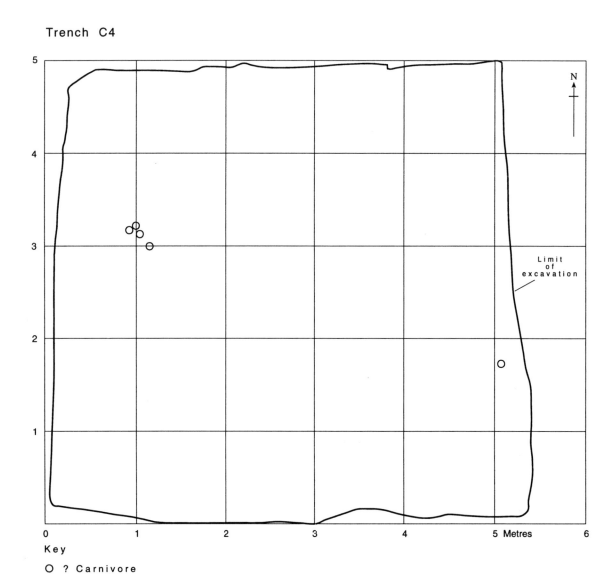

Fig. 13.4. Plan of carnivore footprints in Square C4

The bovid prints closely resembled those deriving from modern domestic cattle, although generally slightly smaller; it was felt that *Bos* was appropriate (see Figure 13.2).

Carnivores. The 'carnivore' prints appeared to belong to the Canidae, and were obviously from a small animal. The prints were small, about 3 cm across. There is one group of four prints to the west, and a solitary print to the south east (see Figure 13.4)

Large mammals. Twenty prints, 20-45 cm across were also noted. Their condition was generally somewhat poorer than the smaller ones, as they appear to have been made when the exposure was covered with shallow waters. However, some were generally rounded, while others appeared to have a trifoliate edge suggestive of toes. No clear grouping appeared. Initially, the rounder prints were attributed to elephant, and those with distinct toes to rhinoceros. However, both animals produce prints with toes, although those of rhinoceros are more pronounced in fresh spoor. The effect of water washing may have been either to enhance or to reduce this difference. Thus, whether these prints pertain to rhinoceros or elephant or both has to remain speculative (Figure 13.5).

Trench C4

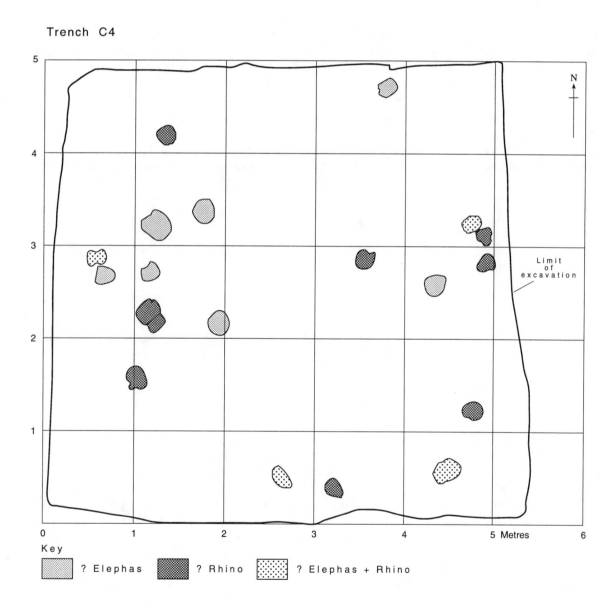

Key

? Elephas   ? Rhino   ? Elephas + Rhino

Fig. 13.5. Plan of large mammal footprints in Square C4

Measurements. The length measurements vary considerably, mainly because many were made when the animal was slipping. For this reason, only the widths have been compared. The results of a comparison of all the Cervid and bovid footprint widths, to the nearest cm are shown in Figures 13.6 A and B, which also include the same dimensions from those positively identified in the original notes. The similarity between the two sets of histograms is striking and suggest that the later identifications fit well with those made when writing the rough notes. That three different groups of animals are involved is clearly suggested by the three peaks in Figure 13.6 the largest pertaining to the Bovidae, the middle group pertaining to *Cervus*, and the smallest to *Dama*.

Spatial patterning. The Cervid prints appear mainly in the north-west corner of the exposure (see Figures 13.1 and 13.3). In this corner, the weaving track of, probably, one animal can be seen. From the analysis of the surface at the time of excavation this was provisionally identified as an adult, with the smaller tracks being those of a foal. Further south, the prints include those of somewhat larger Cervids, with other smaller prints alongside. Two of the western Cervid prints show that the animal had slipped slightly. There are just two Cervid prints on the eastern side of the square, one of the two occurring on a long slip.

The bovids are more widely distributed (see Figure 13.1 and 13.2), and generally appear to be moving to the north-east. That the surface was slippery is shown by the frequent and substantial skid marks. The prints suggest that five or six animals were involved, three or four crossing in a straight line, and being joined in the south-west corner by one animal coming from the west and skidding as it turned to join them. A further one or two may have come from the south-east, and these also skidded. Little can be inferred from the distribution of the carnivore prints (Figure 13.4) other than that such animals were there. Their small size indicates that they were probably living on the leavings from kills made by other predators.

Thus it is clear that a mixed grazing population existed in the area. The baked condition of some of the prints indicates that hot dry periods occurred, presumably in summer, and the sand infilling followed by coarser gravel overlay suggests that the imprinting occurred at the end of the period of Lower Loam accretion.

TRENCH E 1969

Four prints were identified from trench E in the 1969 and 1970 seasons. Two were deer prints (1969 E5; 1970 E33), and two were provisionally identified in the field as possible human footprints (1969 E6; 1970 E35). The two prints from 1969 (E5 and E6) are almost certainly contemporary. The field notes indicate that they were both excavated from a 'greasy loam' capped by a shelly lens. Since the two prints were separated, horizontally, by less than a metre, and vertically by 0.22 m, it is probable that they were part of the same contemporary undulating land surface. The deer print was published by Waechter (1976, 52), and identified as Clacton fallow deer *D. dama clactoniana*. E 33 was also in the 'greasy loam' and is tentatively considered to be contemporary with the 1969 prints, and part of the same undulating surface. No identification was made on the 1970 deer print other than to attribute it to a Cervid. A report on the E6 print by Alan Walker is presented below. The second potential human print (E35) is unlikely to be human.

Although trench E was 32 m away from the main area (see Figure 5.1), it is possible that the surface on which the prints in trench E occurred is contemporary with one of the land surfaces within the Lower Loam in the main area. Two major ones are present within the main area that can still be partially reconstructed from the extant archive; the B3/C3 knapping floor and the sandy horizon in B3 with rain runnels and cavitation hollows (degraded footprints ?, see Chapter 7). The heights for the highest and lowest artefacts in the B3/C3 knapping floor in relation to trench E finds are given in Table 3.3. All heights quoted to OD.

The vertical difference between the lowest C3 artefact on the knapping floor and the highest

E print is 0.80 m over 32 m, which gives a gradient of 1 in 40 or 2.5%. Against this interpretation is the fact that no footprints were recognized on the knapping floor. The shelly sand in B3 was at approximately 25.80 m OD which gives a slightly steeper gradient of 1 in 30 or 3.3% over approximately 36 m (B3 to E). This surface, like the E prints, was covered by a shelly sand. Although it is impossible to be certain which of the two horizons the footprints in E are associated with, it is likely that they are associated with one or the other.

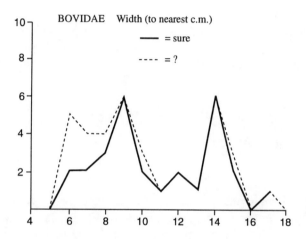

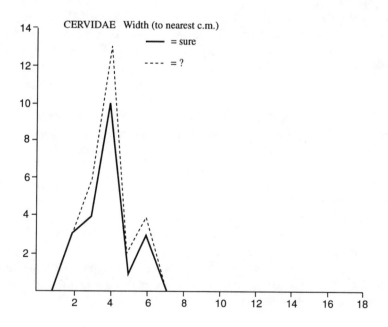

Fig. 13.6. Frequency of Bovid and Cervid footprint widths.

REPORT ON THE SC69 E6 FOOTPRINT

Alan Walker

INTRODUCTION

Apart from an epoxy cast, the only information about the SC69 E6 Footprint that I had to work with was a copy of a letter written by Professor P. R. Davis on 25th February, 1994 and a photocopy of a note and a sketch of the footprint made by Professor Davis in the 1970's on University of Surrey letterhead. I have also seen the photographs on pages 69 and 72 of Waechter (1976) which shows vacuum cleaning of the footprint surface of the Lower Loam and an isolated hoofprint of a fallow deer. Before assessing whether or not this is a human footprint, we should ask what it would tell us if it were.

THE USEFULNESS OF FOOTPRINTS

Apart from their symbolic and emotional value, footprints have been very useful in human palaeontology. The most important prints are those from Laetoli in Tanzania (Leakey and Hay 1979). These are about 3.6 million years old and are important for many reasons, but mostly because they predate the first anatomical evidence of bipedal locomotion in hominids by a few hundred thousand years. In another instance (Behrensmeyer and Laporte 1981) the size of *Homo erectus* footprints confirmed the large stature of early members of this species (Walker 1993). On occasion footprints can reveal a record of dynamic activity that could never be deduced from anatomy or palaeoenvironment. The Laetoli case reveals a fairly mundane activity - walking across a flat, wet ashfield, but does give insights into group structure (Tuttle 1987). A great deal more has been learned about many aspects of dinosaur biology from studying their prints (Gillete and Lockley 1989). But what can be learned from human prints from later time periods? The prints made by early hominids over 3 million years ago are eerily like those of modern people and the structure of the modern human foot is not so dissimilar from that of 1.9 million year old small hominids from Olduvai (Day and Napier 1964). *Homo erectus*, the species generally regarded as being antecedent to our own, is extremely close to us in practically all parts of its postcranial skeleton (Walker and Leakey 1993). It is virtually certain, therefore, that the foot of the Swanscombe early *Homo sapiens* had a structure identical to that of the modern human foot. What, then, would we learn from footprints that were almost certainly identical to those of modern people? We could tell if they had footwear. If the prints were of the complete foot we could estimate their stature with accuracy. If only partial prints were known the accuracy of such estimates would be less. We could tell, if the prints were extremely large, that some of these people were tall. But we could not tell, if the prints were small, that some of them were small, because of the inability to distinguish adult from childs' footprints. We could tell, if there were the tracks of a dramatic confrontation, something about interactions with other animals or humans.

P.Davis & A.Walker

THE SWANSCOMBE PRINT

The Swanscombe print, if shown to be a partial anterior print of a human, would have been made by a medium sized early member of our own species. For the reasons given above, it would tell us nothing about the stature of the population. If it proved to be a human footprint then the individual did not have footwear on at the time. This is probably not surprising, but it does not tell us that these populations never had footwear, because although some of us wear shoes and sandals, people in many societies today do not wear shoes. The print is an isolated one. There is not even a trail from which to estimate stride length, much less a record of a dramatic confrontation.

A small series of experiments were carried out in which prints were made under various conditions of substrate hardness and with varying speed and foot posture. This was undertaken solely to see if anything like the Swanscombe print could be produced by a human foot on damp loam. Because the experiments were not exhaustive and because varying the consistency of the loam proved to be difficult, only a tentative conclusion can be reached. This conclusion is that in order to produce the Swanscombe print a foot would have to be placed and moved in a contorted way that this researcher at least finds impossible to duplicate. A case might be made that at the time the upper surface of the loam was so inhomogeneous that the foot was forced into a contorted position, but this sort of special pleading is not convincing. The SC69 E6 print is extremely deep anteriorly and there is no trace of a heel print. This can only be accomplished by running on tip-toe, but this always produces a strong impression for the head of the first metatarsal. This is conspicuously absent in the Swanscombe print.

CONCLUSION

It is extremely unlikely that the print from Swanscombe was made by a human, and even if it were, there is nothing much useful to be found out from it. It may also be that it is a compound (that is two or more superimposed) hoof or foot print of other animals or even snout mark.

185

14. THE OSTRACOD FAUNA FROM THE WAECHTER EXCAVATIONS

Eric Robinson

Over the years of excavation by Waechter, Wymer and Gladfelter, several samples were taken from the exposures of the Lower Loam to add an ostracod fauna to the exceptionally well-preserved macrofauna, notably the examples of *Potamida Littoralis* with the two valves still articulated suggesting the minimum of disturbance of an ecosystem of fossilisation. Many spot samples confirmed this assumption, the ostracod fauna being a near-perfect association of the smallest juvenile moult stages with the valves of mature individuals. This attests to a low energy, virtually still water environment for the silty loams, which is the sediment infill of the visible channels within the gravels and sands of the site - a deduction to be drawn from the size distribution and preservation of the ostracod, irrespective of their taxonomy.

Invariably, the samples regularly consisted of an abundance of one species, *Scottia browniana* (Jones), which went some way to confirming the first deduction. In the present day *Scottia* is a genus which swarms in marshy fen environments, including the marsh fringes to the Lower Danube in Bulgaria (Danielopol and McKenzie 1977) where it often forms the dominant species in a low-diversity fauna. In the fossil record, *Scottia browniana* similarly dominated the fauna recovered from the Sugworth Cromerian site in Oxfordshire (Shotton 1980). In early discussions of the Swanscombe site, the main contribution from the ostracod faunal record was of stagnant virtually still-water environmental conditions.

Following the clearing of the site towards its present condition as a conserved site (June 1985), the opportunity was taken to resample a short profile through the Lower Loam in the lower part of the Pit, close to a newly established pond. About 70 cm were available for sampling from a low bluff close to the path, with a visible contact with the top of the Lower Gravel below. The location was close to section H, where Hubbard sampled for pollen studies (Waechter *et al.* 1971).

Four bulk samples were taken (each approximately 2 kg) from base to top, each representing a channel sample through some 20-25 cm of the total profile. These samples were easy to disaggregate in water, were washed and wet-sieved, and the ostracod picked from the dried residues down to mesh size 120 (63 µ). The following fauna was obtained and is recorded as number of valves (v) or carapaces (c) when the two valves of the living animal remain articulated after fossilisation. The other notation records adult valves (A) or earlier instars in the life history counting backward from adult, A-I, A-II to as small a stage as A-IV which may be a specimen as small as 0.20 mm.

DISCUSSION

These samples added a diversity to the record from Swanscombe and the Lower Loam which allow a broadening of the environmental interpretation and comparison with other sites and present-day ecology. Each sample contained some ten species, all of them freshwater in their habitat. This is a relatively low species diversity compared with an average lake or pond in a temperate climate, but each species carries signals which lead to a conclusion based upon the facts given below.

Candona neglecta has often been taken as signifying cold temperature but this seems unreasonable as the species is to be found in the soft substrates of most ponds or lakes in Britain. By mode of life, the species is a burrower, commonly found in bottom sediments rich in organic matter such as rotting leaf litter. Juvenile moults and both male and female adults present in most samples indicate a complete life history and an *in situ* role for this species.

Sample 1 (lowermost sample)

Candona neglecta Sars	A-III 5v A male 1v A female 4v
Cypridopsis vidua (Muller)	A-III 2v A-II 2v A-I 8v A 1v
Cyprinotus salinus (Brady)	A-I 2v A 2v
Darwinula stevensoni (Brady and Robertson)	10v
Herpetocypris reptans	A-IV 1v A-III 4v A-II 1v fragts A
Ilyocypris bradyi Sars	A-II 2v A-I 8v A 3v
Ilyocypris gibba (Ramdohr)	3v
Prionocypris serrata (Norman)	A-I 6v A 3v
Scottia browniana (Jones)	A-III 4v A-II 5v A-I 19v A 48v 1c

Sample 2

Candona neglecta Sars	A-I 3v A 5v 1c female
Candona sp	A-I 1v A 1v 1c
Cypridopsis vidua (Muller)	A-II 7v A-I 3v 1c
Darwinula stevensoni (Brady and Robertson)	14v 2c
Herpetocypris reptans (Baird)	3v fragts
Ilyocypris bradyi Sars	A-II 3v A-I 5v A 5v
Ilyocypris gibba (Ramdohr)	2v
Ilyocypris inermis Kaufmann	A-II 2v A-I 2v A 3v
Prionocypris serrata (Norman)	A-IV 1v A-III 1v A-II 3v A-I 3v A 10v
Scottia browniana (Jones)	A-IV 1v A-III 6v A-II 2v A-I 7v A 46v 4c

Sample 3

Candona neglecta Sars	A-II 3v A-I 1v A female 2v
Cypridopsis vidua (Muller)	A-I 1v A 7v
Darwinula stevensoni (Brady and Robertson)	13v 2c
Herpetocypris reptans (Baird)	A-I 4v A fragts
Ilyocypris bradyi Sars	8v
Ilyocypris gibba (Ramdohr)	1v
Ilyocypris inermis Kaufmann	2v
Prionocypris serrata (Norman)	A-I 2v A 2v
Scottia browniana (Jones)	A-IV 1v A-III 1v A-II 6v A-I 20v A 36v 2c

Sample 4 (uppermost sample)

Candona neglecta Sars	A-III 2v A-II 1v A 1v female
Cypridopsis vidua (Muller)	1v 1c
Darwinula stevensoni (Brady and Robertson)	1v
Ilyocypris bradyi Sars	4v
Ilyocypris inermis Kaufmann	3v
Scottia browniana (Jones)	A-III 5v A-II 4v A-I 6v A 6v

Cypridopsis vidua by contrast is an active swimming ostracod, swimming above the sediment interface in ponds and lakes and even capable of swimming in flowing waters of a modest current strength (Nüchterlein 1969; Absolon 1973). Here at Swanscombe it could be taken to indicate open water conditions in a ponded drainage possibly fringed by reed beds. Other fauna could as easily have lived in temporary pools or water films covering water meadows. Size ranges indicate an *in situ* species as opposed to a washed-in element.

Cyprinotus salinus is a species of springs and ponds with a slight saline character, but does not signify the salinity of tidal estuaries. The salinity hinted at in the specific name could be the salinity of mineral springs emerging from the Chalk or the older gravels, and need not be a sodium saltiness. An estuarine connection for the Swanscombe site, linking it with a contemporary Thames, would have involved the presence of the species *Cyprideis torosa* found in incursions to the sequences at Marks Tey and at Clacton in Middle Pleistocene deposits. No such records have been found at Swanscombe.

Darwinula stevensoni is a relatively small ostracod species (valve length less than 0.60 mm in the adult) which occurs in abundance in the banks of ponds, lakes and river channels, where it burrows into soft sediments or organic litter. The occurrence of the species here at Swanscombe with juveniles associated with adults, and with a proportion of carapaces occurring in addition to isolated valves speak of quiet, undisturbed sedimentation and no subsequent erosion. The two valves of *Darwinula* are without any real hingement or articulation, so that on death and the decay of the muscle tissues, the two valves readily fall apart. Their presence in these samples also gives a hint of a margin to the channel or water body within which the Lower Loam accumulated.

Herpetocypris reptans is a large ostracod species, ranging up to 2 mm in length as an adult making it a 'giant' among ostracods. At the same time, its large valves are most delicate and very prone to fragmentation by compaction during sedimentation and lithification of deposits. It is also easy to damage in the processing of samples. For all these reasons, the preservation of adults and the association of juveniles allows some assessment of the energy levels of sedimentation which can be useful lines of reasoning. By habit, the species either clambers upon weed or burrows into soft substrates. The short antennal bristles equip it for these modes of life, but are ineffective for swimming or free movement in an open water setting. It's presence at Swanscombe in the Lower Loam back up the evidence provided by *Candona* and *Scottia* quite usefully.

Scottia browniana is a species which has a similar ecology to *Herpetocypris*, extending to environments which could be called fen and marsh rather than just the margins of openwater lakes. The living species *Scottia pseudobrowniana* (the species *S. browniana* became extinct at the end of the Middle Pleistocene) has been recorded from the Danube marshes where it is associated with rafts of floating vegetation amidst reed beds ((Danielopol and McKenzie 1977). It also occurs in sedgy pools and lochans on Bute. As a fossil *Scottia* species can occur in calc-tufa deposits in which the vegetation could be thickets of *Chara*. *Scottia browniana* was recorded from the Cromerian Sugworth Channel in Oxfordshire, where the interpretation was of an abandoned cut off of an old Thames water course (Robinson 1980). Closer to Swanscombe, *Scottia browniana* was the main element in the fauna of limited diversity from the Clacton Channel of Hoxnian age as exposed in the Butlins site, Clacton (Wymer and Singer 1970).

Prionocypris serrata is a large ostracod species, with habits similar to those recorded for *Herpetocypris* above, namely as a plant-clambering form, found in shallow water bodies. From the type locality in County Durham, the setting could be water meadows subject to temporary flooding (Norman 1861), an environment which always seems unusual for a larger-than-average ostracod (adult length c. 1.65 mm), but demonstrating that ostracods often live crawling in little more than wet grass and can go into a resting phase akin to hibernation when conditions dry out. The species has been recorded as fossils from the sluggish channel deposits of the Pleistocene Thames from Isleworth (Kerney *et al.* 1982), from the Ismaili site in South Kensington (Coope *et al.* in press) and from Marsworth (Green *et al.* 1984).

Ilyocypris bradyi, I.gibba and *I.inermis* are all non-swimming forms thus confirming the general impression conveyed by other species that this was a stagnant pond-like environment rather than a flowing water setting. Ilyocyprids either clamber amongst aquatic vegetation or burrow into a soft substrate after the fashion of candonids. In the Swanscombe samples, they occur with a range of growth stages which indicate that they make up a life assemblage as fossilised rather than an inwashed element in the fauna. This is confirmed by the excellent preservation of the delicately ornamented surface and marginal spines.

In summary, the ostracod fauna from the Lower Loam could well represent an abandoned meander channel marginal to a sluggish river. The material filling visible channel forms being a low energy infill following an initial erosional phase. Reviewing the balance of species from bottom sample to top, the conditions could be judged to have become more sedgy and overgrown with time, the open water conditions favouring *Cypridopsis* giving place to a more closed environment in which *Scottia* became dominant overall. At this point, the conditions could correspond to those of the Sugworth Channel of the Cromerian Thames in Oxfordshire as described by Shotton (Shotton *et al.* 1980). The absence of the accepted lake indicator species such as *Limnocythere* and *Cytherissa* differentiate the Swanscombe site from the undoubted lake basins of Marks Tey and Hoxne where both join with the species listed here to make up a more diversified fauna. At the same time, the fauna from Swanscombe has a higher diversity than the fauna from the Clacton Channel which is virtually a totally *Scottia* dominated association.

In looking for an age for the Swanscombe Lower loam, the one species which has an age significance is *Scottia browniana*. This species was first described by T.R. Jones from Hoxnian interglacial sands from Copford in Essex, close to the fuller interglacial record of Marks Tey (Jones 1850). Subsequently, the record of the species was extended to include Upper Pleistocene and even recent sites before Kempf was able to show in a critical review that two distinct species had been confused. True *Scottia browniana* consistent and conspecific with specimens deposited in the collections of the Natural History Museum are indeed confined to Lower and Middle Pleistocene sites, whilst younger records proved to belong to a new species, *Scottia pseudobrowniana* extending through many Ipswichian sites and into modern fens and Scottish lochans (Kempf 1971.) The distinction has proved to be a very useful one, allowing the validation of several Hoxnian and older deposits including the Clacton Channel and the channel deposits at Barling, also in Essex (Bridgland 1988). it also contributes to an age determination for channel deposits at Stanton Harcourt in Oxfordshire (Briggs *et al.* 1985). One of the fullest accounts of a *Scottia*-dominated fauna is that for the Freshwater Bed at West Runton, Norfolk (De Dekker 1979), but here the associated ostracod fauna give an undoubted Cromerian age to the deposit partly reflected in the channel deposits of the Little Oakley site close to Harwich (*in* Preece *et al.* 1990).

Finer definition of Middle Pleistocene time depends upon the various species of *Ilyocypris* and *Limnocythere* which can occur in the wider range of environments associated with lake basins and spring sites, settings not represented by what was sampled from the Lower Loam at Swanscombe.

15. THE PALYNOLOGICAL STUDIES FROM THE WAECHTER EXCAVATIONS

Richard Hubbard

INTRODUCTION

Palynological sampling was carried out in August 1971 during the Waechter excavations. Five main locations were sampled, namely:

Lower Gravel, on the south face of square A3, and Section H (Figure 15.1)
Lower Loam, south east corner of square B3 (Figure 15.1)
Lower Middle Gravel, squares C4 and B4 (Figure 15.1)
Upper Middle Gravel lower part only in Section G (Figure 6.2)
Upper Loam, in Section LA1 (Figure 6.7)

Pollen was extracted by a modified version of Frenzel's technique (Frenzel 1964) similar to that devised by Bastin and Coûteaux (1966). After acid and alkaline digestions, the sample is shaken with a saturated solution of potassium cadmium iodide (of specific gravity 2.0) in which pollen floats and mineral matter does not. Immediately after the initial decalcification stage, a known quantity of exotic pollen is introduced to each sample so that extraction efficiencies and absolute pollen concentrations can be determined. Pollen floating in the dense liquid after centrifugation is collected on glass-fibre filters in Hirsch funnels. The filters are then destroyed by treatment with hydrofluoric acid, and the residue is stained and mounted. (Traditionally, the pollen is collected on paper filters which have to be destroyed by classic acetolytic methods. Unfortunately this artificially fossilises any modern contaminant pollen grains that may be present.) All apparatus is pollen-sterilised with concentrated chromic or nitric acid before use to ensure that accidental contamination with modern pollen is reduced to a minimum.

Juvigné (1975) has presented evidence that appears to indicate that ancient pollen grains are much denser than recent ones. Her findings are at odds with my own experiments, which showed that free Middle Pleistocene pollen had a specific gravity of about 1.8. This figure is only fractionally higher than that of acetolysed modern pollen exines. One factor involved is the chemical treatment, which affects the size of palynomorphs, and presumably influences their density as well. A much more important consideration is whether the pollen grains were freed from the matrix by preliminary digestions in acid and alkali: if the pollen grains were still attached to the matrix, it would explain why they appeared to have densities similar to that of the minerals.

RESULTS

Lower Gravel

The palynological record from the Lower Gravel (Figure 15.2) is patchy and erratic, some samples showing the low pollen concentrations (and minimal pollen sums) to be expected of a coarse, waterlaid deposit, while others are surprisingly rich and are believed to record temporary land surfaces. The pollen spectra reflect a very open facies of an ordinary early temperate interglacial environment (Zone IIb of Turner and West's 1968 nomenclature). The presence of *Hedera*, like the snail *Lauria*, testifies

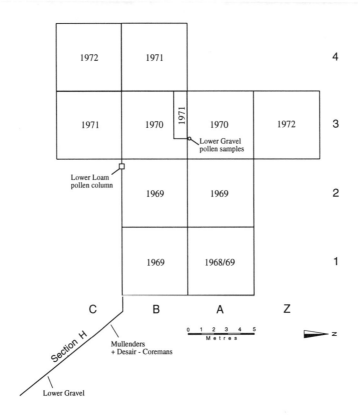

Fig. 15.1. Location of the pollen samples taken in squares A1 to C4

to a mild climate (Iversen, 1944). One sample (33) from 20 cm below the Lower Loam in Section H yielded what appeared to be a fragment of a pollen grain of the unidentified plant named 'Type X' by Turner (1970). If correct, the identification would support the conclusion that the Lower Gravel belongs to the Hoxnian interglacial (*sensu stricto*) but the record must be treated with reserve.

Lower Loam

The results of the pollen analyses from the Lower Loam are shown in Figure 15.2. The difficulties of interpretation of the palynological data will be discussed in more detail below. The essential points are that, although obscured by differential destruction effects inflating the contribution of *Pinus* at the expense of *Quercus* and *Ulmus*, a mixed oak forest with hazel is present throughout the profile: the presence of pollen of 'Type X' and glochidia of *Azolla filiculoides* allow correlation with the Hoxnian interglacial (*sensu stricto*) with some confidence. The change from *Alnus* domination to a predominance of grass and herb pollen about 60 cm from the top of the Lower Loam, is not believed to record a hydrosere, but a change of pollen catchment regime. Also the undisturbed tree-pollen composition during this period of open conditions at the top of Lower Loam show that the episode has no connection with the open conditions of the East Anglian sub-Zone HoIIc (HoIId of West 1966; Turner 1970), the whole sequence being placed within sub-Zone HoIIb. Nor should it be thought that the palynological change in the upper part of the Lower Loam is attributable to the soil-pollen profile that would have been associated with the *sol lessivé* developed on its surface: such pollen profiles rarely extend to half a metre in depth, and therefore would almost certainly be removed by the erosion episode which truncated that soil profile.

R.Hubbard

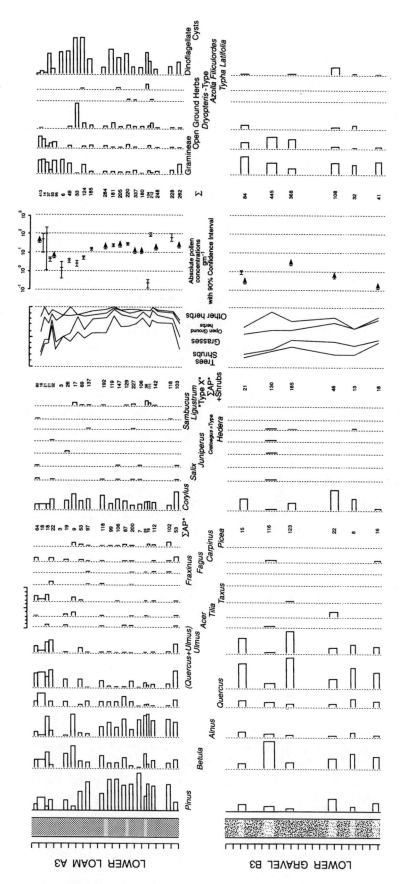

Fig. 15.2. Pollen diagram for the Lower Gravel and Lower Loam

193

The sand lenses in the Lower Loam provide some interesting palynological insights. These sand horizons are the basal fillings of stream channels cut into the Lower Loam (Conway 1970, 90). Three samples (49, 52' and 52) correspond to these horizons; and samples 52' and 52 are particularly interesting as they comprise the sand and the bed of the channel on which the sand was deposited. The pollen of aquatic plants is very rare, except in these stream-bed samples, where *Typha* tetrads are found. Stream channels like this are exactly where *Typha* (cat's tail) likes to grow. *Typha* pollen is found in the sands, but not in the Loam on which the sand was deposited. The tree-pollen spectra from the contiguous samples are, however, virtually identical. These samples, therefore, tell us that the Lower Loam samples can tell very specific and appropriate botanical stories, that they can be correlated on a regional basis even when the herbaceous component is telling a story of extremely local significance; and that even when such coarse-textured matrices are involved, pollen neither moves nor (when carefully sampled) is contaminated by modern air-borne pollen.

Lower Middle Gravel

Only two samples have been analysed from the Lower Middle Gravel. The sedimentology and the aquatic molluscan fauna indicate that the unit was laid down by clear, rapidly-flowing water. Consequently, the absolute pollen concentration is very low (c. 1 grain/gm). Even when the pollen counts are pooled, the pollen sum is only 33 grains. Fortunately, there is no evidence of differential destruction of pollen. With information as scanty as this, one can only draw very generalised conclusions with any degree of certainty.

The pollen assemblage is similar to those from the Lower Gravel. The pollen reflects an open environment, with grass and herbs contributing 75% of the pollen, with the trees and shrubs clearly reflecting temperate conditions. The pollen spectra appear to reflect some kind of interglacial Zone II environment. As is the case with the Lower Gravel pollen spectra, the openness of the environment is almost certainly more apparent than real, as it seems to be a consequence of the prevailing pollen catchment regime (see below).

A comparable tree-pollen spectrum, based on a much more substantial count, was recovered from one of the clay pebbles stratified in the basal Lower Middle Gravel in square C4 (Figure 15.3). The pollen spectrum in this sample differed from those of the surrounding matrices by its lower proportion of herbaceous pollen types and lower percentages of *Corylus*. Being derived, this sample can at best give a *terminus post quem* date for the aggradation of the Lower Middle Gravel. The pollen spectrum does not support the possibility of the clay balls being reworked weathered Lower Loam. In fact fossils from these pebbles, like those from comparable triaxial clay pebbles found in the base of the Lower Loam (Conway 1971, 62), show the clay to be of Eocene age. The pollen spectrum is very clearly not Eocene, however, and the likeliest explanation of the finds is that a Pleistocene weathering profile on an exposure of London Clay was being eroded. We have no guarantee that this weathering is the same as the Stage II land surface on the top of the (Stage I) Lower Loam. (This decalcified surface, bearing animal footprints and trodden-in snails, is the first episode of the second sedimentary cycle. Attempts to recover pollen from the surface were made using monoliths preserving footprints. The attempts were foiled by abundant fungal material, apparently associated with the exposure of the surface, either during excavation or in geological times.) Since the arboreal pollen spectrum in this clay ball sample is closely comparable with the underlying spectra, we may conclude that either admixture of later pollen was minor, or that the arboreal pollen rain of the later component was very similar to that at the top of Stage Id. As the evidence of the molluscan and mammalian fossils corroborates the exiguous direct palynological record, it seems not unreasonable to infer that the Lower Middle Gravel was laid down in Zone II of an interglacial.

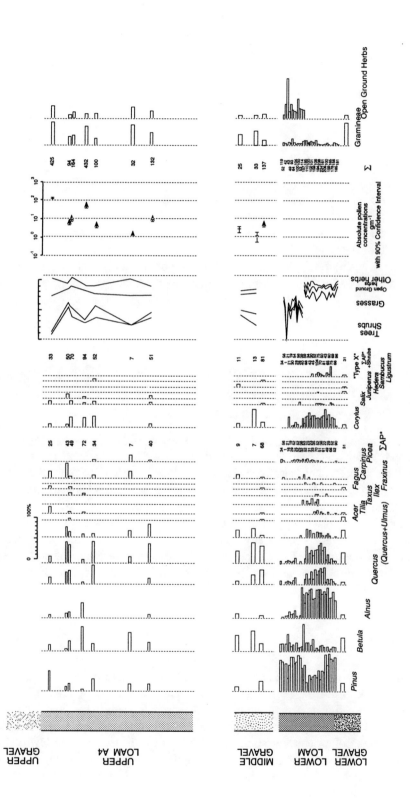

Fig. 15.3. Pollen diagram for Lower Gravel, Lower Loam, Middle Gravel and Upper Loam

Upper Middle Gravel

So far, only one small sample from the Upper Middle Gravel has yielded enough pollen to give any useful indication of the climatic conditions. Allowing for the statistical implications of the low pollen sum involved, the spectrum from this sample (Figure 15.3) is closely comparable with the pollen contents of the Lower Middle Gravel, suggesting an interglacial Zone llb age; and corroborating Conway's deduction (1972, 83-4) that the distinction between the Lower and Upper Middle Gravels is spurious.

Upper Loam

Although pollen has been obtained from the Upper Loam, fungal spores and algal material are frequently encountered, making pollen-analysis difficult. Preliminary studies (Figure 15.3) indicated that the bulk of the Upper Loam in LA1 belongs to the temperate mixed-oak forest Zone IIb of an interglacial, a conclusion supported by the presence of pollen of the thermophile *Hedera* and of the frost-sensitive *Ilex* (Iversen 1944). The high non-tree pollen contribution to the pollen spectra seems to be attributable, once again, to the fluviatile pollen catchment regime involved. A single sample from the top 50 cm of the Upper Loam shows an abrupt and marked increase in *Carpinus*, suggesting an unconformity and deposition during Zone III of the interglacial. *Picea* does not increase and *Abies* is absent.

DISCUSSION

The palynological evidence is controversial for some people, since pollen analyses are not usually carried out on relatively coarse, calcareous, water-laid sediments. In particular, Turner (1985) has argued that ordinary 'reliable' pollen analyses involve samples containing tens of thousands of pollen grains in every gram of matrix, and that the pollen in samples like those from Swanscombe, where the pollen concentrations are hundreds, or tens, or less of grains per gram, is the residual trace of far higher concentrations that were originally present. The extremely high rates of attrition implied by this interpretation cause him to doubt whether any trust can be placed in pollen recovered at concentrations of a few thousand grains per gram or less. The crucial issue is the 'meaning' of pollen concentrations, with the mobility of pollen grains, and the mechanisms involved in their destruction as secondary problems. These problems are discussed below.

Catchment regime

A crucial element in understanding pollen concentrations, and the interpretation of any pollen profile, is a knowledge of the origin of the pollen. In a classic study, Rhona Peck (1973) showed that about 90% of the pollen in lake deposits was brought in by the streams feeding the lake. This pollen, in turn, is derived from the land surfaces by sheet erosion after heavy rainfall has saturated the soil. The streams showed particularly high pollen concentrations as the water level rose to flood levels. Pollen landing from the air - 'pollen rain' in the classical sense - accounts for no more than about 10% of the influx. Her conclusions have been confirmed repeatedly in the subsequent decades. As an example, we may note that absolute pollen influx studies of peats and lake sediments of the present interglacial show that lakes accumulate pollen at 10-15 times the rate of peats (which mainly trap air-borne pollen). Tauber (1977) has concluded that water transport must account for at least 50% of the pollen influx of a lake set in woodland.

It could be argued that the fundamental difference between the palynology of acid lacustrine sediments and alkaline fluviatile deposits such as those at Swanscombe is that in the first case a minor component of uncertain size may be *in situ* pollen, while in the latter case one can be reasonably certain that virtually all the pollen is derived. On the other hand, the short mean lifetime of pollen grains in the well-oxygenated conditions that abound in alkaline environments means that most of the pollen there is contemporary. In contrast, where conditions of pollen preservation are good, there is plenty of non-contemporary pollen to be reworked - which is a contributory reason why their pollen concentrations are so high.

Relatively little work has been done on the effect on pollen spectra of different forms of water transport, and absolutely none on deposits of as coarse a texture as those at Swanscombe. Crowder and Cuddy (1973) studied a river system in Canada, comparing the woodland through which the river flowed with pollen caught in moss clumps from various points between the river's source and its mouth. These included pollen spectra from a mire at its head, river water, alluvium from near its mouth, and sediments from Lake Ontario into which the river debouched. In the light of Peck's work, it is not surprising that Crowder and Cuddy found no simple relationship between the pollen spectra and the vegetation beyond a rough and vague correspondence. The proportion of herbaceous pollen types, however, showed marked (if inexplicable) differences between different contexts. The river water and alluvial spectra had a very low tree and shrub pollen component and (most perversely) very little pollen of aquatic plants. In both respects, the parallel with the Lower Gravel, Middle Gravel and Upper Loam pollen analyses is clear.

The Lower Loam is obviously a somewhat different case. Although obscured by differential destruction (see below) there is a general trend for *Alnus* dominance to be replaced by grass and herb pollen. This superficially resembles a classic hydrosere; but the abrupt *Alnus* peaks at depths of 15-20 and 50-55 cm in the Lower Loam indicate that this interpretation is incorrect. It is suggested that some kind of lacustrine pollen catchment régime is being succeeded by a fluviatile one, as might happen if a river were silting up the freshwater but tidal part of an estuary. The *Alnus* peaks seem to record occasional isolated flooding episodes of the kind that the Thames Barrier is designed to prevent. Because the *Alnus* pollen largely reflects changes in the pollen catchment régime, it has been excluded from the pollen sum used in constructing the arboreal pollen diagram for the Lower Loam.

Interpretation of the pollen diagrams in terms of the catchment régimes thus leads to similar conclusions to those indicated by the ostracods from the Lower Loam; and reconciles several lines of evidence (such as why *in situ* artefacts come to be found in a water-laid sediment) in an agreeably economical way.

The high values for *Ulmus* pollen and the occasional preponderance of *Ulmus* over *Quercus* also seem to be connected with the alkaline fluviatile nature of the catchment régime. These phenomena were also encountered at Caddington (Hubbard, *in* Sampson 1978) and are considered in more detail in that publication. Since the two taxa seem to be complementary, for the purposes of chronological and environmental interpretation and for comparison with other diagrams, a composite (*Quercus* + *Ulmus*) percentage is plotted in the tree pollen diagrams. It may be noted that pollen analyses from the brickearths at Caddington also showed a progressive increase in the herbaceous pollen component comparable with the Lower Loam results, and which likewise is believed to reflect changes not in environment, but in the pollen catchment régime.

Polliniferous deposits whose formation involved moving water reflect processes almost as different from those of peats as those of soil-profiles. In particular, since almost all the pollen arrived by the same process as the mineral component, any interpretation of the pollen concentrations in such sediments must take their granulometry into account. Since Stanley (1969) pointed out that an 'average' fossil pollen grain behaves hydrodynamically as though it were a 5-10 μm quartz particle, a detailed study of pollen concentrations in relation to the proportion of sediment in the 7 phi size grade is called for. No such investigations have ever been made, but the famous tendency of silty-clayey samples to be most palynologically productive is explained by the relationship. The relationship between sedimentology and pollen concentration is well illustrated by the contiguous samples 52' and 52 (between 1.50 and 1.55 cm deep in the Lower Loam). The samples represent the alluvium, and the sand deposited in an evanescent channel cut into it; the spectra are very similar but the concentrations differ by a factor of about 300.

Equally, there are certain anomalous samples that contain extraordinarily high pollen concentrations (for instance, the samples at depths of 50-65 cm and 171-176 cm in the Lower Gravel). It seems likely that these samples are from temporary land surfaces, and in these cases direct rain-out of pollen from the air may play a major part in the catchment régime. If this interpretation were correct, the pollen-spectra from these samples should reflect the vegetation in the immediate vicinity of the site, for the results of soil pollen analyses seem to be heavily biased in favour of plants growing within a radius of a few hundred metres (at most) of the sampling site (Dimbleby 1957). If the land surfaces were exposed briefly and intermittently, it might not be surprising if the resultant pollen spectra were somewhat unusual and showed inconsistent patterns suggestive of local over-representation of various pollen types.

Mobility in a matrix

Any discussion of the meaning of pollen concentrations assumes that pollen grains are immobile in a matrix. If they were free to move, the pollen in any sample would merely reflect transient factors, like the concentration of commuters in a traffic jam. Experiments, however, have shown that pollen grains are bound to the body of material comprising the sample. Even a fresh hyrax dropping only liberated about 12% of its pollen contents after 20 minutes of vigorous boiling and stirring in water (Hubbard and Sampson 1993). Similar experiments have been carried out on acid and alkaline soil samples, with similar results. Although no such experiments have been reported using arid soils, lake muds, or peats, there are grounds for suspicion that pollen grains are no more 'free' in them. At Swanscombe, the sharp definition of the Stage Id-Ie boundary discovered by Mullenders and Desair-Coremans, the abrupt *Typha* and *Alnus* peaks, and the clear palynological distinction between the Lower Loam and Lower Gravel show that vertical and lateral movement of pollen within the deposits under the influence of groundwater percolation or other such agencies is (at worst) less than the resolution of the sampling, even in such a coarse-textured matrix as that of the Lower Gravel, and is probably non-existant. The only source of movement of pollen that needs to be considered here is bioturbation. Learned discussions in the palynological literature about pollen movement in response to osmotic water pressure are almost certainly irrelevant.

Differential destruction

A final complication of the Swanscombe pollen analyses concerns differential destruction. It is clear that some of the pollen spectra from the Lower Loam are distorted by a degradation process to which *Pinus* pollen is particularly resistant and those of *Quercus* and *Ulmus* are particularly sensitive. A recalculation of Desair-Coremans and Mullenders' results, excluding *Alnus* from the tree-pollen sum, strongly implies that the lowest six samples in their pollen column from section H are also affected by differential destruction. That differential destruction of pollen is not caused by transport in calcareous water is shown by the intermittent occurrence of the effect within the Lower Loam and in the Swanscombe pollen spectra in general. Similarly, pollen analyses from calcareous but otherwise conventional contexts in Britain and elsewhere in Europe by no means invariably display signs of differential destruction. Differential destruction seems to occur subsequent to the deposition of pollen in certain circumstances of subaerial exposure that are not well understood, but which are suspected of being connected with percolating oxygenated groundwater.

Destruction of pollen can take place very rapidly in calcareous environments. Dimbleby (Dimbleby and Evans 1974, 119) has suggested that destruction can sometimes be completed within a matter of years; and it seems that this may, in fact, be a simplifying factor in interpreting pollen analyses like those from Swanscombe. While pollen does not seem to be adversely affected by alkaline water and thus can be carried very long distances, its lifetime when stranded and subjected to weathering may be very short. One may compare this with the implications of the excellent conditions of pollen preservation displayed by the environments in which palynological investigations are usually carried out. Thus the relative unimportance of earlier pollen (as, for example, in the case of the spectrum from the London Clay ball in the Lower Middle Gravel) may be directly attributable to the calcareous environment involved.

CONCLUSION

Setting aside the distorting effects of differential destruction of pollen, there is no good reason for treating the palynological evidence from Swanscombe as any less legitimate than the record from other lacustrine and estuarine contexts. Equally, there seems to be no reason to believe that there are fundamental differences in the geographical extent of the pollen catchment or of the extent of the chronological mixing in the influx of pollen. There are good reasons to suspect that some of the pollen spectra from the Lower Gravel are vastly more precise, both in the chronological and regional senses, than the majority of 'conventional' pollen analyses. An unprejudiced reader, therefore, will see that the pollen analyses from Swanscombe are basically reliable. As Samuel Palmer said of Handel, 'no one but a professional musician is unable to understand him'.

Nothing that has been published in the last decade or so inclines me to revise the opinions and conclusions I published in 1982. Indeed, what new facts there are tend to confirm the accuracy of the guesses I had to make then.

16. THE FLINT INDUSTRIES FROM THE WAECHTER EXCAVATIONS

Nick Ashton and John McNabb

INTRODUCTION

The Swanscombe flint industries from the Waechter excavations derive principally from the main excavation area (squares Z3, A1-A3, B1-B4, C2-C4) and from the 1968 Trench B. The artefacts from Trench B are listed in Table 16.1, but it is the assemblages from the main area that form the subject of this report.

The artefacts from the main area have been broadly divided into nine main assemblages on the basis of both context and height within a context. These consist of units 1 to 4 within the Lower Gravel, the midden towards the top of the Lower Gravel, the top of the Lower Gravel, the base of the Lower Loam, the knapping floor within the Lower Loam, the main body of the Lower Loam and finally the Lower Middle Gravel. Explanation of these divisions on the basis of the excavation notebooks, plans and sections is given in Chapter 5.

A thematic approach has been adopted, so that in the first part of the chapter, the condition, raw material and technology of the nine assemblages are compared and contrasted. In the last two sections of the chapter, refitting and spatial studies are examined in more detail, particularly in relation to the evidence from the Knapping Floor.

The artefacts have been studied by an amalgamation of the techniques used by McNabb (1992) and by Ashton (1992). Twelve attributes have been recorded for each flake and a more complex system has been developed for recording cores. This system broadly covers the three categories of condition, raw material and technology. Condition is recorded by abrasion, surface colouration (patination and staining) and surface appearance (gloss/matt). The second category, raw material, has been recorded by type, size (weight) and by the amount of cortex on dorsal surfaces (see Table 16.2).

The third and most important category is technology. The recording system is based on understanding the complex sequence of flake removals from the cores and describing this in a meaningful and comprehensible form (see Figure 16.1). The system is modified from that used on High Lodge (Ashton 1992) and consists of viewing the reduction of each core as one or more 'core episodes'. Each core episode consists of a series of flake removals that form a sequence and naturally follow on from each other. A core episode at its most basic level consists of one flake removal ('single removal' or type A). If further flakes are removed in the same direction as a sequence from a single or adjacent platforms in the same plane, then the core episode is described as 'parallel flaking' (type B).

A more complex core episode is 'alternate flaking' (type C). In its simple form it consists of one or more flakes being removed in a single direction, then the core being turned so that the proximal ends of the first set of removals act as the platforms for the second set of removals. A more complex form of 'alternate flaking' continues on from this sequence, with the core being turned back to its original position and the proximal ends of the second set of removals acting as the platform for a third set of removals. There may be several turns of the core in this way. These two forms have been termed 'simple alternate flaking' (type Ci) and 'complex alternate flaking' (type Cii). In effect, both simple and complex alternate flaking may incorporate several sequences of parallel flaking. Equally, a sequence that starts as parallel flaking may develop into simple alternate flaking and then into complex alternate flaking. These are termed Cip or Ciip.

A subcategory of the complex form is where a single flake is removed, the core turned, a flake removed from the first flake scar, the core turned again, a flake removed from the second scar, and so on, until at least four flakes are removed. This is termed 'classic alternate flaking' (type Ciic).

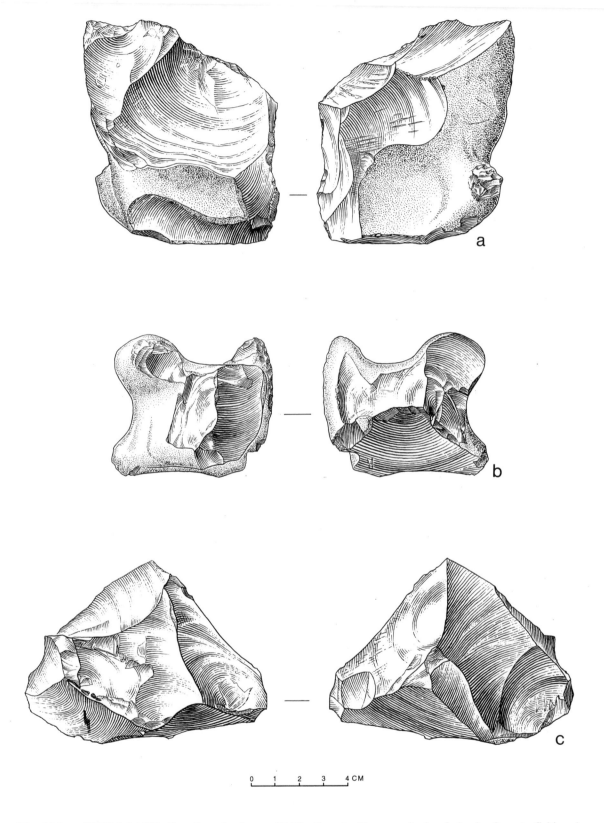

0 1 2 3 4 CM

Fig. 16.1. a. P1989.1-3.1537. Core from the Lower Middle Gravel with one episode of simple alternate flaking. b. P1989.1-3.1297. Core from the Lower Loam with one episode of simple alternate flaking and one episode of complex alternate flaking. c. P1989.1-3.1277. Core from the Lower Loam with one episode of complex alternate flaking, worked discoidally.

This system for describing cores provides a full understanding of the technology. On any one core there may be several core episodes. The first core episode has often been abandoned due to theoretical angle being reached, or new platforms being inadvertently created elsewhere. A different part of the core has then been selected and knapping proceeds. The interaction of two or three core episodes on a single core often makes the final interpretation difficult, but by unravelling the different sequences, the reduction processes can be more fully understood (see Appendix I).

	L.G. (layer 4)	L.L./L.G. (layer 3)	L.L. (layer 1)
Flakes	15	18	113
Cores	2	0	2
Flake tools	0	2	3

Table 16.1. Quantities of flakes, cores and flake tools from trench B.

Information	Recorded details
Condition	Abrasion, Surface colouration, Surface appearance
Raw Material	Type, Weight, Quantity of cortex on dorsal surface
Technology	Butt morphology, Dorsal scar pattern, Relict core edge

Table 16.2. The flake attributes that contribute to an understanding of condition, raw material and technology.

The flakes also contribute to an understanding of the core technology. Three attributes are particularly relevant and include butt morphology, dorsal scar pattern and the types of relict core edge. In the description of the technology they are used to confirm the findings on the cores. A full breakdown of these attributes is given in Appendix I.

The technology of the flake tools is also looked at, and is limited to a straight description. A detailed typological analysis of the flake tools was not attempted, as they are limited to mainly flaked flakes and retouched pieces where further subdivision would be both arbitrary and meaningless. The four bifaces are also described in this section. The quantities of flakes, cores and flake tools for each unit are given in Table 16.3.

CONDITION

The results of the analysis of condition show that the assemblages can be divided into three main groups, particularly on the basis of Tables 16.4 and 6 (see also Table 16.5). The first group consists of Lower Gravel units 1-4, the midden, the top of the Lower Gravel and the base of the Lower Loam. The second group consists of the Lower Loam, including knapping floor, and the third group is the Lower Middle Gravel.

The first group exhibits the characteristics that would be expected of material from sand and gravel contexts. They are moderately to heavily rolled, and are dominated by orange-brown and grey-green colorations. These surface colorations indicate a moderate amount of both staining and

The flint industries from the Waechter excavations

	L.G.4	L.G.3	L.G.2	L.G.1	Midden	Top L.G.	B.L.L.	K.Fl.	L.L.	L.M.G.
Flakes	269	140	190	145	127	61	33	72	115	122
Cores	39	10	13	9	9	5	3	0	7	13
Flake tools	21	12	11	15	10	1	5	6	6	7
Bifaces	0	0	0	1	0	0	0	0	0	3
Chips	0	6	1	0	0	10	0	176	15	6
Total	329	168	217	168	146	77	41	254	143	151

Table 16.3. Quantities of flakes, cores, flake tools, bifaces and chips in each archaeological unit.

	L.G.4	L.G.3	L.G.2	L.G.1	Midden	Top L.G.	B.L.L.	K.Fl.	L.L.	L.M.G.
Cond.										
1	5.3	2.0	0.5	0	3.6	3.2	2.6	94.9	43.0	5.4
2	50.0	40.8	46.3	34.8	56.3	66.1	71.5	5.1	35.5	72.9
3	44.7	57.2	53.2	65.2	40.1	30.6	26.3	0	21.5	21.7

Table 16.4. Percentages of abrasion type by archaeological unit. 1 = fresh condition, 2 = moderately rolled, 3 = very rolled.

	L.G.4	L.G.3	L.G.2	L.G.1	Midden	Top L.G.	B.L.L.	K.Fl.	L.L.	L.M.G.
Colour										
1	14.5	23.2	25.6	22.6	22.6	30.6	13.2	15.4	20.7	15.6
2	6.6	6.0	4.9	7.7	2.9	3.2	5.3	1.3	5.8	7.0
3	9.0	16.6	18.7	16.1	17.5	16.1	15.8	24.4	8.3	8.6
4	25.6	28.5	26.1	10.3	21.2	25.8	34.2	59.0	41.3	32.8
5	4.1	2.0	1.5	0	0.7	0	0	0	0	3.1
6	40.3	23.8	23.1	43.2	34.3	22.6	31.6	0	23.1	32.8
7	0	0	0	0	0.7	1.6	0	0	0.8	0

Table 16.5. Percentages of surface colorations on the flakes by stratigraphic unit. 1 = black, 2 = orange, 3 = brown, 4 = grey, 5 = yellow, 6 = green/grey, 7 = white.

204

patination. The surfaces also have a slight gloss, probably due to abrasion by sand. The inclusion of artefacts from the base of the Lower Loam in this group, might suggest that they were originally derived from the top of the Lower Gravel.

The second group is much fresher in condition. The knapping floor artefacts, in particular, have very little edge abrasion or rolling, often have a matt surface appearance, and are slightly patinated, but unstained, as indicated by the grey colouration. The patination suggests a degree of subaerial exposure which is supported by the sedimentology of the unit (see Chapter 7). The condition of the knapping floor artefacts confirms that they are an *in situ* archaeological entity. The main body of the Lower Loam material share some of these characteristics, although it is more varied in terms of abrasion and surface colouration. Episodes of channelling in the Lower Loam (see Chapter 7) may have incorporated more rolled material, producing a mixed assemblage.

The third group is dominated by moderately rolled pieces with surface colorations suggesting some patination and staining, and moderate surface abrasion. The reduced amount of rolling compared with the first group is probably a reflection of the slightly finer sand and gravel context.

RAW MATERIAL

The raw material is exclusively chalk flint, but as is apparent from the worn cortex, the majority is probably derived from a secondary source such as fluvial gravels. The size of the raw material is reflected by the weight of the artefacts and the degree of cortex. The weights of the flakes show enormous variation (see Table 16.7), but the mean weights are considerably higher for flakes from the Lower Gravel unit 4, and slightly higher for flakes from the Lower Middle Gravel. The weights of the cores show even more variations, but this is based on very small numbers with no meaningful pattern.

The problem arises as to whether the apparent size difference, of the flakes from the Lower Gravel unit 4, is due to human selection or simply size sorting by the river. The two agencies, however, would produce differences in the composition of the assemblages, in particular the flake to core ratio. If human selection was the reason, then it would be expected that larger nodules would not only produce larger flakes, but would also produce a higher ratio of flakes to cores. In contrast, a natural agency, such as fluvial size sorting, on the larger assemblage would produce a lower ratio of flakes to cores, the smaller flakes being winnowed away. The situation in the comparison of unit 4 with the remainder of the assemblages is that the flake to core ratio is considerably smaller for unit 4 (see Table 16.7) suggesting that it is fluvial size sorting that is responsible for the size difference. This is further confirmed by differences in the gravel size between the units, being generally larger in unit 4 (see Chapter 7). This may also explain the higher weights for flakes in the Lower Middle Gravel, confirmed by the low ratio of flakes to cores. This is supported by the interpretation of the Lower Middle Gravel as a lag gravel, with the smaller debitage washed away. The absence of cores in the knapping floor is discussed in more detail below.

The amount of cortex on the flake dorsal surfaces is also an indication of raw material size. There appears to be very little variation between the units, although there is possibly a lower proportion of cortex on flakes from the base of the Lower Loam and from the knapping floor (see Table 16.8). Lower proportions of cortex might suggest either the use of larger raw material or natural/human selection of non-cortical flakes. Study of the weights suggested that raw material size did not vary in these units. It can also be argued that material from the knapping floor is in relatively primary context, as indicated by the condition and refitting of the artefacts and by the nature of the sediment. This could be a hint, therefore, that the knapping floor represents the final stages of knapping, rather than the full reduction sequence, with slightly worked raw material being brought in from elsewhere (see also below). The lower proportion of cortex on flakes from the base of the Lower Loam is unlikely to be explicable in this way. It should also be noted that cores are totally absent from the knapping floor, suggesting that they have been humanly transported elsewhere (see below).

	L.G.4	L.G.3	L.G.2	L.G.1	Midden	Top L.G.	B.L.L	K.Fl.	L.L.	L.M.G.
Surface appear. 1	21.0	9.2	22.7	9.5	9.5	19.3	7.9	61.5	37.2	2.3
2	70.0	84.9	75.4	86.1	86.9	79.0	92.1	38.5	56.2	96.1
3	9.0	5.9	2.0	4.4	3.6	1.6	0	0	6.6	1.6

Table 16.6. Percentages of surface sheen on the flakes by stratigraphic unit. 1 = matt, 2 = slight sheen, 3 = gloss.

	L.G.4	L.G.3	L.G.2	L.G.1	Midden	Top L.G.	B.L.L	K.Fl.	L.L.	L.M.G.
Flakes mean wt.	75.3	41.5	47.7	43.0	37.6	18.9	24.63	51.2	42.7	61.1
S.dev.	106.2	35.7	35.1	45.5	41.6	17.2	22.15	82.7	68.6	77.4
Cores mean wt.	262.7	162.7	301.2	221.4	175.4	52.6	190.5	0	352.9	417.5
S.dev.	180.3	137.5	428.2	278.3	198.6	10.4	184.9	0	329.4	657.0
Flake/ core ratio	7.4	15.2	15.6	17.6	15.2	12.4	12.7	-	17.3	9.9

Table 16.7. Means and standard deviations of the weights of flakes and cores, and the flake/core ratio by stratigraphic unit.

	L.G.4	L.G.3	L.G.2	L.G.1	Midden	Top L.G.	B.L.L	K.Fl.	L.L.	L.M.G.
cortex 1	10.1	9.5	9.6	5.7	9.8	9.7	5.6	8.5	7.8	10.6
2	26.1	25.2	25.8	19.1	18.0	17.7	16.7	21.1	26.7	19.5
3	45.6	46.9	44.4	54.1	48.9	48.4	47.2	36.6	42.2	45.5
4	18.1	18.4	20.2	21.0	23.3	24.2	30.5	33.8	23.3	24.4

Table 16.8. Percentages of cortication categories on flakes by stratigraphic unit. 1 = wholly cortical, 2 = more than 50% cortex, 3 = less than 50% cortex, 4 = no cortex.

TECHNOLOGY

The core technology has been studied by three principal flake attributes and by detailed analysis of the cores (see above and Appendix I). While the cores provide the basis and key to a full understanding of the reduction processes, the flakes confirm those findings. Unfortunately, the low quantities of cores in many of the units, make it necessary to rely on the flakes for comparisons between units and for quantitative assessments, while the cores provide a more qualitative backup.

Flakes

The flake attributes that contribute to an understanding of the technology include butt morphology, dorsal scar patterns and relict core edges (see Appendix I). These are detailed in Tables 16.9 to 16.11 which indicate a remarkably consistent pattern right the way through the sequence with only minor variations. Each of the attributes is considered in more detail below.

The butts are generally wide, which together with the bulb and other flake characteristics (e.g. pronounced point and cone, thick flakes) are typical of hard hammer flaking (see Figure 16.2). The butt morphologies are dominated by plain butts (type 1) and by cortical butts (type 3), with only small percentages of other butt types (see Table 16.9). Facetted butts are totally absent, while butts indicating soft hammer flaking are only present in very small proportions in the Lower Middle Gravel.

Plain and dihedral butts are the types that would be expected from the use of both parallel and alternate flaking. The high proportion of plain as opposed to dihedral butts suggests that the knappers tended to favour flat surfaces as a platform, rather than the junction of two flake scars. Some of the butts have relict core edges, but these are examined in more detail below. Only occasionally is there any evidence of platform adjustment.

The dorsal scar patterns give further information about the core reduction processes. The patterns indicate that 80% of the flakes have removals which derive from either the proximal end and/or from one of the lateral edges (see Table 16.10 and Figure 16.2). This again would be expected from the use of both parallel and alternate flaking. It may also suggest that the core episodes normally occur as discrete units, and backs up the system of analysis. Occasionally where two core episodes have impinged on each other, flake removals from the distal end are present on the dorsal scar pattern.

A more accurate indication of the relative importance of the different types of core episodes lies in the study of the types of relict core edge. These are summarised by types 1 to 6 (see Table 16.11 and Figure 16.2). Types 1 to 3 (Figure 16.2a-b) indicate the removal of a previous core episode, in one case parallel flaking, and in the other two simple and complex alternate flaking. Types 4 to 6 (Figure 16.2c-e), on the other hand, indicate the current use of parallel flaking technique, or a change of flaking direction in either simple or complex alternate flaking.

The relative proportions of types 1 to 3 should be a genuine reflection of the use of the techniques. This suggests that simple and complex alternate flaking have been used two or three times more frequently than parallel flaking. This is also the conclusion reached from study of the cores (see below).

The same comparison can not be used for types 4 to 6. Type 4 flakes could be produced from either parallel flaking, or a sequence of parallel flaking within alternate flaking and therefore, cannot be used for direct comparison. This explains the much higher proportion of type 4 flakes. Nonetheless they are a further demonstration on the flakes of the use of these techniques and both illustrate the use of parallel flaking within episodes of alternate flaking.

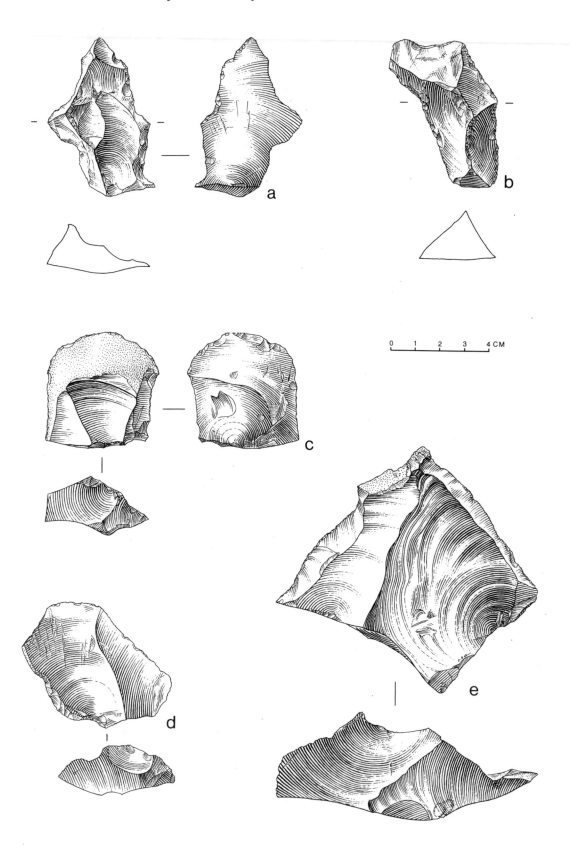

Fig. 16.2. a. P1989.1-3.893. Flaked flake from the Lower Gravel with a type 1 relict core edge. b. P1989.1-3.708. Flake from the Lower Gravel with a type 3 relict core edge. c. P1989.1-3.156. Flake from the Lower Gravel with a type 6 relict core edge. d. P1989.1-3.934. Flake from the Lower Gravel with a type 4 relict core edge. e. P1989.1-3.1348. Flake from the Lower Loam with a type 5 relict core edge.

	L.G.4	L.G.3	L.G.2	L.G.1	Midden	Top L.G.	B.L.L	K.Fl.	L.L.	L.M.G.
Butt										
1	68.6	67.8	68.6	75.8	76.2	76.8	71.0	65.4	69.5	64.2
2	10.8	7.4	7.0	2.4	6.2	2.3	9.7	5.5	8.4	5.7
3	18.4	21.5	20.1	18.0	10.2	7.0	16.1	25.5	17.9	16.0
4	1.3	1.7	1.9	2.3	0.8	7.0	3.2	0	0	1.9
5	0.9	0.8	1.9	1.6	6.8	4.7	0	1.8	3.2	11.3
6	0	0	0	0	0	0	0	0	0	0.9
7	0	0.8	0.6	0	0	2.3	0	1.8	1.1	0

Table 16.9. Percentages of butt types by stratigraphic unit. 1 = plain, 2 = dihedral, 3 = cortical, 4 = natural, 5 = marginal, 6 = soft hammer, 7 = mixed (eg cortical/plain). Also see Appendix I.

	L.G.4	L.G.3	L.G.2	L.G.1	Midden	Top L.G.	B.L.L	K.Fl.	L.L.	L.M.G.
Dorsal scar patt.										
1	31.4	31.0	31.6	45.9	31.8	39.7	35.3	35.8	34.5	48.0
2	15.3	16.2	10.0	6.7	10.9	13.8	23.5	22.4	20.0	8.8
3	2.9	1.4	3.7	0	0.8	0	0	0	0.9	0.8
4	3.6	0.7	2.1	3.0	2.3	1.7	2.9	1.5	1.8	4.8
5	18.6	18.3	17.4	14.8	21.7	12.1	14.7	19.4	18.2	8.0
6	2.9	2.8	5.3	4.4	1.6	0	2.9	3.0	3.6	3.2
7	2.2	3.5	1.6	3.0	3.9	5.2	0	0	1.8	0
8	2.6	2.1	5.8	2.2	3.1	0	5.9	0	1.8	0
9	0.4	0	0	0	0	1.7	0	0	0	0
10	19.3	21.1	20.5	20.0	20.2	24.1	14.7	11.9	16.4	23.2
11	0.4	0	0.5	0	0	1.7	0	1.5	0	0
12	0.4	2.8	1.6	0	3.9	0	0	4.5	0.9	0.8

Table 16.10. Percentages of dorsal scar patterns by stratigraphic unit. For key see Appendix I.

	L.G.4	L.G.3	L.G.2	L.G.1	Midden	Top L.G.	B.L.L	K.Fl.	L.L.	L.M.G.
Relict core edge										
1	3	2	3	0	3	0	0	0	1	0
2	6	2	9	7	4	0	4	0	2	1
3	2	2	4	1	0	1	0	0	0	2
4	33	24	23	17	21	11	8	14	17	19
5	10	7	9	6	3	3	2	0	3	4
6	10	2	4	5	3	0	1	1	2	5

Table 16.11. Quantities of relict core edge type by stratigraphic unit. See Appendix I for key.

Cores

The system of analysis for the cores is described above and in more detail in Appendix I and cores are illustrated in Figure 16.1. A list of the types of core episode from each unit is given in Table 16.12. The quantities of cores tend to be very low for most units, so that comparison between the units is problematic. Generally there appears to be little variation between the units and where variations do occur this is more likely to be due to low samples, rather than meaningful distinctions. There are still no clear distinctions even when the units are grouped together into their stratigraphic beds (Table 16.13). The lack of variation in the flake data also confirms that there is no technological difference between the Lower Gravel, the Lower Loam and the Lower Middle Gravel. Therefore, for the purposes of the technology, the cores have been grouped together into these three stratigraphic units.

Table 16.13 indicates that for all the stratigraphic units, the cores are dominated by alternate flaking, particularly the simple form, with lesser quantities of parallel flaking and single removal. It should also be noted that there are very low quantities of classic alternate flaking. Table 16.14 indicates that there tend to be between 1 to 3 core episodes per core and that each core episode consists of 2 to 4 removals. By looking at the sequence of each core episode it can be further demonstrated that the cores tend to be turned after 1 to 2 flake removals. Where sequences of parallel flaking have been identified either as core episodes, or as part of alternate flaking, these tend to consist of 2 to 3 removals.

These figures should, however, be treated with some caution, as it is only the final flake removals that are represented on the cores, which may not be entirely representative of the technology.

The weight of the cores varies enormously from 24g to 2,604g, with mean weights between 52g and 417g. The modal weights lie between 100-199g for the Lower Gravel and Lower Loam, and between 0-99g for the Lower Middle Gravel (see Tables 16.15-17), but in the latter case, as with the Lower Loam the sample size is very small and should be treated with some caution. Given this reservation, the data suggests that there is no relationship between the weight of the cores and the number and type of core episodes on each core. This seems to indicate that the extent or the form of the knapping tends not to be affected by the size of the original nodule or evolving core, but is rather determined by the quality of the flint and the opportunities presented through the knapping of the core. In other words large and small nodules are knapped by the same variety of techniques.

Equally there is little patterning in the association of types of core episode (see Table 16.18). The figures merely show that core episode type C dominates and is frequently associated with further episodes of type C or often with type A or B. The undertaking of a first technique on a core appears not to determine the form of the next technique. Again the lack of patterning in this way suggests that it is the form and nature of the evolving core that determines the sequence and type of flake removals, rather than a predetermined form of flaking.

In some instances it could be argued that a core shape has emerged from the flaking. In nine instances the cores have been worked discoidally. In effect all these cores have been worked by extensive alternate flaking which has been continued right the way round the core. The lack of this type of patterning on any of the other cores, suggests that this is fortuitous, rather than predetermined.

	L.G.4	L.G.3	L.G.2	L.G.1	Midden	Top L.G.	B.L.L	K.Fl.	L.L.	L.M.G.
Core episode type										
A	17	0	1	1	2	0	1	3	0	6
B	12	5	0	1	1	2	1	0	0	3
C	9	2	6	6	1	2	2	0	0	9
Ci	12	2	2	1	3	0	3	0	4	0
Cip	9	2	4	0	4	2	0	0	2	3
Cii	4	2	3	2	2	0	1	0	1	1
Ciip	5	2	1	1	1	0	0	0	3	2
Ciic	1	0	2	0	1	0	1	0	0	0
D	4	1	1	0	1	0	0	0	0	0
Total	73	16	20	12	16	6	9	13	0	24

Table 16.12. Quantities of types of core episode by stratigraphic unit. A full explanation of the core episode types is given in Appendix I

Core episode types	L.G.	L.L.	L.M.G.
A	21	4	6
B	21	1	3
C	26	2	9
Ci	20	7	0
Cip	21	2	3
Cii	13	2	1
Ciip	10	3	2
Ciic	4	1	0
D	7	0	0

Table 16.13. Quantities of core episode types on cores by stratigraphic unit.

	L.G.	L.L.	L.M.G.
Cores	85	10	13
Mean no. core episodes per core	1.7	2.2	1.8
Mean no. removals per core episode	2.8	2.7	2.5
Mean no. removals before turning	1.5	1.2	1.4
Mean no. removals in seq. of parallel	2.4	2.2	2.1

Table 16.14. Quantities of cores, mean number of core episodes per core, mean no of removals prior to turning cores, and mean number of removals in sequences of parallel flaking, by stratigraphic unit.

	0-99	100-199	200-299	300-399	400-499	500 +
Core episode types						
A	3	6	3	4	4	1
B	7	8	1	4	0	1
C	24	39	16	4	3	8
D	1	1	1	1	1	1

Table 16.15. Quantities of core episode types by weight categories on cores from the Lower Gravel.

	0-99	100-199	200-299	300-399	400-499	500 +
Core episode types						
A	1	0	2	0	0	2
B	1	0	0	0	0	0
C	1	7	4	1	0	2
D	0	0	0	0	0	0

Table 16.16. Quantities of core episode types by weight categories on cores from the Lower Loam.

	0-99	100-199	200-299	300-399	400-499	500 +
Core episode types						
A	3	2	1	0	0	0
B	0	1	1	0	0	1
C	4	2	4	1	2	2
D	0	0	0	0	0	0

Table 16.17. Quantities of core episode types by weight categories on cores from the Lower Middle Gravel.

	L.G.	L.L.	L.M.G.
AA	1	0	0
AB	1	0	1
AC	9	2	3
ABC	4	0	0
ACD	1	0	0
BB	1	0	0
BC	7	1	0
BCD	1	0	0
CC	15	4	4
CD	3	0	0

Table 16.18. Association of core episodes types A, B, C and D

Flake tools

In total there are 90 flake tools from the excavations, the quantities of which are shown in Table 16.19 for each major stratigraphic unit. As with the technology, there appears to be only limited variation in the types between the units. Any variation that is apparent may be due to the low sample numbers, such as in the Lower Middle Gravel.

The flake tools are dominated by flaked flakes (92%), a type which has been described in detail by Ashton *et al.* (1991). The flaked flakes from Swanscombe are typical, in that there is enormous variation in their form (see Figures 16.2a, 16.3 and 16.4a). The flakes vary enormously in size, ranging from 6 to 447 g in weight and with a mean weight of 73.6 g. The latter falls within the upper part of the range of the mean weights of all the flakes (see Table 16.7) and suggests that size is not an important factor in blank selection. The removal or removals are detached from lateral, proximal or distal edges and from both dorsal and ventral faces (see Table 16.20). It has been argued (Ashton *et al.* 1991) that although most should probably be interpreted as tools, some of the particularly larger examples might best be viewed as cores.

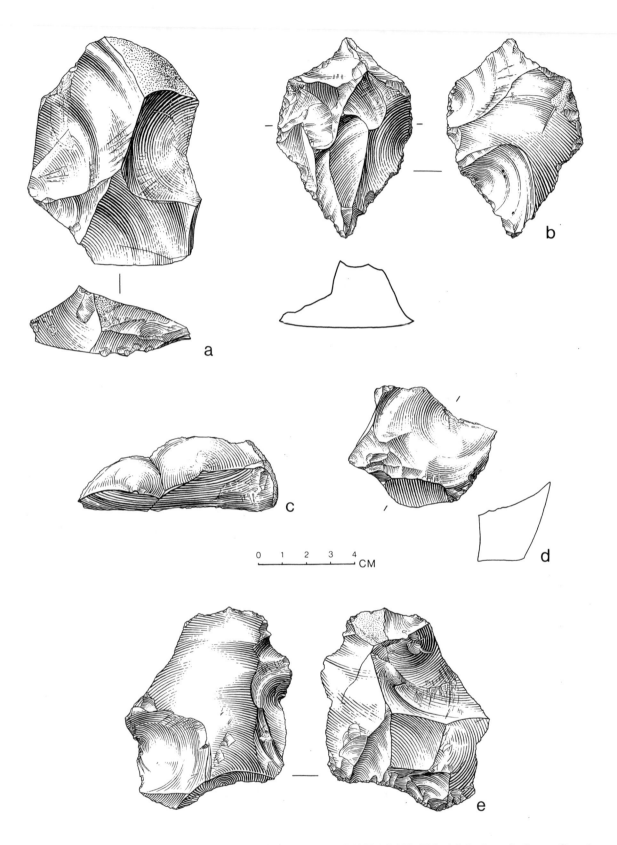

Fig. 16.3. a. P1989.1-3.919. Flaked flake from the Lower Loam. b. P1989.1-3.110. Flaked flake from the Lower Gravel. c. P1989.1-3.1226-1227. Two refitting flaked flake spalls from the Lower Loam knapping floor (complex 22, Group I). d. P1989.1-3.1251. Flaked flake from the Lower Loam knapping floor (complex 22). e. P1989.1-3.1396. Flake flake from the Lower Loam

	L.G	L.L	L.M.G.
Flaked flakes	66	13	6
Pieces with scraper retouch	5 (3)	1	1 (1)
Pieces with uneven retouch	3 (1)	1 (1)	0
Denticulates	2 (2)	1	1 (1)
Retouched notches	2	0	1
Wedge	0	1 (1)	0
Bifaces	1	0	3
Total	73	15	10

Table 16.19. Quantities of tool types. The numbers in brackets are flaked flakes with additional retouch

	L.G.	L.L.	L.M.G.
Flakes removed from			
Dorsal	92	18	10
Ventral	34	8	9
Left lateral	39	13	11
Right lateral	29	3	3
Proximal	22	5	4
Distal	36	5	1
Mean no. rems/piece	1.91	2.00	3.17

Table 16.20. Removals on flaked flakes and mean number of removals per piece

One flaked flake from the knapping floor (P1989.1-3.1188 - Figure 16.4a) also bears some retouch and has additionally been used as a wedge with characteristic shattering. An attempt has also been made to remove a further flake from the butt as shown by the incipient cones.

The four denticulates are distinctive from the flaked flakes in that the retouch spalls are smaller, forming a sequence of at least three removals to create a denticulated edge (see Figure 16.4). In terms of function there might be little difference between the denticulates and other pieces with uneven retouch (see below).

The three retouched notches, although distinct in manufacturing technique, may have been used for similar tasks as the flaked flakes, suggested by their similar edge morphology. In one example the

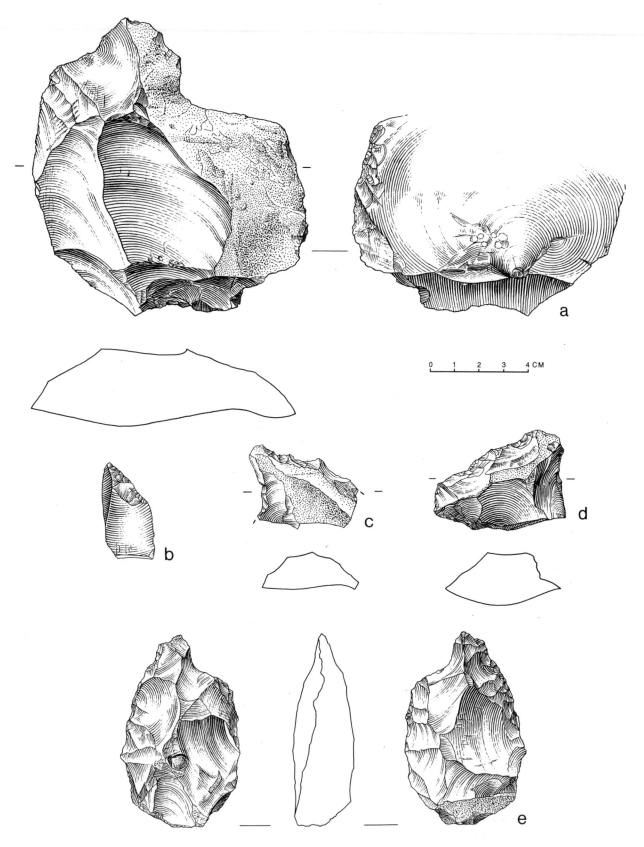

Fig. 16.4. a. P1989.1-3.1188. Flaked flake with retouch, probably used as wedge from Lower Loam knapping floor, square C3. b. P1989.1-3.1246. Retouched flake fragment from Lower Loam knapping floor (complex 22 refitting to complex 19, Group B - see Figure 16.8a). c. P1989.1-3.1233. Denticulate from Lower Loam knapping floor (complex 21). d. P1989.1-3.846. Retouched flake from the Lower Gravel. e. P1989.1-3.795. Biface from the Lower Gravel

retouch may be resharpening of a flaked flake removal.

The retouch on the remaining tools is largely of a miscellaneous nature whereby the retouch is often an addition or a modification to a flaked flake; in two cases the retouch has continued on from a flaked flake removal along an edge (see Figure 16.4a). In another case a flaked flake spall has removed part of a scraper edge from the original flake. In other examples the retouch is sporadic or occurs in isolated areas and is sometimes of an uneven nature or steeply angled, perhaps suggesting a function other than scraping (see Figure 16.4a-d). There are no examples where the tools could simply be described as formalised scrapers.

One difference between the stratigraphic units that may be significant is the proportion of flake tools to useable flakes (flakes > 4cm). For the Lower Gravel and Lower Middle Gravel the proportions are 7.6% and 6.7% respectively, while for the Lower Loam it is as high as 19.1%. This difference may reflect the type of context from which they were found. Although the artefacts from the Lower Gravel and Lower Middle Gravel are somewhat derived, it is reasonable to suggest that core knapping and tool manufacture were taking place close to the river, using the aggrading gravel beach as the source of raw material. In other words the assemblages could be regarded as predominantly reflecting primary manufacturing with perhaps additional *ad hoc* use of the flakes and tools.

In contrast, the Lower Loam artefacts (particularly those from the knapping floor) are in a relatively primary context with the knapping taking place some distance from the source of raw material (see Raw Material section, above, and Spatial Distribution section, below). In this type of situation, where the raw material has been moved to a distinct location, a different type of assemblage might be expected. It has already been suggested from the cortex studies above that the knapping floor assemblage represents the later stages of core reduction. It is likely that this reduction was taking place for a specific purpose at that location which might explain the higher proportion of flake tools. Similar models can be used to explain the higher proportion of flake tools in the remainder of the Lower Loam.

The general approach to flake tool manufacture reflects in many ways the approach to core technology, whereby a set of techniques are applied and adapted according to immediate circumstance. Rather than a formalised approach, tools are manufactured within set parameters, but in an *ad hoc* fashion, dictated by the form of the initial blank and the type of tool required to undertake the immediate task.

Bifaces

There are a total of four bifaces, one from the Lower Gravel and three from the Lower Middle Gravel. The one from the Lower Gravel (P1989.1-3.795, Figure 16.4e) is generally ovate in shape, quite thick and may have been reduced by soft hammer. It is quite rudimentary in its manufacture with a larger flake removed from one of the lateral edges near the tip giving an asymmetrical outline to the piece. The biface is in a similar condition to other artefacts from the same context and there is no evidence that the piece 'dropped in' from a higher context, as has been verbally claimed since the excavation. For a full discussion of the background to the recovery of this biface see McNabb and Ashton (1992).

The three bifaces from the Lower Middle Gravel are equally small and rudimentary in their manufacture. The first (P1989.1-3.1462, Figure 16.5a) is thick with a pointed tip. It bears little evidence of soft hammer flaking and is again asymmetrical in outline. The base is largely unworked and retains a small area of cortex.

The second biface (P1989.1-3.1475, Figure 16.5b) is thick and pointed, and probably made on a flake. It has minimal hard hammer working with 4 flakes removed on one face and eight on the other. The base is minimally worked with some cortex.

The final piece (P1989.1-3.1538, Figure 16.5c) is a thick ovate with an S-twist, produced with a soft hammer, retaining a plano-convex cross-section. In contrast to the others, it is considerably more rolled and abraded.

The bifaces, rather than adhering to a specific typological form, reflect the size and shape of the original raw material. In most cases they appear to be made with a minimum number of removals and perhaps like the flake tools represent an *ad hoc* response to a situation

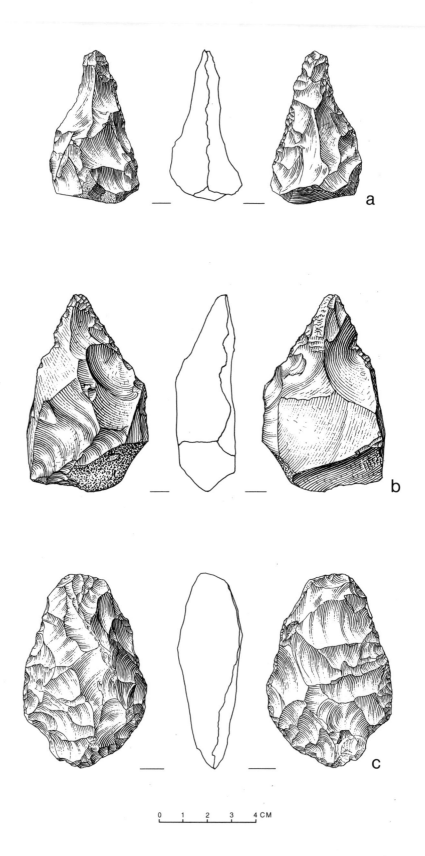

0 1 2 3 4 CM

Fig. 16.5. a. P1989.1-3.1462. Biface from the Lower Middle Gravel. b. P1989.1-3.1475. Biface from the Lower Middle Gravel. c. P1989.1-3.1538. Biface from the Lower Middle Gravel

REFITTING FROM THE KNAPPING FLOOR

The artefacts from the knapping floor have been argued to be an *in situ* assemblage. They are, therefore, more likely to represent specific knapping events, rather than a collection of artefacts derived from a number of locations through fluvial sorting. As can be seen from Tables 16.9-12, however, there are few differences between the technology of this unit and those of the other beds. The only exception is the absence of cores, which is discussed below. This tends to confirm that even though the other units consist in most instances of fluvially sorted material, they appear to be representative of the technology.

The knapping floor assemblage is also of further use, as many of the artefacts refit. The refitting artefacts can be divided into 12 groups. In the descriptions given below the term composite is used for fragments or flakes that have been reconstructed out of a number of different shatter pieces but which do not form part of a group of refitting flakes. These have not been described in the text because they only retain a limited amount of information on flaking strategies.

Complex 19 (Table 16.21)

This complex is composed of two main groups of refitting flakes, (Groups A and B) as well as a smaller number of other associated flakes and fragments that have not been refitted. The details of complex 19 are given in Table 16.21. The plan of complex 19 is shown in Figure 16.6 and the relationship with other complexes in Figure 16.10. Unfortunately some of the material originally present within complex 19 has subsequently been lost (including pieces 19M, F, Q, N).

Group A. The group consists of four large flakes (P1989.1-3.1184-1187) and some fragments, and has previously been published by Newcomer (1970). It should be noted that the interpretation put forward here, is slightly different to that published by Newcomer. In addition to the four flakes, there is evidence of ten previous removals. All 14 flakes appear to have been removed as a sequence of complex alternate flaking from either side of a ridge, the axis of which shifted slightly as knapping progressed. The flake scars are numbered sequentially (Figure 16.7) in the probable order in which they were removed and are described as being removed from two directions (A and B).

Although it is certain that flake 1 was removed before flake 2 and that both were removed in direction A, flake 3 may have been taken off before, during or after these removals, and came from direction B. Two flakes (4 and 5) were then removed from direction A and at this point the axis of the ridge shifted. The core was turned again with the removal of flake 6 from direction B and turned a further time to take off flakes 7, 8 and 9 from direction A. Flake 10 was removed from direction B, probably followed by one of the refitting flakes (-1186). Flakes -1185 and -1184 were then removed from direction A and the core was turned a final time for the removal of flake -1187 from direction B. In this last phase it is possible that flake -1186 was removed after -1185 as there is no direct relationship between the two.

The whole sequence involves at least six, and potentially eight, turns of the core with the removal of 14 flakes. Within the sequence there are at least two and possibly four sequences of parallel flaking (flakes 4 and 5; flakes 7, 8 and 9; possibly flakes 1 and 2; possibly flakes 10 and -1186). The complex nature of this knapping illustrates the difficulties of interpreting knapping strategies purely from cores and flakes without the aid of refitting.

Group B. Group B is composed of two refitting flakes, and two fragments of a flake (Table 16.21). As far as can be reconstructed, this block consists of a sequence of six flake removals from a cylindrical shaped nodule of flint (Figure 16.8a). The two refitting flakes are the second and fourth removals in the sequence, and the two refitting fragments are part of the fifth removal. One of these (P1989.1-3.1246) was found in complex 21/22 and has been retouched (see spatial analysis). Removals

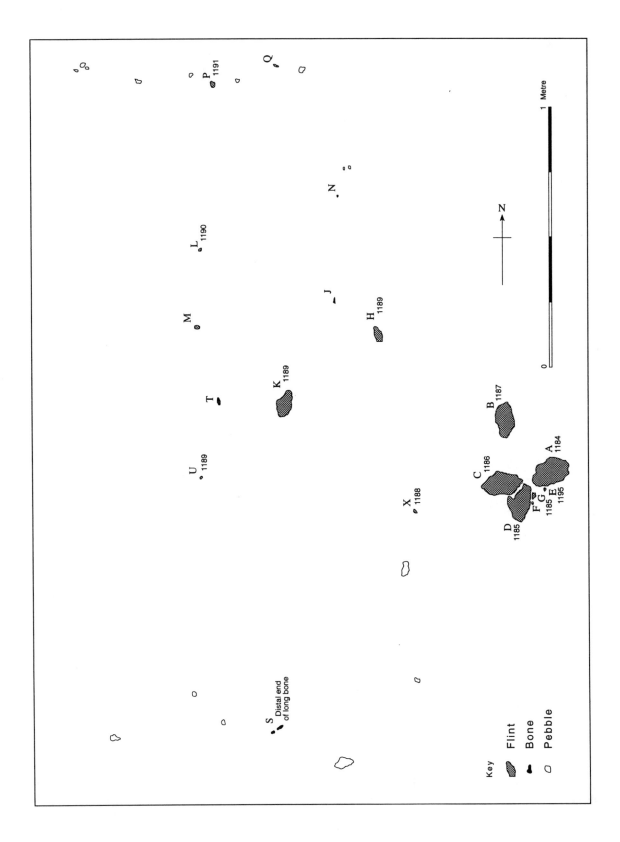

Fig. 16.6. Plan of complex 19

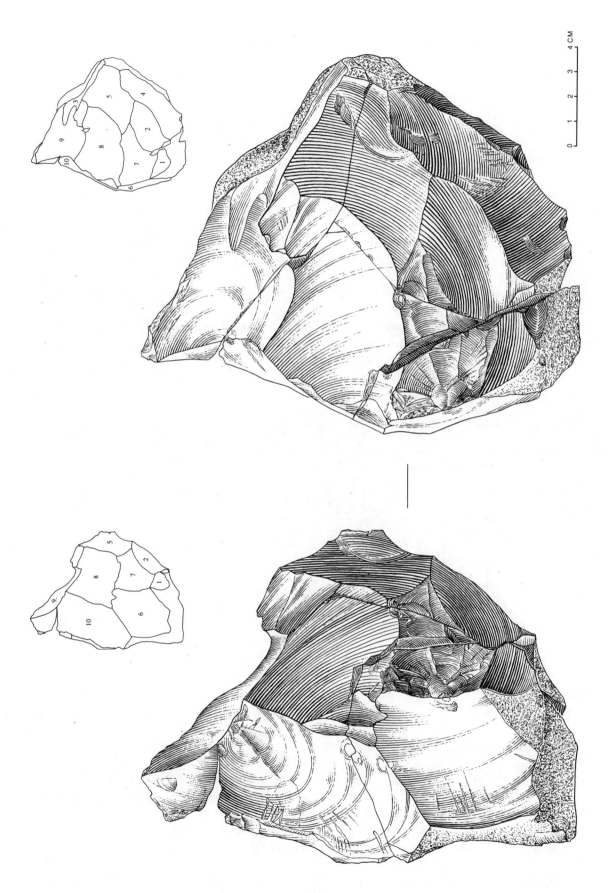

Fig. 16.7. Refitting Group A. Removals numbered sequentially

one, three and six were not present in the complex, nor were they recovered in the excavation. Previously this has been termed 'salami slice technique' (Newcomer 1970).

The evidence for the removal of the first flake in the sequence is preserved on the dorsal face of flake number two (P1989.1-3.1188). The first flake was a single detachment (possibly all or mostly cortical) that removed the end of the nodule from a cortical platform. The knapper then rotated the cylindrical nodule a quarter turn to the right and struck off the second flake. This flake, like all the remaining flakes in the sequence, also had a cortical platform. Percussion damage on the cortex of the second flake indicates that the knapper had to strike the surface several times before the flake came off. This probably explains the atypical nature of the flake's ventral surface, as well as the shattering of the flake as it came off. The knapper then rotated the nodule another quarter turn to the right before removing the third flake in the sequence. The fourth removal was preceded by a half turn to the left. The flake is composed of three fragments and either represents two separate detachments (19+H/19+U followed by 19+K) from the same spot, or, as is tentatively supported here, a single detachment 19+K accompanied by shatter on the dorsal. The fifth removal (P1989.1-3.1246 and Figure 16.4b) consists of two fragments of the proximal end of a flake and indicate that the knapper rotated the nodule an eighth of a turn back to the left for its removal. This piece has also been retouched. The missing sixth flake was detached in the same direction, as shown by the dorsal scar of the fifth removal, but might simply be shatter from this removal.

The knapping strategy followed in the reduction of Group B was one that was determined by the knappers appreciation of the difficulties inherent in the reduction of a nodule of that particular shape. The approach is very different to that noted in complex 19 main group.

B.M. Reg. No. P1989.1-3.	Type	Excavation No.
1184	Refitting Group A	19A
1185		19D,G
1186		19C
1187,1192		19B,19.5,19.7
1188	Refitting Group B	19+V,19+W,19+X
1189		19+K,19+H,19+U
1194		19
1191	Flakes	19P
1193		19.8
1190	Fragments	19L
1195	Chips	19O,19J,19E,196,?

Table 16.21. Provenance details for complex 19 (1184-1195).

Complex 20 (Table 16.22)

This complex consists of two refitting groups (P1989.1-3.1196 = Group C; P1989.1-3.1197 + 1199 = Group D), a composite piece, and 11 other flakes and fragments. Details are given in Table 16.22. Although no plan of the complex has survived, a sketch plan, drawn to scale, has been reconstructed from Waechter's published photograph of the complex (1970 plate 2b) (Figure 16.9). Both refitting groups appear to be from the same nodule of flint (see spatial analysis).

Group C. Initial parallel flaking removed at least four and possibly five small flakes, accompanied by shatter, using a natural flint surface as a striking platform. The knapper then rotated the block a quarter turn clockwise and removed at least four flakes (again accompanied by shatter) by parallel

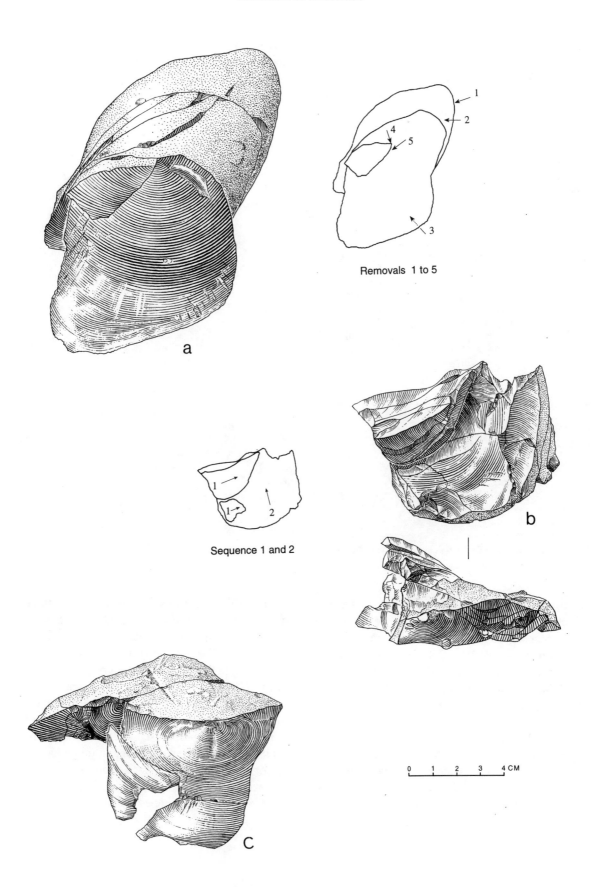

Removals 1 to 5

Sequence 1 and 2

a

b

C

Fig. 16.8. a. Refitting Group B. b. Refitting Group C. c. Refitting Group D

flaking, in the same direction, but at right-angles to the previous sequence. This second sequence of flakes was taken from a plain platform with a relict percussion cone at its edge (see Figure 16.8b). Two interpretations are possible. Either the refitting flakes have been removed from the butt and ventral surface of a very large flake, or the percussion cone is an incipient fracture formed by a failed attempt to remove a flake and exposed accidentally, prior to the removal of the second sequence. Without further refitting either interpretation could be correct.

B.M. Reg. No. P1989.1-3.	Type	Excavation No.
1196	Refitting Group C	20R,20J,20B,20C,20W 20G,20E,20?,20R
1197	Refitting Group D	20O,20?
1199		20Y,20K,20U
1198	Composite	20F,20H
1200	Flakes	20A
1201		20P
1202		20L
1203		
1204		20T
1206		
1205	Fragments	
1207		
1208		20Z
1209		20Q
1210		
1211	Chips	(X 30)

Table 16.22. Provenance details for complex 20 (1196-1211).

Group D. The two flakes in this group are the second and third removals in a sequence of three detachments. The first removal has not been recovered, but was a large flake as identified from the dorsal scar of the second removal, detached from a cortical platform. After a quarter turn clockwise, the second flake (P1989.1-3.1197) was detached, again from cortex. The impact point was too far away from the edge and the resulting flake (-1197) was short, wedge shaped and accompanied by shatter. One large shatter fragment/flake associated with the removal of -1197 formed the main dorsal scar of the next flake to be removed in the sequence (P1989.1-3.1199). This third flake was removed after the knapper turned the block back anti-clockwise. It broke into three fragments as it was removed, two of which (20U and 20Y) were found to one side of the main concentration (see Figure 16.8c). The approach to the flaking of the nodule or block in Group D is the same as that described in the reduction of Group B in that the knapper rotated the block, looking for a suitable place to strike, but did not turn the nodule over as in alternate flaking. The knappers appreciation of flaking angles in this refitting group is poor, although that may only reflect the reduction of awkwardly shaped nodules.

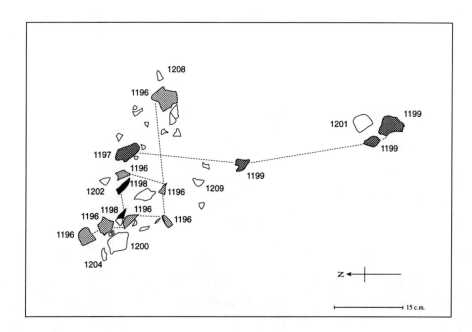

Fig. 16.9. Plan of complex 20

Complexes 21 and 22 (Table 16.23)

Refitting demonstrates that complex 21 and the various sub-complexes that comprise 22 (= 22, 22A1, 22B1, 22C1) are part of the same knapping scatter. This complex consists of eight different refitting groups, each of two to three flakes, possibly representing several nodules (see spatial analysis). Figure 16.10 shows the relationship with complexes 19 and 20

Group E. A refitting group of three small flakes with shatter, removed by parallel flaking.

Group F. A refitting group of two flakes and a flaked flake spall. The two flakes were removed by parallel flaking, one from directly in front of the other and were the first removals from the nodule on that part of the core. The nature of the cortex suggests that the block is a river cobble (see spatial analysis). The first flake (P1989.1-3.1214) was modified into a flaked flake on several occasions in the same place. Newcomer (1970) described the refitting spall as a first sharpening spall, and considered that the piece had been retouched four times in all. There are two separate retouch scars present which post-date the refitting spall, but it is not possible to determine whether they represent deliberate individual removals, or one removal accompanied by shatter.

Group G. This refitting group consists of two cortical flakes removed as part of a sequence of parallel flaking from the surface of a nodule or block. The knapper was working from right to left from a plain platform. The larger of the two flakes (P1989.1-3.1218), the second to be removed, has evidence of preparation on its butt.

Group H. This group preserves an identical sequence and situation to the previous group. Three flakes are present, representing removals two, three, and four. Evidence of the first flake in the sequence is preserved on the dorsal face of the second flake. Knapping proceeded from right to left with the four flakes being removed by parallel flaking from a plain platform on the outer surface of a nodule.

Group I. This refitting group presents a modification on the same theme as that demonstrated in the last two groups. Parallel flaking from left to right is responsible for the removal of two flaked flake spalls from the ventral face and distal end of a large flake.

B.M. Reg. No. P1989.1-3.	Type	Excavation No.
1212	Refitting Group E	22C1,21,21
1213,1214,1215	Refitting Group F	21,21,22C1
1218,1219	Refitting Group G	22B1,21
1220,1221,1222	Refitting Group H	22B1/21,22C1,22C1
1226,1227	Refitting Group I	22B1,22C1/22C1
1231,1232	Refitting Group J	22C1,21
1261,1262	Refitting Group K	Sq. B3 #35,22B1
1228,1229 1216,1217,1223 1224,1225,1230	Composites	22C1,22/22A1/22B1/22C1 22B1,22B1,22B1 22B1,21,22C1
1237,1238,1242 1244,1251	Flakes	21,21,22A1 22A1,22C1
1233-1236,1239 1241,1243 1246 1247-1249 1253-1256	Fragments (Group B)	21 22A1 22B1 22B1 22C1
1240 1245 1250 1257 1258	Chips	21 (x34) 22A1 (x9) 22B1 (x27) 22C1 (x6) 22 Rolled (x44)

Table 16.23. Provenance details for complex 21 and 22 (1212-1258).

Group J. This group of conjoins is another example of parallel flaking. The knapper worked from right to left to detach two flakes from the outer face of a nodule.

Group K. These two conjoining flakes have been detached by parallel flaking, the first one (P1989.1-3.1261) coming from the distal end of a flake scar. The presence of several incipient cones demonstrate that a number of attempts were made to detach the next flake. One of these attempts resulted in shatter which exposed a large incipient cone, the surface of which became the platform for the removal of the second flake in the sequence (P1989.1-3.1262). This explains the atypical, almost negative, appearance of the flake's ventral surface. Flake -1261 was not recovered on the knapping floor but from 30 cm below it. The implications of this are discussed below.

The technological information present in complex 21/22 shows a high incidence of parallel flaking, especially from the outer surfaces of nodules or blocks, although whether this is in relation to parallel flaking *sensu stricto* (ie. type B, see Appendix I), or to sequences of parallel flaking within alternate flaking (type C), is not clear from the data.

226

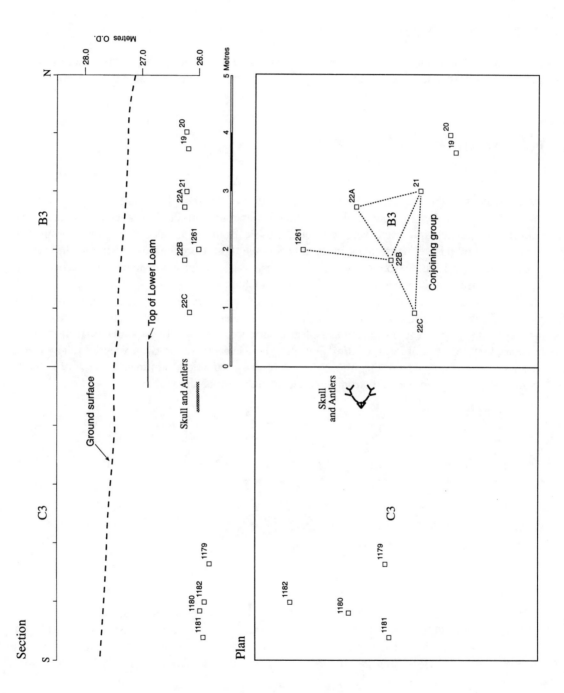

Fig. 16.10. Schematic plan and section of the knapping floor in squares B3 and C3

Summary of the knapping floor technology.

The knapping floor shows a range of different reduction strategies, all entirely consistent with those noted in the other units. The technology demonstrates the knappers adapting strategies to suit platforms and nodule surfaces. The high incidence of parallel flaking is a response to plain platforms. Although some of the flaking shows a poor appreciation of flaking angles, not all of the shatter is attributed to bad knapping. The high incidence of refits showing the removal of the outer surface of nodules and blocks by parallel flaking along the length of a platform is curious, but not necessarily indicative of a deliberate strategy associated with a particular form of knapping or tool manufacture.

SPATIAL ANALYSIS

The spatial analysis of the artefacts is limited by the nature of the recording system employed during excavation. This is described in more detail in Chapter 5. Generally, artefacts excavated from the Lower Gravel were recorded by spit depth and grid square, those from the midden and Lower Loam were normally recorded by three dimensional grid reference, while those from the Lower Middle Gravel were simply recorded by grid square. In terms of overall comparison, a rough estimate of artefact density has been calculated based on the excavation details given in Chapter 5.

The densities are given in Table 16.24 for each stratigraphic unit, except in the cases of the Lower Gravel/Lower Loam interface and the base of the Lower Loam. In these latter two cases there is insufficient data to give a realistic estimate of artefact density. Table 16.24 shows that most of the units have artefact densities of between $3/m^3$ and $7/m^3$. However, there are two exceptions. The Lower Loam has a density of only $0.5/m^3$ that may either represent a reduction in human activity, or could be that the depositional regime was not strong enough to carry artefactual material.

	L.G.4	L.G.3	L.G.2	L.G.1	Midden	Top L.G.	B.L.L.	K.Fl.	L.L.	L.M.G.
Artefacts per m^3	7.2	3.6	4.7	3.0	6.5	?	?	31.2	0.5	3.1

Table 16.24. Density of artefacts per m^3 by stratigraphic unit.

However, the high density in the knapping floor ($31.2/m^3$) does appear to show a real difference and is a further demonstration that the knapping floor artefacts are a discrete episode of knapping. In contrast, the midden in terms of the flintwork appears to have a far more dispersed distribution. The distributions of material from both the knapping floor and the midden are discussed in more detail below.

The extent of the knapping floor

The northern edge of the knapping floor can probably be identified on the A3/B3 interface where a series of contemporary, small stream banks, left by successive episodes of channelling, would have provided a natural limit. Furthermore, in A3 and A2 there is little flintwork in comparable condition to that in B3 from within the Loams.

The eastern, southern and western limits of the knapping floor are more problematic. In B2, B3 and C3 there are other artefacts that come from the same horizon as the knapping floor, but do not derive from the complexes (see Table 16.25). Although the heights vary (26.25-25.82), differences of this nature may be accounted for by Waechter's suggestion that the knapping floor was an undulating surface. Even within the B3 complexes there are small differences in heights (Figure 16.6), while a flake from sub-complex 22B1 (1262), was refitted to a flake about 0.25 m. below the knapping floor, and 1.60 m. to the west of it, apparently from a different stratigraphic level (1261; see Table 16.23).

There are other pieces from a wider range of squares (B1-B4, A2, A3 and Z3, see Table 16.26) which on grounds of condition, cortex and flint type are similar to material from the floor in B3. Again there are height differences, although they do come from a broadly similar horizon as can be seen in cross-section (see Figure 16.6). Definitive evidence of the extension of the knapping floor into these squares could only be found through refitting, but as yet no refits have been identified.

The material found in C3 is particularly notable as it was found on the same stratigraphic horizon as the knapping floor and is a major southerly extension. Two large flakes (P1989.1-3.1179 and P1989.1-3.1180) were identified along with a skull and antler rack of fallow deer and two pebbles. The flakes appear to have been from the same nodule and the larger one (-1180) was modified into a flaked flake and was additionally used as a wedge (see above and Figure 16.4a). The smaller of the two pebbles in C3 (P1989.1-3.1182, 109g) showed no evidence of battering, but the larger (P1989.1-3.1181, 401g) had a flake taken out from one of its flat faces. This is tentatively interpreted as a flint hammerstone. Its stained scar, suggests it was already broken before it was brought to the knapping floor. A further flint pebble (Sc70 B2, 34) was also recovered from the knapping floor. There was no battering on this piece.

In summary, the knapping floor was an uneven surface which dipped to the south and was delineated by a small stream to the north with a series of flaking episodes adjacent to this small stream. Why the knappers chose this position is impossible to say. Near the junction between B3 and C3, the skull and antlers of a Clacton fallow deer were excavated from the floor horizon. The remainder of the animal was not present. It is possible that the carcass attracted the knappers to this spot.

B.M. Reg. No. P1989.1-3.	Type	Excavation No.
1263	Retouched piece	B3
1179	Flakes	C3, #76
1180		C3, #71
1259		21, B3
1260		22, B3
1264		B3
1266		B3
1268		B3
1183	Fragments B2, #120	
1265		B3
1267		B3
1269		B3
1181	Hammer Stone?	C3, #74
1182	Pebbles	C3, #75
Unreg.		B2, #34
1270	Chips	B3, X21

Table 16.25. Provenance details for material associated with the knapping floor but not excavated from the B3 complexes.

Square	BM. Reg. No. P1989.1-3.
B1	1303-1307,1318,1322,1324
B2	1330,1332,1341
B3	1345
B4	1347-1350,1352-1358,1367-1368
A2	1290,1297
A3	1302
Z3	1376-1378

Table 16.26. Material from B1, B2, B3, B4, A2, A3 and Z3 possibly associated with the knapping floor

The spatial distribution and behavioural implications of the knapping floor

Medium to large flint clasts are not native to the Lower Loam, so any flint found had to be either introduced by humans or through natural agencies such as fluvial deposition. For complexes 19 to 22 the refitting material preclude the latter explanation. The presence of rolled material (44 chips and a flake - P1989.1-3.1258 and 1259) recorded as being associated with the knapping floor is here suggested to have already been present as a part of the Loam surface prior to the knapping.

The knapping floor in B3 consists of three complexes with a total of 12 refitting groups (see above). There are probably a minimum of 9 nodules, and possibly several more. The description and contexts of these nodules are given in Table 16.27. The history of each nodule is assessed in terms of what state it was brought into the area, how and where it was knapped, what flakes were modified, and whether the core was removed from the area. This information is summarised in Table 16.28 and discussed below.

Previous knapping. In some instances it is possible to assess the amount of knapping that took place on a nodule prior to being introduced to the area. Nodule 1 had at least 10 flakes removed before being knapped in complex 19. Nodules 8 and 9 were probably partially knapped, whereas nodules 2, 4 and 5 were largely unknapped, when introduced into the area. In contrast, the two flakes from nodule 6 were possibly knapped elsewhere and then brought into C3.

Sequence of knapping. The relationship between the different complexes can be assessed by the refits and by study of the different nodule types. There are numerous refits between complexes 21, 22A1, 22B1 and 22C1 indicating that these scatters are closely associated and should probably be regarded as a single complex. In addition, there is a refit between complexes 19 and 22C1. In this case a flake from nodule 2 (Group B) was knapped in complex 19, it broke, a fragment was left behind, and a larger fragment was retouched and taken to complex 21/22. A further flake was also found in complex 21/22 that appears to be from nodule 2. There are also two flakes in complex 20 that appear to be from nodule 7 which is predominantly in complex 21/22. Without refitting it is difficult to reconstruct whether these two flakes were knapped in complex 20 or simply taken there from complex 21/22. However, all these links between the different complexes do suggest that they are contemporary.

There is little information on the sequence in which the knapping of the nodules occurred in B3. The exception is the relationship between nodules 1 and 2 (see Figure 16.6). The four flakes of nodule 1 were recovered lying on top of two of the three shatter fragments (19+V and 19+W) of the second flake from nodule 2 (P1989.1-3.1188). 19X, the third shatter fragment, was found to the west of the main complex. The three pieces that form the fourth flake from nodule 2 (P1989.1-3.1189) were recovered to the north-west of the main group and were in a north-east to south-west line (see Figure 16.6). There are several potential interpretations. Nodule 2 was knapped first, and some of the material was scattered either by shatter or by the knapper selecting and throwing out some of the larger debitage (or both), and then knapping nodule 1 directly on top. Alternatively, this complex may represent the sweeping up of some of the larger pieces from the reduction of both nodules 1 and 2.

Modification of flakes. There are three flaked flakes (one with a refitting spall), one retouched flake, one denticulate and two flaked flake spalls from the complexes and C3 (see Table 16.29). These pieces have been described above in the technology section. Some of these pieces also show evidence of movement from outside and within the area. The fifth flake in nodule 2 (P1989.1-3.1246 and Figure 16.4b), as described above, was retouched and truncated by a break, and at some point was taken from complex 19 to 21/22. In C3 one of the flakes (P1989.1-3.1180 and Figure 16.4a) appears to have been used as a wedge and has also had a single flake removed. This piece was probably brought into C3,

Nodule	Description	Location	Groups	B.M. Reg. No. (P1989.1-3.)
1	Grey,bizoned, mottled flint with dark grey/ brown cortex	19	A	1184-1187,1192
2	Brown/grey, flint with slightly speckled, brown cortex	19+21/22	B	1188-1195,1246,1253
3	Grey, bizoned, flint with speckled, thin white/brown cortex	20	C+D	1196-1199,1201,1204,1208,1210
4	Black flint with dark brown/green cortex	21/22	F	1213-1215
5	Dark grey flint with inclusions and thin brown cortex	21/22	J	1231,1232
6	Dark-light grey mottled flint with inclusions and white/grey cortex	C3		1179,1180
7	Dark grey bizoned flint with light grey inclusions and whit/grey-brown cortex	21/22+20	E,G,H+I	1202,1200,1212,1216-1219,1226, 1227,1230,1234,1242,1247,1251, 1256
8	Dark grey bizoned flint with thin white/grey cortex	21/22		1220-1222,1228,1229,1233,1241
9	Brown/grey, slightly speckled with thin white/ grey cortex	21/22	K	1261,1262

Table 16.27. Suggested associations between flint complexes and the nodules that were knapped on the Lower Loam knapping floor.

Nodule	Previous knapping	Knapping in B3/C3	Flake modification	Core history
1	Knapped extensively prior to knapping in complex 19	4 flakes removed in complex 19 by alternate flaking with parallel	None	Core removed from area
2	Almost complete nodule, at least one flake removed	Knapped in complex 19 by 'salami slice'. One flake (1253) either taken to or knapped in 22C	Flake fragment (1246) retouched and taken to complex 22B	Core removed from area
3	?	Knapped in complex 20 by 2 episodes of parallel flaking and possibly by 'salami slice'	None	Core removed from area
4	Largely unknapped nodule	Knapped in complex 21/22 by parallel flaking	Flake modified into flaked flake by several removals. One spall recovered	Core removed from area
5	Unknapped nodule	Knapped in complex 21/22 by parallel flaking	None	Core removed from area
6	Two flakes possibly brought already knapped to C3	Possibly no knapping in C3	None	Core possibly never in area
7	?	Knapped in complex 21/22 and either further knapped in complex 20 or flakes taken to complex 20	Flake modified into flaked flake (1251) 2 flaked flake spalls (1226-7) removed from large flake which was taken from area	Core probably removed from area
8	Partially knapped nodule	Knapped in complex 21/22 by parallel flaking	Flake made into denticulate (1233)	Core removed from area
9?	Partially knapped nodule	Knapped in complex 21/22 by parallel flaking	None	Core removed from area

Table 16.28. The knapping history of nodules 1 to 9 from the Lower Loam knapping floor.

having been knapped elsewhere. The two flaked flake spalls from the distal end of a flake (P1989.1-3.1226 and 1227 and Figure 16.3c) were removed in complex 21/22, but the flaked flake was taken and possibly used elsewhere. In contrast, a different flaked flake (P1989.1-3.1214 and 1215) was knapped, modified and resharpened in complex 21/22. The same is probably the case with the denticulate (P1989.1-3.1233 and Figure 16.4c) and the flaked flake (P1989.1-3.1251 and Figure 16.3d), both found in complex 21/22. The last flaked flake (P1989.1-3.1263) was associated with the knapping floor in B3, but was not related to any individual complex.

Four of the six flake tools and all of the flaked flake spalls were recovered from complex 21/22. What the significance of this is remains unclear, but might suggest concentrated use of the tools, as well as knapping, in this area.

The presence of the fallow deer skull and antlers in C3 may give a clue to at least some of the activities on the knapping floor. The absence of any other skeletal parts in such a fine-grained context suggests that they were taken away in an articulated form. The absence is unlikely to be due to non-human scavenging, but is more likely to be an indication of human butchery with the larger joints of meat removed elsewhere. It might even be suggested that the wedge, found in close proximity, was used to sever the spinal column, while the sharp edges provided by the flaked flakes and unretouched flakes were used for the cutting of the hide, meat and sinews. Unfortunately there is no evidence of cutmarks or microwear to test this.

The post-knapping movement of artefacts. The presence of small chips, shatter fragments, as well as the refitting of flakes from discrete complexes (especially complex 20) clearly indicate that knapping took place in B3. The absence of cores, therefore, implies that they were knapped and taken elsewhere. A latex mould was made of the shape of the core from Group A (nodule 1) which showed that there was considerable potential for further reduction (Newcomer 1970). It was presumably taken elsewhere for knapping. Such reconstructions can also be suggested for nodules 2-5 and 8-9, where the absence of cores suggests that they were removed from the area. For nodule 7 it is less certain whether the core was removed, as there is a certain amount of shatter, whereas for nodule 6, the core was probably never in the area. It should be noted that some cores, in mint condition, were recovered from the other B trenches. They are very similar in condition to the material from B3 (see Table 16.24), but as yet no refits have been found.

Tool type or Retouch type	Complex	Nodule	B.M. Reg. No. P1989.1-3.	Description
Wedge and flaked flake	C3	6	1180	Large flake with macro damage suggesting use as a wedge and with a flake removed from the distal end
Flaked flake and spall (refitting)	21/22	4	1214/1215	First of three flaked flake spalls to be removed from right lateral edge of flake. Other two spalls missing
Flaked flake spalls (refitting)	21/22	7	1226/1227	Two refitting flaked flake spalls from the ventral surface and distal end of a large flake
Flaked flake	21/22	7	1251	Flake with large flake removed from distal end
Retouched piece	B3	?	1263	Large flake retouched on distal end, with a break caused by the retouching
Denticulate	21/22	3/4	1233	Broken flake with four small notch removals on distal end creating a denticulate
Retouched piece	21/22	2	1246	Flake fragment with retouch on proximal end

Table 16.29. The location, registration number and description of flake tools and spalls on the Lower Loam knapping floor and associated areas.

The Midden

This feature was initially discovered in 1968, at the junction between the Lower Loam and the Lower Gravel. Excavations in trench A revealed faunal remains apparently associated with a distinct horizon (Waechter 1968). The real nature of the feature was not identified until 1969. The history of the excavation of the feature is described in Chapter 5, and the geological context and interpretation of the feature is given in Chapter 7.

Geologically, the feature is interpreted as a muddy hollow in a channel system (see Chapter 7). The archaeological material recovered from this context does not conflict with this interpretation;

however, it does not support Waechter's suggestion that the accumulation of fauna and flintwork is a direct result of human activity. On balance, the evidence suggests that most of the fauna and flintwork is derived, and that the character of the assemblage is, for the most part, a reflection of fluvial deposition as opposed to human action.

The condition of the artefacts strongly supports this interpretation of fluvial deposition. Of the 145 pieces of struck flint found on the midden (see Tables 16.3 and 4), 96.4% has been rolled of which 40% is heavily rolled. The only *in-situ* flintwork at the site was the Knapping Floor in the Lower Loam where 94.5% is unrolled. This is the exact opposite of the evidence from the midden. This situation is paralleled in the faunal assemblage where a high percentage of the bone is rolled (Schreve pers. comm.; see also Chapter 11). In addition, over 90% of the midden artefacts possess a sheen which in this situation is likely to be due to fluvial transport. This is almost identical to the results from the Lower Gravel unit 1, the fluvial deposits directly below the midden. By comparison only 38% of the material from the Lower Loam knapping floor has a sheen which may have been acquired during the subsequent burial of the knapping floor.

Furthermore, the composition of the midden assemblage, in terms of density of artefacts and the lack of refits and small chips, suggests fluvial deposition (see Table 16.3). The results show a closer affinity with the remainder of the Lower Gravel assemblages rather than the in-situ Lower Loam knapping floor. Although excavation strategy may account for the absence of chips, some relatively small flakes were recovered from the midden as were small fragments of bone. The lack of small material may therefore be a result of a genuine absence, as would be expected in a derived assemblage, and/or subsequent winnowing prior to burial.

The only evidence that might suggest *in situ* human activity on the midden, are the large unknapped flint blocks found in squares A3 and B2. It was suggested (Waechter *et al.* 1970), that these were too big to be emplaced by fluvial action. Many of the larger bones (e.g. the bear skull in A2) are also too big to have been easily transported. However, both the condition and composition of the midden assemblage indicate that virtually all the material is derived and moved by fluvial action. This is supported by the geological interpretation of the unit (see Chapter 7) and is also adopted to explain the accumulation of most of the fauna (see Chapter 12).

DISCUSSION

For the past sixty years the Swanscombe archaeological sequence has been the main component of the British Lower Palaeolithic framework. The stratification of Clactonian core and flake industries from the Lower Gravel and Lower Loam, beneath Acheulian handaxe industries from the Middle Gravels and Upper Loam formed a natural evolutionary sequence that mirrored, albeit later, that of the Oldowan, developed Oldowan and Acheulian in East Africa. Over the last ten years, excavations at Boxgrove (Roberts 1990) and High Lodge (Ashton *et al.* 1992) together with have shown that Acheulian industries also pre-date the Clactonian and have highlighted the difficulties of using typology either to date assemblages or to form the basis of a cultural framework. This has been leant further weight by a detailed technological study of the principal assemblages (McNabb 1992). Meanwhile, recent excavations at Barnham have shown the contemporaneity at the same site of industries that were previously interpreted as Clactonian and Acheulian (Ashton *et al.* 1994)

In the light of this new work then, how should the Swanscombe industries be interpreted? The Waechter excavations recovered three industries, two previously interpreted as Clactonian from the Lower Gravel and Lower Loam, and the last previously interpreted as Acheulian from the Lower Middle Gravel. What is remarkable about the three industries is the similarity of the core working technology, the range of flake tools and to some extent the bifaces.

The core working consists of a range of techniques which are encompassed by single removal, parallel flaking and alternate flaking. Given the small sample numbers in some assemblages, there are few differences between them (see Tables 16.12 to 18). The absence of cores from the knapping floor is a special case and is discussed below. This is confirmed by the dorsal scar patterns, butts and relict core edges on the flakes (see Tables 16.9-11).

Equally, the flake tools consist predominantly of flaked flakes with occasional retouched notches, denticulates and scrapers (see Table 16.19). Again, although the sample numbers are low, there are no differences in the range of flake tools being made, and few differences in the relative proportions. The main difference is in the high proportion of flake tools, compared to the total number of larger flakes, from the knapping floor. This is again discussed below.

Of the four bifaces from the excavations, one was recovered from the Lower Gravel, and three from the Lower Middle Gravel. According to the traditional interpretation there should be no bifaces from either the Lower Gravel or Lower Loam, so the presence of even one, questions the validity of the division between the industries. Furthermore, in terms of the technological processes involved in the manufacture and their size, there are few grounds for distinguishing between them. All the bifaces are small, quite thick and have been usually made with a minimum of flaking (see above and Figures 16.4-5). Where they do vary is in their typology. Two of the bifaces are generally ovate in shape, one with an S-twist being from the Lower Middle Gravel, and the other deriving from the Lower Gravel. Of the remaining two, one is pointed, while the other is a non-classic (Ashton and McNabb 1994). The important point is that within the Lower Middle Gravel there is such an apparent diversity in the range of types. This in itself suggests that the variation is non-cultural, but may well be due to variation in nodule shape (*ibid.*).

One further variation that should be discussed is the difference in quantities of biface between the Lower Gravel and Lower Middle Gravel. This is discussed in more detail below.

Despite the similarities between the assemblages, can the slight variations that do occur be explained through a cultural interpretation? To answer this it is necessary to understand the effects of other factors, such as assemblage formation processes, the type and location of the raw material, the type of functions that might vary in a changing landscape, and simple human idiosyncrasy. If the variation can be explained through these factors, then it would be unnecessary to evoke cultural explanations.

One difference that occurs between the Lower Loam knapping floor and all the other units is the lack of cores in the area and the higher proportion of flake tools. The knapping floor is the only area where specific knapping events can be reconstructed, and some detail given to the movement of flint into and out of the area. Here, it is quite clear that the source of raw material is some distance from the knapping area, and that partially worked nodules have been brought to that location, knapped and then the cores taken elsewhere. With all the other units it is impossible, because of the nature of the preservation, to reconstruct events in this detail. Consequently, the other assemblages consist of a number of different knapping events, that have become intermixed, producing more amorphous assemblages and masking some of the subtle differences that may have originally occurred.

In addition, the fact that the raw material was some distance away from the knapping floor might explain the higher proportion of flake tools. As was discussed in the Knapping Floor section (see above) it is not unreasonable to suggest that the assemblages from the Lower Gravel and Lower Middle Gravel were made on raw material from those gravels. Knapping may have been taking place on a gravel bar at the edge of the river, on the source of raw material, as a primary manufacturing area. In contrast, the knapping floor assemblage consists of artefacts that have been moved from the primary manufacturing area, presumably with greater emphasis placed on their use. This might explain the higher proportion of flake tools on the knapping floor, and is supported by the presence of the fallow deer antler and skull, but the absence of other skeletal parts (see above). Although much of this model is based on conjecture, it is the type of local situation that causes assemblage variation.

It is this sort of model that might explain the variation in the number of bifaces. It could be argued that the raw material was generally less suitable for biface manufacture. This explains both the low numbers of bifaces in the different units, and also their small size. The variation that does occur could at least in part be due to very localised differences in the quality of that raw material. Equally, variation in function could also play a role. Unfortunately it is now impossible to reconstruct the types of function that were taking place along the edges of the river, and even more difficult to reconstruct the changing landscape and its impact on function variation. But as an example, localised changes in forestation may have had an important effect on hunting or scavenging patterns. Or the role of the river as a resource may have changed as fresh, eroding flint from nearby Chalk bluffs was exposed and then covered over. Unfortunately, the geological, faunal and floral evidence gives only a generalised picture of the environment, without the resolution necessary to support such reconstructions. In the absence of solid evidence, it is only possible to put forward function and the changing environment as likely important factors.

It is clear that through conjecture, and a limited amount of evidence, that the variation that occurs between the assemblages at Swanscombe could be explained by factors such as assemblage formation, raw material, function and the changing landscape. On this basis there is no clear evidence for the identification of distinct cultures at the site. Although at Swanscombe there is only limited concrete evidence for the explanation, at a different site, Barnham, Suffolk, similar explanations have a much more solid foundation.

At Barnham, the source of raw material has been clearly identified and the variation in the assemblages can be directly related to the proximity of the raw material (Ashton *et al.* 1994). The knapping occurs on the edge of a river channel with a lag gravel clearly forming the source of raw material. Against a background of general core-working, there is one distinct location where the debitage from perhaps only three or four bifaces has been recovered. The manufacture of bifaces at this spot may have been due to the presence of several larger nodules, or may simply reflect a one-off scavenging opportunity. The debitage is generally from the earlier stages of the process, but in a different area on a dry landsurfacc some distance from the raw material source, the final finishing flakes have been identified. At Barnham the variation in the assemblages can be understood within the framework of the overall landscape. This type of scenario might well explain the type of variation that can be seen at Swanscombe, rather than using a purely cultural interpretation.

17. SUMMARY

Bernard Conway, John McNabb and Nick Ashton

The Waechter excavations (1968-72) examined a series of geological exposures, in and around the National Nature Reserve at Barnfield Pit, Swanscombe, examining units from the basal Lower Gravel up to the topmost unit, the Higher Loam. Archaeological excavation concentrated on the Lower Gravel and Lower Loam within the NNR, with additional work on the Lower Middle Gravel. This has been the only formal area excavation of these lower units. A summary of the geological, palaeoenvironmental and archaeological work is presented below and in Figure 17.1.

GEOLOGICAL AND PALAEOENVIRONMENTAL HISTORY

The geological work opened a series of sections, some lying outside the NNR (Chapter 6) revealing the complete sequence, and others lying inside the NNR (Chapter 7) concentrating on the lower units. Additional environmental information was obtained from work on the vertebrate fauna (Chapters 9 - 11), ostracods (Chapter 14) and pollen (Chapter 15). The geological and palaeoenvironmental history has been reconstructed from this work.

During the latter part of the Anglian glaciation a river channel running west to east was cut through Thanet Sand to the south and through Chalk to the north. This channel was subsequently infilled by the Stage I deposits of the Lower Gravel and Lower Loam. At the base of the Lower Gravel a solifluction unit was probably deposited at the end of the Anglian (Stage Ia). The overlying sands and gravels that form the bulk of the Lower Gravel (Stage Ib) are fluvial in origin. The contained molluscs, mammals and pollen indicate fully temperate conditions with a mixture of wooded and open environments. A small, shallow channel (Stage Ic) was cut in the top of the Lower Gravel, aggraded with a shelly sand, and into which a large collection of bone accumulated. The molluscs and mammalian fauna are similar to those from the remainder of the Lower Gravel, indicating interglacial conditions.

The Lower Loam (Stage Id and e) rests in a channel cut into the top of the Lower Gravel and indicates a low-energy regime. Several interruptions in the deposition are indicated by channel recutting and by temporary dry-land surfaces. The dry surfaces are confirmed by at least one footprint horizon (Chapter 13) and by the presence of *in situ* knapping scatters (Chapter 16). The molluscs and ostracods reflect the low-energy deposition indicating a variation between clear-running water and more stagnant, marshy conditions. The pollen and terrestrial molluscs again suggest mixed oak forrest with some open areas. The identification of pollen Type X helps to confirm that the Lower Loam was formed during the Hoxnian interglacial.

At the top of the Lower Loam (Stage Ie) a land surface has been identified on which a soil profile developed. This has again been confirmed by a footprint horizon (Chapter 12). The pollen and molluscs suggest more open conditions than the remainder of the Lower Loam.

The top of the Lower Loam was truncated by fluvial activity and it is this surface at 27.5 m OD that is interpreted as the bench on which the Boyn Hill terrace deposits were laid down. Equivalent deposits have been recognised at Upminster on the north side of the Thames, resting on a bench cut into Anglian till at a similar height.

The Lower Middle Gravel (Stage IIa) forms the lowermost unit of these terrace deposits and consists of a medium sandy-gravel. This was overlain by the cross-bedded sands of the Upper Middle Gravel, both indicating fluvial deposition. The molluscs particularly in the Lower Middle Gravel include 'southern' species implying a warm climate and perhaps the development of a link between the Thames and the Rhine river systems. Whereas the terrestrial molluscs in the Lower Middle Gravel suggest a more wooded environment, those from the Upper Middle Gravel indicate open conditions with perhaps a cooling of the climate. The Upper Middle Gravel (Stage IIb) was interpreted by

STAGE	STRATIGRAPHY	VERTEBRATES	MOLLUSCS	OSTRACODS	POLLEN	PALAEOENVIRONMENT	LITHICS
IIIe	Higher Loam					Poorly understood	
IIId	Upper Gravel					Solifluction with ice wedge casts cutting IIIc	
IIIc	Upper Loam				sparse - temperate, mixed oak forest	Fluvial, overbank(?) sediment	Some bifaces - mainly ovates
IIIb	Upper Sand					Cold climate fluvial sands with cryoturbation and ice wedges cutting Ia (solifluction)	
IIIa							Some bifaces - mainly ovates
IIb	Upper Middle Gravel	Lemming & Musk ox - cooler climate? Open environment with some woodland	Cooling of climate 'Rhenish' species present Aquatic species predom. Open environment		sparse - temperate, open environment - some mixed, oak woodland	Fluvial aggradation perhaps under cooler conditions	Core and flake industry with bifaces - mainly pointed forms
IIa	Lower Middle Gravel		Temperate Aquatic species predom. First 'Rhenish' species Open environment		sparse - temperate, open environment - some mixed oak woodland	Fluvial aggradation under temperate conditions	Core and flake industry with bifaces - mainly pointed forms
Ie	Surface Lower Loam	Temperate woodland with open grass areas	Open, temperate environment Dry land surfaces	Drier Still, shallow pools	Mixed oak forest with hazel	Temperate	Core and flake industry Knapping Floors
Id	Lower Loam					Slow/still water conditions interrupted by dry land surfaces	
Ic	Midden	Temperate, open woodland	Aquatic species Temperate woodland and some open areas		sparse - temperate, open environment with some mixed oak woodland	Fluvial aggradation under temperate conditions	Core and flake industry Occasional bifaces
Ib	Lower Gravel						
Ia	Basal Gravel	Temperate?				Solifluction - cold?	Cores and flakes

Marston as the infilling of a major channel that cut through the underlying deposits down to within 0.3 m of the Thanet Sand. Although an erosional surface has been recognised at the top of the Lower Middle Gravel, there is no evidence for this channel.

All the units from the Lower Gravel to the Upper Middle Gravel were deposited during interglacial conditions. On this basis, these units have been interpreted as Hoxnian, currently argued to be Oxygen Isotope Stage 11 of the deep sea sequence. Amino acid ratios also suggest a Stage 11 date (Bowen *et al.* 1989).

The top of the Upper Middle Gravel is cryoturbated and was overlain by solifluction material (Stage IIIa) and the newly recognised fluvial Upper Sand (Stage IIIb) under periglacial conditions; well developed ice-wedge casts are visible at several levels. The Upper Sand passes conformably up into the Upper Loam (Stage IIIc) which contains sparse pollen, suggesting interglacial conditions. The overlying Upper Gravel (Stage IIId) is a further solifluction unit, with cold conditions indicated by the ice-wedge casts at its base. Finally this unit is overlain by the also newly recognised, but poorly understood Higher Loam (Stage IIIe).

The sequence from the Upper Sand to Upper Gravel suggests a change in climate from cold to warmer and back to cold conditions. This has been interpreted here as representing Oxygen Isotope Stages 10 to 8, equivalent to the first stadial, first interstadial and second stadial of the Saalian glaciation.

ARCHAEOLOGICAL SEQUENCE

The archaeological work at the site is reported in Chapter 5 and the flint industries are described and interpreted in Chapter 16. Traditionally, the sequence at Swanscombe was thought to consist of a Clactonian (core and flake) industry in the Lower Gravel, a sterile Lower Loam, overlain by an Acheulian (biface) industry in the Lower Middle Gravel. The Waechter excavations have demonstrated that there is very clearly a core and flake industry in the Lower Loam, but also that the interpretation of the Swanscombe industries as representing at least two different cultures, is difficult to maintain.

In terms of the core working and flake tool technology the knapping from the Lower Gravel, Lower Loam and Lower Middle Gravel is virtually identical. Where slight differences do occur, these can be explained in terms of fluvial size-sorting, slight changes in the availability of the raw material, or slight variation in function (see Chapter 16). The main difference between the assemblages is in the proportion of bifaces (1/1105 artefacts for the Lower Gravel and 3/151 for the Lower Middle Gravel).

These differences are clearly quantitative, rather than qualitative in nature which suggests that a non-cultural explanation is more likely to account for the variation. As discussed in Chapter 16, slight differences in the raw material might be one explanation, or changes in the landscape leading to variation in the activities on the river margins might be another. At Swanscombe these types of factor are now difficult to assess, although at the site of Barnham (Ashton *et al.* 1994) they have been shown to have a demonstrable effect on assemblage composition. There are good reasons to believe that similar effects account for the variation at Swanscombe.

In addition, the Lower Loam knapping floor has yielded important behavioural information. There it can be demonstrated that partially worked cores were brought into the area and knapped. From the debitage a variety of tools were made and probably used prior to being discarded. In particular, the skull and antlers of a fallow deer, in the absence of other skeletal remains, suggest that initial butchery may have been one of the activities in the area. All the cores were removed from the area, presumably for knapping elsewhere. This is one of only a handful of examples from the Lower Palaeolithic of Britain where evidence of perhaps only twenty minutes of human activity has been preserved.

The study of these assemblages has highlighted the changes in archaeological approach and direction. The main thrust of study until recently was the creation of a cultural framework which documented the progress and changes in one aspect of material culture, namely stone tools. Waechter undertook these excavations very much with this in mind, but he also had the foresight to realise that gathering behavioural information was also important, hence his concentration on the excavation of the knapping floor. The behavioural information that has been gleaned from the knapping floor reflects the research questions that are now coming to the forefront. What state was the raw material in when it was brought to the area? What knapping took place? Was the flint used? Was it taken away for use elsewhere? All these are questions that lead to a reconstruction of human activity. Answering such questions leads to further questions, such as what foresight or planning was involved in early human behaviour? Did they hunt or scavenge? Or how did humans adapt to the environment? It is only through such an approach that there is any hope of beginning to understand the Lower Palaeolithic. Does it matter about the first Acheulian, or the earliest Englishman? The first humans, most definitely yes.

APPENDIX I

Nick Ashton and John McNabb

The methodology for the flint analysis used in Chapter 16 is summarised below.

FLAKES AND CORES

Condition

1.   Fresh condition. Sharp edges with no evidence of natural abrasion or edge damage.

2.   Moderately rolled. Edges with clear abrasion and damage. Arrêtes on dorsal slightly rounded.

3.   Very rolled. Edges considerably rolled and abraded. Clear rounding of arrêtes on dorsal surface.

Surface colorations

1. Black
2. Orange
3. Brown
4. Grey

5. Yellow
6. Green/Grey
7. White

White/grey colorations are usually indicative of patination, orange, brown and yellow suggest iron or manganese staining, while black usually indicates little surface alteration.

Surface sheen

1. Matt
2. Slight sheen
3. Gloss

This is an indication of abrasion. From matt usually being unabraded to gloss being considerably abraded.

In addition, it was also noted whether each flake or core was whole or broken.

FLAKES

Cortex

1. Wholly cortical
2. > 50% cortex
3. < 50% cortex
4. No cortex

Butt types

1. Plain. Flake removed from a single flake scar.

2. Dihedral. Flake removed from the intersection of two flake scars.

3. Cortical. Flake removed from cortical surface.

4. Natural. Flake removed from natural (but non-cortical) flint surface (eg frost shatter surface etc).

5. Marginal. Flake removed from edge of core, forming narrow, indeterminate butt.

6. Soft hammer. Flake removed with antler/bone/wood hammer forming diffused bulb of percussion, wide point of percussion and often with a lip at the contact between the butt and the ventral surface. The butt is often very thin and in these cases frequently associated with shattering.

7. Mixed. Flake removed from a combination of natural and flake surfaces (eg cortical/plain or natural/plain).

Dorsal scar patterns (see Figure 1)

Previous flakes, as indicated by the dorsal scar pattern, removed in the following directions with the flake orientated with the butt at the base.

1. Flakes removed from proximal end only.
2. Flakes removed from proximal and left only, or proximal and right only.
3. Flakes removed from proximal, left and right.
4. Flakes removed from proximal, distal and right only, or proximal, distal and left only.
5. Flakes removed from either left only, or right only.
6. Flakes removed from distal.
7. Flakes removed from proximal and distal.
8. Flakes removed from right and left.
9. Flakes removed from proximal, right, left and distal.
10. Dorsal wholly cortical or natural.
11. Flakes removed right, left and distal.
12. Flakes removed from distal and right only, or distal and left only.

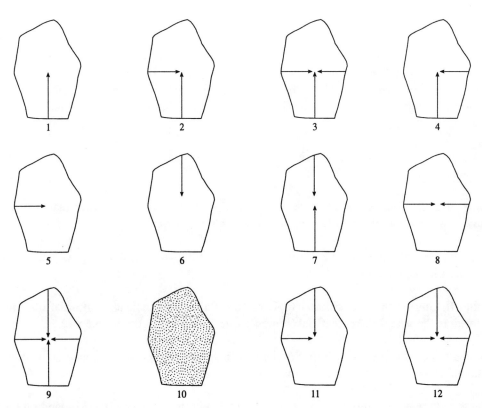

Fig. 1. Dorsal scar patterns

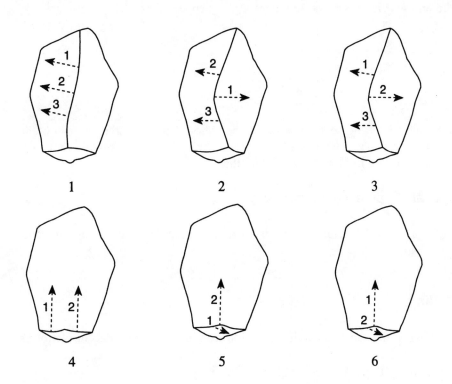

Fig. 2. Relict core edges

Relict core edges (see Figure 2)

Where a part of a core edge, showing negative bulbs of percussion, is preserved on a flake, this is termed a relict core edge. They can be divided up into two main types: types 1-3 where the core edge is preserved on the dorsal of the flake and forms part of a seperate sequence to that flake; and types 4-6 where the core edge is on the butt of the flake. For the full definition of the core flaking types, see cores, below.

1. Parallel flaking on the dorsal. Two or more flake scars indicating parallel removals from a single or adjacent platforms.

2. Simple alternate flaking on the dorsal. A sequence of flake scars showing that one or more removals formed the platform for one or more further removals.

3. Complex alternate flaking on the dorsal. Similar to 2, but involving showing evidence of at least one more turn of the core.

4. Parallel flaking on the butt. Similar to 1, but the flake scars indicate removal from the same platform as the actual flake, that flake being the last removal in that sequence.

5. Simple alternate flaking on the butt. Similar to 2, but the sequence is positioned on the butt, with the actual flake forming the last removal in the sequence.

6. Complex alternate flaking on the butt. Similar to 3, but the sequence is positioned on the butt, with the actual flake forming the last removal in the sequence.

In addition to the above information, each flake was assessed as to whether it was a soft or hard hammer flake and whether there was any platform adjustment present.

CORES

The system of analysis of the cores is based on the notion that core reduction can be divided up into a number of different stages, each described as a core episode. Each core-episode consists of a series of removals that naturally follow on from each other.

Single removal, Type A (see Figure 3.1)

This consists of a single flake removal from a natural surface or from flake scars that are part of a different core episode.

Parallel flaking, Type B (see Figure 3.2)

Two or more flakes removed in a parallel direction from the same or adjacent platforms.

Alternate flaking, Type C (see Figure 3.3-3.5)

One or more flakes removed in parallel form the platform or platforms at their proximal ends for the next on or more removals. They in turn may form the platform or platforms at their proximal ends for further removals in the same direction as the original set of removals. The core may be turned several times in this way. This can be divided into several types:

Simple alternate flaking, Type Ci (see Figure 3.3). The core is turned just once, with one or more removals forming the platform for the second set of removals.

Complex alternate flaking, Type Cii (see Figure 3.4). The core is turned at least twice and consists of at least three sets of removals.

Classic alternate flaking, Type Ciii (see Figure 3.5). A single flake forms the platform for the second flake which in turn forms the platform for the third flake. Several more flakes may be removed in this way.

If episodes of parallel flaking occur as part of Ci or Cii, then they are termed Cip or Ciip.

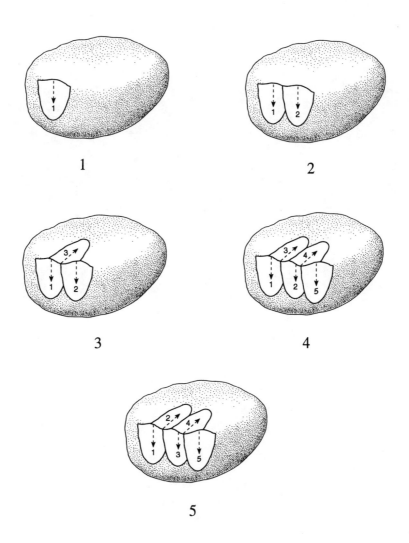

Fig. 3. Core episode types

APPENDIX II

Editors Note

In 1965 Marston told B.W. Conway that he had written a second paper on the Barnfield Pit deposits, following that published in the *Journal of the Royal Anthropological Institute* (Marston 1937A), but that it had been mislaid when it was submitted for publication. In 1976 a typescript copy of Marston's unpublished paper came into Conway's possession having apparently been discovered among off-prints and papers at a saleroom.

The typescript, which is a carbon copy, shows marginal notes in pencil made by a referee/editor and notes (answers) made in ink by Marston, some of which he has initialled. These are indicated in their approximate positions by numbers in brackets and the notes are listed at the end of the text.

An additional note on the Stratigraphy of the Barnfield deposits by A.T.M. Marston, December 1937.

The Barnfield deposits have usually been considered as a part of the right bank terrace of the Lower Thames, the corresponding and contemporary left bank of which is to be found on the Essex side of the present river. An alternative view may be considered.

Instead of being merely a right bank terrace, the Barnfield deposits may be considered as the infilling of an old river bed which was cut down for a distance of about fifty feet (1, 2) through the overlying Tertiary deposits almost to the surface of the Chalk. This river bed was infilled by an ascending sequence of sub-terraces contained within the banks of the original channel, and was ultimately capped by a Boyn Hill flood plain deposit which reached its maximum at Swanscombe in the twisted ovate stage of the neighbouring New Craylands Pit.

Both of the original banks of the Barnfield river are visible. The east bank shows in section, on the Craylands Lane side of the pit near to the allotments. The west bank is exposed as it rests upon the slope of the Thanet Sands at the extreme western end of the pit.

The width of the Barnfield channel is about 1,400 feet (A.T.M. Nov. 14 1937). The width of the Thames at:

Oxford	150 feet
Teddington	250 feet
London Bridge	750 feet
Gravesend	2150 feet
Between Sheerness and Shoeburyness	5½ miles

(3 and 4)   (Enc. Britt., 14th edit., Vol 22, p.16a)

In Ricksons Pit, Swanscombe, the channel can be seen cutting down into the Chalk on the side of the pit nearest to the footpath from Stanhope to Ebbsfleet.

In the Stone Court Pit at Horns Cross, about one and a half miles west of Barnfield, a classic section of an infilled river bed which is cut down below the surface of the Chalk, shows along the face of the east side of the pit, below the road from Horns Cross to Stone Railway Station. This channel is not to be considered as contemporary with the Barnfield channel; there is no lower loam, and the direction of the channel, West by N.W. to East by S.E., and the difference in base levels, indicate different ages for the two channels. The base of the gravel at Horns Cross is given as 110 feet above

O.D.. The height of the Chalk bank between this channel and the present Thames would be about 130 feet.

In the three instances given, the old river beds are separated from the present Thames by Chalk which is at a higher level than the floors of these channels. These were therefore cut before the excavation of the present valley of the Thames with its descending sequence of terraces, began. At Barnfield, the Chalk rises on the east and is higher under New Craylands Pit than under Barnfield.

A discrepancy appears as to the height usually given of the solid shelf underlying the gravel deposit at Barnfield. The Dartford Memoir (1924) gives the level of the Lower Loam as 83 ft OD. Allowing a thickness of 10 feet for the Lower Loam and the Lower Gravel, the base of the terrace at Barnfield must be 73 ft OD, instead of 90 ft OD. The top of the Chalk at Ingress Vale is given as approximately 83 ft, and the chalk shelf at New Craylands Pit as just over 90 ft OD.

At Barnfield, the Chalk is capped by the Thanet Sands, and the Bull Head Bed between the Chalk and the Thanet Sand has been found to be *in situ* wherever the junction of the Chalk and the Thanet Sand has been examined. Further downcutting below this stage therefore did not occur at Barnfield during the course of the infilling of the Barnfield channel. This becomes obvious to an observer standing on the floor of the Chalk pit below Barnfield with his back to the north, and looking upwards to see the Barnfield channel stranded above at the top of the Chalk face.

At the period of the deposition of the basal bed of the Lower Gravel, the Barnfield river can be visualised as coursing down a channel which was at least fifty feet below the surface of the land, since in spite of the subsequent surface denudation due to peri-glacial and other causes, the land on the western side of the channel rises more than 50 feet above the base of the deposits.

Upon the floor of the channel rests a layer of fine gravel from which the very small and often highly lustrous Clacton type flakes and implements were obtained. Some of these, the single and double concave side-scrapers, points, etc. have typologically and eolithic facies. Among the thousand or so of these small flakes and implements I have several which manifest differing degrees of white patination, which suggests shallow water conditions at some time during this stage. This layer is not uniformly preserved throughout the pit. In places it has been eroded or displaced by the coarse gravel layer which lies above it and contains scratched flakes suggestive of solifluxion conditions, and it is to be expected that a solifluxion layer would erode, to some extent, the finer gravel of the basal layer. It was in this fine basal layer that in the summer of 1937 we found the solid portion of a tusk of Elephas antiquus (?) eight and a half feet in length.

As regards the second and coarse, red gravel layer, from it I have obtained flakes with striations in the one direction only, which certainly supports the view that they were embedded in a semi-frozen (5) sludge which had found its way along the floor of the channel. They are usually coated with a tenacious brown clay which has to be washed off before the flakes can be judged for the presence of secondary work.

I would suggest that here we have evidence that the small lustrous Clacton flakes and implements from the lowest layer, and the contents of the second layer, i.e. the scratched flakes, the lustrous greenish Clacton flakes and the Strepy implements, belonged to an earlier stage which was separated from the Barnfield Middle Gravel stage by the intervention of peri-glacial conditions which were favourable for the deposition of a solifluxion layer.

I am inclined to the view that a certain amount of redistribution of the Lower Gravels occurred after the deposition of the solifluxion layer, and that the beds above this layer and up to the Lower Loam belong to a later stage. The layer above the solifluxion layer contains in places a large proportion of flint nodules freshly derived from the Chalk, and nodules of rolled chalk, sometimes as heavy as one can lift, occur; in places the gravels are almost cemented by chalk wash-out. The flakes tend to become larger and more typically Clactonian, that is, with a straighter ventral cleavage face, with less diffuse bulbs of percussion, and the colour to pass from the green through the yellow green to the rich brown. I am also of the opinion that the brown Clacton flakes although often they have been considered to have been derived, are not necessarily older than the green Clacton flakes, but that they became so patinated by being subjected to redistribution within the same terrace. It is noteworthy that the brown Clacton flakes preponderate in section F at Barnfield where the Lower and Middle Gravels are mixed during the infilling of the Middle Gravel Erosion Stage.

The capping of the Lower Gravels and the shell bed (6) by the deposition of the Lower Loam as a silt, may be considered as the end stage of the Lower Gravel Terrace (7 and 8). It marks a definite pause in the history of the river. For some reason or other, the flow of water in the Barnfield channel ceased. The mud silt layer, 2 to 6 ft in thickness became a land surface upon which plants grew, land snails lived, and Clacton flakes remained sufficiently long to become patinated white by sub-aerial exposure. I have over 70 of these large white Clacton flakes.

What happened to the water? Was the drying up of the Barnfield river bed due to

a.   prolonged dry period?
b.   the water being diverted along another channel?
c.   the water being tied up in ice?

The last condition, a peri-glacial interlude, is at variance with the warmth loving mammalian fauna of the Lower Gravel shell bed from which I have obtained Lion, Rhinoceros, Elephant and Deer.

If the second possibility were entertained, we should still have to ask why, if the river found a path of less resistance elsewhere and was able to cut down the supposed ..... into the Chalk to 20 ft OD, it should have again returned to its former bed 63 feet higher up (9), to become subjected anew to the difficulties which it had sought to evade? And further, if a period of land elevation were to be invoked of such intensity as to cause the cutting of the Little Thurrock and Clacton channels at this stage, would not the rejuvenated river first have scoured its own floor and have removed the Lower Loam which was still sufficiently plastic to allow Clacton flakes and cores from its surface to sink within it? And in the case of a river of the width of the Barnfield channel, could we not expect that any violent change in the system of drainage which could institute this scouring of a new bed through 63 feet of solid Chalk, would have found it easier to erode the loosely held silt, sand, and gravel which comprises the Lower Gravels, before it could become actively engaged in cutting down through the solid. At Barnfield, positive as contrasted with negative evidence of a stage of down-cutting from the surface of the Lower Loam at this stage, is absent.

But, by whatever means the hiatus at the stage of the weathering of the surface of the Lower Loam be explained, the next stage of the infilling of the Barnfield channel brings a new factor into the situation, namely, the Chelles-Acheulean type of implement. The Dartford Memoir (1924) states of the Middle Gravel implements:

> Palaeolithic implements were numerous but mostly of 'pear-shape' and of rather rough workmanship. Those from the lower beds are of Early Chelles type; the upper layers yield more advanced work, with one or two ovates approaching the St. Acheul form. The Middle Gravel may therefore represent the whole of the Chelles period and the transition to that of St. Acheul.

Note. The Dartford Memoir came into my hands for the first time in September 1937 and after my paper containing the suggestion that the Older Middle Gravels be recognised as an Abbevillian horizon had gone to press. My own opinion was independent and was based on practical experience in the pit, uninfluenced by theoretical or academic considerations.

While I am conscious that my view that the Older Middle Gravels should be considered an Abbevillian horizon will encounter criticism, and also that the raising of debatable issues may obscure that which I wish to clarify to the utmost, namely, the very precise horizon of the Swanscombe skull, the sole object of this additional note on the stratigraphy of the Barnfield deposits, is to allow the very precise Acheulean horizon of the skull to be the more accurately estimated and appreciated, in the Pleistocene time-sheet. (A.T.M.)

I have divided the Middle Gravel Stage into the Older Middle Gravels and the Later Middle Gravels, the two being separated by the Middle Gravel Erosion Stage.

During the deposition of the Lower Gravels, the Lower Loam, and of the Older Middle Gravels, the Barnfield river had neither deepened its bed nor widened to any great extent its banks. Its western bank did not overflow, for here the Thanet Sands rise higher than the Upper Loam. These conditions may be correlated with a continued period of land subsidence. Although the river flowed with sufficient force to transport gravels and large blocks of stone, the ordinary scouring action of water borne detritus was negatived by the fall of land level. The land sank faster than the river and the aggradates accumulated.

After the deposition of the Older Middle Gravels, there is evidence of the existence of a Middle Loam, a whitish mud-silt, which is relatively rich in Acheulean, as distinguished from Abbevillian, implements which occur in mint condition. Clacton type flakes and cores in the same condition are found in this layer, the Acheulean implements being more numerous. Sometimes such flakes show an incipient white patination, just a smear of white. This silt layer is not continuous. The inference may be made that it suffered erosion, as indeed may have the higher layers of the Older Middle Gravels, during the channelling and oscillations of the later phases of the Boyn Hill flood plain. The Older Middle Gravels, capped by the Middle Loam may be considered as a further terrace within the Barnfield Channel.

Note. Treacher and White (1909, 198) consider that the smaller implements from Furze Platt upper pit may with some reason be referred to the Chellian and the lower to the Acheulean stage.

For some reason or other, either a period of land elevation, or of greatly increased volume of water, a major channel was cut which passed through the whole depth of the Older Middle Gravels, through the Lower Loam, and down through the Lower Gravels, actually reaching in one place at least in section F, the original level of the Thanet Sand floor of the main channel.

It should be emphasised, that in the early stage of this down-cutting, in the first oblique bank which was left stranded as the channel was cut lower, is the horizon of the Swanscombe skull.

The skull horizon was subsequent to the Older Middle Gravel Stage, and prior to the stage of infilling of the Middle Gravel Erosion Stage.

At this point it is of interest to note the apparent declination in the bedding of the Older Middle Gravels from the north-east to the south-west, and also that the centralisation of the new channel was carried nearer to the western than the eastern side of the pit. In this respect too, it is of interest to note that the Chalk level east of Barnfield, and under and beyond New Craylands Pit, rises higher than under Barnfield. Is it possible that the modification of relative land level, (elevation?) which inaugurated the Middle Gravel Erosion Stage, was accompanied by some degree of land tilt along this approximately north-east to the south-west line, which modified the system of drainage and caused the main river to swing to the north side of the present Thames, and in its later system of Boyn Hill flood plain meanderings to have deposited gravels with Acheulean implements, which at Hornchurch, could rest upon the eroded surface of the Chalky-Jurassic Boulder Clay.

EVIDENCE OF THE MIDDLE GRAVEL EROSION STAGE

a.   In order to establish the connection between the down-cutting evidenced by the oblique seams at the skull site in section D, with the erosion of the Lower Loam in section F, in September 1937 I sank a pit at the extreme west end of section D. The surface of the Lower Loam at that spot sank to 4ft 6ins below the floor of section D. It was covered by a seam of coarse sharp gravel about 9 inches thick, which yielded a stone-struck hand-axe (conchoidal flake scars). This seam was covered by a seam of finer gravel about 6 inches thick. Above this was only fine whitish current-bedded sand. The erosion had reduced the whole depth of the Older Middle Gravels from 10-12 feet to approximately 1 foot.

b.   I have a photograph taken in the winter of 1935 not sufficiently good for reproduction, which shows the absence of gravels above the floor level and their replacement by sands alone, in the west corner of section D. This feature will be remembered by those familiar with the pit in 1933-35. It is now obscured by falls of the top-brown clay.

c.   Plate 3a (10) in the Proceedings of the Geologists' Association Vol. XLVI, 1935. A photograph by Mr A.L. Leach shows the Lower Loam to be absent in this part of section F.

d.   Not only does the hard white state of preservation of the bones in the Older Middle Gravels differ from the softer bones, often brown, of the Later Middle Gravels, and the workmanship of the Older Middle Gravel differ from the more advanced implements of the Later Middle Gravels, but the relative proportions of Chalk and Tertiary derived pebbles and flints differs in the Older and the Later Middle Gravels.

e.   On Sunday December 12 1937, I was trying to satisfy myself that the Bull Head Bed was in situ below the Thanet Sand under section F, a part of the pit now no longer worked and which has been covered by a dump of Thanet Sand from a neighbouring Chalk-pit. The surface of the Chalk was cleared and the Bull Head Bed was found to be in situ. However, resting upon the undisturbed Barnfield Thanet Sand some feet higher up, I found a layer of undisturbed sharp gravel which was similar to the fine gravel seam noted in paragraph "a". This seam I explored, expecting to find as its position suggested, flakes, but to my surprise found an Acheulean ovate, which was black, lustrous, and unabraded. The patination and condition were the same as that on an Acheulean implement found in 1934 at floor level in the western corner of Section D where the gravel seams disappear from above the (11) working floor of the section, and the working face consists only of the current bedded yellow sands. It is important to recognise that this implement was found on the level of the Thanet Sand, and that although from its position it might have been misjudged as a Lower Gravel implement, it was in reality an implement of the post-Older Middle Gravel Stage, which had reached this position as the result of the Middle Gravel Erosion Stage. This implement connects the down-cutting at the skull site in section D with the down-cutting through the Lower Loam, in section F.

Note. The implement has been sent to the British Museum, Bloomsbury, to be recorded and photographed.

THE STAGE OF THE LATER MIDDLE GRAVEL INFILLING

Aggregates to the depth of about 45 feet (12) accumulated and filled the channel. These covered the skull site, where they are represented by gravels and sands above the horizontal seam of silt which caps in the oblique seams, and they feathered out over the surface of the Older Middle Gravels to become merged into the hard laminated sands of the Upper Loam. (13)

This infilling of the Middle Gravel Erosion channel may be regarded as still another stage in the ascending sequence of terraces in the Barnfield river bed.

It did not complete the ascending sequence, however. From the working floor within the Upper Loam white patinated flakes and Acheulean implements which are still below the twisted ovate stage, indicate a period of sub-aerial exposure. Doubtless minor oscillations affected the upper layers of the deposits about this time.

It has been felt that among the implements found in the far west end of the pit, section F, are some which are later than those found even on the surfaces of sections A and D. Some such implements are typologically identical with those obtained from the channel which crosses the floor of Pearson's Pit, Dartford Heath, differing only in that the latter are often more abraded and show signs of being, or having been, patinated white.

Other implements from section F resemble those from the Wansunt channel, Dartford, and which are showing Plates 16 and 17 (*Proc. Geol. Assoc.*, Vol. XXIII) to illustrate the paper by Messrs Chandler and Leach. I have four implements of the Plate 17 figs 1 and 2 types.

From the examinations of the sections in Pearson's Pit, Heath Street, Dartford, and in Bowman's Pit, Dartford Heath, from the implements from the former and from the levels in which the implements occur I would assign a later date to the whole depth of the deposits in these two pits than the Barnfield Older Middle Gravels, and to a somewhat later stage than even the Acheulean working floor within the Barnfield Upper Loam.

The fact that implements which are found unabraded in the later stages of the Barnfield sequence occur abraded in the earliest stage of Pearson's Pit, Dartford, is of importance in establishing the Dartford Heath gravels as Boyn Hill flood plain deposits, and as appreciably later than the horizon of the Swanscombe skull.

NEW CRAYLANDS PIT

A still later aggradative stage of the Boyn Hill terrace than Barnfield is to be recognised in the deposits of the New Craylands Pit, a now disused pit on the east side of Craylands Lane, and immediately adjacent to the Barnfield Pit.

Men who were engaged in this pit while it was being worked have told me that twisted implements were found 13 feet below the surface against a seam of blue clay. "All the implements in this pit had twists and were worked smooth".

The Dartford Memoir describes the twisted Acheulean ovates which were found on the surface of the current bedded sandy gravel. This pit is at a slightly higher level than most of the Middle Gravel at Barnfield Pit. The twisted ovates from Rickson's Pit, Swanscombe, would probably correspond with the New Craylands Stage.

SUMMARY

The stratigraphical sequence of the Barnfield deposits which I have thus visualised, may be summarised as follows:

Stage 1	(14) Early stage of down-cutting during which the Barnfield Lower Gravel channel were cut down at least 50 feet below the existing land surface and down into the solid to about 73 ft OD.
Stage 2	Lower Gravel Aggradative Stage, containing Strepy and Clactonian artifacts, but no Abbevillian. This stage may probably be further subdivided into i. up to the surface of the solifluxion layer. ii. from it up to the surface of the Lower Loam.
Stage 2a	Resting phase of the surface of the Lower Loam. Flakes become patinated white.
Stage 3	Older Middle Gravel Aggradative Stage, with implements representing the whole of the Chelles or Abbevillian period and the transition to that of St. Acheul.
Stage 3a	Resting phase of the surface of the Older Middle Gravels and Middle Loam (?). Occasional white patinated Acheulean and Clactonian implements. The habitation level of Swanscombe Man.

| Stage 4 | (15) Middle Gravel Erosion Stage. The formation of a series of descending, oblique, overlapping seams. The erosion, gradual at first, accelerated later. The horizon of the Swanscombe skull was in the first bank to be left stranded. |

| Stage 5 | Later Middle Gravel Aggradative Stage. The infilling to the level of the Acheulean working floor within the Upper Loam. Still below the twisted ovate stage. |

| Stage 5a | Resting phase of the Upper Loam. Implements and flakes patinated white. |

| Stage 6 | New Craylands Pit Aggradative Stage. With twisted ovates. The maximum of the Boyn Hill flood plain at Swanscombe. |

At the end of stage 5, the deposits of a sandy nature had spread out beyond the confines of the original Barnfield channel. The stratified nature of the fine and compact sandy Upper Loam, in which each strata at Barnfield may have been represented higher upstream by a layer of gravel, suggests the existence of an appreciable time interval between stages 5 and 6.

In regard to this, the New Craylands stage is of interest. The aggradates in New Craylands Pit are coarse gravels overlain by current bedded gravel and sand. We have still to ask why a sand deposition river such as formed the Barnfield Upper sandy Loam should have become rejuvenated into a gravel transporting river?

On the west side of New Craylands Pit a Coombe Rock appears to underlie the gravel; on the east side a Coombe Rock overlies the gravel; and north of the pit and showing in the railway cutting approaching Swanscombe Halt Station, a Coombe Rock underlies the gravel (16). In some sections of the face no chalky rubble shows either above, in, or below the gravel. Did a peri-glacial interlude therefore intervene between stages 5 and 6?

In this sequence, the horizon of the horizon of the Swanscombe skull, which is definitely placed as occurring later than the Barnfield Older Middle Gravel Stage, and at the beginning of the Middle Gravel Erosion Stage, was antecedent to the establishment of the Boyn Hill Flood Plain.

Although the skull was found 24 feet below the surface at Barnfield, this figure alone does not fully convey an adequate idea of its antiquity. But when it is visualised that after the Swanscombe skull horizon the deep aggradates in Bowman's Pit, Dartford Heath, were formed, then a new meaning is added to the horizon of the skull.

Thanks are expressed to the management of the Barnfield Pit for the facilities extended during 1937; to the workmen in the pit who have removed my debris and have cleared the top-sand above the bone site; and to my voluntary workers, Messrs J. Jones, W. Carter and J. Capon who have worked with me on the site.

Alvan T Marston December 1937

Marginal Notes

Ref = referee or editor (unknown). ATM = A. T. Marston.

1.	Ref.	What is the figure of 50 ft based on?
2.	ATM.	Answer. At the far end of Section F the position of the ovate was quite 50 ft below surface. Chandler says surface is about 125 ft OD.
3.	Ref.	This is the width of the actual water surely, not that of the channel.
4.	ATM.	Granted.
5.	Ref.	? partly.
6.	Ref.	Which? Not mentioned previously.
7.	Ref.	Can you really regard this as a terrace? Infilling.
8.	ATM.	Yes if it can be shown there is a hiatus between the Lower and Middle Gravels.
9.	Ref.	Where are these figures obtained from?
10.	Ref.	3b?
11.	Ref.	Present day
12.	Ref.	Is the channel really 45 ft. deep?
13.	Ref.	Not very clear.
14.	Ref.	Pre-Boyn Hill Erosion Stage.
15.	Ref.	Inter-Boyn Hill Erosion Stage.
16.	ATM.	The Coombe Rock overlies the gravels. Mr Oakley is of the opinion, after examining the railway cutting, that the gravel showing here is a solifluxion gravel and <u>later</u> than the current bedded sands and gravels of New Crayland Stage.

254

BIBLIOGRAPHY

Absolon, A. 1973. Ostracoden aud einigen profilen spät-und postglazialer karbonatablagerungen in Mitteleuropa. *Mitt. Bayer. Staatsamml. Paläont. Hist. Geol.* 13, 47-94.

Anon, 1931 (c/f Dewey 1959)

Ashley-Montagu, M.F. 1948. Report on expedition to Swanscombe, Kent: 26th May-13th Sept. 1948. *The Archaeological Newsletter for April 1948.*

Ashley-Montagu, M.F. 1949. A report of archaeological work at Swanscombe and Galley Hill, Kent, England: June to September 1948. *Bull. Philadelphia Anthropol. Soc.* 2, 2-3.

Ashton, N.M., Dean, P. and McNabb, J. 1991. Flaked flakes: what, where, when and why? *Lithics* 12, 1-11.

Ashton, N.M. 1992. The High Lodge flint industries. *In* Ashton, N.M., Cook, J., Lewis, S.G. and Rose, J. (eds) *High Lodge. Excavations by G. de G. Sieveking 1962-68 and J. Cook 1988.* British Museum Press. London.

Ashton, N.M., Cook, J., Lewis, S.G. and Rose, J. (eds) 1992. *High Lodge. Excavations by G. de G. Sieveking 1962-68 and J. Cook 1988.* British Museum Press. London.

Ashton, N.M., McNabb, J., Irving, B., Lewis, S. and Parfitt, S. 1994. Contemporaneity of Clactonian and Acheulian flint industries at Barnham, Suffolk. *Antiquity* 68, 585-589.

Ashton, N. and McNabb, J. 1994. Bifaces in perspective. *In* Ashton, N. and David, A. (eds) *Stories in Stone.* Lithic Studies Occasional Paper No. 4, 182-191.

Ashton, N.M., McNabb, J. and Bridgland, D.R. 1995. Barnfield Pit, Swanscombe (TQ 598743). *In* Bridgland, D.R., Allen, P. and Haggart, B.A. (eds) *The Quaternary of the Lower Reaches of the Thames.* Quaternary Research Association Field Guide. Preliminary edition.

Bamber, H.K. 1908. Portland Cement. *Proc. Inst. Civil Engineers*, 1907-1908.

Bastin, B. and Couteaux, M. 1966. Application de la méthode de Frenzel a l'extraction des pollens dans les sédiments archéologiques pauvres. *L'Anthropologie* 70, 201-203.

Baumel, J.J., King, A.S. Lucas, A.M., Breazile, J.E. and Evans, H.E. (eds). 1979. *Nomina Anatomica Avium.* Academic Press. London.

Behrensmeyer, A.K. and Laporte, L.F. 1981 Peistocene hominid in northern Kenya. *Science* 289, 167-169.

Bordes, F. 1950A. Principes d'une methode d'étude des téchniques de débitage et de la typologie du Paléolithique ancien et moyen. *L'Anthropologie* 54, 19-34.

Bordes, F. 1950B. L'Evolution buissonnante des industries en Europe occidentale. Considérations théoriques sur le Paléolithique ancien et moyen. *L'Anthropologie* 54, 393-420.

Bordes, F. 1956. Some observations on the Pleistocene succession in the Somme Valley. *Proc. Prehist. Soc.* 22, 1-5.

Bordes F. and Bourgon, M. 1951. Le complexe Mousterien; Mousteriens, Levalloisien, et Tayacien. *L'Anthropologie 55,* 1-23.

Bowen, D.Q., Hughes, S., Sykes, G.A. and Miller, G.H. 1989. Land-sea correlations in the Pleistocene based on isoluecine epimerization in non-marine molluscs. *Nature* 340, 49-51.

Boyd Dawkins, W. 1910. The arrival of man in Britain in the Pleistocene age. *J. Roy. Anthropol. Inst. Gr. Brit. Ir. 40,* 233-263.

Breuil, H. 1932. Les industries a éclats du Paléolithique ancien, I: Le Clactonien. *Prehistoire* 1, 148-157

Bridgland, D.R. 1988. The Pleistocene fluvial stratigraphy and palaeogeography of Essex. *Proc. Geol. Ass.* 99, 291-314.

Bridgland, D.R. 1994. *Quaternary of the Thames.* Chapman and Hall. London.

Bridgland, D.R., Gibbard, P.L., Harding, P., Kemp, R.A. and Southgate, G. 1985. New information and results from recent excavations at Barnfield Pit, Swanscombe. *Quaternary Newsletter* 46, 25-39.

Bridgland, D.R., Allen, P. and Haggart, B.A. 1995. *The Quaternary of the Lower Reaches of the Thames.* Quaternary Research Association Field Guide. Preliminary edition.

Briggs, D.J., Coope, G.R. and Gilbertson, D.D. 1985. *The chronology and environmental framework of Early Man in the Upper Thames Valley.* Brit. Archaeol. Rep., British Series 137. Oxford.

British Birds, 1993. *The 'British Birds' list of English names of Western Palearctic birds.* British Birds. Blunham. Bedford.

British Museum. 1902. *A Guide to the Antiquities of the Stone Age.* British Museum. London. 1st edit.

British Museum. 1911. *A Guide to the Antiquities of the Stone Age.* British Museum. London. 2nd edit.

British Museum. 1926. *A Guide to the Antiquities of the Stone Age.* British Museum. London. 3rd edit.

Brodkorb, P. 1964. Catalogue of fossil birds. Part 2. (Anseriformes through Galliformes). *Bull. Florida State Mus. Biol. Sci.* 8, 195-335.

Bull, A. J. 1942. Pleistocene chronology. *Proc. Geol. Ass.* 53, 1-20.

Burchell, J.P.T. and Reid Moir, J. 1933. East Anglia: Implementiferous Deposits. *Man* 33, 31-31.

Bury, H. 1942. Reply to Bull (1942). *Proc. Geol. Ass.* 53, 20.

Campbell, S. and Bowen, D.Q. 1989. *Quaternary of Wales.* Geological Conservation Review Series. Nature Conservancy Council.

Carss, D.N. and Brockie, K. 1994. Prey remains at osprey nests in Tayside and Grampian, 1987-1993. *Scottish Birds* 17, 132-145.

Castell, C.P. 1964. The non-marine Mollusca. *In* Ovey, C. (ed) *The Swanscombe Skull. A survey of Research on a Pleistocene Site. Roy. Anthropol. Inst. Gr. Brit. Ir. Occasional Paper No. 20,* 77-83.

Chandler, R.H. 1928/29. On the Clactonian industry at Swanscombe. *Proc. Prehist. Soc. East Anglia* 6, 79-116.

Chandler, R.H. 1931A. The Clactonian Industry and report of field meeting at Swanscombe. *Proc. Geol. Ass.* 42, 175-177.

Chandler, R.H. 1931B. Types of Clactonian implements at Swanscombe. *Proc. Prehist. Soc. East Anglia* 6, 377-378.

Chandler, R.H. 1932. The Clactonian Industry and report of field meeting at Swanscombe (II). *Proc. Geol. Ass.* 43, 70-72.

Chandler, R.H. 1935. The Clactonian industry and report of a field meeting at Swanscombe (III). *Proc. Geol. Ass.* 46, 43-44.

Chandler, R.H. 1942. Reply to Bull (1942). *Proc. Geol. Ass.* 53, 21.

Chandler, R.H. and Leach, A.L. 1912. On the Dartford Heath Gravel and on a Palaeolithic implement factory. *Proc. Geol. Ass.* 23, 102-111.

Clements, J.F. 1991. *Birds of the World: a Checklist.* Ibis Publishing Company. Vista, California.

Collins, D.A. 1986. *Palaeolithic Europe: a Theoretical and Systematic Study.* Clayhanger Press. Tiverton.

Conway, B.W. 1968. Preliminary geological investigation of Boyn Hill Terrace deposits at Barnfield Pit, Swanscombe, Kent, during 1968. *Proc. Roy. Anthropol. Inst. Gr. Brit. Ir. for 1968.* 59-61.

Conway, B.W. 1969. Geological investigation of Boyn Hill Terrace deposits at Barnfield Pit, Swanscombe, Kent, during 1969. *Proc. Roy. Anthropol. Inst. Gr. Brit. Ir. for 1969.* 90-93.

Conway, B.W. 1970. Geological investigation of Boyn Hill Terrace deposits at Barnfield Pit, Swanscombe, Kent, during 1970. *Proc. Roy. Anthropol. Inst. Gr. Brit. Ir. for 1970.* 60-64.

Conway, B.W. 1971. Geological investigation of Boyn Hill Terrace deposits at Barnfield Pit, Swanscombe, Kent, during 1971. *Proc. Roy. Anthropol. Inst. Gr. Brit. Ir. for 1971.* 80-85.

Conway, B.W. and Waechter, J d'A. 1977. Lower Thames and Medway Valleys-Barnfield Pit, Swanscombe. *In* Shephard-Thorn, E.R. and Wymer, J. (eds) *South East England and the Thames Valley. Guide book for excursion A5, X INQUA Congress, Birmingham.* Geoabstracts. Norwich. 38-44.

Corbet, G.B. and Harris, S. 1990. *The Handbook of British Mammals.* Published for the Mammal Society. Blackwell Scientific Publications. Oxford. 3rd edit.

Cotton, M.A. 1938. Report on the Committee's excavations in the Barnfield Pit in June, 1937. *Swanscombe Committee. Report on the Swanscombe Skull. J. Roy. Anthropol. Inst. Gr. Brit. Ir. 68,* 48-54

Cramp, S. and Simmons, K.E.L. (eds). 1977. *The Birds of the Western Palearctic, volume 1.* Oxford University Press. Oxford.

Cramp, S. and Simmons, K.E.L. (eds). 1979. *The Birds of the Western Palearctic, volume 2.* Oxford University Press. Oxford.

Crowder, A.A. and Cuddy, D.G. 1973. Pollen in a small river basin: Wilton Creek, Ontario. *In* Birks, H.J.B. and West, R.G. (eds) *Quaternary Plant Ecology.* Blackwells. Oxford. 61-77.

Currant A.P. 1986. Man and the Quaternary interglacial faunas of Britain. *In* Collcutt, S.N. (ed) *The Palaeolithic of Britain and its Nearest Neighbours; Recent Trends.* Department of Archaeology and Prehistory, Sheffield University. J.R. Collis Publications. Sheffield. 50-52.

Currant, A.P. 1989. The Quaternary origins of the modern British mammal fauna. *Biol. J. Linnean Soc. London* 38, 23-30.

Danielopol, D.L. and McKenzie, K.G. 1977. *Psychrodromus* gen n (Crustacea, Ostracoda) with rediscription of the Cyprid Genera *Prionocypris* and *Ilyodromus. Zoologica Scripta* 6, 301-322.

Dansgard, W., Johnsen, S.J., Clausen, H.B., Dahl-Jensen, D., Gundestrup, N.S., Hammer, C.U., Hvidberg, C.S., Steffensen, J.P., Sveinbjörnsdottir, A.E., Jouzel, J. and Bond, G. 1993. Evidence for general instability of past climate from a 250-kyr ice-core record. *Nature* 364, 218-220.

Day, M.H. and Napier, J.R. 1964. Hominid fossils from Bed I, Olduvai Gorge, Tanzania. *Nature* 201, 967-970.

De Dekker, P. 1979. Middle Pleistocene ostracod fauna of West Runton Freshwater Bed, Norfolk. *Palaeontology* 22, 293-316.

Dewey, H. 1930. Palaeolithic Thames deposits. *Proc. Prehist. Soc. of East Anglia* 6, 147-155.

Dewey, H. 1932. The Palaeolithic deposits of the Lower Thames Valley. *Quart. J. Geol. Soc. London* 88, 35-56.

Dewey, H. 1959. *Palaeolithic deposits of the Thames at Dartford Heath and Swanscombe, north Kent.* Unpublished, edited text of Henry Stopes memorial lecture for the Geologists Association in 1959.

Dewey, H. and Smith, R.A. 1914. The Palaeolithic sequence at Swanscombe, Kent. *Proc. Geol. Ass.* 25, 90-97.

Dewey, H., Bromhead, C.E.N., Chatwin, C.P., and Dines, H.G. 1924. *The Geology of the country around Dartford. Mem. Geol. Surv.*

Dimbleby, G.W. 1957. The pollen analysis of terrestrial soils. *New Phytol.* 56, 12-28.

Dimbleby, G.W. & Evans, J.G. 1974. Pollen and landsnail analysis of calcareous soils. *J. Archaeol. Sci.* 1, 117-133.

Dines, H.G. 1938. A general account of the 100-ft terrace gravels of the Barnfield Pit. *Swanscombe Committee. Report on the Swanscombe skull. J. Roy. Anthropol. Inst. Gr. Brit. Ir.* 68, 21-27.

Dines, H.G. and Edmunds, F.H. 1925. *The geology of the country around Romford. Mem. Geol. Surv.*.

Duff, K.L. (ed) 1985. *The story of Swanscombe man.* Kent County Council and Nature Conservancy Council.

Edmunds, C.N. 1983. Towards the prediction of subsidence risk upon Chalk outcrop. *Quat. J. Eng. Geol.*, 261-266.

Evans, J. 1860. On the occurrence of flint implements in undisturbed beds of gravel, sand and clay. *Archaeologia* 38, 280-307.

Evans, J. 1863. Account of some further discoveries of flint implements in the drift of the continent and in England. *Archaeologia* 39, 57-84.

Evans, J. 1897. *The Ancient Stone Implements, Weapons and Ornaments of Great Britain.* Longmans, Green, and Co. London. 2nd edit.

Frenzel, B. 1964. Zur Pollenanalyse von Lossen. *Eiszeitalter und Gegenwart* 15, 5-39.

Fortelius, M., Mazza, P., and Sala, B. 1993. *Stephanorhinus (Mammalia: Rhinocerotidae)* of the western European Pleistocene, with a revision of *S. etruscus* (Falconer 1868). *Palaeontographica Italica* 80, 63-155.

Green, C.P., Coope, G.R., Currant, A.P., Holyoak, D.T., Ivanovich, M., Jones, R.L., Keen, D.H., McGregor, D.F.M., and Robinson, J.E. 1984. Evidence of two temperate episodes in Late Pleistocene deposits at Marsworth, UK. *Nature* 309, 778-781.

Greenland Ice-core Project (GRIP) Members. 1993. Climate instability during the last interglacial period recorded in the GRIP ice core. *Nature* 364, 203-207.

Gillette, D.D. and Lockley, M.G. 1989. *Dinosaur Tracks and Traces.* Cambridge University Press. Cambridge.

Gibbard, P.L., Whiteman, C.A. and Bridgland, D.R. 1988. A preliminary report on the stratigraphy of the Lower Thames valley. *Quaternary Newsletter* 56, 1-8.

Grootes, P.M., Stuiver, M., White, J.W.C., Johnsen, S. and Jouzel, J. 1993. Comparison of oxygen isotope records from the GISP2 and GRIP Greenland ice-cores. *Nature* 366, 552-554.

Guy, T. 1975. *Swanscombe 1825-1975.* Blue Circle. Northfleet.

Harrison, C.J.O. 1979. Pleistocene birds from Swanscombe, Kent. *London Naturalist* 58, 6-8.

Harrison, C.J.O. 1985. The Pleistocene birds of south-eastern England. *Bull. Geol. Soc. Norfolk* 35, 53-69.

Harrison, C.J.O. 1988. *The History of the Birds of Britain.* Collins. London.

Hawkes, C.F.C. 1938. The industries of the Barnfield Pit. *Swanscombe Committee. Report on the Swanscombe Skull. J. Roy. Anthropol. Inst. Gr. Brit. Ir.* 68, 30-47.

Havinga, A.J. 1963. A palynological investigation of soil profiles developed in cover sands. *Mededelingen van de Landbouwhogeschool te Wageningen, Nederland* 63, 1-93.

Hinton, M.A.C. and Kennard, A.S. 1905. The relative ages of the stone implements of the Lower Thames Valley. *Proc. Geol. Ass.* 19, 76-100.

Holmes, T.V. 1894. Further notes on some sections of the new railway from Romford to Upminster, and on the relations of the Thames valley beds to the boulder clay. *Quart. J. Geol. Soc. London* 50, 443-452.

Hubbard, R.N.L.B. 1971. An interim report on the pollen record at Swanscombe. *Proc. Roy. Anthropol. Inst. Gr. Brit. Ir. for 1971.* 79.

Hubbard, R.N.L.B. 1982. The environmental evidence from Swanscombe, and its implications for Palaeolithic archaeology. *In* Leach P.E. (ed) *Archaeology in Kent to AD 1500. Counc. Brit. Archaeol. Res. Rep. 48,* 3-7.

Hubbard, R.N.L.B. and Sampson, C.G. 1993. Rainfall estimates derived from the pollen content of modern hyrax dung: an evaluation. *South African J. Sci.* 89, 199-204.

Irving, B. G. (1994). *Zooarchaeology and Paleoecology of the Middle and Upper Pleistocene Ichthyofaunas of the British Isles.* Unpublished Ph.D thesis. University of London.

Irving, B. G. (in prep). Seasonality in the atlantic salmon *Salmo salar* (L), myth or reality ? *In Archaeological Seasonality.* Association for Environmental Archaeology Conference Proceedings, The Netherlands 1994.

Iversen, J. 1944. *Viscum, Hedera* and *Ilex* as climatic indicators. *Geol. Forens. Stockholm Forh.* 66, 463-483.

Jamieson, I.G., Seymour, N.R. and Bancroft, R.P. 1982. Use of two habitats related to changes in prey availability in a population of ospreys in northeastern Nova Scotia. *Wilson Bull.* 94, 557-564.

Jollie, M. 1977. A contribution to the morphology and the phylogeny of the Falconiformes. Part 4. *Evolutionary Theory* 3, 1-141.

Jones, T.R. 1850. Description of the Entomostraca of the Pleistocene beds at Newbury, Copford, Clacton and Grays. *Annal. and Mag. Nat. Hist.* 6, 25-28.

Juvigne, E. 1975. Note on pollen extraction from coarse sediments. *Quaternary Res.* 5, 121-123.

Kelley, H. 1937. Acheulian flake tools. *Proc. Prehist. Soc.* 3, 15-28.

Kemp, R.A. 1985. The decalcified Lower Loam at Swanscombe, Kent: a buried Quaternary soil. *Proc. Geol. Ass.* 96, 343-355.

Kemp, R.A. 1995. Soil formation in the Swanscombe Lower Loam. *In* Bridgland, D.R., Allen, P. and Haggart, B.A. (eds) *The Quaternary of the Lower Reaches of the Thames.* Quaternary Research Association Field Guide. Preliminary edition. Durham. 142-143.

Kempf, E. 1971. Ökologtie, taxonomie und verbreitung der michtmarinen ostrakoden - Gattug *Scottia* im Quatär von Europa. *Eiszeitalter und Gegenwart* 22, 43-63.

Kerney, M.P. 1971. Interglacial deposits at Barnfield Pit, Swanscombe, and their molluscan fauna. *J. Geol. Soc. of London* 127, 69-93.

Kerney, M.P., Gibbard, P.L., Hall, A.R., Robinson, J.E. and Coope, G.R. 1982. Middle Devensian river deposits beneath the 'Upper Floodplain' terrace of the river Thames at Isleworth, West London. *Proc. Geol. Assoc.* 93, 385-393.

King, W.B.R. and Oakley, K.P. 1936. The Pleistocene succession in the lower parts of the Thames Valley. *Proc. Prehist. Soc.* 2, 52-76.

Kukla, G.J. 1977. Pleistocene land-sea correlations. I. Europe. *Earth Sci. Rev.* 13, 307-374.

Leakey, L.S.B. 1951. *Olduvai Gorge.* Cambridge University Press. Cambridge.

Leakey, M.D. and Hay, R.L. 1979 Pliocene footprints in the Laetolil Beds at Laetoli, Northern Tanzania. *Nature* 278, 317-323.

Leakey, M.D. and Harris, J.M. 1987. *Laetoli: a Pliocene Site in Northen Tanzania.* Clarendon Press. Oxford.

Lepiksaar, J. 1983. *Osteologia. I. Pisces.* Privately distributed, Goteborg.

Lister, A.M. 1986. New results on deer from Swanscombe, and the stratigraphical significance of deer in the Middle and Upper Pleistocene of Europe. *J. Archaeol. Sci.* 13, 319-338.

Lundelius, E.L. 1989. The implications of disharmonious assemblages for Pleistocene extinctions. *J. Archaeol. Sci.* 16, 407-417.

Marston, A.T. 1937A. The Swanscombe skull. *J. Roy. Anthropol. Inst. Gr. Brit. Ir.* 67, 339-406.

Marston, A.T. 1937B. An additional note on the stratigraphy of the Barnfield deposits. Unpublished manuscript; Appendix II of this volume.

McBurney, C.B.M. 1953. Review of Adam's Ancestors by L.S.B. Leakey. *Proc. Prehist. Soc.* 19, 127.

McNabb, J. 1992. *The Clactonian: British Lower Palaeolithic flint technology in biface and non-biface assemblages.* Unpublished Ph.D thesis. London University.

McNabb, J. and Ashton, N.M. 1992. The cutting edge: bifaces in the Clactonian. *Lithics* 13, 4-10.

Millward, R. and Robinson, A.H.W. 1971. The cement industry of Lower Thameside. *In* Millward, R., and Robinson, A.H.W. (eds) *South-east England: Thameside and the Weald.* Macmillan. London.

Morales, A. & Rosenlund, K. 1979. *Fish Bone Measurements: An attempt to standardise the measuring of fish bones from archaeological sites.* Steenstrupia. Copenhagen.

Moreau, R. 1972. *The Palearctic-African Migration Systems.* Academic Press. London.

Mourer-Chauviré, C. 1975. Les oiseaux du Pléistocène moyen et supérieur de France. *Documents ces Laboratoires de Géologie de la Faculté des Sciences de Lyon* 64, Fascicule 1.

Newcomer, M.H. 1969. The method of excavation at Barnfield Pit, Swanscombe (1969). *Proc. Roy. Anthropol. Inst. Gr. Brit. Ir. for 1969*, 87-89.

Newcomer, M.H. 1970. Conjoined flakes from the Lower Loam, Barnfield Pit, Swanscombe (1970). *Proc. Roy. Anthropol. Inst. Gr. Brit. Ir. for 1970*, 51-59.

Newton, I. 1979. *Population Ecology of Raptors.* T. and A. Poyser. London.

Norman, A.M. 1861. Dredging report: crustacea. *Nat. Hist. Soc. Trans. of Northumberland and Durham* 1.

Nüchterlein, H. 1969. Susswasserostracoden aus Franken: ein Beitrag zur Systematik und Ökologie der Ostracoden. *Inter. Review Ges. Hydrobiol* 54, 223-287

Oakley K.P. 1939. Field meeting at Swanscombe, Kent. *Proc. Geol. Ass.* 50, 357-361.

Oakley, K.P. 1952. Swanscombe Man. *Proc. Geol. Ass.* 63, 271-300.

Oakley, K.P. and Leakey, L.S.B. 1935. Fossil human occipital bone from Thames gravels. *Nature* 136, 916-917.

Oakley, K.P. and Leakey, M.D. 1937. Report on excavations at Jaywick Sands, Essex (1934), with some observations on the Clactonian industry, and on the fauna and geological significance of the Clacton channel. *Proc. Prehist. Soc.* 3, 217-260.

Ovey, C.D. (ed) 1964. *The Swanscombe skull. A survey of research on a Pleistocene Site. Roy. Anthropol. Inst. Occasional Paper No. 20.* Roy. Anthropol. Inst. Gr. Brit. Ir. London.

Paterson, T.T. 1940. The Swanscombe skull: a defence. *Proc. Prehist. Soc.* 6, 166-169.

Peck, R. 1973. Pollen budget studies in a small Yorkshire catchment. *In* Birks, H.J.B. and West, R.G. (eds) *Quaternary Plant Ecology.* Blackwells. Oxford. 43-60.

Penk, A. and Bruckner, E. 1909. *Die Alpen im Eiszeitalter.* Leipzig.

Poole, A.F. 1989. *Ospreys: a Natural and Unnatural History.* Cambridge University Press. Cambridge.

Preece, R.C. 1990. The molluscan fauna of the Middle Pleistocene interglacial deposits at Little Oakley, Essex, and its environmental and stratigraphic implications. *Phil. Trans. Roy. Soc. London* B328, 387-407.

Pugh, P. 1988. *The History of Blue Circle.* Cambridge Business Publishing. Cambridge.

Renault-Miskovsky, J., Bui-Thi-Mai and Girard, M. 1985. *Palynologie Archéologique.* Editions du C.N.R.S.. Paris.

Roberts, M.B. 1990. Day 3, Stop 6, Amey's Eartham Pit, Boxgrove. *In* Turner, C. (ed) *SEQS The Cromer Symposium, Norwich 1990. Field Excursion Guidebook September 5th-7th.* Quaternary Research Association. Cambridge. 62-81

Robinson, J.E. 1980. The ostracod fauna of the interglacial deposits at Sugworth, Oxfordshire. *Phil. Trans. Roy. Soc. London* B289, 99-106.

Sackett, J.R. 1981. From de Mortillet to Bordes: a century of French Palaeolithic research. *In* Daniel, G. (ed) *Towards a History of Archaeology.* Thames and Hudson. London. 85-99.

Sampson, C.G. (ed) 1978. *Paleoecology and Archeology of an Acheulian site at Caddington, England.* Southern Methodist University. Dallas.

Schafer, W. 1972. *Ecology and Palaeocology of Marine Environments.* Oliver and Boyd, Edinburgh.

Schreuder, A. 1950. Microtinae from the Middle Gravels of Swanscombe. *Annals and Magazine of Nat. Hist. (12th series)* 13, 3, 629-635.

Shackleton, N.J. and Opdyke, N.D. 1973. Oxygen isotope and palaeomagnetic stratigraphy of Equatorial Pacific Core V28-238, Oxygen Isotope temperatures and ice volumes on a 10^5 year - 10^6 year scale. *Quaternary Research* 3, 39-55.

Shephard-Thorn, E.R. and Wymer, J. 1977. *South East England and the Thames Valley. Guide book for excursion A5, X INQUA Congress, Birmingham.* Geoabstracts. Norwich.

Sher, A.V. 1990. Actualism and disconformism in studies of ecology of Pleistocene mammals. *J. General Biol.* 51, 163-177 (In Russian).

Sher, A.V. 1991. Problems of the last interglacial in Arctic Siberia. *Quaternary International* 10-12, 215-222.

Shotton, F.W., Goudie, A.S. and Briggs, D.J. 1980. Cromerian interglacial deposits at Sugworth near Oxford, England, and their relation to the Plateau Drift of the Cotswolds and the terrace sequence of the Upper and Middle Thames. *Phil. Trans. Roy. Soc. London* B289, 55-86.

Smith, R.A. 1912. On the classification of Palaeolithic stone implements. *Proc. Geol. Assoc.* 23, 137-147.

Smith, R.A. and Dewey, H. 1912. Unpublished notes. British Museum archive.

Smith, R.A. and Dewey, H. 1913. Stratification at Swanscombe: report on excavations made on behalf of the British Museum and H.M. Geological Survey. *Archaeologia* 64, 177-204.

Smith, R.A. and Dewey, H. 1914. The High Terrace of the Thames: report on excavations made on behalf of the British Museum and H.M. Geological Survey in 1913. *Archaeologia* 65, 187-212.

Stanley, E.A. 1969. Marine palynology. *Oceanography and Marine Biol. Ann. Rev.* 7, 277-92.

Stuart, A.J. 1982. *Pleistocene Vertebrates of the British Isles.* Longman. London and New York.

Sturge, W.A. 1908. Presidential address. *Proc. Prehist. Soc. East Anglia* 1, (1908-1914), 9-16.

Sturge, W.A. 1909. The chronology of the Stone Age. *Proc. Prehist. Soc. East Anglia* 1, (1908-1914) 43-105.

Sutcliffe, A.J. 1964. The mammal fauna. *In* Ovey, C. (ed) *The Swanscombe Skull. A Survey of Research on a Pleistocene Site. Roy. Anthropol. Inst. Occasional Paper No. 20.* Roy. Anthropol. Instit. Gr. Brit. Ir. London. 85-111.

Sutcliffe, A.J. and Kowalski, K. 1976. Pleistocene rodents of the British Isles. *Bull. Brit. Mus. (Natural History) Geol.* 27, 31-147.

Swanscombe Committee, 1938. *Report on the Swanscombe Skull: prepared by the Swanscombe Committee of the Royal Anthropological Institute. J. Roy. Anthropol. Inst. Gr. Brit. Ir.* 68, 17-98.

Spurrell, F.C.J. 1883. Palaeolithic implements found in west Kent. *Archaeol. Cantiana* 15, 89-103.

Tauber, H. 1977. Investigations of aerial pollen transport in a forested area. *Danm. Bot. Ark.* 32, 1-121.

Treacher, Ll. and White, H.J.O. 1909. Excursion to Maidenhead. *Proc. Geol. Assoc.* 21, 198-201.

Trigger, B.G. 1989. *A History of Archaeological Thought.* Cambridge University Press. Cambridge.

Turner, C. 1970. The Middle Pleistocene deposits at Marks Tey, Essex. *Phil. Trans. Roy. Soc. London* B257, 373-440.

Turner, C. 1985. Problems and pitfalls in the application of palynology to Pleistocene archaeological sites in western Europe. *In* Rcnault-Miskovsky, J., Bui-Thi-Mai, and Girard, M. (eds) *Palynologie Archeologique.* Editions du C.N.R.S.. Paris. 347-373.

Turner, C. and West, R.G. 1968. The subdivision and zonation of interglacial periods. *Eiszeitalter und Gegenwart* 19, 93-101.

Tuttle, R.H. 1987. Kinesiological inferences and evolutionary implications from Laetoli bipedal trails G-1, G-2/3, and A. *In* Leakey, M.D. and Harris, J.M. (eds) *Laetoli, A Pliocene Site in Northern Tanzania.* Clarendon Press. Oxford.

Vaufrey, R. 1939. Review of Swanscombe Committee. Report on the Swanscombe skull 1938. *L'Anthropologie* 49, 363-365.

Waechter, J.d'A. 1952. Review of Olduvai Gorge vol. 1 by L.S.B. Leakey. *Man* 52, 24.

Waechter, J.d'A. and Conway, B.W. 1968. Swanscombe 1968. *Proc. Roy. Anthropol. Inst. Gr. Brit. Ir. for 1968.* 53-61.

Waechter, J.d'A., Newcomer, M.H. and Conway, B.W. 1969. Swanscombe 1969. *Proc. Roy. Anthropol. Inst. Gr. Brit. Ir. for 1969.* 83-95.

Waechter, J.d'A., Newcomer, M.H. and Conway, B.W. 1970. Swanscombe 1970. *Proc. Roy. Anthropol. Inst. Gr. Brit. Ir. for 1970.* 43-64.

Waechter, J.d'A., Hubbard, R.N.L.B., and Conway, B.W. 1971. Swanscombe 1971. *Proc. Roy. Anthropol. Inst. Gr. Brit. Ir. for 1971.* 73-85.

Waechter, J.d'A. 1976. *Man Before History.* Elsevier, Phaidon. London.

Walker, A. and Leakey, R. (eds) 1993. *The Nariokotome Homo erectus Skeleton.* Harvard University Press. Cambridge.

Walker, A. 1993. Perspectives on the Nariokotome Discovery. *In* Walker, A. and Leakey, R. (eds) *The Nariokotome Homo erectus Skeleton.* Harvard University Press. Cambridge.

Walsh, P.T., Edler, G.A., Edwards, B.R., Urbani, D.M., Valentine, K. and Soyer, J. 1973. Large-scale surveys of solution subsidence deposits in the Carboniferous and Cretaceous limestones of Great Britain and Belgium and their contribution to an understanding of the mechanisms of karstic subsidence. *Proc. I.A.E.G. Symposium. Sink Holes and Subsidence.* Hanover. T2 A1-10.

Warren, S.H. 1902. On the value of mineral condition in determining the relative age of stone implements. *Geological Magazine* 9, 97-105.

Warren, S.H. 1922. The Mesvinian industry of Clacton-on-Sea. *Proc. Prehist. Soc. East Anglia* 3, 597-602.

Warren, S.H. 1923. The *Elephas-antiquus* bed of Clacton-on-Sea (Essex) and its flora and fauna. *Quat. J. Geol. Soc. London* 79, 606-634.

Warren, S.H. 1924. Pleistocene classifications. *Proc. Geol. Ass.* 35, 265-282.

Warren, S.H. 1926. The classification of the Lower Palaeolithic with especial reference to Essex. *Trans. South-East Union of Sci. Soc. for 1926. South East Naturalist.* 38-51.

Warren, S.H. 1933. The Palaeolithic industries of the Clacton and Dovercourt districts. *Essex Naturalist* (vol. for 1932-1935) 24, 1-29.

Warren, S.H. 1951. The Clacton flint industry: a new interpretation. *Proc. Geol. Ass.* 62, 107-135.

Watson, W. 1949. *Flint Implements.* British Museum Publications. London. 1st edit.

Watson, W. 1956. *Flint Implements.* British Museum Publications. London. 2nd edit.

Weigelt, J. 1927. *Rezente Wirbeltierleichen und ihre Paläobiologische Bedeutung.* Verlag von Max Weg, Liepzig. (English translation, 1989, *Recent Vertebrate Carcasses and their Paleobiological Implications.* University of Chicago Press. Chicago.)

Weightman, G. and Humphries, S. 1983. *The Making of Modern London 1815-1914.* Sidgwick and Jackson. London.

West, R.G. 1956. The Quaternary deposits at Hoxne, Suffolk. *Phil. Trans. Roy. Soc. London* B239, 265-356.

West, R.G. and McBurney, C.M.B. 1954. The Quaternary deposits at Hoxne, Suffolk, and their archaeology. *Proc. Prehist. Soc.* 20, 131-154.

Wheeler, A. 1969. *The Fishes of the British Isles and North West Europe.* MacMillan. London.

Wheeler, A. and Jones, A.K.G. 1989. *Fishes.* Cambridge Manuals in Archaeology. Cambridge University Press. Cambridge.

Wrigley, E.A. and Schofield, R.S. 1981. *The History of Population in England 1551-1861.* Arnold. London.

Wymer, J. 1961. The Lower Palaeolithic succession in the Thames Valley and the date of the ancient channel between Caversham and Henley, Oxon. *Proc. Prehist. Soc.* 27, 1-27.

Wymer, J. 1964. Excavations at Barnfield Pit, 1955-1960. *In* Ovey, C. (ed) *The Swanscombe Skull. A Survey of Research on a Pleistocene Site. Roy. Anthropol. Inst. Gr. Brit. Ir. Occasional Paper No. 20.* 19-61.

Wymer J. 1968. *Lower Palaeolithic Archaeology in Britain as represented by the Thames Valley.* John Baker. London.

Wymer, J. and Singer, R. 1970. The first season of excavations at Clacton-on-Sea, Essex, England: a brief report. *World Arch.* 2, 12-16.

Zeuner, F.E. 1955. Loess and Palaeolithic chronology. *Proc. Prehist. Soc.* 21, 51-64.

Zeuner, F.E. 1959. *The Pleistocene Period: its Climate, Chronology, and Faunal Successions.* Hutchinson. London. 2nd edit.